Ted and Amy Cunningham have written the perfect antidote for the busyness of everyday modern life. *Come to the Family Table* provides encouraging devotionals, interesting questions, and recipes as a way to bind your family together over a meal. If you're looking for a way to increase the conversation and the laughter in your house, make sure this book makes its way onto your dinner table.

JÁNA GUYNN
Director of MarriedLife at North Point Community Church

Do yourself a favor and devour this book like you would your favorite meal. It's an amazing read! Thank you, Ted and Amy, for providing insight into family, love, relationships, food, fun, and laughter. You have filled these pages with great content, recipes, conversations starters, and devotions . . . it literally has it all. This book is an excellent tool for any family that wants to move in the direction of health. Thank you for blessing my family and our table time. This is a gift that will serve so many. Well d

DOUG FIELDS
Pastor, author, and speaker

Ted and Amy Cunningham offe. . . challenge to return to a time when "dinner time" was not just about quickly downing the food but about relaxing together as we connect with friends and family. *Come to the Family Table* is a must for every newlywed couple as they anticipate building a rich life together. Filled with creative ideas, recipes, and ways to foster discipleship and intimacy as a family, this book invites readers to give attention to how they are nurturing those closest to them. Ted and Amy teach with ease that intentional hospitality—integrated with simplicity and love—is vital as we seek to leave a lasting footprint in the lives of those we invite into our homes.

DANA YEAKLEY
Author of *The Gentle Art of Discipling Women*

We all know food impacts the body. Ted and Amy Cunningham make a compelling and deeply personal argument that food can impact your family and even your soul. They will show you how gathering around the table as family and friends might not just be good for you— it might even heal you. This is a fascinating read.

CAREY NIEUWHOF
Author and founding/teaching pastor at Connexus Church

How thrilled would you be to find a $1,000 bill under a napkin at your kitchen table? *Come to the Family Table* will fill you with warm feelings of belonging and help you build rich memories with your family. Consider this book permission and energy to enjoy what we should never have lost—joy around meals and hospitality that makes sharing Jesus way more natural. Our families deserve so much more than what they get in this hurried, food-for-fuel world. This book rocks when it comes to reviving hope, fun, and virtue in our busy families.

JEFF KEMP
Vice president of FamilyLife and author of *Facing the Blitz*

I loved this book! I felt welcomed to Ted and Amy's dinner table as they shared stories, advice, and ideas for a more vibrant and intentional way of doing family. If you want to connect more deeply with your kids, God, and your community, read this book!

SHANNON ETHRIDGE
Life/relationship coach and author of twenty-two books, including the bestselling *Every Woman's Battle* series

One of the highlights of our day is sitting down together as a family of six for dinner. With four boys, most meals are filled with energy, laughs, and loud noises, but not a lot of intentional conversation. *Come to the Family Table* by Ted and Amy Cunningham reminds us of the value of making memories and raising disciples together around our kitchen table. This book will help you transform the way you view the precious times you have together with your spouse, kids, friends, and family. In our fast-paced, go-go-go culture, *Come to the Family Table* will challenge the way you view food, meals, and even time with your family. The book is based on God's Word and is practical, creative, and ready to be applied!

SCOTT KEDERSHA
Director of premarital and newly married ministries at Watermark Community Church

If the kitchen is the center of the house, then the dinner table is the heart of the home. In *Come to the Family Table*, Ted and Amy Cunningham remind us that part of being a healthy and intentional family is regularly gathering together for meals. Wise parents prioritize "table" opportunities to build into their children as well as reach out to others. *Come to the Family Table* presents a practical, biblical, intentional, and fun approach to loving your family and friends.

MICHAEL KAST
Family minister at Southeast Christian Church in Louisville, Kentucky

A simple book with a powerful message. Every family needs to come to the table. Ted has been a champion for marriage and family in the church for years. Now he brings it home to the family table. The book is a great blend of wisdom, stories, games, recipes, and simple tips to make deep connections with family and friends. It's a book everyone can engage with—the kind you would want to take on a family road trip or read out loud around the fire on a holiday. I wish someone had encouraged me to spend more time at the family table when we were raising our kids.

GREG WEAVER
Director of development at FamilyLife

I highly recommend this book! The format is engaging and easy to follow. Each chapter has compelling and simple illustrations of ways to incorporate the family table into real life. Best of all, Ted and Amy speak to the heart, reinforcing what is good at home and stirring up what can be even better.

CHRISTINE DENTE
Singer/songwriter, Out of the Grey

Ted and Amy are two of my favorite foodie friends. There is probably no better way to experience community than around a common table. *Come to the Family Table* gives a very practical way to create intentional shared experiences with your family. This book is #DateNightWorks approved and will keep you and your family laughing and loving at every meal!

TIM POPADIC
President of DateNightWorks and creator of Date Night Comedy Tour

From the Family Table of

_____

Come to the family table

*Slowing down
to enjoy food, each other,
and JESUS*

Ted & Amy Cunningham

A NavPress resource published in alliance
with Tyndale House Publishers, Inc.

NAVPRESS⊙.

NavPress is the publishing ministry of The Navigators, an international Christian organization and leader in personal spiritual development. NavPress is committed to helping people grow spiritually and enjoy lives of meaning and hope through personal and group resources that are biblically rooted, culturally relevant, and highly practical.

For more information, visit www.NavPress.com.

Come to the Family Table: Slowing Down to Enjoy Food, Each Other, and Jesus
Copyright © 2016 by Ted and Amy Cunningham. All rights reserved.
A NavPress resource published in alliance with Tyndale House Publishers, Inc.

NAVPRESS and the NAVPRESS logo are registered trademarks of NavPress, The Navigators, Colorado Springs, CO. *TYNDALE* is a registered trademark of Tyndale House Publishers, Inc. Absence of ® in connection with marks of NavPress or other parties does not indicate an absence of registration of those marks.

Cover photograph copyright © Alie Lengyelova/Stocksy. All rights reserved.

The Team:
Don Pape, Publisher
Caitlyn Carlson, Acquiring Editor
Mark Anthony Lane II, Designer

All Scripture quotations, unless otherwise indicated, are taken from the Holy Bible, *New International Version,® NIV.®* Copyright © 1973, 1978, 1984, 2011 by Biblica, Inc.® Used by permission. All rights reserved worldwide.

Scripture quotations marked NET are taken from the NET Bible,® copyright © 1996-2006 by Biblical Studies Press, L.L.C. http://netbible.com All rights reserved.

Scripture quotations marked ESV are taken from *The Holy Bible*, English Standard Version® (ESV®), copyright © 2001 by Crossway, a publishing ministry of Good News Publishers. Used by permission. All rights reserved.

Scripture quotations marked NASB are taken from the New American Standard Bible,® copyright © 1960, 1962, 1963, 1968, 1971, 1972, 1973, 1975, 1977, 1995 by The Lockman Foundation. Used by permission.

Scripture quotations marked NLT are taken from the *Holy Bible*, New Living Translation, copyright © 1996, 2004, 2007, 2013 by Tyndale House Foundation. Used by permission of Tyndale House Publishers, Inc., Carol Stream, Illinois 60188. All rights reserved.

Some of the anecdotal illustrations in this book are true to life and are included with the permission of the persons involved. All other illustrations are composites of real situations, and any resemblance to people living or dead is purely coincidental.

Library of Congress Cataloging-in-Publication Data
Names: Cunningham, Ted, author.
Title: Come to the family table : slowing down to enjoy food, each other, and Jesus / Ted and Amy Cunningham.
Description: Colorado Springs : NavPress, 2016. | Includes bibliographical references. | Description based on print version record and CIP data provided by publisher; resource not viewed.
Identifiers: LCCN 2016019754 (print) | LCCN 2016015619 (ebook) | ISBN 9781631463679 (Apple) | ISBN 9781631463686 (E-Pub) | ISBN 9781631463693 (Kindle) | ISBN 9781631463662
Subjects: LCSH: Dinners and dining—Religious aspects—Christianity. | Families—Religious life.
Classification: LCC BR115.N87 (print) | LCC BR115.N87 C86 2016 (ebook) | DDC 249—dc23
LC record available at https://lccn.loc.gov/2016019754

Printed in the United States of America

22	21	20	19	18	17	16
7	6	5	4	3	2	1

We want to honor the family tables of our grandmothers:

Lorraine Freitag
Austin, Minnesota

Erliss Kelzenberg
Owatonna, Minnesota

Mary Jane Ludwig
Naperville, Illinois

Mildred Cunningham
Elizabethtown, Pennsylvania

CONTENTS

Acknowledgments

It takes an army of people to make a book successful. Many folks gathered around many tables to make the dream of this book a reality.

Thank you to all of our friends at NavPress and Tyndale House Publishers. Thank you, Don Pape, for reaching out and asking if we would be interested in writing a family discipleship book. You are a great friend, and we love working with you. Caitlyn Carlson is the most inspiring and encouraging editor in publishing. We've never worked with anyone as talented as you, Caitlyn. Your skills and passion are on every page.

Thank you to Melissa Myers, Stephanie Wright, Pat Reinheimer, Jeff Rustemeyer, Robin Bermel, and David Geeslin for believing in this message and seeing it through to print.

Thank you to Woodland Hills Family Church. So many of our stories flow from the work and ministry in Branson, Missouri. Most of our thoughts, chapters, and books start as sermons. We are grateful to serve a church that believes it is important for the message to go beyond the walls of the castle we call our church building. Our church staff leads well. Denise Bevins, Stephanie and Andy Watson, Corey and Mesa Mitchell, Mickey Pitman,

Matt and Katie Gumm, Donna Seiler, David Everson, and count-less leaders and volunteers lead the mission of marriage and fam-ily at Woodland Hills. We are also grateful for our elders, Travis Brawner, Doug Goodwin, Mike Gattis, Doug Hayter, Bryan Bronn, and R. G. Yallaly.

We have many foodie friends who share our passion for food and fellowship. We share our stories of meals with them through-out the book. Thank you.

Our parents inspired so much of this book. Thank you to Ron and Bonnie Cunningham and Dennis and Linda Freitag, for the power and influence of your family tables.

Introduction

AMY

The year 2014 was heart changing for us. Our physical and nutritional depletion was finally becoming obvious to us, although it had been obvious to those around us for quite some time. Our souls were now exhausted, and it was time to make some changes. Ted and I had several emotional breakdowns and deep moments of discussion and prayer. After identifying our inevitable burnout, we knew everything had to be on the table—our calling, our ministry, our home, and the way we do life. The realization that we had a diminishing margin for relationships with others and one another made our hearts ache. Our family yearned for more. We had slid into this lonely place. But God intended us for relationship with him and others. Jesus said the most important thing we should do is love God and love other people (Mark 12:30-31). Both of these priorities are simply impossible without intentional margin in your life. Our family certainly does not have it all figured out now, but we work hard to say no a lot and edit our schedules often. As a couple, we strive to decide our way into health and relationships. It is crucial to Ted and me that we model this for our kids. The most intentional method in modeling how God intended relationships is our approach to the family table. It is a timeless tool that can be used to prove that you place high value on the ones you love.

I used to have a terrible habit of clearing the table as soon I was done with my food—often when everyone else was still only halfway through the meal! I just wanted to get the dishes done so I could relax. But part of being intentional with our family table means taking the time to relax *during* the meal.

So we rearranged some furniture. I know me—if the dishes are in my peripheral vision, I am just not going to be able to relax. Now instead of eating in our kitchenette, we eat in the dining room with no view of the kitchen. This simple decision changed my life—and led to many little changes that made a big difference at our family table.

Since the dining room is a little more formal, we prep the environment as if honored guests are on the way over. And honored guests *are* coming—our family! We light candles and put out the nice dishes. We think through and prepare for conversation, games, special desserts, and devotions.

How many of us have a dining room and don't use it? Why not invite your family into this underused space each night and enjoy a meal together? Even if you don't have a dining room, try to find a way to set the table apart. Consider sitting with your back to the kitchen and maybe purchasing a screen or curtain to separate you from the mess. The dishes probably won't bother the kids nearly as much as they bother you.

Our journey toward a more intentional family table began when our kids were five and seven. At first their questions went along the lines of "What is this?" or "How many bites do I have to eat?" or my favorite, "Do we have to have a fancy meal?" I often got discouraged and lost my resolve. But four years later, we have a twelve-year-old who asks regularly what is for dinner and if we are going to all eat together at the table. Now, our ten-year-old son is at a different place on the journey. He prefers Kraft mac and cheese to almost anything else offered to him. But he doesn't mind sitting at the dining room table as long as he can have a comfy chair and light the candles himself. He is progressing. The family table requires intentional, consistent resolve from parents. Don't give up.

We work hard to keep our kids at the family table. We play board games and question games, have place mats they can color or do crossword puzzles on, and do family devotions. And the goal of all of these games and activities is to foster conversation. The intentional time spent together gives us all the opportunity to share what's on our hearts.

Food and family bring us to the table. Stories, games, and laughter keep us there for hours. Thoughtful food and conversations create meals worth repeating. We want our children to leave home and establish family tables of their own. We want them to enjoy spending time around their tables as they talk about time they spent around our table.

That is the purpose of this book: to inspire you in creating a family table that your children and guests will talk about for a lifetime. Then, as a result, they will be motivated to bless others by inviting gatherings that build relationships around their own tables.

Starting Your Meal

We've crafted this book with the same care we craft our time at the family table. At the end of each chapter we leave you with a family recipe, a game, a devotional with conversation starters, and a prayer. Every piece that you'll read has been used at our family table. Our desire is that each chapter gives you the content and tools necessary to enjoy a slow, refreshing meal with your family.

How you use this book will be unique to your individual family. Sometimes families will read the chapters together. In other cases, parents will read the chapter to connect on the theme and discuss how it fits their family. Some families will cook the recipe together, while others may have a parent or child exclusively prepare the meal. We encourage everyone to play the game around the family table and end the meal together with the devotional, discussion, and prayer.

Thank you for prioritizing your family's table. We hope your time together will impress upon each family member's heart a love for one another, your community, and the Lord.

the family table is for us

CHAPTER I

SPACE AROUND THE TABLE

The family table is a much-needed break in the midst of the grind.

> *God never hurries. There are no deadlines against*
> *which He must work. Only to know this is to quiet*
> *our spirits and relax our nerves.*
>
> A. W. TOZER, *THE PURSUIT OF GOD*

Take It Slow

AMY

If you've spent any time in an airport, you know that travel means hurry, delay, run, sit, and "throw all of your plans out the window—you're sleeping in a chair tonight at gate D31." Ted speaks at marriage conferences and date night challenges around the country, so we travel often as a family. And we used to eat way too much junk food on the road. We would go to the nearest chain restaurant, quickly order, ask for the check as the food arrived, and eat everything on our plate. Planning margin to enjoy a meal was not even a consideration. It wasn't long before we found ourselves a few pounds heavier and depleted nutritionally and emotionally.

Something needed to change. I picked up magazines in airports on cooking healthy and eating real food. Then came the cookbooks. Eventually I gathered several recipes with fresh ingredients and bold flavors.

While home for extended periods of time, I prepared the new dishes. We spent less time watching the Food Network and more time in the kitchen. Good, wholesome food on the table slowed us down too. The time, preparation, and care put into a meal made us savor it.

This new take on food challenged us to step up to the plate when we traveled. We now google farm-to-table, locally sourced restaurants in the area. We schedule our travel around having wholesome, longer meals upon arrival in a new city. Ted, Corynn, and I find ourselves anticipating great meals in new places. We talk about it leading up to the meal. Most times, it is not forgotten once consumed. We relive the meal days, months, and years later. Sure, the food is important to us, but the experience becomes a memory that we savor and hold on to. The equation? Good conversation with family and friends + environment + service + good food = a blessed memory to enjoy together.

The desire to slow down the pace of our kitchens, tables, and homes is catching on. The Slow Food Movement launched in 1989, three years after Carlo Petrini, an Italian journalist, condemned McDonald's for moving next door to a Spanish gourmet restaurant. Fast food in Rome? What would this do the health and culture of Italy?[1]

The Slow Food Manifesto states,

> We are enslaved by speed and have all succumbed to the same insidious virus: *Fast Life*, which disrupts our habits, pervades the privacy of our homes and forces us to eat Fast Foods. To be worthy of the name, *Homo Sapiens* should rid himself of speed before it reduces him to a species in danger of extinction. . . . May suitable doses of guaranteed sensual pleasure and slow, long-lasting enjoyment preserve us from the contagion of the multitude who mistake frenzy for efficiency. Our defense should begin at the table with *Slow Food*. Let us rediscover the flavors and savors of regional cooking and banish the degrading effects of *Fast Food*. . . . Slow Food guarantees a better future.[2]

While we appreciate the passion in this manifesto, we are not fanatics. There are few choices and no fine dining options between Tulsa, Oklahoma, and Springfield, Missouri. We've had more than a few cheeseburgers from McDonald's on that route. We joke, "Let's call it 'quick-service food' instead of 'fast food' to make ourselves feel better about this."

Balance is our goal. Speed is the enemy of intimacy. We do not want our meal pace to reflect our work pace. The family table is best served slow, not fast. In the midst of the grind of life, God wants us to pause, slow down, and enjoy what He provides. Ecclesiastes 3:12-13 says, "I know that there is nothing better for people than to be happy and to do good while they live. That each of them may eat and drink, and find satisfaction in all their toil—this is the gift of God." Just as Jesus reclined at the table of a Pharisee (Luke 7:36) and with His disciples at the Last Supper (Luke 22:14), we recline at the family table to give children and parents room to breathe. The drive-throughs of the fast-food movement escalate our chaotic schedules. Intentionally slowing down around the family table provides much-needed balance in the home through creating space for margin, safety, and laughter.

The Family Table Creates Margin

Comedian Tim Hawkins jokes about the fact that everyone today is in a rush. When someone needs to use your bathroom, they ask, "Could I use your restroom real quick?" When was the last time someone asked, "Could I use your restroom for a really long time? I don't know what's going to happen in there"?[3] We have forgotten why it is called a restroom. We should rest while we are in there. Why are we in such a big hurry? Whatever happened to margin?

Author Richard Swenson describes margin as "the space that once existed between ourselves and our limits."[4] The benefits of margin are "good health, financial stability, fulfilling relationships, and availability for God's purposes."[5] Our homes need it. We fizzle and fade without it. We are grumpy when we don't get enough of it. Too much of it and some consider us lazy.

Margin means room to breathe. It's a reserve. Have you ever felt panic and anxiety and helplessness in the face of being almost out of gas and unable to find a gas station? Margin keeps a little fuel in the tank. Margin refuses to run on fumes. It does not rush from one errand or meeting to another.

Margin is the gap between your load and your limit—and the family table increases the space between your family's load and limit. Our family used to say yes to every request for a meeting or counseling appointment, every invitation to a party, every meal invite. But we are a much happier and healthier family when we say no to other good stuff and yes to time around the table.

Never allow your load to be dictated by anyone else. After all, you are the expert on your limit. There's not another person on the planet who understands or controls your limit. No one knows you better than you. The understanding of your physical, emotional, and relational limits determines your necessary margin.

Scripture calls us to a margin-filled life. God rested after creating for six days. Jesus ministered to multitudes, and then He rested. We read in Mark 6:30, "The apostles gathered around Jesus and reported to him all they had done and taught." They were running full steam in their ministry, giving the reports to Him. He told them, "Hey, let's break away and chill for a while. Let's rest our bodies and our emotions. Let's take some time away so we can be more effective for

COME TO THE FAMILY TABLE

ministry." (Okay, that's our paraphrase of Mark 6:31, but you get the idea.)

We humans rebel against the whole idea of rest, so God had to command it: "Remember the Sabbath day by keeping it holy" (Exodus 20:8). *Holy* means set apart. The Sabbath looks nothing like the other six days of the week. It has a different pace and rhythm: "Six days you shall labor and do all your work" (verse 9). For six days God wants us to work and provide for our family. Productivity is part of God's plan for the family. "But the seventh day is a sabbath to the LORD your God. On it you shall not do any work" (verse 10). We need to slow down the pace of home, table, and kitchen and provide margin to rest and relax.

The Family Table Provides Safety

Consider for a moment your posture at the table. Is it warm and inviting or cold and distant? Do your children approach the table excited to spend time with you, or do they question your mood and passively resist you? Do your family and friends feel emotionally safe at your family table? Safety exists at the table when slowing down creates intentional space to communicate value to those who sit there.

Recently a pastor challenged us with how others feel in our presence. He said that there are two ways to enter a room. The first way is rooted in self and says, "Here I am." The second is concerned about the well-being of others and says, "There you are." When you walk into a room or conversation, do you look for ways to bless the one standing right in front of you? Even if it is a quick conversation, the quality of that time includes both verbal and nonverbal communication.

Relationship experts teach that 7 percent of our communication is verbal and 93 percent is nonverbal. Your approach and the way you sit at the table communicate to people how much you value them. Before you speak your first word, others know where they stand (or in this case, sit) with you. Consider the following nonverbal ways to create safety around your family table:

- Eye contact says, "I am interested and focused on what you are saying." Looking over the other person's shoulder says, "I wonder if there is someone more interesting to talk to" or "That conversation over there looks like more fun than this one." Looking at your watch or mobile device shows people that you would rather check the time or social media than talk to them. (And by the way, you are fooling no one with your phone sitting on your lap during dinner.) The look in our eyes can also communicate many things—sadness, curiosity, surprise, joy, relief, confusion, anticipation. Proverbs 15:30 says, "Bright eyes gladden the heart" (NASB). "Bright eyes" expresses excitement to the one you are greeting. People know when our eyes say, "There you are— I'm so glad to see you," and they also know when they say, "Oh boy, they're going to take up way too much of my time."

- Facial expressions honor others too. A wink says, "I get what you're saying." Raising your eyebrows shows excitement, shock, and intrigue. Gritted teeth can portray fright. A simple smile lets the other person know that you enjoy their presence, story, or joke. A furrowed brow and straight lips show empathy. Flat faces are the enemy of enthusiasm.
- Your mannerisms communicate an open or closed spirit. Folded arms say, "I'm not receiving your critique." Arms at the side are nonthreatening and communicate openness to the feedback of another. Sitting on the edge of your seat and leaning forward shows interest and enthusiasm, but too much of it can come across as aggressive. Slouching down in your chair is a sure sign that you are tired and ready for bed.
- Your proximity to the other person is an often overlooked nonverbal. Consider where each guest will sit and how the seating will impact conversation. We have a dear senior friend whom we always place between us because she is hard of hearing. She wants to hear all the conversation but can't do so sitting at the end of the table.
- Physical touch is a type of nonverbal communication that shows forgiveness, companionship, and even romance. Parents hold hands with their children to protect and lead them across a busy street. A husband shows chivalry by placing his hand on the small of his

wife's back as she walks through the door he opened for her. A gentle hand on the shoulder can say, "Will you forgive me?" Appropriate physical touch shows love.

The Family Table Invites Laughter

Great laughter lingers at the table because slowing down allows us to relax. Laughter is never in a rush to get away. It is contagious. One joke leads to another. Just watching someone laugh makes you want to laugh. Ever walk into a room and hear laughter and immediately start laughing before you ask, "What did I miss?"

You know that book *The Five Love Languages*?[6] I think laughter should be the sixth love language. There are a lot of ways to help bring humor to the family table.

Embrace everyone's personality. Not everyone has the same sense of humor, but everyone has something to offer. For example, Dr. Kevin Leman teaches that last-born children are natural comedians.[7] Your favorite standup comedian is probably the youngest in their family. I (Ted) was the last born in my family, and humor, comedy, and laughter are my passion. Our younger child, Carson, is our family's comedian and keeps it light around our table. So let the comics in your family cut loose at mealtime!

The comics may keep the jokes rolling, but make sure there's space for everyone else to enjoy laughter too. Our daughter, Corynn, might not be the comic Carson is, but we love it when she throws a line or two out for a laugh. She asked me the other day, "Dad, is the song 'Friends in Low

Places' by Garth Brooks about Florida or hell?" She tried to convince me that it was a serious question, but I convinced her that she has great wit.

And encourage those who think they struggle with being funny! Amy convinced herself years ago that she does not have the timing necessary for good joke telling. Not true. She has learned to lean into her timing issues and make that part of her routine. We get many miles out of the same joke. After I tell a joke, we often work on how Amy would deliver it. With passion, she delivers the punch line and gives us all the look that says, "You'd better laugh."

Don't ask for performance. We get the biggest kick out of our kids reciting movie lines or song lyrics at the table. We can see a movie one time as a family and the kids memorize a dozen or so lines. We've become those parents who say, "Do that one line from . . ." You may have experienced this. But when we ask our kids to perform, they shut down. Wait and let it flow out of the overflow of their hearts. Keep the mood light and you will have plenty of laughter.

Discover everyone's laugh style. Our family regularly takes inventory of our personal laughing styles. We love the "Tripp and Tyler Laughing" video,[8] where they categorize dozens of laughs like the chuckle, the wheezer, the clapper, and the machine gun. I have a "slow machine gun" laugh. Corynn calls her laugh the "clogged machine gun." Carson considers his laugh a "cute slow machine gun." Amy has a "silent, tilt the head back" laugh. I call it patriotic because she always places her hand over her heart when she is about to lose it. It's her way of holding it in. I tell her, "Like a sneeze, it's dangerous to try to hold it in. You've got to let it out."

We hear these four laugh styles every day in our home. Discovering everyone's laugh style is a great way to remove the vacuum of laughter from your home. However, this does come with a caution. Make sure your children know not to identify the laugh styles of guests visiting for a meal. That can be quite awkward. Wait until they leave, then cut loose. (Just kidding.)

Use humor to soften the blow. Humor can help us cope with the demands of this life. My all-time favorite quote on humor, attributed to nineteenth-century preacher Henry Ward Beecher, is, "A person without a sense of humor is like a wagon without springs. It is jolted by every pebble in the road. Good humor makes all things tolerable." Laughter at the table provides a necessary break at the end of a difficult or challenging day.

Additionally, humor can play a valuable role in helping guide people into and through difficult conversations. I recently received an e-mail from a senior woman in our church. She has served in the same international ministry for sixty years and has been a member of our church for fourteen years. After a challenging sermon, she wrote,

> Your humor at the beginning allowed for what was to follow. I have noted often how you get us to laugh at your candid experiences, then point us to Scripture that shows all of us that sin is not funny.

Your sharing allows us to identify and relate the
points to ourselves and say, "Yeah, I've said that,
done that, felt that way."

Now, while humor can be an effective way to navigate difficult situations, it isn't always the right response. My glaring weakness as a pastor is using too much humor at inappropriate times. When I feel the congregation wrestling with a deep truth or conviction, my pastor's heart wants to rescue them (and me). As a husband, I often use humor to diffuse conflict. As a dad, I sometimes use it to get the kids to like me again after discipline. These approaches aren't healthy. There is a fine line and skill involved in using humor to soften a difficult conversation. Humor should never be used as a distraction from something that needs to be worked through. Sometimes we must wrestle with difficult issues at mealtime and need to guard our tongues from sarcasm and jokes.

Allow humor to cultivate health in your home and relationships. When you walk into a home and hear laughter, you know immediately that people are enjoying one another. I love when my children laugh together, and I believe it pleases our Father when we enjoy one another in fellowship. Humor brings down walls and bonds us to one another, even those of us from different backgrounds, cultures, and denominations.

Proverbs 17:22 says, "A cheerful heart is good medicine, but a crushed spirit dries up the bones." Laughter heals us emotionally. And according to Ecclesiastes 3:4, there is "a time to weep and a time to laugh, a time to mourn and a time to dance." Emotionally healthy families experience a wide range of emotions. Some seasons bring sorrow and mourning. Other seasons bring joy and laughter. Expressing these emotions around the table ministers to the well-being of the entire family.

Set the Pace

You don't need to have a three-hour dinner every night to slow down the pace of your home. Start slowly increasing margin in your home and at your table. Set a limit on the number of fast-food stops each week. Consider Taco Tuesdays or Pizza Fridays at home and allow every member of your family to participate in the preparation of the meal. Open your hearts to one another. Laugh together. Declaring one special day a week for a long, slow meal increases your desire for more of it. It creates space in your life for God and others.

Your Family Table

Recipe: One-Pot Apple Cider Chicken Bake

AMY

In my quest to find simple, healthy meals that my family and guests enjoy, this fall dinner choice has become one of our favorites. If you don't own a French oven yet, I highly recommend it! In my opinion, it is a gift to the home-cook and worth every penny invested. I have come to love this particular tool so dearly, I would probably grab it on the way out the door in a fire. The French oven cooks food and merges flavors in a way that can't be replicated without a lot more effort from other traditional cookware. I use a 12-inch round French oven that is three inches deep. Since the whole meal is prepared and served in one pot, Ted doesn't have to scrub lots of pots and pans at the end of the night!

Recipe serves 3–4.

INGREDIENTS:
- 2 tablespoons canola oil
- 1 tablespoon butter
- 4–6 boneless, skinless chicken thighs
- 1 large yellow onion, chopped
- 1 cup apple cider, divided
- 1 large sweet potato, peeled and cut into 1-inch cubes
- 1 large apple, cut in 1-inch cubes
- 2 cups of kale leaves, chopped (discard stems if you wish)
- salt and pepper to taste

INSTRUCTIONS:

Preheat oven to 350 degrees. Pour oil and butter in a French oven or large skillet that can also be placed in the oven. On stove top, heat oil and butter over medium heat. Season chicken thighs on both sides with salt and pepper and place in hot oil. Cook on both sides for about 2 minutes. Do not fully cook the chicken.

Remove the chicken and set aside. Set the pan on

medium heat. Add the onion and ½ cup of apple cider to the remaining oil. Cook until onion is nearly translucent. Add sweet potatoes and apples and stir often for 4–5 minutes. Add chopped kale and keep stirring for another minute. Place browned pieces of chicken back into the pot so they lie on the bottom of the pan, spreading out as much as possible. Pour the remaining apple cider over the chicken and vegetables. Place in the oven for about 30 minutes, or until chicken cooks through and sweet potatoes are fork tender.

The "Who Am I?" Game

1. Pick a famous person, but don't tell anyone who you are.
2. Become that person.
3. When it is your turn, give a brief bio (four to five sentences) on who you are. Don't give too much away.
4. Impersonate your chosen person through body posture, tone, accent, gestures, and mannerisms.
5. Everyone around the table can ask you questions.
6. Have everyone reveal their guesses at the same time.[9]

Devotional

My beloved is to me a cluster of henna blossoms from the vineyards of En Gedi.

SONG OF SONGS 1:14

Hurry is one of the family's greatest enemies. It kills the soul and quality time together. We run too fast. We do too much. We like to max out our lives and squeeze out the margin to get the most out of life. But God wants us to enjoy a life in which time is not the enemy.

In Scripture, En Gedi was a lush desert oasis providing rest, rejuvenation, and relaxation to weary travelers—a place for them to slow down, to stop, to recover from the busy journey. Here are some practical ways to create a family table that refreshes and rejuvenates each member of the family at the end of a long, hard day:

Refreshing homes refuel us physically, mentally, and emotionally. Unplugging from the hustle and bustle of life gives our minds and bodies rest. Sitting down to eat and drink gives our bodies nourishment. When we are physically worn down, our moods are affected. A good meal restores the stomach and soul.

Refreshing homes create judgment-free zones. The world throws enough criticism at us—we don't need to be bombarded with it at home. Take time to listen and validate the feelings of your family rather than telling them how they're doing it wrong.

Refreshing homes have time for games and hobbies. Some parents say, "Family fun when the chores are done." Good idea. Every home needs the trash picked up, laundry sorted, meals prepared, lawn mowed, and homework completed. The sooner you get your work done, the sooner you can relax.

The Bible does not command us or encourage us to manage time. It calls us to redeem time, and we can do that by creating a slower home that is a place of refreshment and rest for all who enter. The most important question you must ask is, "What am I going to say no to?" The word *no* is the best way to protect your breathing room and guarantee time around the table. It keeps you going on more than just fumes.

Discuss
- Is our load exceeding our limit?
- How would you best describe your limit? Physical limit? Emotional limit? Mental? Relational?
- What should we trim from our family calendar to create more margin in our lives and to make more time for the family table?
- How do you best recharge and refuel at home?
- If you could change one thing about our home to make it more refreshing, what would it be?

Prayer
Father, slow us down. We run too fast and squeeze You out of our lives. This is not our intention. We just allow it to happen. For this, we confess our busyness, speed, and hurried spirits to You. We do not want to rush from one thing to another and miss life altogether. Help us say no more often so we can say yes to the most important people around our table and find rest and refreshment together. Help us to not take ourselves so seriously.

May our home and table all be a safe place where we create space for family and friends. We want to create space for You to work in our family. You are an invited guest at our family table. In Jesus' name, amen.

CHAPTER 2

A PLACE FOR MEMORIES

The family table creates memories worth repeating for generations.

AMY

Food takes us back. Smells and tastes and textures can remind us of special moments, events, seasons of life, friends, and family. For example, sweet memories flood my mind whenever I smell cocktail meatballs simmering in the crockpot. You know that smell, right? The combination of chili sauce, cranberry sauce, a little brown sugar, and minced onion? The smell of meatballs takes me back to Grandma Freitag's house on Christmas Eve. My fondest memories in childhood took place on this day every year.

My extended family lives in Minnesota. My family lived there until I was five years old, when my dad transferred with Hormel Foods to Fremont, Nebraska. This was a tough move for me. Returning to Minnesota every year to be with grand-parents and cousins was a cherished time. When Christmas rolled around, we loaded up the blue station wagon and headed for Austin, Minnesota. This long road trip was a much-anticipated part of every Christmas. We rarely ate out as a family, so a smoked-filled truck-stop diner and a short stack of pancakes along the way was a thrill. And the closer we got to Austin, the giddier I became. All I could think about was time with family. The "Welcome to Minnesota" sign is branded on my mind and heart forever.

When we walked in the door of Grandma Freitag's house, the smell lifted us out of our shoes. A crockpot full of cocktail meatballs. Now, there is nothing all that special about cock-tail meatballs, right? Most of the time, they come precooked and frozen. You defrost and heat them in the crockpot along with a plethora of canned ingredients. But anything served in an environment of love, safety, and family feels like it comes from a four-star Michelin restaurant, even if it actually comes from a can.

My grandma Freitag is truly one of the most precious people I know. She loves her family, and everything she did was to care for those she loved. We no longer make it back to Minnesota for Christmas, but that doesn't stop us from eating meatballs on Christmas Eve. The memory lives on.

TED

My favorite job in college was that of snow shoveler for a con-tractor in Naperville, Illinois. Every Christmas break, I prayed for snow. The contractor secured hundreds of contracts to remove snow from commercial and residential properties in the suburbs of Chicago and employed a hundred guys on shovels and plows every time it snowed. He said he wanted hard workers who didn't need sleep, and he paid his shovelers sixteen dollars an hour. I signed up immediately.

My record shift was thirty hours straight. We shoveled outside banks, stores, restaurants, and apartment complexes. I was wiped out after thirty hours, but my weariness subsided when I counted the $480 paycheck. Better yet, the forecast showed another storm front moving in. At the end of the shift, the boss told me to stick close and wait for the next call. I was too tired to drive back to where I lived, so I crashed on Grandma Mary Jane Ludwig's couch.

After a few hours of sleep, I woke up to find Grandma fixing me breakfast in the kitchen. Her specialty was cinnamon toast. It was light on cinnamon and heavy on sugar and butter. That and a hot cup of coffee was comfort to me. Grandma told me how proud she was of her hardworking grandsons. She grew up during the Great Depression, when her entire family worked very hard to make ends meet. Watching her grandsons develop a strong work ethic meant a lot to her.

As we ate, talked about life, and watched the snow fall, the phone rang. It was my boss calling me back to work. He assigned me to go shovel everything I had cleared the previous day. I hugged and kissed Grandma like I always did and headed out for another marathon shift.

I did not leave her house empty-handed. She sent me out the door with the same coffee can she had sent to work with my grandpa twenty years earlier. And in the can? Snacks. She was always one step ahead of me. My brother and cousins received the same can on their side jobs too. It was her way of passing on my grandpa's work ethic to his grandsons. Her motto was "Work hard, snack well."

When I think about my grandma, Proverbs 11:24-25 comes to mind: "One person gives freely, yet gains even more; another withholds unduly, but comes to poverty. A generous person will prosper; whoever refreshes others will be refreshed." My grandma lived simply so that she could be generous. She gave away as much as she could. She loved blessing people in her life even when she didn't have a whole lot.

As the years go by, I want my kids to remember that our mealtimes came with real food, rich conversation, and unconditional love. What will they think about when they are forty years old? What smells will they remember? What memories will stick? Creating an intentional family table means creating memories that will last our families a lifetime. We're products of our grandparents' and parents' tables and the memories of time spent around them—and one of these days, we'll be the grandparents encouraging lasting memories in the next generation.

What about Your Grandma's Table?

Many of us have memories of our grandparents that made their family table particularly special. When I asked friends on Facebook to share with me their favorite memories around grandma's table, I was overwhelmed with responses. Over a hundred people left a memory of grandma. I read every one and enjoyed the stories immensely. Some made me laugh out loud. Some made me *verklempt*. All of them took me to grandma's family table.

So what sort of memories come out of our family tables? Our memories help us learn what an intentional family table looks like.

The family table is where we make room for others. My cousin Cal Samstag is the oldest of Grandma Ludwig's grandsons. We have many common memories around Grandma's table. He wrote,

> I was blessed with two fantastic grandmas. I always
> enjoyed coffee with both at their kitchen tables.
> Both would drink coffee at any time, day or night.
> Grandma Mary Jane had a sign in her kitchen
> that read, "It does not matter where I entertain
> my guests. They always seem to like the kitchen
> best." Ted, we have great memories in her kitchen;
> however, the thing that makes me smile most about
> eating with her was at Grandma Sally's Restaurant.
> Leo [Grandma's boyfriend] insisted on a round table
> to encourage and stimulate conversation. Their
> largest table sat six people comfortably, but we
> always fit ten or more on a busy night. Wednesday
> was Leo's family night. I swear there were nights

when I was at least two feet back from that table, trying to eat and not crowd others.

The family table is where we play games. Amy's dad, Dennis Freitag, said,

> One of my grandma's favorite meals was mashed potatoes, dark gravy, scalloped corn, and roast beef. She loved to play the card game Euchre with Grandpa, me, and Linda.

The family table is where secrets are kept. Our children's director at Woodland Hills, Stephanie Watson, revealed,

> My grandma used to make these wonderful scalloped potatoes but wouldn't give us the recipe because it was "secret." When she was past the point of cooking, she finally agreed to tell the secret. They were from a box! Now my sister gets the honor of making the potatoes every Thanksgiving.

The family table is where we honor our elders. Amy Hanstein Smith's brother esteemed his grandma as highly valuable:

> My grandma made her special batch of homegrown green beans for my brother every time we visited because "they were his favorite." My brother doesn't

like green beans, but every time she serves them, he eats them and says they are delicious. He is nearly forty and she is eighty-five, and I suspect she will never know.

The family table is where we indulge from time to time. Angie Mabe indulged at Grandma's:

Both my grandmas were intent on filling our bellies (still are at eighty-four) each time I visited them. My grandparents from my mom's side would get up and make a stack of pancakes fifteen high! Grandma would slather them in butter, then drench them in syrup. Meals are always big at her house. We simply didn't eat like this at home. You can see the love and happiness in her eyes when we eat. That's her way of caring for us and loving us.

The family table can be thrifty. How many of us had grandmas who used margarine and Cool Whip tubs for everyday bowls? Julie Seymour Lanham wrote,

My grandmother used to wash and reuse Styrofoam plates!

The family table is where we learn to laugh at ourselves. Our family friend Heather Jenkins recounted,

It's not a sweet memory but one of our funniest. At Thanksgiving one year, Grandma sat at the kids' table with us. She was a large woman, and when all the kids got up, the table flipped upside down—food and all. I can still remember the look on her face and the table on top of her. I'm glad she liked to laugh and was able to do so with us.

The family table cultivates adventurous culinary spirits. Woodland Hills Family Church member Katy Gray shared,

My grandma always used to let me try to come up with "new" recipes. One time I mixed lemon juice, pickle juice, and milk. She gave it a try. I now know how much love that must have taken.

Mesa Mitchell's grandma combined laughter and adventure:

My grandma, Mary Jane Tollefson, was one of a kind. I could tell stories about her for hours and it would be a fantastic ab workout. One of the things she always did when I would visit was try new recipes from one of her magazines. She was so excited about the surprise of something new she'd never tried. Corey and I still laugh about the final recipe she ever prepared for us: "Weenie Casserole." I will never look at hot dogs and baked beans the same again.

The family table has scraps for everyone. Jenelle Pettigrew recalls,

> We spent a lot of time at Grandma Irene's house, and she baked cakes from her home. Oh, the smell of cake and sweet icing. When she would stack cakes for weddings, she would slice off portions to make them sit even and put those pieces in a bowl for anyone wanting a taste . . . and we'd *taste*!

The family table inspires us to do the best with what we have. Our friend Marcia Phillips says,

> I have so many wonderful memories of my grandma Martha Webster! My mom's side of the family is pretty big, and there were always little ones running around. I have fond memories of sitting at the "kids' table" with all my cousins, being loud in Grandma's kitchen, and laughing at the "black-bottom biscuits" she always made. She would never take them out of the oven until she could smell them burning! We learned to always just peel the bottom layer off! Luckily, she didn't use the same timer for her hummingbird, Milky Way, and pineapple upside-down cakes. Yum! Two things I will always remember about her dining room table: She always had a stick of butter in a beautiful butter dish, and she always had fresh flowers, usually

carnations. "I know they're cheap," she'd say, "but they're pretty!"

The family table shares recipes. To this day, my grandma Millie Cunningham's meatloaf is still my favorite. It was simply hamburger, egg, milk, saltine crackers, chopped onion, salt, and pepper. One extra ingredient kept my brother from eating it. When Andy was two years old my family visited my grandparents. Grandma made meatloaf, knowing it was my dad's favorite meal, along with mashed potatoes and lima beans. Andy didn't touch his. Mom discreetly told him he would like it because it was just like hers. He told her he wasn't eating it because it had something growing in it. Grandma added parsley to it. Forty years later, my mom still uses Grandma Millie's recipe but leaves out the parsley.

The family table ignites our faith and gives us a place to come back to. Author, speaker, and friend Sundi Jo Graham reminds us that life around the table is where our faith is forged:

> I remember a season of my childhood where we would have family brunches around the large dining room table in my grandmother's Victorian-style house. She always made homemade biscuits. As a lonely child, I desired those family meals every day. I couldn't wait for Sundays. But my grandma was a bitter woman most of my life, and our family meals abruptly stopped.

Fourteen years ago I ran away from my hometown, vowing I'd never go back. But God has changed that, and He's slowly changing the hearts of my family—including my grandma. In the last year, she has devoted her life to Jesus, and there's a peace I've never seen in her. She's traded her bitter heart for joy.

In a recent conversation, after announcing with many tears that I was moving back, I asked her, "If I move back, can we start having Sunday brunches again like we used to?"

She smiled and said, "Yes."

It's a picture of God's love for me. I look forward to those homemade biscuits, but more importantly, I look forward to getting to know the grandma I've always desired to have, around the table.

Creating Memories Worth Repeating

AMY

The Herschend family founded Silver Dollar City in Branson, Missouri, over fifty years ago. This family theme park has a great mission statement: "Creating memories worth repeating." They want to inspire family memories passed down from generation to generation. Some of our best family memories are in that park, and our emotional connection to Silver Dollar City runs deep. I can still remember watching the Christmas parade on a cold December night with four generations of my family like it was yesterday. We sipped hot chocolate, shared funnel cakes, and made our own s'mores. That was more than five years ago, but every Christmas our hearts and minds go back to that night with a growing desire to create more memories worth repeating.

Some might call Ted and me "experience parents," but we prefer the term "memories parents." Creating and repeating memories reminds us to honor each other and our past. We stay grounded when we stay connected to the past. Memories teach our children how to prioritize family and faith. Recounting defining moments in life brings us face-to-face with our rich heritage.

Like many of our parents and grandparents, my mom grew up on a farm. Animals have always been a part of her life. And since I love animals too, you would think that when our daughter, Corynn, started talking about her desire to raise chickens, I would jump on the idea. But my experience has been with furry creatures—I knew nothing of the feathered variety. I also knew nothing about farming. I was shocked to learn that Corynn was able to get her dad on board with this adventure way before she had me convinced. But when I thought about my mom and grandparents and their farm, I started to get excited about the thought of a hobby farm. This would be a great way to connect our family with our heritage. I was in.

A week later, we stopped at our local Sam's Club to pick up a few things in bulk. I went to the produce section, and Ted took the kids to wander around and look at more exciting stuff. About twenty minutes into the trip, I came around the corner to find them all staring at a chicken coop. When Ted looked at me, I knew what he was thinking: *Come on—we only have the kids for a short time—let's be adventurous!* I instantly felt stressed and overwhelmed. The planner in me knew we had not done the proper amount of research necessary for such a big decision.

"It's three hundred dollars, and the eggs we get will pay us back in two years," Ted said. That's how his brain works. Not mine. I thought about buying the chicks, feeders, fencing, heat lamps, shavings, and food.

We bought the coop that day, and the research began. I found some beautiful books filled with pictures of chickens in English gardens and read how the chickens would eat ticks and other bugs and keep weeds out of our yet-to-be-planted garden. The books also included pictures of beautiful chicken coops surrounded by elaborate landscaping. The more I read, the more I realized that our Sam's Club chicken coop was not going to provide our chickens the comfort and safety they would need—or cut it as the backdrop for our new landscaping and garden. So I started a Pinterest board for chicken coops (really, guest cottages with nesting boxes). After a few weeks of pinning and reading, I informed Ted that we needed to start from scratch.

While some local carpenters built our chicken chateau, we went over to Tractor Supply Company to buy baby chicks and load up on gear. We bought troughs to house the chicks, heat lamps to keep them warm, food and water dispensers, and pine shavings to give them comfort during cold nights. According to my research and checklists, we were hitting all the marks of true farmers.

When the chicks arrived home, my motherly instinct kicked in. I woke up every few hours to check on the little balls of fluff. Early the next morning, my greatest fear involving the chicks came true. One of them hadn't made it through that first night. I wondered if I was cut out for the huge responsibility of caring for these eleven chicks. Going with the flow is not my forte. Control is my friend. Faced with my powerlessness, I started making plans to return everything to the farm store. I was mad they sold stuff to us to begin with. Shouldn't you have to have a license of some sort to be a farmer?

After I got a good night's sleep and got over my anxiety attack, I realized that the loss of a baby chick in a group that size is normal. We didn't lose any more after that first night. A year later we still have all eleven chickens.

Our hobby farm is a family affair. We all take turns feeding, filling water jugs, checking for eggs, and cleaning out the coop. I love watching our children put on their rubber boots and get their hands dirty. The chickens provide us with almost a dozen eggs daily. We have done more baking and cooking in the last several months than ever before. And as a result, we share our table with others more often. It's fun sending our dinner guests home with a dozen eggs. We started this journey to create memories with our daughter. It has turned out to be one of the coolest adventures we have had as a family. Raising these chickens together is a memory our kids will never forget.

Ted and I have a strong desire to create memories for all who visit our home. We love practical application and a hands-on approach to teaching and learning. The goal of great teaching and parenting is to take complex, difficult-to-understand ideas and make them easy to grasp and apply. Memories illustrate the life principles we want our children to leave home with. As Dick Foth wrote,

> Our experiences shape the way we think, the way we interact with each other, and the way we live. They add richness and depth and meaning to our days. You can give your children toys today that quickly end up in tomorrow's trash. Or you can deliver a living, breathing experience that shapes their souls, enriches their lives, and makes their world and yours a doorway to tomorrow.[1]

The family table creates memories that will live on long after the meal ends.

Your Family Table

Recipe: Super-Simple Giant Stuffed Meatballs

Sad to say, we lost my grandma's meatball recipe. My family doesn't care for my traditional recipes. When they hear *meatballs*, they want Italian meatballs with marinara sauce.

I finally stopped trying to persuade them to like them. Now we enjoy Italian meatballs.

So here is our favorite original family meatball recipe. These meatballs have more of your traditional Italian flavors. We often enjoy them with my parents, as this is my dad's all-time favorite food. I am pretty sure it has something to do with the fact that my mom made him meatballs and spaghetti for their first meal together when they were dating. This is a great dish to make ahead, freeze, bring to a friend, or serve to adults and kids alike. Who doesn't enjoy the comfort and flavors of meatballs—especially super-sized and stuffed with cheese?

Can meatballs create memories? Absolutely! When you share your home, your food, and your family with someone, you create memories with others and for your family.

Recipe serves 8–9.

INGREDIENTS:
    1 pound ground turkey (at least 93% lean)
    1 pound Italian pork sausage
    1 cup grated Parmesan cheese
    ½ cup breadcrumbs
    2 teaspoons onion powder
    2 teaspoons red pepper flakes
    1 egg, beaten
    ½ pound shredded mozzarella
    1 tablespoon olive oil

salt and pepper to taste
2 jars of your favorite marinara sauce

INSTRUCTIONS:
Preheat oven to 350 degrees.

In a large mixing bowl, combine the ground turkey, sausage, Parmesan cheese, breadcrumbs, onion powder, and red pepper flakes. Beat the egg in a separate bowl and then add to the mixture. Work it all together with your hands.

Once the mixture is thoroughly combined, form your meatballs. Make a 4- to 5-inch diameter ball. Use your thumbs to push in on the ball and form a pocket at the center for the cheese. Stuff with mozzarella (my family says there can't be too much!). Once the pocket is stuffed with cheese, reform the meatball. You should be able to make 8 to 9 giant meatballs.

Heat olive oil in a 2-inch-deep skillet or a French oven. (This will need to go directly from the stove top to the oven, so make sure it is ovenproof.) Once the oil is heated, place your meatballs in the pot and lightly brown them on each side, about 1 to 2 minutes on each side. Salt and pepper each side as well. Browning them will keep your meatballs juicy and help them hold together as they are drenched in sauce. Drain oil. Add 2 jars of marinara sauce to the pot. You will want plenty of sauce, however you choose to serve them. A little extra sauce and a sprinkle of Parmesan make the whole dish more flavorful. Place them in the oven for 30 minutes, then serve on pasta, in toasted subs, or with vegetables. Bon appétit!

The "Or" Game

Our family enjoys this game, which involves players asking one another to choose between two options. It's the perfect spontaneous, rapid-fire game. You can launch into it at a moment's notice, and it only takes a minute or two to play. Anyone can shout out two options:

Beach or mountains?
Six Flags or Disney World?
Pepsi or Coca-Cola?
Kale or spinach?
Milk chocolate or dark chocolate?
Fries or fruit?
Bacon or ham?
Baseball or basketball?

Devotional

They broke bread in their homes and ate together with glad and sincere hearts.

ACTS 2:46

The first-century church met together in one another's homes to pray, study the Scriptures, partake in the Lord's Supper, worship, and sing. They gathered around family tables to enjoy food, each other, and Jesus. The family table is about the quality of fellowship and the memories made there, not just the need to eat.

An open door and a thoughtful, prepared meal says, "You

are valuable to me and to our family." Esteem your guests as highly valuable by asking them great questions, speaking a blessing over them, and serving them from the moment they step over your threshold.

Create memories by slowing down the pace of the table. Great fellowship is never rushed. It is slow. Speed and hurry are the enemies of intimate gatherings. One test of great fellowship around the family table? When it's over and you look at your watch and say, "I can't believe how fast time went."

To make intentional spiritual memories around your family table, center the conversation around the Lord. Begin the meal with a prayer of thanksgiving. Every breath we take and every morsel we eat come from God.

Use these questions to encourage your family to think through how to create lasting memories around the family table:

Discuss

- What are some of your favorite family meals? Be specific.
- Is the guest experience in your home creating good memories for others? How?
- Do you remember an awkward moment around the family table? What made it awkward, and what could you do to keep it from happening again?

Prayer

Father, You are the Creator and Sustainer of life. Thank You for our home. Thank You for this table. May there always be a place here for family, friends, and strangers to make lasting memories. You have given us the family table to be shared with others. We desire to be a family that loves You and one another. Years from now, may we look back on this time with joy. Bless our conversation and the food that is provided around this table from this day forward. In Jesus' name, amen.

CHAPTER 3

FOOD, WINE, AND GOD'S FAVOR

The family table is where we receive food and wine
as good gifts from our Lord.

TED

Brownies are my weakness. Amy knows this. Joy floods my soul when I walk in the house and a pan of fresh-baked goodness rests on our kitchen counter. The clouds open and I hear angels singing, "Hallelujah!"

One afternoon, several years ago, the angels did not sing. As I cut into the pan, my heart raced and my hands trembled in anticipation. The first bite is usually the best bite. Chewy chocolate stuck to your teeth and the roof of your mouth makes subsequent bites all the better. But this first bite? It was almost my last.

As I chewed, Amy walked into the kitchen and asked, "What do you think?"

It walks like a brownie and it talks like a brownie, but this most certainly is not a brownie. I was speechless.

Her next words brought me to my knees. "I put spinach in it," she said.

What? You did what? Who puts spinach in brownies? This goes against everything I believe! I thought.

Amy sneaks healthy food into my diet every chance she gets. Flax and chia seeds go undetected. Protein powder hides itself in small doses. But spinach is another story, especially in large doses. Comedian Jim Gaffigan says, "Can we knock it off with all the kale propaganda?" but I say, "Could we please knock it off with all the covert operations in the kitchen?"

The brownie incident was a turning point in our marriage. Do or die, I had to state my case: "Amy, you can put flaxseed in our pancakes and protein powder in our smoothies, but for all that is good and right, leave the brownies alone." I wanted to add, "Thus saith the Lord," but didn't. But brownies are a particularly good gift from God, if I do say so myself.

Enjoying God's Good Gifts

Food and fellowship are linked. Enjoying a meal with others is part of daily living. The family table receives food and wine as gifts from the Lord. King Solomon implored us to "go, eat your food with gladness, and drink your wine with a joyful heart, for God has already approved what you do" (Ecclesiastes 9:7). God approves of enjoying food and wine around the table! We receive the gifts on our family table with thanksgiving and guard against lies and demonic spirits that deny us these gifts:

> They forbid people to marry and order them to abstain from certain foods, which God created to be received with thanksgiving by those who believe and who know the truth. For everything God created is good, and nothing is to be rejected if it is received with thanksgiving, because it is consecrated by the word of God and prayer.
>
> 1 TIMOTHY 4:3-5

When we eat and drink together, we pause and remember that the Lord provided it all (Deuteronomy 6:10-12). At the end of each day, we rest from our labor and enjoy one another around the table. Solomon asked the question:

> What do workers gain from their toil? . . . I know that there is nothing better for people than to be happy and to do good while they live. That each of them may eat and drink, and find satisfaction in all their toil—this is the gift of God.
>
> ECCLESIASTES 3:9, 12-13

Food and wine are gifts not to be abused. Too much food leads to gluttony. Too much wine leads to drunkenness. Both are sin. We should enjoy wine paired with great food with no temptation to indulge. When we stop viewing these things as gifts, we misuse them. The overconsumption is the sin, not the food and wine.

Jesus provided one of these gifts at a wedding. His first miraculous sign blessed a couple and their gathered guests with more wine. In that day, weddings lasted for days. Providing food and drink for that long of a party was costly. Look how Jesus handled the shortage and blessed those in attendance:

> On the third day a wedding took place at Cana in Galilee. Jesus' mother was there, and Jesus and his disciples had also been invited to the wedding. When the wine was gone, Jesus' mother said to him, "They have no more wine."
>
> "Woman, why do you involve me?" Jesus replied. "My hour has not yet come."
>
> His mother said to the servants, "Do whatever he tells you."
>
> Nearby stood six stone water jars, the kind used by the Jews for ceremonial washing, each holding from twenty to thirty gallons.
>
> Jesus said to the servants, "Fill the jars with water"; so they filled them to the brim.
>
> Then he told them, "Now draw some out and take it to the master of the banquet."
>
> They did so, and the master of the banquet tasted the water that had been turned into wine. He did not realize where it had come from, though

the servants who had drawn the water knew. Then he called the bridegroom aside and said, "Everyone brings out the choice wine first and then the cheaper wine after the guests have had too much to drink; but you have saved the best till now."

JOHN 2:1-10

Jesus created 120 gallons of wine. In today's measurements, He produced over six hundred bottles of wine. That's at least twelve thousand dollars in wine in today's market! And because the master of the banquet called the wine the "best," we must assume it would have been a lot more than that. What a great gift!

The Lord started and ended His earthly ministry by blessing others gathered around the table. At the Last Supper, He reclined at the table with His disciples. He blessed the bread and the wine, and as they ate and drank He told them that this would be His last meal with them:

On the first day of the Festival of Unleavened Bread, the disciples came to Jesus and asked, "Where do you want us to make preparations for you to eat the Passover?"

He replied, "Go into the city to a certain man and tell him, 'The Teacher says: My appointed time is near. I am going to celebrate the Passover with my disciples at your house.'" So the disciples did as Jesus had directed them and prepared the Passover.

When evening came, Jesus was reclining at the table with the Twelve. . . .

While they were eating, Jesus took bread, and when he had given thanks, he broke it and gave it to his disciples, saying, "Take and eat; this is my body."

Then he took a cup, and when he had given thanks, he gave it to them, saying, "Drink from it, all of you. This is my blood of the covenant, which is poured out for many for the forgiveness of sins. I tell you, I will not drink from this fruit of the vine from now on until that day when I drink it new with you in my Father's kingdom."

When they had sung a hymn, they went out to the Mount of Olives.

MATTHEW 26:17-20, 26-30

When Jesus gave His disciples the bread and the wine, He was foreshadowing the good gifts of His body and blood. He commemorated His death on the cross. He also left them with this hope: "I tell you, I will not drink from this fruit of the vine from now on until that day when I drink it new with you in my Father's kingdom." We will enjoy the good gifts of bread and wine one day with our Savior: "Blessed are those who are invited to the marriage supper of the Lamb" (Revelation 19:9, ESV). His death and resurrection guarantee that we will recline at a table with Him and enjoy all He has done and all He has provided.

It saddens us when people look upon food and wine with

disdain. The Lord provides everything we enjoy around the family table. He is our Creator, Salvation, and Sustainer. This is why we offer a prayer of thanksgiving around the family table before every meal. We receive it with gratefulness and refuse to abuse or misuse it.

The Fear of Loving Food

AMY

As far back as I can remember, I had a love-hate relationship with food. Loving the taste, the experience, the recreation of it. Hating how I felt when I ate too much. Hating that good-tasting food denied me the perfect body. Hating that my beanpole friends could eat anything they wanted and not gain weight. Hating that I felt like I should pretend to be full when I was still hungry.

I remember being eight years old and secretly hoping my friend Michelle would invite me over to her house. Lunch at her house meant creamy peanut butter and grape jelly sandwiches on white Wonder Bread with a side of Nacho Cheese Doritos or extra salty potato chips. For dessert, a cold glass of milk and frozen Oreos! Seriously, what could be better than that? I worked hard to control my excitement. I would try not to eat too fast, making sure to stay one bite behind my friend, partly to savor the food and partly because I just knew if I let myself I would inhale it all in three big bites.

None of this food was in my family's pantry. It was an indulgence for me to eat like a "normal kid." In her book

Bread and Wine, Shauna Niequist talks about how her mom ate and cooked healthy before it was cool to do so. That was my mom. Wheaties, whole wheat bread, crunchy peanut butter (what kid likes crunchy peanut butter?), fruit, and an occasional Tab cola were treats in my childhood home. For an extra special treat we rode four miles round trip on our bikes to the health food store, where they served the new eighties phenomenon frozen yogurt. I am pretty sure that none of my friends secretly wished they could eat lunch at my house.

Now I realize and appreciate the effort and expense my mom put into keeping us healthy. Regardless, I still struggled with food. I wondered why everyone else didn't seem to love it as much as I did. I was not overweight, but I was always bigger than my friends. I wore bigger size jeans, shoes, and shirts. I often found myself daydreaming of being smaller and skinnier just like everybody else. Of course, my view of myself and others was a bit warped.

I don't ever remember making the decision to have an eating disorder. I do remember being fed up with my body and feeling out of control. I tried not to eat, and that didn't go over so well. Did I mention how much I enjoy food? So bulimia seemed like a good alternative to not eating. I could have my cake and eat it too. I would just need to get rid of it when it was gone. I did this for a few years in high school. I didn't eat breakfast. I would eat a salad for lunch, and then when I got home I'd eat what I wanted and purge. I lost weight, but I also lost energy and drive. It was hard for me to stick to any particular sport because I didn't eat enough calories to sustain any sort of active lifestyle.

My parents caught on to what I was doing and took me to a doctor. The doctor pressed me about what I was doing to my body, but she wasn't telling me anything I didn't already know. I had read and studied all about it and understood the risks.

Unfortunately, it took some serious circumstances to get my attention. The summer after my senior year in high school, I was pulled over for driving while intoxicated and had to do some jail time. It was humiliating and forced me to see that I was completely out of control. I wanted to be done with the bulimia and with partying with my friends. Living for myself proved to be empty and aimless. I prayed that the Lord would take these desires from me and replace them with a desire for Him. He answered my prayer and filled every void in my life. My life verse became 2 Corinthians 12:9: "But he said to me, 'My grace is sufficient for you, for my power is made perfect in weakness.' Therefore I will boast all the more gladly about my weaknesses, so that Christ's power may rest on me."

The desire to binge, purge, and drink too much was taken from me. As I write this, I am reminded that it is good to look back and reflect on what the Lord has done. It's such a good reminder of His hand of protection and His faithfulness (Psalms 126:3; 118).

We live in a nation that loves food and drink too much. Finding joy in food and wine is good, but consuming too much is where we fall short. I like what Jim Gaffigan says about it:

If anything defines American eating, it is the quantity of food we consume. This would explain why the "All-You-Can-Eat Buffet" is such an American phenomenon, and it makes perfect sense that it started in Las Vegas. Some of the most amazing restaurants in the world are in Las Vegas, but the real local specialty is the All-You-Can-Eat Buffet. Buffets are as common in Vegas as glitter and regrettable behavior. The Vegas casino buffets are expansive and ridiculous. In other words, completely American. You can get sushi, mac and cheese, and doughnuts all in the same meal. God bless America. One of the main reasons that the all-you-can-eat buffet is a perfect fit for casinos is because the all-you-can-eat buffet is the food equivalent of gambling. And like all other forms of institutional gambling, it's rigged for the house.

The all-you-can-eat buffets always feel like a challenge. "All-YOU-can-eat." The unspoken rule of the all-you-can-eat buffet is that you must eat the food value of more than the cost of the buffet.[1]

For us, food and wine around the family table are balanced with moderation. We prioritize quality over quantity. More is not always better. What is better? Actually enjoying it together. As J. R. R. Tolkien once said, "If more of us valued food and cheer and song above hoarded gold, it would be a merrier world."[2] Gathering to enjoy a meal is a gift from our

Lord. He is present when we enjoy one another and all that He has provided.

⇾Your Family Table

Recipe: Linda's Zucchini Coconut Bars

AMY

As I mentioned earlier, my mom had a thing for healthy food. Mom and Dad gardened every year. The garden in our backyard was big and divided into neat, orderly sections of tomatoes and squash, potatoes and carrots. Strawberries were my favorite part of the garden until it became my job to pick them every late morning in the blazing heat of the sun. The yield didn't seem to be worth the effort.

Another plant found in a lot of gardens? Zucchini! For those of you who have never had zucchini in baked goods, never fear. You won't taste the vegetable. The zucchini simply provides moistness to the cake. I must forewarn you: If you are not a food texture person, this is not for you. However, those of us who like to chew and crunch and savor a bunch of flavors and textures at once love this cake!

Recipe makes 12 very thin bars.

INGREDIENTS:

   ¾ cup softened butter
   1 cup brown sugar
   ¼ cup white sugar
   2 eggs

1½ teaspoons vanilla

1¾ cups light flour (like White Lily)

2 teaspoons baking powder

2 cups shredded zucchini (with peel)

1 cup shredded coconut

1 cup chopped almonds

FROSTING:

1½ cups powdered sugar

¼ teaspoon allspice

¼ teaspoon nutmeg

¼ cup softened butter

2 tablespoons milk

1 teaspoon almond extract

INSTRUCTIONS:

Cream butter and sugars together. Add eggs and vanilla. Stir in flour and baking powder; mix in zucchini, coconut, and almonds. Grease and flour a 9 x 13 cake pan. Pour batter in. Bake at 350 degrees for 40 minutes, until edges begin to brown and a toothpick inserted in the center comes out clean. Cool.

In my opinion, the cake tastes great unfrosted, but the frosting just takes it to a whole new level. Combine all dry ingredients. In a separate bowl, mix softened butter, milk, and almond extract with an immersion blender or fork. Mix them all together. Store-bought cream cheese frosting also works really well.

The "If" Game

Enjoy exploring these what-if questions together as a family!

1. If you could visit any country tomorrow, where would you go and what would you do?
2. If you could become proficient in one musical instrument overnight, what would the instrument be? What is the first song you would play?
3. If you were only allowed to eat vegetables for the rest of your life, what would you grow in your garden?
4. If you were asked to pray at the White House, what would be the first line of your prayer?
5. If you could invite any US President (living or dead) over for dinner, who would you invite?
6. If you knew tonight was your last night on earth, what would you do?
7. If you had to leave your home forever with only one small suitcase, what would you take with you?
8. If you could learn three foreign languages in the next three weeks, which ones would you choose?
9. If you were asked to coach a professional sports team, which team would you choose and what changes would you make?
10. If you were asked to create a theme park, what would you name it?
11. If you had to wear one outfit for the rest of your life, describe what it would be from head to toe.

12. If you could have been an extra in a movie that has already been released, which movie and scene would you be in?
13. If you could choose a different ending to a movie, which movie would you change and how?
14. If we were told we had to relocate to a big city tomorrow, which city would you choose?
15. If you had to choose between living on a farm or in a big city, which would you choose and why?
16. If you were forced to dance in front of a group of people, who would you bust a move for?
17. If you could write yourself into a novel, which book would your choose and what would your character do?
18. If you could preach a sermon at your church, which topic or passage would you choose?
19. If you were asked to downsize to a tiny house, what is the minimum amount of square footage you could live in?
20. If you were a master carpenter, what piece of furniture would you want to build for your family?

Devotional

Eat your food with gladness, and drink your wine with a joyful heart, for God has already approved what you do.

ECCLESIASTES 9:7

Scripture links food and enjoyment. God favors us when we sit down and enjoy the food He created. God gives us cows for milk and chickens for eggs. He created the herbs we use to season the meat of both cows and chickens. The seas are full of great fish to eat. He planted the first vegetables to give our bodies the nutrition necessary to enjoy long life upon the earth. Yes, God wants you to enjoy broccoli, asparagus, beets, carrots, and kale.

God also created the vine and the grapes that give us good wine. Comedian John Branyan makes this humorous observation: "Do you really think God is up in heaven telling the angels, 'Look what they're doing with grapes!'" He made them, and he knows what they are capable of.

There are many ways to eat with gladness and a joyful heart. First, you can begin each meal with a prayer of thanksgiving. You can also applaud as a family as the food arrives at the table. Compliment the hands that prepared it. If you really want to show your excitement, you can end the meal with more applause and a standing ovation.

Spend some time around the family table discussing where the food on the table came from. Farmers planted and harvested the food. Truck drivers delivered it to your town. Grocery store employees unpacked it and organized it on shelves. Someone you love prepared it for you to eat.

Discuss

- What are some ways our family can prevent boredom at mealtime?

- Why do you think God wants you to enjoy eating good food?
- What are your favorite foods?

Prayer

Lord, thank You for the good gifts of food and drink around our table. You enabled us to work so we could buy this food. You gave us the knowledge to prepare it. We are grateful. We receive with thanksgiving all that is on this table. Use it to nourish our bodies, souls, and spirits. Refresh us with what you have created so that we may better serve you. May our table be life-giving to all who dine here. In Jesus' name, amen.

CHAPTER 4

TOGETHER, WHEREVER

The family table is anywhere we are together.

TED

Years ago, a mentor shared with me, "Every marriage needs a daily delay, weekly withdrawal, and annual abandon." He told me to prioritize these three dates if I wanted a thriving marriage for a lifetime. This structure works not only for our marriage, but for our family as well, which is why our family enjoys meals around town and out of town.

The daily delay assures quality, not just quantity, time. A weekly withdrawal gets us out of the house away from chores and routine. An annual abandon gives us adventure away from the familiar settings of our hometown. Prioritizing quality time says to family and friends, "Our family is important." Just being together in a non-rushed, tech-free setting communicates that we love one another enough to block the world out for a little bit and re-center our family.

Daily Delay

Our home is an oasis and a fortress. We need a lush, relaxing, rejuvenating oasis that refreshes us from the grind of life and work. We also need a safe fortress where we can be ourselves in a judgment-free zone. In relationships, we can tend to avoid issues and stuff conflict until we explode like a volcano. And we do not feel better immediately following the eruption. It takes some time to repair and heal the home after months of neglect.

There is a much better way. Securing a daily delay keeps things from building up. The daily delay is an intentional time every day where we as a family step away from the distractions around us simply to focus on and talk to each other. For us, this happens during the meal.

Instead of waiting weeks or months to discuss sensitive subjects, take the time each day to keep short accounts. We want little to no gap between what we expect and what we receive (reality). When expectations are not met, we get frustrated. Left unchecked, the primary emotion of frustration turns into the secondary emotion of anger. A big gap between what we expected and what actually happened equals big anger.

You want as small of a gap as possible. Reducing the gap happens one of two ways: You can either adjust your expectations to be more healthy and realistic or choose to change your reality. Quality family time can happen in the gap between expectations and reality. The daily delay gives you time to work through differences and come to a win-win for all members of the family. You want everyone involved to walk away from the table feeling like a winner.

Here are some questions and conversation starters we find helpful in making the most of our daily delays:

1. What was the hardest part of your day?
2. What was the best part of your day?
3. If we played hooky tomorrow, we would

            _____ .
4. What was your biggest distraction today?
5. Did you talk to anyone interesting today?
6. If you could change one thing about your day, what would it be?
7. Did you say anything today that you wish you could take back?
8. If you knew you couldn't fail, what would you wake up tomorrow and do?
9. If I handed you a check for ten million dollars, what would you do first thing tomorrow morning?
10. If your job let you work and live anywhere in the world, where would you choose to live and why?
11. What could I do this week that would make you feel extra special?
12. What people group, organization, cause, or mission would you most want to give to over the next twelve months?

13. How do you desire to serve others this year, either in the community or at church?
14. Who is one person you would like to seek counsel from?
15. What do you want to get better at?
16. What are some things you always wanted to do but haven't done yet?
17. Describe the person you want to be five years from now.
18. This will be a relaxing evening if we _____ _____ .

A daily delay protects fun times around town by ensuring that expectations and other practical family items are in their proper place. Leave the chores at home. When we go out, we don't need to spend time working out schedules or budgets. We can unplug and enjoy one another.

Weekly Withdrawal

Our family's favorite spot for a weekly withdrawal is at the library lounge at the Chateau on the Lake here in Branson, Missouri. Our vacation spot is four high-back leather chairs around a coffee table next to the fireplace. Winter, summer, spring, or fall, it is the perfect getaway. We order light, usually appetizers. You have not lived until you've tried their avocado fries. Dipped in ranch and smothered with salsa, there's no better way to eat fruit.

Our favorite time to enjoy this lounge is on a Monday

night. This is Amy's most stressful day of the week. She spends the day at a home school cooperative with Carson. It is a very social day, and she is out of words by 4:00 p.m. Of all the places to eat out in our town, this lounge is the one place where our family never seems to be in a rush to leave. We never run into people we know, so conversations are limited to polite nods toward tourists. It often feels like we're hiding, and that is okay.

A weekly withdrawal is intended to help our family disconnect from the world around us and reconnect with one another. This can look like time with the whole family or special date nights just for mom and dad.

The Family Table around Town

A weekly withdrawal should provide the opportunity for us to connect as a family as well as a context to honor and love those around us. How does your family handle themselves in public? Do you have a plan for around town? Before your family goes out, do you talk through courtesy, manners, and hospitality? Do you care for the needs of those around you?

Picture the following scene. A family of five is taking up eight seats at the gate in the airport. They are sitting in five seats and using three seats for luggage. Dad and Mom are checking e-mails and texts. The children are playing games on various devices. A golf cart pulls up, and the driver assists a senior couple to the gate area. There are no seats available, and the family has not noticed them.

If this was your family, what would you do? Would you keep your head buried in technology, or would you offer your seats? Better yet, would you reach for the bags and escort the couple to the seats? When you're out with your family, seek opportunities to be alert and practice hospitality. Show your concern for others by offering a lending hand wherever and whenever you can. Here are some practical ways to practice courtesy, hospitality, and good manners around town:

1. Give up your place in line for seniors and those with disabilities.
2. Give up your seat when you see a mom or senior adult standing.
3. Be patient with those who move a little slower than you do.
4. Exchange your four-person table at Starbucks (that you are sitting at alone) for a two-person table (that four people are crowded around).
5. Pick up trash off the floor in restaurants and stores.
6. Open and hold doors for strangers going into stores and restaurants.
7. Consider those behind you in line and expedite your questions, checkout, and payment to keep the line moving.
8. If you see someone is hurting physically or emotionally, ask, "Are you okay? Is there anything I can do for you?"

9. Treat waiters and waitresses well by staying off technology, looking them in the eyes, and ordering for yourself off the menu with a clear, strong voice.
10. Engage in conversation with people standing in line with you.

What are some other ways to show people how valuable they are when your family is spending time in town? What distractions do you need to remove to be more alert and aware of the people around you? Is there a neighbor or family friend you know needs a little extra help around the house? How can you best reach out to them? While the weekly withdrawal is a great way to disconnect from people and recharge, be sure you do not disconnect from common courtesy and manners. You may not have the energy to engage in a lengthy conversation, but a nod and a quick "hello" may be just the trick.

Dating around Town

Family time around town is important, but a weekly date for mom and dad is just as important. When mom and dad get some time together to have fun and talk, there is more balance around the family table. Children need parents who are well rested and ready for the demands of parenting. The entire family wins when mom and dad get a weekly withdrawal.

In Song of Songs, we watch as Solomon picks up the Shulammite woman for a night on the town:

Listen! My beloved!
Look! Here he comes,
leaping across the mountains,
bounding over the hills.
My beloved is like a gazelle or a young stag.
Look! There he stands behind our wall,
gazing through the windows,
peering through the lattice.
My beloved spoke and said to me,
"Arise, my darling,
my beautiful one, come with me.
See! The winter is past;
the rains are over and gone.
Flowers appear on the earth;
the season of singing has come,
the cooing of doves
is heard in our land.
The fig tree forms its early fruit;
the blossoming vines spread their fragrance.
Arise, come, my darling;
my beautiful one, come with me."

SONG OF SONGS 2:8-13

If you are brand new to studying Hebrew poetry, you might be thinking, *This guy's a peeping Tom.* That's not the case at all. "He stands behind our wall, gazing through the windows, peering through the lattice," not because he is inappropriate but because he is filled with excitement and can't wait for the date. Dating here is portrayed as going from winter to spring. The workweek might feel like winter, but a date means you get a taste of spring on Friday night!

This weekly withdrawal creates memories worth repeating. Planning the date fills us with anticipation. Nothing stands in our way when it comes to prioritizing date nights. The two most common objections to married dating are child care and finances. Couples say, "We have children and no money." Child care is not insurmountable but does require creativity. Try swapping child care with friends and neighbors. Take advantage of date nights provided by churches— often those events come with child care. When your parents visit from out of town, that is a great week to plan a couple of dates. And spending time together does not mean spending large sums of money. Here are ten date ideas for under twenty dollars:

1. Go to a movie before 5:00 p.m. (matinee price) and share a soda.
2. Enjoy pizza and drinks at a nearby park.
3. Go for a hike.
4. If you have fruit farms in your area, pick fruit together.
5. Bake a blueberry pie together from scratch and invite another couple over for a double date.
6. Go to your local flea market with ten dollars apiece and have a contest for who can find the best item for under ten dollars.

7. Wander around your local bookstore and find a book to read together.
8. Get a guest pass to a nearby gym (or go to your gym if you're a member) and play tennis or racquetball together.
9. Go to your town's website to check for local free or inexpensive concerts and other events that may be happening around town.
10. Find a restaurant with live music on the weekend.

Challenging couples at Woodland Hills Family Church to date has become part of our mission statement. When you visit our website (woodhills.org) you'll find hundreds of questions, fill-in-the-blanks, and conversation starters to help couples plan fun on their dates. We talk about ideas for play dates, laugh dates, adventure dates, and dream dates. We even have a downloadable discussion guide for double dates.

This was such a hit that one of our teaching pastors, Adam Donyes, envisioned a year of dates he called #52in15. In the pulpit, he challenged every married couple to go on fifty-two dates in 2015. It was a huge success. Couples really got into it. Within the first three months, we had 1,250 dates posted on Facebook, Twitter, and Instagram. This so inspired us that we wrote a parody set to the tune of Darius Rucker's "Wagon Wheel." (Don't just read the chorus. Sing it out loud.)

Rock your date night, leave the kids at home
Rock your date night, turn off your phone

Hey, rock your date night
Rock your date night, like tonight's your last
Rock your date night, take it slow not fast
Hey, rock your date night

Amy and I are extremely grateful for parents who love being grandparents. My parents, Ron and Bonnie Cunningham, and Amy's parents, Dennis and Linda Freitag, live minutes from our home. We get a weekly date night because they love spending time with Corynn and Carson and they know how important dates are for a great marriage. We know our date night is possible because of grandparents. Thank you, Mom and Dad. Once a week, you let us leave the kids at home, unplug from technology, and enjoy a slow-paced meal.

Annual Abandon

AMY

As we're writing this book, our family is on a ten-day trip to several different cities. February is "love month" in our family. It is our busiest travel month, with Ted speaking on marriage and family around the country. Planes, freezing-cold weather, small hotel rooms, worn-out mattresses, heavy bags, school on the road, and a busy schedule can sometimes contribute to limited patience and overall discontentment.

I was feeling a bit that way one day when we arrived in Chicago around lunchtime. Normally, I would be so thrilled to be in Chicago, but this time, I was in a funk when I got off the plane. Ted read it all over me. He knew exactly what to say as we were waiting for our luggage.

He said, "You have one job: Find us a good place to eat lunch."

Game on! Something in me ignites over such a challenge. First off, I have serious directional issues. Without fail, when I walk out of a hotel room, elevator, or airport terminal, I go left when I am supposed to go right. Ted has found great entertainment in holding back a bit and letting me lead the way until I turn around and find him back where I started, pointing in the opposite direction.

So when it comes to finding the best place to enjoy lunch in an unfamiliar city, I have to overcome this obstacle. My trusty Zomato app is one of the first places I go. That day, we ate at a quaint Italian neighborhood eatery. As the host greeted us with a strong, authentic accent, we felt as if we were about to experience a treasure that only locals probably really knew about.

We were given a long description of the specials, which included everything from house-made pasta and gnocchi to lamb shanks with a red wine reduction. We all ordered something different to share. During the meal, we all started to talk about the host and how he seemed to take pride in the menu. We guessed that these were probably his family recipes that had been handed down from generation to generation.

Our family dreamed of visiting Italy. For months prior to this lunch, Corynn had been pinning pictures of Venice. My son could live on pasta and bread alone. Ted and I longed to visit the vineyards and imitate an Italian way of life. So, as we were served our bread and drinks, Ted asked the host where he, as an Italian, would recommend we visit in Italy. The host giggled and said, "I am not Italian. I am Polish."

Our faces displayed our shock. Little did he know that we had pretty much just made up a whole story of his life! He went on to share about his experience in Italy. He told us that we needed to stay in bed-and-breakfasts and go through a touring company, especially if we go with the kids. He talked about the vineyards and the cooking classes in Tuscany. I silently forgave him for his non-Italian heritage and approved of him once more for his experience and knowledge of Italy. I now could enjoy my authentic Italian food since he had been there and participated in our dreaming of our future trip to Italy.

Our goal is to make the most of the family table on the road. Restaurants and vacations need not hinder our time together. Experiencing the family table in different cities and cultures enhances the family's appreciation for new and different ways of sharing a meal. Just as the weekly withdrawal is a disconnect from the responsibilities of home, the annual abandon is a break from the pace of hometown living. It is a break from school activities, sporting schedules, errands, and community participation. We all need to get away to a place where no one knows us and we are free to roam, both as a family and as a couple.

The Family Table out of Town

Traveling is a great adventure. Our family invests in experiences, more than stuff. Life on the road breaks us out of routine, forces us to be spontaneous, and gives us a reason to take risks we normally would avoid in our regular routine. The family table out of town should be an adventure too. Whether you take a day trip to a neighboring town or you plan on driving home for the holidays, here are a few ways to craft an adventure for your family:

1. **Try a new route.** If you take the same road or highway every time on a familiar trip, invite Google Maps to offer you a few route choices. You'd be surprised how an extra fifteen minutes of driving brings a whole new world to life. Besides, have you ever noticed that the same cluster of fast-food chains repeat every few exits? Boring. Travel the unbeaten path.

2. **Try something new.** Our family avoids chain restaurants altogether when out of town because, living in a small Midwest town, we do not normally get to experience other cultures' cuisines. So when you're traveling with your family, consider Thai, Indian, Mediterranean, or Vietnamese. Many of these restaurants are owned by families. While they serve you, ask questions about their culture and family history.

3. **Don't eat all of your courses at one sitting.** Eat light bites and spread it out throughout the journey. At home, we call this a progressive meal. On the road, we call this a progressive journey. This is why we love the Food and Wine Festival that Disney's

Epcot Center hosts every year. We love snacking our way around eleven countries. That is an event that should be on every family's bucket list.

4. **Keep a journal of your favorite spots.** I know we have emphasized trying something new, but sometimes a restaurant is so good you want to return to try something from the 90 percent of the menu you did not experience. Create a folder called "Dining Experiences" on your phone's camera roll. This is a great way to relive old experiences and plan for new ones.

Our family enjoys visiting hot spots from Guy Fieri's hit show *Diners, Drive-Ins and Dives* on the Food Network. From Detroit to Dallas, and Phoenix to New York City, we trust Guy's taste buds. If you have not seen the show, Chef Fieri visits a local favorite and goes into the kitchen with the owner and chef. They usually cook three of the patrons' favorite dishes. Then the viewer gets to watch them sample each dish. It's torture for me, and I don't recommend watching the show late at night. When our family visits one of these Triple D diners, we say, "We will take one of everything Guy made on the show."

Dating out of Town

TED

Some meals out of town are too long to make our children endure them. So Amy and I make a mental note and plan to return one day, just the two of us. Since one of the greatest gifts you can give your children is a mom and dad who enjoy each other, prioritizing an annual abandon with some long meals is a gift for our children.

Some parents shy away from a couple's vacation because it feels selfish. You hear friends say, "We've got plenty of time for that when our children leave home" or "We would hate to miss one of their games." If you attend 85 to 95 percent of your child's sporting activities, then I would say you are a fantastic and attentive parent. Missing a game does not mean you are neglecting your children.

Amy and I regularly discuss how excited we will be to watch our grandkids for an extended period of time so Corynn and Carson can head out of town with their spouses. This is one reason why Amy wants me to work out. She says, "You need to be healthy and mobile so we can watch our grandkids for a week without you having a heart attack." That makes me want to walk a few laps around the block!

After you have been married for a while, you know how important it is to get out of town often. The Shulammite woman invited her busy husband out of town for a passionate time of intimacy:

> Come, my beloved, let us go to the countryside,
>   let us spend the night in the villages.
> Let us go early to the vineyards
>   to see if the vines have budded,

if their blossoms have opened,
and if the pomegranates are in bloom—
there I will give you my love.

SONG OF SONGS 7:11-12

The annual abandon date ignites intimacy and adventure. "There I will give you my love" means this couple will enjoy each other physically. It even alludes to physical intimacy in the great outdoors.

If given the choice between the big city, the beach, or the mountains, Amy chooses the big city. Her ideal annual abandon involves walking ten to fifteen miles on the streets of the city and ending the day with a fine, slow meal.

On a recent trip to New York City, we walked over ten miles before watching the Broadway musical *Matilda*. We planned dinner at Marc Forgione's signature restaurant in the financial district three and a half miles from the theater. We planned on using Uber after the show, but I had a spontaneous romantic moment as we walked out of the theater.

"Amy, what if we walked to dinner?" I asked. She lit up. We walked at a brisk pace and she smiled the entire time. She was in what we call her "happy spot."

At the restaurant, we were seated next to the big open bifold doors. So we got the best of both worlds—the comforts of the indoors with the feeling of the outdoors.

We ordered drinks that came with freshly picked mint leaves. Our spunky waitress encouraged us to rub the mint leaves on our lips and faces to take in the whole experience.

Amy laughed—she knows I'm a foodie, but sometimes we take it a little bit too far. This was one of those times. Rubbing herbs on my face seemed a little extreme, but we talk about it to this day.

Throughout dinner we noticed Food Network chef Marc Forgione step out of the kitchen several times to watch people enjoy his food. The mohawked chef is all professional, and his food was fantastic.

Had the day ended there, we would have said, "Perfect day!" But one more cool surprise awaited us. I asked the waitress to add one of the chef's cookbooks to the bill. Within a few minutes Chef Marc was standing at our table, asking, "How was everything?" Intending to keep the conversation short because we didn't want to impose on his time, we complimented everything quickly. Then—I'll never forget this part—he sat down next to Amy and they discussed sauces. I took their picture together, and he signed his book and headed back to the kitchen. That's how you plan and stumble into the perfect annual abandon.

⯈Your Family Table

Recipe: Blueberry-Lemon Muffins

When friends and family come to town, there are a few places in the Ozark Mountains that we really enjoy taking them to. The Bohner Family Persimmon Hill Farm is a memorable experience that gets repeat business from our family each summer. It is a forty-minute drive from our home. As you enter the property, you drive through several acres of blue-berries, raspberries, blackberries, and gooseberries. The berry plants are planted in rows set apart wide enough so you can pick them for yourself. The onsite restaurant offers blueberry pancakes with homemade blueberry syrup in the morning and pulled pork sandwiches in the afternoon. They have homemade barbecue sauces with raspberries, blackberries, and blueberries added in. However, the most famous food they serve is the Thunder Muffin. Jumbo in size and filled with moist, buttery goodness, this muffin is one of our regu-lar cravings. Since we always have blueberries in our freezer, I've experimented with some of our favorite blueberry com-binations in a basic muffin recipe. We particularly love this blueberry-lemon muffin. You have been warned!

Recipe makes 6 jumbo muffins.

INGREDIENTS:
   2 cups all-purpose flour
   2 teaspoons baking powder
   ½ teaspoon salt
   ½ cup butter, softened
   1 cup sugar
   2 eggs
   ½ cup milk
   1 teaspoon vanilla
   1 teaspoon pure lemon extract (optional, makes it more
      lemony)

1 tablespoon lemon zest

2 cups fresh blueberries (frozen can be substituted)

TOPPING:

2 tablespoons sugar (raw sugar is great as well)

½ teaspoon ground cinnamon

GLAZE:

1 tablespoon pure lemon extract or lemon zest

1 cup powdered sugar

3 tablespoons milk

INSTRUCTIONS:

Line six 3½-inch (jumbo) muffin cups with paper baking cups or spread butter in pan to prevent sticking; set aside. In a medium bowl, combine flour, baking powder, and salt; set aside.

In a large mixing bowl, beat butter with electric mixer for 30 seconds. Add 1 cup of sugar; beat until well combined. Beat in eggs, milk, vanilla, pure lemon extract, and lemon zest. Stir in flour until just moistened (batter should be lumpy). Gently stir in berries.

Spoon batter into prepared muffin cups, filling each one nearly full. In a small bowl, combine the sugar and cinnamon. Sprinkle sugar mixture over batter.

Bake in preheated 350-degree oven for 35–40 minutes or until golden brown and wooden toothpick inserted in center comes out clean. Cool in muffin cups on a wire rack for 5 minutes.

Combine all glaze ingredients in a small bowl and drizzle on cooled muffins. Remove from muffin cups; serve warm. These muffins are also delicious with a little vanilla ice cream and whipped cream! This is the perfect dessert to be shared.

The "Write Someone's Story" Game
As you dine out, look around the restaurant for individuals or couples who stick out to you. In an honoring way, imagine a story about them.

- Where are they from?
- What do they do for a living?
- How much money do they make?
- What is their house like?
- What kind of car do they drive?
- Are they a people of faith?

It's even fun to put words in their mouth as they speak. If you are bold and adventurous, you might introduce yourself to them after the meal and see how close you were to getting their story straight.

Devotional
Now listen, you who say, "Today or tomorrow we will go to this or that city, spend a year there, carry on business and make money." Why, you do not even know what will happen tomorrow. What is your life? You are a mist that appears for a little while

and then vanishes. Instead, you ought to say, "If it is the Lord's will, we will live and do this or that."

JAMES 4:13-15

Tomorrow is not guaranteed. The brevity and uncertainty of life are themes throughout all of Scripture. Moses said,

Our days may come to seventy years,
    or eighty, if our strength endures;
yet the best of them are but trouble and sorrow,
    for they quickly pass, and we fly away.

PSALM 90:10

If life is short and trouble follows us everywhere, should we bury our heads in the sand and do nothing? Since life is fleeting and burdensome, should we not find ways to enjoy the time we do have?

In Ecclesiastes, Solomon wrestles with these same questions and ultimately ends with the firm conviction that we should "fear God and keep his commandments, for this is the duty of all mankind." Solomon calls this the "conclusion of the matter" (Ecclesiastes 12:13). But leading up to this conclusion, he also says, "Go, eat your food with gladness, and drink your wine with a joyful heart, for God has already approved what you do" (9:7) and "it is appropriate for a person to eat, to drink and to find satisfaction in their toilsome labor under the sun during the few days of life God has given them" (5:18).

Wherever you journey in life, take time to enjoy the good gifts of food God has given you. Whether at home, at a restaurant, or on a trip, thank the Lord that he gives you food to enjoy during the years you have upon this earth.

Discuss

- What is your favorite meal at home?
- If you could only eat at one restaurant the rest of your life, which would it be?
- Next time you travel to a big city, what country's food do you want to try?

Prayer

Father, what a journey our family has been on lately. You have provided for us in so many ways. We thank You. May our time at home around the family table refresh us and bring us closer to You and one another. When we eat out, may our family be a testimony to the world. We are known by the way we love one another. May our love be evident whether we are at home or out and about. In Jesus' name, amen.

CHAPTER 5

THE FAMILY CONSTITUTION

The family table is where we convene to discuss
what we believe about God and life.

TED

The United States of America declared independence with the words, "We hold these truths to be self-evident, that all men are created equal, that they are endowed by their Creator with certain unalienable Rights, that among these are Life, Liberty and the pursuit of Happiness."

Raised in Illinois, the Land of Lincoln, I learned the famous words of Abraham Lincoln's Gettysburg Address at an early age: "Four score and seven years ago our fathers brought forth on this continent, a new nation, conceived in Liberty, and dedicated to the proposition that all men are created equal." Those words forged a doctrine of equality in our country that has been fought for, argued over, discussed, legislated, picketed, and died for. Many presidents since have fought for this freedom around the globe and have come to the defense of liberty when it was threatened.

In classrooms and at ballgames, we teach our children to stand, remove their hats, place their hands over their hearts, and say, "I pledge allegiance to the Flag of the United States of America, and to the Republic for which it stands, one nation under God, indivisible, with liberty and justice for all." We want to raise children who seek to contribute to rather than take from their nation. We all remember President John F. Kennedy's famous challenge: "And so, my fellow Americans: ask not what your country can do for you—ask what you can do for your country."

These decisions, proclamations, statements, and beliefs shaped our nation. Presidents will be remembered in history for them. Citizens will go back to them for generations to come. Future generations will gain perspective through our history, good and bad.

Men and women have fought and died for what they believe. The least we can do as a family is know what we believe and why we believe it. Friends on college campuses tell me that they see many Christian kids who are clueless about what they believe. These kids know many Bible stories and have attended countless Christian concerts, but they cannot articulate their beliefs.

Knowing your beliefs is important, and doing so within your family is vital. Ask your children, "What do we believe as a family?" Just as the Christian church has looked to creeds over the years, our family has simple belief statements in a family constitution. It is a work in progress. There is great strength, support, and unity when a family comes together and declares what they believe.

The Benefits of the Family Constitution

Gathering your family around the table and involving them in the process of creating a family constitution unites your family and creates a lifelong bond that will continue for generations.

A family constitution prioritizes truth over emotions. When our family runs on empty and everyone needs a nap, we remind ourselves that our feelings do not determine our love for one another. Love is a decision, not an emotion. We decide to say and do the right thing even when we don't feel like it.

A family constitution keeps anger low and reduces escalated arguments. Anger is a secondary emotion triggered by the primary emotions of hurt, fear, and frustration. When we disagree, what we believe requires us to make amends and seek forgiveness. We allow mistakes but want to quickly make things right after we offend a member of our family.

A family constitution reduces stress and creates safety. Parents and children find comfort in stability and knowledge of the rules. Discipline is not based on a parent's mood. Children are not surprised by consequences.

Mom and dad serve as the judge when arguments occur between siblings, but just like judges in our country, they interpret and apply the law. As a family, we decide together what we believe, and mom and dad enforce our family decisions. When kids have buy-in to the beliefs of the family, mom and dad serve as the loving and firm reminders and consequence enforcers. This creates safety for children because the "rules" are not always changing. The bull's-eye is the same today as it was yesterday. If there is something in the constitution that starts to irritate you, the family table is your legislative session. Use that time to speak and share your appeal. Everyone weighs in. Everyone decides.

You may be asking, "Is our home a democracy?" No. Absolutely not! The Constitution of the United States was written after the Declaration of Independence, our nation's founding document. Our elected officials gather to write laws and govern, but they can't change our founding document. Life, liberty, and the pursuit of happiness are still the goals. We debate and legislate to that end.

Our family's founding document is the Bible. We will not add or take away anything that is contrary to Scripture. Everything we say and do is filtered through God's Word. So, before anything is added or subtracted, go to your first and final authority. A family constitution is like a creed and is secondary to the Scripture.

A family constitution needs to be displayed in the home. Many homes already display pictures and calendars with Scripture verses. The family constitution is a daily reminder of a family's most important values and beliefs, just as Moses and the Israelites had a daily reminder of God's provision with a jar of manna.

The Cunningham Family Constitution

At the urging of Dr. Gary Smalley, our family wrote a family constitution a few years ago. It states what we believe and how we intend to live. It connects our beliefs with our behaviors. Jim Daly, president of Focus on the Family, once challenged me to make sure that my orthodoxy (belief) lines up with my orthopraxy (conduct). We must be careful not to prioritize orthodoxy without aligning it with orthopraxy. Matching faith with practice helps our family know what we believe and what we will do because of our beliefs.

Feel free to use this example in whole or in part to form your own constitution. Allow your entire family to be a part of the process. If your family does not have a regular devotional time, this is a great place to start. When you are finished, print out a copy and hang it on your wall. Let it be a daily reminder of your family's commitment to one another.

1. We will love the Lord with all our heart, soul, mind, and strength. This is number one. The Lord is the Boss, and He will be the Boss of this home. We will strive to love Him in everything we do.

> Hear, O Israel: The LORD our God, the LORD is one. Love the LORD your God with all your heart and with all your soul and with all your strength.
>
> DEUTERONOMY 6:4-5

> Jesus replied: "'Love the Lord your God with
> all your heart and with all your soul and with
> all your mind.'" MATTHEW 22:37

Each family member must decide to love Jesus personally. This is not a decision a parent can make for a child. At best, parents influence children to love Jesus. He is our Source of Life and the primary message of our home.

We humble ourselves and cry out to Jesus every day. We know that it is impossible for us to create or produce love, power, and forgiveness. It comes to us from God. We receive, then give.

2. We will speak words of high honor over one another every day. Our home is a judgment-free zone. It's going to be a safe place for us to gather and care for one another. Honor is a decision to esteem as highly valuable. Each member of our family is personally autographed by God. We will speak words that validate that honor.

> Love your neighbor as yourself.
>
> MATTHEW 22:39

> Gracious words are a honeycomb,
>   sweet to the soul and healing to the bones.
>
> PROVERBS 16:24

3. We will read and memorize Scripture together. The Bible will be our primary source of truth. All of our traditions, emotions, and experiences will be filtered through Scripture. The Bible is our founding document. If we change any articles of this constitution, it will be done with the Word of God as our guide.

> Do your best to present yourself to God as one approved, a worker who does not need to be ashamed and who correctly handles the word of truth.
>
> 2 TIMOTHY 2:15

> Blessed is the one
>   who does not walk in step with the wicked
> or stand in the way that sinners take
>   or sit in the company of mockers,
> but whose delight is in the law of the LORD,
>   and who meditates on his law day and night.
> That person is like a tree planted by streams
>   of water,
>   which yields its fruit in season
> and whose leaf does not wither—
>   whatever they do prospers.
>
> PSALM 1:1-3

4. We will pray together every day. Before bed each night, we will pray to close out the day. We will

thank God for all that He provides, confess sins one to another, and pray for the hurting in our family, church, and community.

Pray continually.   1 THESSALONIANS 5:17

This, then, is how you should pray:

> "Our Father in heaven,
> hallowed be your name,
> your kingdom come,
> your will be done,
>   on earth as it is in heaven.
> Give us today our daily bread.
> And forgive us our debts,
>   as we also have forgiven our debtors.
> And lead us not into temptation,
>   but deliver us from the evil one."
>
> MATTHEW 6:9-13

5. We will offer grace for mistakes and avoid repeating the same mistakes. We all make mistakes. We want to learn from them and move on. When someone makes a mistake, we will forgive that person. We will not hold it against him or her.

> As a dog returns to its vomit,
>   so fools repeat their folly.
>
> PROVERBS 26:11

"In your anger do not sin": Do not let the sun
go down while you are still angry, and do not
give the devil a foothold.

EPHESIANS 4:26-27

Get rid of all bitterness, rage and anger,
brawling and slander, along with every form
of malice. Be kind and compassionate to
one another, forgiving each other, just as in
Christ God forgave you.

EPHESIANS 4:31-32

6. We will work hard, give generously, save wisely, and
spend sensibly. We will work and give as an antidote
to attitudes of selfishness and entitlement. Jesus
is our ultimate Boss. We will live on less to enjoy
more. We want to be a family that refreshes others.

Go to the ant, you sluggard;
consider its ways and be wise!

PROVERBS 6:6

A generous person will prosper;
whoever refreshes others will be refreshed.

PROVERBS 11:25

The wise store up choice food and olive oil,
but fools gulp theirs down.

PROVERBS 21:20

7. We will love and support and serve our church.
   Faithful attendance and giving to the church is a
   highly regarded value in our family. We will love
   the church as the Bride of Christ. Sports, hobbies,
   and community activities will not take priority
   over our church. We are in no way legalistic about
   this, but we want time in biblical community to
   refresh us.

   > And I tell you that you are Peter, and on this
   > rock I will build my church, and the gates of
   > Hades will not overcome it.
   > MATTHEW 16:18

   > Husbands, love your wives, just as Christ
   > loved the church and gave himself up for her.
   > EPHESIANS 5:25

8. We will laugh together every day. We will enjoy
   life together. We want to cultivate a great sense of
   humor as a family. We want to take God seriously—
   ourselves, not so much. We will avoid at all costs a
   lack of intimacy, fun, and laughter.

   > A cheerful heart is good medicine,
   >   but a crushed spirit dries up the bones.
   > PROVERBS 17:22

A time to weep and a time to laugh,
a time to mourn and a time to dance.
ECCLESIASTES 3:4

9. We will take 100 percent personal responsibility for
our emotions, words, and actions. I am responsible
for my heart, not yours. We will avoid blaming one
another for our feelings, words, or actions.

Above all else, guard your heart,
for everything you do flows from it.
PROVERBS 4:23

But the things that come out of a person's
mouth come from the heart, and these defile
them. MATTHEW 15:18

10. We will live in the moment, not on technology. We
will not miss the important moments for the sake
of social media. We will seek permission from other
family members before posting private moments.
Above all else, we will limit the amount of time we
spend staring at a screen.

We take captive every thought to make it
obedient to Christ.
2 CORINTHIANS 10:5

Discretion will protect you,
and understanding will guard you.

PROVERBS 2:11

Our family is allowed to add to, delete from, or change our family constitution at any time. Keeping these beliefs and practices before us is the goal. Our hope and prayer is that each line would be a message branded on our hearts. We want the overflow of our lives to reflect a deep love for Jesus and one another.

Drafting Your Family's Constitution

We encourage you to spend intentional time crafting a family constitution together. If you'd like, use our family constitution as a template. If you see something missing from our constitution, add it to yours. Meditate on the passages of Scripture. Write down a few discussion questions for dinner tonight or for the drive to school.

Here are some questions to help you draft your family's constitution. These are just conversation starters. Give each member of the family time to share from the heart. You may want to take on one item at a time. Even if this process takes a month, it is well worth the time.

1. What do we believe about God? Has each member of this family placed faith in Jesus? How strong is your walk with Christ? How does a love for the Lord sustain our love for one another?

2. How do we prioritize our relationship with the Lord above all others?

3. Is forgiveness easy in this home? Do we carry unresolved anger towards others or one another? What steps will we take to keep short accounts with one another?

4. How do we make meaningful touch part of our home?

5. Since our desire is to be a close-knit family, what can we do to prioritize quality and quantity time? How many meals at home will we commit to as a family? What about a family date night? What would that look like, and how often should we schedule it?

6. Do we have a plan for earning, giving, saving, and spending?

7. How do we best appreciate our differences? Do you ever feel like your personality is not appreciated? If so, what do we say or do that makes you feel unsafe? What unique perspective do you feel you bring to this family?

8. We commit to spend _____ – _____ minutes a day in a distraction-free setting for meaningful communication with one another. What distractions do we need to remove so the conversation flows? Describe the posture, facial expressions, and tone of someone who is listening well.

9. What do I say and do that makes you feel most cared for?

10. Picturing a special future for our family includes seeing the best in one another, offering grace, learning from mistakes, and making plans for days down the road. What is our vision for this family? How can each of us support the vision God has given for your life?

Financial expert Dave Ramsey is known for saying, "The Ramseys don't borrow money." His kids grew up hearing that from their dad. Decisions have power, and making power statements is a great way to keep your family's beliefs out there for all to practice. So lead out in conversation tonight with, "Our family believes," and discern together what your family will hold to be true in your home.

⋟Your Family Table

Recipe: Sweet or Savory Crepes

AMY

The idea of working with what you have is key to home cooking. Our family has eggs. A lot of eggs. Our eleven chickens provide us with about eleven eggs almost every day. It's a good thing we all enjoy them! When we first started collecting eggs, we scrambled them and then topped them with shredded cheese every morning. We ate in awe knowing they came from chickens raised in our backyard. Ted and I were proud of ourselves for providing our kids with a warm, healthy, protein-filled, farm-to-table breakfast.

About a month into cheesy scrambled eggs for breakfast every morning, Corynn and Carson came to me and asked for pancakes. What? I'll admit, initially their request frustrated me because I'd taken such pride in our eggs. But once I got over myself, I decided to get out the cookbooks and learn what else we could do with eggs. We have since experimented with quiche, soufflés, and custard. Currently, our family favorite is crepes.

Crepes are unique because of their endless possibilities. This basic recipe can be used to create both sweet and savory entrees and desserts. Each member of your family can create his or her own favorite combinations.

A crepe bar is a huge hit at a party. Prepare the crepes and ingredients ahead of time. Have guests fill their crepes and place on an oven-safe dish lined with wax paper. Write each person's name on the wax paper with a sharpie. Stick the prepared crepes in a 325- to 350-degree preheated oven to warm all at the same time, and everyone will be ready to enjoy together in about ten to fifteen minutes.

Crepes also make leftovers a gourmet delight. My favorite crepes include leftover roasted vegetables topped with a creamy white-wine sauce.

Recipe makes approximately six crepes.

INGREDIENTS:

    2 large eggs

    1 cup all-purpose flour

    2 teaspoons sugar

    2 teaspoons salt

    1 cup whole milk

    2 tablespoons butter

INSTRUCTIONS:

In a large mixing bowl, beat the eggs. Add the flour, sugar, and salt and whisk together. Slowly add the milk and 1 tablespoon melted butter. Use a hand mixer or blender and mix until light and frothy. Let sit for 10 minutes or cover and refrigerate overnight. Heat a 10-inch skillet or crepe pan on low to medium heat. Place 1 to 2 teaspoons of butter in the pan and melt. Pour ¼ cup of batter into the pan and swirl the pan to spread the batter. Cook until the edges are browning slightly. Flip with an extra-wide spatula. Cook on the other side for 45 seconds to a minute. Stack on a plate with wax paper in between each crepe. Continue with the rest of the batter and add a little butter to grease the pan in between each crepe.

Crepes will refrigerate well overnight. To get your creative culinary juices flowing, here are the top picks of crepe fillings from our family members:

Ted: "The Farmer" (scrambled eggs, crumbled sausage, various cheeses, topped with maple syrup)

Amy: Roasted veggies and white-wine sauce (recipe below)

Corynn: "Monte Cristo–like" (shaved Black Forest ham, buttery cheese such as Muenster or fontina, and strawberry-rhubarb or red raspberry jam inside the crepe; fold the crepe and top with a little more cheese and jam; microwave for 30 seconds)

Carson: Nutella and sliced bananas or plain with warm maple syrup

WHITE-WINE SAUCE INGREDIENTS:
1 cup heavy whipping cream
1 cup white wine (chardonnay is best)
2 tablespoons all-purpose flour
2 teaspoons salt
2–4 teaspoons pepper (according to your taste)

VARIATIONS: (ONE OR BOTH)
2 teaspoons of your favorite herbs, such as thyme or rosemary (optional)
½ cup of your favorite grated cheeses

INSTRUCTIONS:
Combine ingredients in a small saucepan over medium-high heat. Stir until it comes to a soft boil. Reduce heat to low and simmer until the sauce thickens. If adding herbs and cheeses, do so once the heat has been reduced.

The Telephone Game

One way to enforce the power of communicating what we believe is to demonstrate how quickly we can get it wrong. The telephone game, also known as the gossip game, involves relaying simple information from one person to another in a group. For example, take the phrase, "Molly Jane went to school in the Midwest before marrying and moving to the East Coast, where she started her family," and whisper it to the person to your right. Each subsequent person whispers what they think they heard to the person on their right until the phrase gets to the last person at the table. Then that person shares the phrase—which has likely gotten pretty garbled by this point!—out loud with the group. Compare it to the original phrase shared by the first person. This game helps us realize that information often gets lost in translation.

Devotional

> I am the LORD your God, who brought you out
> of Egypt, out of the land of slavery.
>
> EXODUS 20:2

The "Hear, O Israel" of Deuteronomy 6:4 is referred to as the Shema, a sort of nickname used to refer to the whole verse. Hebrew children learn this as the centerpiece of their prayers. There are four truths in the Shema. One, there is a God. Two, there is only one God. Three, He is the Lord. Four, He is our Lord. This verse is sometimes alternately translated as "The LORD is our God, the LORD alone" (NLT).

To the Jew, the Shema is considered essential to knowing who God is and what their response to Him should be.

Deuteronomy 6:4 is the declaration of the children of Israel that God will be their God. The Ten Commandments, which God gave His children, detailed their relationship with Him and with one another. In a way, the Ten Commandments are like Israel's family constitution. It guided them in the devotion and commitment to God and their values as a people.

God gave the Ten Commandments to Moses to lead the people of Israel. Jesus did not come to earth to "abolish the Law" (Matthew 5:17). He taught us,

> "Love the Lord your God with all your heart and with all your soul and with all your mind." This is the first and greatest commandment. And the second is like it: "Love your neighbor as yourself." All the Law and the Prophets hang on these two commandments.
>
> MATTHEW 22:37-40

The first four of the Ten Commandments are linked to the greatest commandment (love God), and the last six are linked to the second greatest commandment (love others).

THE TEN COMMANDMENTS

1. There is only one God, and He is the Lord.

   You shall have no other gods before me.

   EXODUS 20:3

2. Don't make anything that looks like God.

> You shall not make for yourself an image in
> the form of anything in heaven above or on
> the earth beneath or in the waters below.
> EXODUS 20:4

3. Don't mess with His name.

> You shall not misuse the name of the LORD
> your God, for the LORD will not hold anyone
> guiltless who misuses his name.
> EXODUS 20:7

4. Don't mess with His day. Rest your soul so you can
be productive six days out of seven.

> Remember the Sabbath day by keeping it
> holy. Six days you shall labor and do all your
> work, but the seventh day is a sabbath to the
> LORD your God.   EXODUS 20:8-10

5. Honor your parents. Respect for authority begins
at home.

> Honor your father and your mother, so that
> you may live long in the land the LORD your
> God is giving you.   EXODUS 20:12

6. You shall not murder. (Exodus 20:13)

7. You shall not commit adultery. (Exodus 20:14)

8. You shall not steal. (Exodus 20:15)

9. You shall not give false testimony against your neighbor. (Exodus 20:16)

10. You shall not be jealous of what your friends or neighbors have.

> You shall not covet your neighbor's house. You shall not covet your neighbor's wife, or his male or female servant, his ox or donkey, or anything that belongs to your neighbor.
>
> EXODUS 20:17

Discuss
- How does our relationship with God affect our relationship with one another?
- Are the Ten Commandments relevant in our culture today? Why or why not?

Prayer
Father, thank You for guiding our family in truth. Align our beliefs with our behaviors. Keep hypocrisy far from our lips and

hearts. We seek to walk in Your ways. What do You ask of us? To fear You. To love You. To serve You. To walk in obedience with all of our hearts, souls, minds, and strength. We will observe all that You have commanded. This is for our good and to Your glory. In Jesus' name, amen.

the family table is for others

CHAPTER 6

HOSPITALITY AT THE TABLE

The family table welcomes family, friends, and strangers.

*Long before the church had pulpits and baptisteries,
she had kitchens and dinner tables.*

MAX LUCADO, *LIFE TO THE FULL*

The Tool Is the Table

TED

For years, Amy wanted a ginormous farm table a minimum of
ten feet long to entertain fourteen to twenty people at a time.
And what my baby wants, my baby gets. So I researched,
studied . . . and realized that these tables are super pricey.

So I came up with a solution.

"Babe, I'm going to make you a farm table," I said
enthusiastically.

"Hmmm," she responded.

"You don't need to say a thing. You're welcome," I said.

The schematics were in my head. About a week before Thanksgiving, I went to Lowe's and purchased four ten-foot-long one-inch by twelve-inch boards and a couple of four-foot-long one-by-fours. No saw cuts necessary. All it took were a few screws and a drill and *shazam*—Amy had a ten-foot farm table to set on top of our existing table. It's one huge table leaf. Deep down, Amy was impressed. She had her farm table for ninety dollars. All she needed were two overlapping tablecloths to hide the roughness, and no one would know the difference.

One reason I was excited to make the farm table, other than the fact that I served my wife, was that it eliminates the kids' table. Now everyone is around the same table. We can minister to our guests without splitting everyone up.

The table is a place where community happens. In Acts 2:46-47, we read that the home was central to the launch and expansion of the first-century church:

> Every day they continued to meet together in the
> temple courts. They broke bread in their homes and
> ate together with glad and sincere hearts, praising
> God and enjoying the favor of all the people. And
> the Lord added to their number daily those who
> were being saved.

Many different languages and backgrounds were present when the church started in the first century. How do you bring diverse people together? The answer is simple: food. As we read in Acts 5, "Day after day, in the temple courts and from house to house, they never stopped teaching and pro-claiming the good news that Jesus is the Messiah" (verse 42). The message is Jesus, and the tool is the table.

The table is still the place where we bring uncommon people together. God uses the home and our table to bring different backgrounds together, whether rich or poor, conservative or liberal, regardless of religion or past or present. We are all about inviting people to church, but what about inviting people into our homes? Around the dinner table walls come down. This is the beauty of hospitality. God can use you and your home. As Max Lucado says,

> Not everyone can serve in a foreign land, lead a relief effort, or volunteer at the downtown soup kitchen. But who can't be hospitable? Do you have a front door? A table? Chairs? Bread and meat for sandwiches? Congratulations! You just qualified to serve in the most ancient of ministries: hospitality. . . . Something holy happens around a dinner table that will never happen in a sanctuary. In a church auditorium you see the backs of heads. Around the table you see the expressions on faces. In the auditorium one person speaks; around the table everyone has a voice.[1]

Hospitality Is an Open Door

Do you remember a time when you were invited to someone's home and felt welcomed? Paul and Beth Etheridge, members of our church, hosted our elders' Christmas party a few years ago. It was one of the most memorable evenings of our married life. They requested that we show up and bring nothing. They prepared a multicourse meal and served us through every course. Gourmet doesn't come close to describing this beautiful, relaxing, high-end experience. We started with the first course at 6:00 p.m. Dinner lasted over four hours, and it felt like thirty minutes. Good hospitality makes time fly and leaves you wanting more.

But have you ever been in someone's home and felt like they really didn't want you there? Awkward, right? Gracious hosts project warmth in everything they say and do. Here are a few statements you don't want to hear when you are a guest in someone's home:

"Tonight almost didn't happen because it has been a crazy week."

"My husband tried talking me out of tonight because he knows how crazy I get preparing for parties."

"I hope you enjoyed the salmon. It was on sale."

"I just threw something together."

"I really don't enjoy cooking, but for you I thought I'd fire up the grill."

"Just throw your coats on the bed."

Open-door hospitality sets you at ease and helps the conversation flow. Your invitation to dinner should be more than "I enjoy your company, and I would like to get to know you better." You really want your guests to hear, "You are highly valuable and more than worth the effort."

The Gift of Priority

AMY

One of the most familiar stories in the New Testament is the one about Martha and Mary in Luke 10. You probably know it. Jesus was invited into the home of Martha, who was preparing the meal, and He ended up rebuking her—but not for her actions or hospitality. He didn't say preparations are not important. After all, the Scripture says that "Jesus and His disciples" were there, which could have meant many hungry mouths to feed. Martha had great intentions in her desire to bring Jesus and His followers into her home, but her motives got a little bit skewed: "Martha was distracted by all the preparations that had to be made" (verse 40).

I for one can validate Martha's actions because I have been there. Preparations did need to be made. Entertaining our guests and preparing to have family, friends, neighbors, or strangers over involves a lot.

But let's be honest. How many times have we been distracted by the preparations? The night ends and we never had a chance to enjoy it. We regret not taking more time to relax and talk.

When Martha came to Jesus and asked, "Lord, don't you care that my sister has left me to do the work by myself? Tell her to help me!" He answered, "Martha, Martha, . . . you are worried and upset about many things" (verses 40-41).

One of the greatest takeaways for me in this interaction between Jesus and Martha is that guests take priority over preparations: "Few things are needed—or indeed only one. Mary has chosen what is better, and it will not be taken away from her" (verse 42).

So how can we enjoy hospitality more? How can we not allow the preparations to overwhelm us so we can enjoy our guests?

1. **Be prepared.** The more you can do on the front end, the better. Before the guests ever show up, have as much of the prep work done as possible. Your menu determines much of this. Consider a dessert that can be prepared in individual parfaits rather than a four- or five-step process after dinner.

2. **Declutter.** Make the place a little more comfortable for your guests so they don't have to cram themselves into all your stuff. When I was growing up, our kitchen had a junk drawer. It wasn't because we were lazy. Most guests to our house entered through the kitchen. The junk drawer allowed us to do a twenty-second sweep through the kitchen and stuff everything in the drawer.

3. **Be aware.** You may have advanced social skills compared to the rest of your family. You are aware and concerned for the relationships and emotions around you. Good hosts work to keep the conversation flowing, but they also see when it's about to take a bad turn. Jump in. Change the subject. Offer seconds or pour everyone more

water. Check on the kids. Keep a pulse on the conversation by asking great questions.

You know the hot-button topics. Be aware when the conversation is headed there and divert it. So as your parents start talking about their health and bowel movements, you know Obamacare is coming right after that, so let's just gradually take that back off the table. We want to enjoy one another, and hot-button topics have a way of derailing that.

4. **Avoid one-upping your guests.** You also need to be aware of when you are taking over the conversation. Don't respond to every story with a story of your own. Ask questions for greater understanding of their story.

5. **Be spontaneous.** This is one for all the Marthas who have been preparing and thinking things through. I've been part of the families where all Christmas day was planned out and then one uncle decides everyone should go see a movie. Spontaneity is a way to value those with personalities different from yours.

6. **Include everyone.** And this means kids too! There are three ways we tend to treat children around the family table.

   a. *Not including the kids at all.* The kids' table is a must for some family gatherings because space is limited. But this keeps the kids away from adult conversation and from a great opportunity to learn communication and social skills.

b. *Centering the gathering and conversation around the kids.* Rather than learning to lean into the guests and ask questions, children are the center of attention. We've been those parents who solicit entertainment from the children: "Hey Carson, sing those goofy songs Tim Hawkins does." But children should rather participate in the flow of the gathering. Leading them into conversation is a better approach: "Corynn, what do you think about what was just said?"

c. *Including the kids.* We believe this is the balanced approach. If possible, rid your home of the kids' table and squeeze everyone around one table. Be sensitive to the more reserved child and find ways to bring him or her into the discussion. Ask great follow-up questions to keep the interaction alive.

We have one friend who is incredible at this. I've never seen someone do a more masterful job of including everyone in the conversation. No one dominates the time together. The kids are not the center of the gathering, but they are included in it. During a recent dinner, he asked both Corynn and Carson multiple questions about school, hobbies, friends, and church.

Children learn how to do conversation by watching adults do it. Once you bring them to the table, don't rush past their contribution. If they go awhile without saying anything, ask them their thoughts on the subject.

7. **Share Christ.** When you have created an environment where people enjoy one another and their borders and defenses are down, you have an opportunity to share Christ. Let Jesus, not political issues, have priority in the conversation. One simple way to share Christ is to ask each person around the table to share something they are thankful for. This will give some the opportunity to share heartfelt gratefulness for salvation, Christ's death, and resurrection.

Recently, I attended a dinner where most of the guests barely knew one another. The hostess was the thread that brought us all together. One of the ladies at the table asked us all one simple question: "How did each of you end up in Branson?" She started off by sharing her story, which included her salvation testimony. Hours later, we had heard each person's story. This one simple question prompted some deep moments as we all got to know one another. Amid many tears and bursts of laughter, Christ was shared. One person took a risk with vulnerability, and because of that we all left with new friends.

Another aspect of prioritizing one another can be a bit harder, and that is discerning the best way to graciously end a gathering. Thinking through this by reflecting on those who are in your home—or those whose home you are in—serves others well. We have friends who exit the home just as the party gets cranking and others who stay through countless yawns and stretches. I have no problem admitting that I am wiped out by 9:00 p.m. By 10:00 p.m., I'm in a coma. We start our gatherings a little earlier so as not to rush the time. Here are a few considerations to help hosts and guests land softly on an ending time:

- Know the hosts and guests. Are they morning people or night owls?
- Include a start and stop time with the invitation.
- Be mindful of the children's bedtimes. Ask when the kids go to bed. Leave enough time for evening rituals like baths, teeth brushing, and tuck-ins.
- If you notice the host is yawning, thank them for a great evening and head for the door.
- If there are no previously discussed plans for after dinner, consider leaving thirty to sixty minutes after dessert.
- If the host is at the sink doing dishes, this is a good sign. If they finish the dishes and begin mopping, you have overstayed your welcome.

We are dear friends with a senior lady who simply gets up from the table and retires to her bedroom when she is done for the evening. She retires early and we love giving her a hard time about it. She learned this from her father. He enjoyed meals with extended family and invited them to stay as long as they liked. All he requested was that they turn off the lights and lock the door when they left. That's one way of leaving the exit strategy open.

Intentionally Developing Hospitality

AMY

In 1 Peter 4:8-9 we read, "Above all, love each other deeply, because love covers over a multitude of sins. Offer hospitality to one another without grumbling." This should be in the heart of every Christian. But there are some who have been given an extra measure of faith in hospitality, and we call that a spiritual gift. Following the spiritual gifts list of Romans 12, we read, "Share with the Lord's people who are in need. Practice hospitality" (verse 13). Our church defines the spiritual gift of hospitality as "the divine enablement to care for people by providing fellowship, food, and shelter." While some may be gifted with a measure of grace to show hospitality, every follower of Jesus is called to hospitality as Christian service.

Seven years ago, we experienced a meal that we desired more of. And after partaking in it several times since, we desire to give a similar experience to others. It was New Year's Eve, and we were invited to a party at the home of some friends. I have to admit—when they told us who else would be there, I really did not want to go. There were only two couples we kind of knew. My kids were young at the time, and I remember being very picky about our nights away from them. I wanted to be alone with my husband on a date rather than at a party with a few friends and strangers. But somehow, Ted convinced me that it would be good for us. I am so glad he did. It changed us forever.

Dave White greeted us at the door of their new lake home. He and his wife, Jennifer, had recently moved to Branson from Louisiana. Dave always dreamed of having a home in the Ozark Mountains, and this home was something special with its sprawling ceilings, massive stone fireplace, detailed woodwork, and floor-to-ceiling windows. As we entered the home, I immediately lost myself in its warmth.

Dave took us into the kitchen where Jennifer greeted us, poured us a drink, handed us a recipe card, and pointed us to our workstation. I have to admit, I was taken aback. *What? I have to cook at your house?* It was 7:00, and I was hungry! I was used to eating dinner with my toddlers around 5:30 p.m., and by 7:00 p.m. we were usually ready for bed. Little did I know that the next two and a half hours would be some of the best fun and fellowship we had ever experienced.

We all chopped and diced, stirred and seared, refreshed drinks, and snacked on hors d'oeuvres. The goal that night was not to have a perfect dinner all set and ready to go. The goal was to enjoy the experience, preparations and all. We sat down to dinner at 9:30 p.m. I was happy to sit, but my soul was already full.

Ted and I talk about that evening often. That kind of hospitality—intentionally designed to foster relationships and to bless those who took part—was new to us. By the end of the night, we had new friends and a desire to do hospitality for the sake of blessing others. David and Jennifer are great examples of hospitality—it's Jennifer's spiritual gift, and it pours out of her life.

I desire to be a great host. To be hospitable, to be welcoming, to give others the opportunity to be who they are in a judgment-free zone. I want to provide an experience that makes people want to seek more of it, because seeking more godly fellowship will result in seeking more of Christ. But hospitality doesn't pour out of me as a spiritual gift. I get stressed! I get wrapped up in making sure everything—the house, the food, the kids, my appearance—is perfect. I hate that part of me, so I have decided to study those who offer hospitality with graciousness and ease.

My friend Jill is one of those people you feel like you have known your whole life. I remember the first time we had dinner with her and her husband. I found myself remarkably at ease sharing personal stuff, and Ted felt just as comfortable in her husband's presence. Jill asked us questions about our pasts, families, and ministry, our kids and our dreams. We answered those questions in detail and returned her questions right back at her. We became fast friends that first night. On the way home, Ted and I wondered if we had over-shared. Being in ministry for twenty years, we have learned to ask questions and not talk about ourselves, so everything about this experience took us off guard. We decided that the next time, we would only ask questions and not let it be about us. But that was impossible. You see, Jill has the spiritual gift of hospitality. It flows out of her. When you are with someone with this gift, you just can't help but put your feet up and stay awhile.

Even though I don't have the same spiritual gift, I observe and study and try to apply what I learn from my hospitality mentors. One major common principle applies in every situation: It's not about us! We don't invite someone into our homes to show off our design, cooking, or cleaning skills. We don't have to clean every room in the house to have people over for dinner.

You know what helps me with this? Deliberately sabotaging my need for perfection. I may purposely leave a basket of (clean, folded) laundry in a place where I know my guests will see it. Or I may intentionally leave the garage door open, knowing that the guests may enter through our atrocious garage. I plan a simple menu, making sure I don't spend all of my energy on the food in an effort to make myself look good. I have to be very intentional, but I am getting over my insecurities and practicing the true meaning of hospitality.

I'm also studying a few friends who practice the ultimate act of hospitality. Proverbs 31:20 describes them well: "She extends her hand to the poor, and reaches out her hand to the needy" (NET). Our friends Stephanie and Andy, Kari and Travis, and Kristin and Tom have opened their homes to foster children who were truly in need, both physically and emotionally. These families inspire me. They have been stretched and blessed.

Their stories have challenged our family to step up. Our family devotions around the table often find us discussing what kind of hospitality God asks us to show to those in need. We are all in a different place with this question, so we are trusting that God will unite us on what He calls us to do in His perfect timing. In the meantime, we can come alongside these families and help meet their needs. We can have them into our homes, provide encouragement, and love on them as they serve Him in this amazing capacity.

Not all of us will have the opportunity to make such an impact with our hospitality. You may not be able to serve those in need on a regular basis, but what about inviting someone who doesn't have family nearby over for a holiday meal?

I know holidays are sacred. I am not a really sentimental person, but when it comes to the holidays I have way too many traditions and expectations. My poor husband used to bring up having people over, and I would bite his head off. All I could think about was the cleaning and preparation that I would need to do to get everything perfect, and I would be completely overwhelmed and exhausted just considering it.

Imagine the look on his face when after eighteen years of marriage, I brought up inviting a family or person that does not have a place to go for Thanksgiving. I know he had to restrain himself from acting out on the shock he was feeling. The day after we discussed doing this, a family from our church posted the following question on Facebook: "Where could we get a great Thanksgiving meal in Branson? It will just be the four of us so I don't want to cook a big meal just for our little family."

So we invited them, and they accepted! We had a great time preparing as a family. My kids made place cards and set the table. They went through old toys to see what the younger guests would enjoy playing with. I spent hours in the kitchen in the days leading up to Thanksgiving, wondering why I hadn't done this before. I plan and prepare meals for every holiday. It really doesn't take any more time just to double recipes.

We all talked around the dinner table for seven hours. Food, wine, family, friends, and the Lord at the center of it all. Our kids got to practice hospitality, placing the younger children's wants and desires before their own. Carson and Corynn served the children drinks and snacks, colored, jumped on the trampoline, watched a movie, and cleaned up after them. Our kids were wiped out at the end of it all, but the next day they both asked when we could have the family back again. We were overwhelmed with gratitude on this Thanksgiving. We hope that one day our children will want to open their own homes and dinner tables as a tradition of blessing others.

≥Your Family Table

Recipe: Jill's Chicken Soup

AMY

One of the reasons I consider Jill one of my favorite hostesses is her lack of fuss over the food. Don't get me wrong—everything I have ever eaten in her home is delicious! She just has a way of choosing recipes that are simple and full of flavor. This practice reflects the priority of being fully present when guests are in our homes. If we are staring at a cookbook, setting timers, and stir-frying vegetables all at the same time, we won't have much capacity for our guests.

Recently our family took a trip to Washington, DC, where we spent time with Jill, David, and their two precious girls. Because of David's Hebrew heritage, most of their meals are kosher. Jill served us chicken soup with matzo balls. We savored every bite! The secret is in the parsnips. Most people do not know what they are even looking for when they go to the grocery store for parsnips, which look like white carrots but actually were used as a sweetener in Europe before the arrival of cane sugar. The parsnips alongside seasoned chicken and broth mean you get a little sweet with the savory in this soup. Cooking the chicken overnight makes for easy preparation the next day.

Recipe serves 8.

INGREDIENTS:

    1 whole chicken (3–4 pounds), cleaned and rinsed
    3 32-ounce containers chicken broth
    1 large onion, chopped
    5 large carrots, peeled and sliced thin
    2 stalks celery with leaves, cut in half
    2 large parsnips, peeled and cut in half
    1 bunch of fresh dill, chopped
    ½ tablespoon sea salt

INSTRUCTIONS:

Place chicken in a large stock pot, breast side down. Add chicken broth. The broth should cover the chicken completely. If it doesn't, add water to cover. Add the rest of the ingredients listed. Bring all to a boil, then turn the chicken and simmer for twelve hours (cooking overnight works best). Remove the chicken from the pot and carefully debone. Do not shred. Make small strips. Remove the celery, parsnips, and dill, leaving only the onions, carrots, and broth. Add the chicken pieces into the soup. You can add noodles of your choice or add matzo balls. Enjoy!

The "Grateful For" Game

Give everyone around the table three to four slips of paper. Ask each person to write down something, someone, or some place that they are grateful for. No need to write down your name. Pass around a coffee mug or bowl and have everyone insert their slips. Then, keep passing the mug or bowl around the table and have each person read one slip until they're gone. The goal is not to identify who said it, but rather to find ways for everyone to be grateful for that person, place, or thing.

Devotional

> Contribute to the needs of the saints and seek to show hospitality. ROMANS 12:13, ESV

Dan Cathy, the CEO of Chick-fil-A, shared at a conference years ago that the word *restaurant* comes from a French word meaning "to restore." A good meal restores you 70 percent in the heart and 30 percent in the stomach. (In jest, he said that formula is flipped for teenagers: 30 percent in the heart and 70 percent in the stomach.)

Chick-fil-A desires to serve the heart of the customer. The leaders at Chick-fil-A want people to experience remarkable service at their restaurants. They want people to tell their family and friends things like, "You won't believe what happened to me at Chick-fil-A today," "Everyone behind the counter was smiling and seemed genuinely happy to be there," and "The owner even helped me to my car with an umbrella over my head."

You and I can practice this type of hospitality every day. Hold the door open for a stranger. Allow a senior adult to move ahead of you in line. Help a senior up a flight of stairs by walking alongside and gently holding his or her arm. Assist someone in the parking lot by loading groceries into their car trunk. Buy coffee for the person in front of you in line by announcing to the cashier, "I've got her order covered." Ask a mom struggling with multiple children, "Is there anything I can do to help?" Entertain a screaming child on an airplane rather than turning on your noise-canceling headphones.

Look for opportunities to care for people in unique, fun, and surprising ways. You may run into resistance because our culture is experiencing less and less of this kind of gracious hospitality. Don't let that stop you.

Discuss

- Do you ever allow perfection to trump hospitality?
- What are some remarkable ways we can serve guests in our home?

- How do you react to someone who shows you
  kindness? Do you resist? Do you accept? Do you resist
  at first, then hesitantly accept?

Prayer

*Father, You have called us to care for our family, strangers,
widows, and orphans. We want to share You with those who
don't know You. Let our family table be the place where people
feel comfortable asking us questions about You. Let our home
refresh every person who enters it. We love You and want to serve
You in our home and at our table. In Jesus' name, amen.*

CHAPTER 7

A SIMPLE TABLE

The family table prioritizes relationships over food.

*Better a small serving of vegetables with love
than a fattened calf with hatred.*

PROVERBS 15:17

TED

Have you ever heard of North Platte, Nebraska? There's a story about that place that makes me think of simple hospitality. During World War II, the people there began baking cookies and other sweets for the troops coming through the tiny train station in their tiny town. It had started as a way to encourage the Nebraska National Guard, but soon the women in the town were organizing baked goods for every train filled with troops. Over the course of four and a half years, over fifty thousand women from the surrounding communities baked to provide for every train that came through, sometimes up to thirty-two trains a day. Mind you, this was during the war, so the women were using their own rations to bake for the soldiers! Over six million troops were fed in North Platte, and those soldiers never forgot it.[1]

The simple generosity of a cookie or a slice of cake sticks with a person. Simplicity prioritizes love and relationships over money and possessions. Who is gathered around the table is more important than what is on the table. What you do around the table is more important than what you eat off of the table. Fellowship is greater than food. Discussion is greater than drink.

Simplicity is fueled by love. When love and rich conversation are present, what we eat doesn't really matter. Words like *more*, *fancy*, and *fine* are nice but unnecessary when a family prioritizes love. Simplicity looks different for everyone, but the pursuit of it has the same roots.

In Ecclesiastes, Solomon shares with us a foundation for pursuing simplicity:

> Whoever loves money never has enough;
> > whoever loves wealth is never satisfied with
> > their income.
> This too is meaningless.

> As goods increase,
> > so do those who consume them.
> And what benefit are they to the owners
> > except to feast their eyes on them?

The sleep of a laborer is sweet,
    whether they eat little or much,
but as for the rich, their abundance
    permits them no sleep.

I have seen a grievous evil under the sun:

    wealth hoarded to the harm of its owners,
        or wealth lost through some misfortune,
    so that when they have children
        there is nothing left for them to inherit.
    Everyone comes naked from their mother's
        womb,
        and as everyone comes, so they depart.
    They take nothing from their toil
        that they can carry in their hands.

This too is a grievous evil:

    As everyone comes, so they depart,
        and what do they gain,
        since they toil for the wind?
    All their days they eat in darkness,
        with great frustration, affliction and anger.

ECCLESIASTES 5:10-17

Notice it says, "Whoever loves money never has enough," not, "Whoever has money never has enough." Money is not evil. The love of money is evil. Greed is a sin. So simplicity is different for each family. Your means determine your definition of simplicity. A simple meal may be takeout pizza or an omelet cooked with eggs and vegetables from your farm. Or perhaps simplicity means a meal with two courses instead of five.

These verses probe us to ask, "When is enough, enough?" Abundance permits no sleep because the more you have, the more you have to take care of. Every square inch you own owns you. There is absolutely nothing wrong with wealth building, but managing wealth can be quite stressful. Hold wealth loosely, because you will leave this earth in the same fashion in which you entered. You came in with nothing, and you will leave with nothing. Tough truth, yes. But it sets us up for an application in simplicity: Simplicity does not mean poverty; rather it means choosing to enjoy what we work for.

> This is what I have observed to be good: that it is
> appropriate for a person to eat, to drink and to find
> satisfaction in their toilsome labor under the sun
> during the few days of life God has given them—for
> this is their lot. Moreover, when God gives someone
> wealth and possessions, and the ability to enjoy
> them, to accept their lot and be happy in their toil—
> this is a gift of God. They seldom reflect on the days
> of their life, because God keeps them occupied with
> gladness of heart.
>
> ECCLESIASTES 5:18-20

Simplicity and contentment are bedfellows. Routine is not always a bad thing. Boredom sets into your daily grind when you stop appreciating the simple things in your life. When you combine simplicity, contentment, and appreciation, you begin to accept each day as a gift.

In seminary, professors led us verse by verse through entire books of the Bible in a few short months. Some outlines I memorized the first time they were shared and never forgot. I can still remember the practical commentary on Ecclesiastes 5. I've forgotten the title of the class and the professor, but his words stuck with me. To paraphrase, he said, "Life is hard. You will experience very difficult days throughout your life and ministry. Some of you will toil and sweat trying to make a name for yourself and grow large ministries. Don't lose sight of the joy in life. There's nothing better than getting up and working hard, coming home and enjoying an evening with your family, making love to your spouse, going to sleep, and getting up the next day to do it all again."

Psalm 90:10 says, "Our days may come to seventy years, or eighty, if our strength endures; yet the best of them are but trouble and sorrow, for they quickly pass, and we fly away." In the midst of the grind of life, it is good for you and me to gather around the table and eat, drink, and enjoy life.

You can't change your past, and worrying about your future strips today of its power. So enjoy today while picturing a special future for your marriage and family. When families enjoy food and drink and finding satisfaction in their daily toil, "they seldom reflect on the days of their life, because God keeps them occupied with gladness of heart" (Ecclesiastes 5:20). When your formula for life is simple and content, God keeps you occupied with gladness of heart. Work hard, provide for your family, and live a simple lifestyle, enjoying the company of others and prioritizing relationships. God "richly provides us with everything for our enjoyment" (1 Timothy 6:17).

A few years ago, our church did a summer sermon series called When Someone I Love. Sermons in that series included "When Someone I Love Gives Up and Walks Away," "When Someone I Love Is Diagnosed with Cancer," and "When Someone I Love Dies." The goal of the series was to equip the saints for the work of ministry.

One of the most precious videos in that series was that of Randy Kuenzle and his family. The year prior, Randy had been diagnosed with pancreatic cancer. I will never forget his words: "This is a win-win for me. If the Lord heals me, He gets the glory. If He takes me home, He gets the glory." His eternal perspective on life challenged our entire congregation. Randy was a retired pastor who loved his family dearly. At his funeral, I heard so many great stories with the same theme. He was a simple man who knew how to be content. His daughter, Kristen, wrote me a letter that I shared with our congregation during a sermon on simplicity:

> My dad loved to keep things simple, such to the point we said his life's motto was "pack light." He didn't want to overcomplicate things and he didn't need

much. More than anything, he loved to just spend time with his family, eating good food and relaxing together. When prompted to write a Christmas wish list, he would hand over a piece of paper with items on it like duct tape, Roundup, and socks.

We would laugh and say, "Dad, this is so boring. We can't buy you this stuff." To which he would respond, "Well, I just don't need anything."

He didn't ask for much, but he sure gave a lot. When my husband and I got engaged, Dad offered to build our first home for us. Free of any contracting fees, our mortgage would only include the building supplies and costs.

This past spring, my dad went home to be with Jesus, but his spirit of giving hasn't left us. My mom continues to be the same generous force my parents always were, giving time and energy, resources and needs, demanding nothing in return.

This year, when I asked Mom what she wanted for Christmas, she responded with, "I don't need anything. I just want to spend time with my kids and grandkids this year."[2]

Keeping it simple sets our hearts at peace.

What Do We Need?

If your family downsized, what is the smallest house you could live in? When you think about the rest of the world, that question seems ridiculous. Our family is obsessed with the Tiny House Movement, which involves singles, couples, and families moving into homes ranging in size from 150 to 600 square feet. Our family has no plans of moving into 187 square feet anytime soon, but the Tiny House Movement has us asking great questions about what we truly need in our lives.

The average size of a new single-family home is 2,662 square feet, up from 983 square feet in 1950.[3] Through the eighties and nineties our houses grew larger as Baby Boomers expanded their businesses, companies, careers, and investment portfolios. They created the modern banking system that gave first-time home owners generous mortgages and waived the traditional 20 percent down payment so families could afford bigger spaces to store more stuff.

A tiny house is simple. When you walk into a tiny house, your first thought is, *They have what they need without the extras.* A tiny house is built for function. One tiny house owner recently said, "If it doesn't serve multiple purposes, we kick it to the curb." A tiny house is easy to maintain.

A generous company came to Branson, Missouri, years ago and bought empty theaters for churches. When an abandoned 2,500-seat theater came on the market, many of our church members said, "We need to get that theater." When anyone asked me about the property, I responded with "Have you ever vacuumed a football field?"

"No,'" was the usual answer.

"Well, that theater has ten football fields," I'd tell them.

"Can we count on you to volunteer for facilities?" Most of my friends responded with a smile and "I get it."

Think of all the time you would free up if you didn't need to clean thousands of unnecessary square feet in your house. What would your family do with the extra time you used to spend on mopping, vacuuming, dusting, mowing, pressure washing, and raking?

Another way a tiny house helps you simplify? It doesn't allow hoarding. My wife and I are often shocked by the amount of stuff people keep in storage. We throw away or give away as much as we possibly can. Amy lives by the motto, "If you haven't used it in the last month, throw it away." She once asked me while cleaning out the garage, "When was the last time you used this hammer?"

We can learn a few things from the Tiny House Movement as we plan our gatherings and set our family table. Keep simplicity in mind when you plan spaces and serve your guests. Less is often more. Not every gathering requires a large spread and a four-course meal. Try a dessert gathering. Send out an invite for friends and family to join you for a morning coffee with pastries.

Our seventy-six-year-old friend Norma Smalley figured out simplicity years ago with her annual chili dinner on October 31. Knowing that most families go trick-or-treating, she made a vat of chili and hosted a drop-by party. It was simple, fun, and fast. After a quick bowl of chili, she hugged each child, handed them a personalized bag of candy, and sent them down the street to ring those doorbells. We never turned down her invitation because we appreciated the simplicity. What other holidays, special occasions, and family gatherings could benefit from this type of hospitality?

⇗Your Family Table

Recipe: Grandma Erliss's Molasses Cookies

What is more simple and appreciated than a fresh plate of cookies? Whether they're for new neighbors moving in, the kids after a long day at school, or family and friends at Christmas, homemade cookies are always a hit.

I have searched for years for a go-to cookie recipe, struggling to find something consistent and delicious. We've all been there, right? If we are going through the effort and expense of gathering all the ingredients, preparing the dough, and baking the cookies, we want to be sure they will turn out as intended—scrumptious and mouthwatering.

Well, search no longer. Grandma Erliss spent a lot of time in the kitchen. She didn't bother much with measuring cups and spoons—"a scoop of this and a pinch of that" was more her style. I don't believe I ever saw her looking at a cookbook. So imagine my surprise when my mom came home with Grandma's recipe box shortly after she passed away. I felt like she was bringing me a lost treasure box. It was filled with recipes like some meaty casseroles and Grandma's favorite Jell-O "salads." (I always thought it was funny that they were called "salads" when the main ingredients were Jell-O and Cool Whip!) The first cookie recipe I came across was Grandma's molasses cookies. I was so excited—these were a part of my childhood Christmases. We have enjoyed them several times since and have never been disappointed. I hope you enjoy them and pass them on as well.

Recipe makes about 20 cookies.

INGREDIENTS:
   ¾ cup canola oil
   ¼ cup molasses
   1 cup sugar
   1 egg
   2 cups flour
   ½ teaspoon cloves
   ½ teaspoon cinnamon
   ½ teaspoon ginger
   ½ teaspoon salt
   2 teaspoons baking soda

INSTRUCTIONS:
Beat first 4 ingredients well in mixer. In a separate bowl combine the remaining ingredients and add to the mixer bowl. Cover and refrigerate for at least 1 hour. Make into 1½-inch balls and then roll in sugar. Place on ungreased non-stick cookie sheet. Bake at 375 degrees for 8 to 10 minutes.

The "Would You Rather . . . ?" Game

"Would You Rather . . . ?" can give some great insight into people's personalities and preferences! Enjoy asking one another these questions around the table.

Would you rather . . .

- own your own boat or your own plane?
- be able to fly or be invisible?
- speak every language in the world or play every instrument?
- live in the future or in the past?
- live without a telephone or a television?
- meet the president of the United States or your favorite movie star?
- be a rabbit or a horse?
- go to the beach in the summer or skiing in the winter?
- win an Academy Award or an Olympic Gold Medal?
- raise chickens for eggs or sheep for wool?
- live on a houseboat or in an RV?
- live in space or under the sea?
- be totally covered in hair head to toe, or completely bald?
- always have to enter rooms backward or always have to somersault out?
- always have the same song stuck in your head or always have the same dream at night?[4]

Devotional

This is what I have observed to be good: that it is appropriate for a person to eat, to drink and to find satisfaction in their toilsome labor under the sun during the few days of life God has given them—for this is their lot. Moreover, when God gives someone wealth and possessions, and the ability to enjoy them, to accept their lot and be happy in their toil— this is a gift of God. They seldom reflect on the days of their life, because God keeps them occupied with gladness of heart.

ECCLESIASTES 5:18-20

We spend too much time looking for satisfaction in *more* rather than *enough*. Do we really need more stuff, or could we get by with less and enjoy more? Enjoying what God provides us leads to contentment.

There are many ways to reflect on our days. We can sit around frustrated that we don't have everything we want. We can look at our friends' and neighbors' stuff and wish we had what they have. Some who have nothing want more. Some who have much want less. Funny how that works.

To find balance in living a simple life, work hard and enjoy what God blesses you with. When your attitude reflects gratefulness for the simplicity of God's provision, you will seldom reflect on the days of your life because you will be content and "occupied with gladness of heart."

COME TO THE FAMILY TABLE

Discuss

- Could we get rid of half of what we own? What would that look like?
- If our closet shrank by 90 percent, what clothes would we donate to Goodwill?
- If each person were allowed to bring only one cedar trunk into a tiny house, what would be in your trunk?

Prayer

Lord, help us fight the desire for always wanting more. We desire to find our joy in You. Teach us to enjoy the simple things around us every day. Help us scale back our thirst for more. We do not want to live a life defined by selfishness or entitlement. We want peace of mind, gladness of heart, and contentment. In Jesus' name, amen.

CHAPTER 8

A LAVISH TABLE

The family table wows family and friends.

TED

Delivering *wow* is more about the unexpected than it is the
unaffordable. My grandma Mary Jane knew how to wow
people. At most meals, she left a five-dollar bill under the
place mat for her grandsons. We knew it was coming, but
we always left feeling extra special.

In honor of my grandma, I preached a Christmas series
called Vintage Christmas at our church two months before
she left this earth. Each Sunday the stage was set up with a
scene from her home. Her kitchen table was my favorite and
made for a special sermon. I don't know what was harder—
preaching from the spot where I sat as a child in her home
or watching my mom cry in the seventh row.

To prepare for the series, I solicited my family's help around the table that Thanksgiving. As we shared stories of grandma, I couldn't control my excitement for what I had planned—a surprise that no one saw coming. Amy was the only one who knew.

This was going to be our first big holiday around our big farm table—the first time to have eleven family members gathered around one table. The place mats were set; chargers sat under the dinner plates; cloth napkins were folded; utensils, water glasses, and wine glasses were positioned perfectly.

On my way home from church the day before Thanksgiving, I stopped by the bank and asked for twelve fresh five-dollar bills. When I arrived home and showed Amy, she agreed that this would be a fun and special surprise. Our plan was to go around the table and share one thing we each are grateful for. Then we would follow that up with our favorite Mary Jane story. To end, I would ask everyone to look under his or her place mat.

When I asked everyone to look under the right corner of the place mats, half of our family did, and the others delayed because they thought it was a joke. Who puts money for their guests under a place mat? Why five dollars? After all, I was reliving a memory that was thirty years old. Maybe I should have considered a ten-dollar bill.

I had built up this reveal in my mind so much that the reception of it did not meet my expectations. But that's okay. We still talk about it two years later. For us, that is the test of wow. If we are still talking about it years later, then we achieved our goal.

Lavish hospitality seems to be in sharp contrast to the simple hospitality we talked about in the last chapter, but we believe they complement each other. Together they say, "Everything doesn't have to be perfect or expensive to give your guests a meal they will never forget." Lavish hospitality delivers the *wow*. Simple hospitality allows for greater frequency of the *wow*. If every meal that delivered *wow* was expensive and took weeks to plan, you would throw a party once or twice a year. When you keep it simple, you can entertain a couple of times a month.

Lavishing Love

Lavish means extreme generosity to the point of extravagance. Have you ever practiced generosity to the point of extravagance? Would your guests use the word *lavish* to describe your hospitality? Lavishing love on your guests means going the extra mile and trying some new, unexpected ideas. It does not always mean expensive.

In John 12, Jesus received an act of extreme generosity. While He was a guest in Lazarus's home, Mary did something that redirected the conversation around the table. As you read this story, picture yourself seated at the table, watching Mary bless Jesus while listening to the conversation of the gathered guests:

> Six days before the Passover, Jesus came to Bethany, where Lazarus lived, whom Jesus had raised from

the dead. Here a dinner was given in Jesus' honor. Martha served, while Lazarus was among those reclining at the table with him. Then Mary took about a pint of pure nard, an expensive perfume; she poured it on Jesus' feet and wiped his feet with her hair. And the house was filled with the fragrance of the perfume.

But one of his disciples, Judas Iscariot, who was later to betray him, objected, "Why wasn't this perfume sold and the money given to the poor? It was worth a year's wages." He did not say this because he cared about the poor but because he was a thief; as keeper of the money bag, he used to help himself to what was put into it.

"Leave her alone," Jesus replied. "It was intended that she should save this perfume for the day of my burial. You will always have the poor among you, but you will not always have me."

JOHN 12:1-8

Consider that all of this took place at Lazarus's house. Lazarus was a dead man until Jesus brought him back to life, and this table scene takes place after his resurrection. We have no record of the discussion that followed, but how do you move off of that story?

Conversation flowed around the table as Martha prepared food in the kitchen. Everyone was reclining at the table, relaxed, kicked back, and enjoying one another. This meal was in honor of Jesus. And then in walked Mary, and everything changed.

Mary washed the feet of Jesus with "about a pint of pure nard, an expensive perfume" and "wiped his feet with her hair." This was an act of worship. In that day and in that culture, the only person a woman would let her hair down for was her husband. There was nothing sensual about this scene, but it was an act of intimacy and spontaneous love. She was worshiping Jesus extravagantly. Everyone in the house knew what was happening because the "house was filled with the fragrance of the perfume."

Mary spent up to a year's wages on this act of lavishing love, but that was nothing close to what Jesus has poured out on all of us through His death on the cross. Mary took all that she had available, all that she had there with her to bless her Messiah.

Love lavishers will experience objection. Extreme generosity makes people feel uncomfortable. It can even bring out judgmental spirits. Judas objected to Mary's generosity. We all have those people in our lives who have strong opinions about the way we're living and worshiping, but no action in their lives backs up what they're saying. Judas thought that the perfume should have been sold and the money given to the poor. But it was not the poor he was thinking about. He wanted to line his pockets with some of the proceeds. Jesus knew this. That's why He said, "Leave her alone." Jesus welcomed her worship. Her heart was more valued than her action.

As you sit around this table, who do you relate the most

to, Mary or Judas? Do you want to be the one blessing your guests with extreme generosity or the one questioning it? When you lavish love on others in the name of Christ, you may ask yourself, "Is this worth it?" Planning a dinner party and blessing our guests with extreme generosity seems like too much effort for only a few hours. Is it worth it? Yes.

When we think about lavishing hospitality on guests, the Ritz-Carlton comes to mind. They are world renowned for their five-star hospitality. While you may never stay at one of their properties, you can still gain much from the way they serve their guests.

In Joseph Michelli's book *The New Gold Standard: 5 Leadership Principles for Creating a Legendary Customer Experience Courtesy of the Ritz-Carlton Hotel Company*, he shares the principles he learned from the unprecedented access he was given behind the scenes. The Cunningham home does not have the amenities or staff of the Ritz-Carlton, but we can apply the principles outlined by Joseph Michelli to each guest who visits our home. Here are the five "Ritz" principles we now consider as we entertain guests.

#1 Define and Refine

We seek to understand the ever-evolving needs of our guests. Keep a mental file on your family and friends. Note what they enjoy and eat, and even what hobbies they regularly participate in. E-mail your guests before they arrive and ask about special dietary needs or the kids' favorite ice cream flavor.

Ted's mom is an expert on understanding people's needs.

We are convinced that Bonnie Cunningham has a mental file on hundreds of people. She knows which Disney characters each child likes. She buys little gifts for her guests perfectly suited to their interests and tastes. She never forgets a conversation, so she knows how to tie it all together no matter what the topic.

Gary Smalley was also an expert in this area. Years ago, he created a list of all the reasons why his wife, Norma, is valuable. He regularly returned to it to remind himself and honor her. One way to honor your guests is to prepare a list of the reasons you value them and read it to them over dinner. Honor esteems people as highly valuable. At your next dinner, tell your guests why they are valuable. The mental file will help you write and grow that list. It blesses your guests to learn you think about them when you are not together.

#2 Empower through Trust

Treat each guest with the utmost respect. You've heard the saying, "The customer is always right." I know business owners who would disagree with that, but the idea guides our courtesy and kindness nonetheless. Trust is the "firm belief in the reliability, truth, ability, or strength of someone."[1] Let your guests know that you believe in them and that you are pulling for them. Point out actions you've witnessed that point to their trustworthiness. Here are some practical statements that empower your guests with trust:

"I've always known you to be a compassionate person. I love the way you care for your parents."

"You always speak highly of your spouse. You enjoy being married, don't you?"

"You've worked for that company for more than twenty years. I know you've faced many challenges there, but I'm so inspired by how you stick with it and maintain a positive attitude."

"You have such high integrity. Doing the right thing is not something I ever question in you."

Recently, one of our guests was discussing a sticky situation that required many decisions around some gray areas of life. Our friend struggled with making the right decision. I looked him right in the eyes and said, "You are the most black-and-white person I know. Your desire to always do the right thing is a great testimony to your family. Whatever you decide, I stand with you because I know your integrity and deep conviction to please the Lord."

This caught him off guard. He responded with, "I don't know what to say to that." He didn't need to say anything. We all knew his heart. Even if it is obvious, say it anyway. Spoken words are powerful and make a lasting impression when delivered with grace.

At your next gathering, make a bold proclamation of trust to each of your guests and watch what it does to their spirits. They will leave your table and home with a full heart and open spirit.

#3 It's Not about You

This a core value of the Ritz-Carlton and the first line in the book *The Purpose Driven Life* by Pastor Rick Warren. I remember reading that line and thinking, *That one statement is worth the entire price of the book.* It became a core value at our church and in our home.

The Ritz anticipates a customer's need. In our home, we strive to anticipate the needs and desires of others before they are expressed. Amy is the best at this. She has already talked about her struggles with perfectionism in hospitality, but I remind her not to abandon that compulsion altogether. The reason companies like the Ritz-Carlton and Disney make moments magical is because they direct all of their energies and focus toward the guest experience.

You've probably experienced the restaurant that makes you feel like you are in the way. When you request something, it is as though you are inconveniencing the server or the kitchen staff. Amy cracks up at me when I request something of a waiter because my tone is always apologetic. I cringe when Amy asks for a condiment with boldness. She knows I would rather go without. I've eaten entire meals that were prepared for another table. Imagine the server's shock when he learns I received the wrong meal and ate it anyway. I won't say a word.

Compare that to the restaurant that customizes any meal you want. Our friends at the Chateau on the Lake here in Branson know that my son loves a good breakfast sandwich.

At dinner, they'll ask, "Carson, what would you like on your sandwich?" A menu is just a suggestion for them. They go out of their way to make it about the one dining, not the one serving. This is a secret of success for any business owner.

I love watching Amy watch our guests. She knows how much coffee they have, how they feel about the temperature of the house, and what portion of the meal they ate the quickest and might like a little bit more of. She observes more than asks questions. She's tending to the needs of others, not her own.

#4 Deliver Wow

Give your guests a personalized experience. Unexpected acts of love deliver the *wow*. It doesn't need to be expensive to be lavish. Ask any grandparent—a handwritten card from a grandchild is better than a store-bought card any day. And for a mom, dishes cleaned by her little ones is worth more than a diamond necklace.

Our family loved the television show *Extreme Makeover: Home Edition*. When it was on the air, we watched an episode every Sunday night. Why? Because it delivered extreme, extravagant, lavishing love.

We always cried the first five or six minutes of the show when they told the family's story. We felt like the family in need deserved whatever they wanted. The Extreme Makeover team tore the house down and built a new one, furnishing it from top to bottom. From the furniture to the utensils in the kitchen, it was a spectacular punch of *wow*.

Then the family came back from an all-expenses-paid trip

to Disney for the big reveal. Talk about a special moment. As they walked around the house, each person was in shock. After being wowed in every room, they exited the house to even more amazing news: "Chevy wants to give you a brand new SUV" or "We decided to give you a pool with a water park" or "They also want to pay off your mortgage with this check for $250,000." Every minute one-upped the minute before. It was an emotionally exhausting show. That is what we mean by *wow*. What can we do that leaves our guest saying, "Wow, I didn't see that coming"?

#5 Leave a Lasting Footprint

If your guests leave with the *wow*, you leave a lasting footprint. For Christians, a lasting footprint is our testimony. Jesus said, "Your love for one another will prove to the world that you are my disciples" (John 13:35, NLT). Love lavishers are known to the world. We want guests to leave saying, "That was a great night. Talk about feeling special. They definitely do that."

How do you know if you leave a lasting footprint? If your guests discuss the last time they were with you the next time they see you. A year or two later, if they still bring that night up, you achieved lasting footprint.

We experience this at churches, too. When you leave a church, did you feel welcomed and accepted or judged and ignored? Churches that create warm, inviting environments leave lasting footprints. Guests want to return. They talk about it until the next time they visit.

Here are ten unexpected, affordable ways to wow your guests and leave a lasting footprint:

1. Welcome sign—A personalized sign with your guests' names over the front door or on the mailbox is a great way to welcome friends and family.

2. Place cards—Writing out each person's name on a mini chalkboard or index card marks every person's seat. It allows the host to think through conversation as well.

3. Folded napkins—Nothing says fun like a paper towel or cloth napkin folded like a wave, flower, basket, or tower. You can google many websites that give step-by-step instructions on dozens of designs and patterns.

4. Multi-course meal—This doesn't require extra food. We are accustomed to serving multiple items on one plate all at one time. Try smaller portions on smaller plates over three to four courses. This is the secret to a slow meal and lingering conversation.

5. Plate their food—If you don't want multiple courses, invite your guests to be seated, pray, then serve each guest a plated meal. No buffet or passing of bowls and plates. Get creative with the plating. Drizzle sauce.

6. Playlists—Pick ten or so of your favorite songs that fit the theme of the night. If you are

serving Mexican food, pick some classic Spanish songs. If you are serving a favorite meal from a favorite city, pick songs that fit. For example, a backyard cookout with Chicago hotdogs requires "Sweet Home Chicago," "Go Cubs Go," and at least one Blues Brothers tune. If you serve New York–style pizza, go with Sinatra and a Broadway classic.

7. Hire musicians—If you really want to step up the music, find an up-and-coming band or an artist at church and offer them a fair rate to play for your guests for an hour or two.

8. Custom desserts served individually—This is our favorite. A slice of pie or cake is a traditional choice, but mousse in a mini mug or champagne glass delivers the "I didn't see that coming."

9. Take-home gifts—Give your guests something to remember the night by. We love sending guests home with the centerpiece of flowers or a dozen eggs from the chickens.

10. Picture—Take a picture of the group around the table and print it out before everyone heads home.

May this list serve as a starting point for you and your family table. Add to it throughout the years. Unexpected gestures that wow your guests keep them coming back to your table.

≥Your Family Table

Recipe: Sweet or Savory Popovers

I will never forget the first time our family laid eyes on these pastry puffs of goodness! We were in Phoenix, Arizona, and dined at one of the most wonderful restaurants: French chef Laurent Tourondel's BLT Steak. It was love at first sight. The oversized light fixtures, the playful artwork, the clean lines of the décor, and generously padded booths made me want to move in. The environment was perfect. I couldn't wait to look at the menu. It did not disappoint. I do not remember everything we ordered that night, but I do remember over ordering. We wanted to try everything on the menu. When the jumbo popovers arrived at the table, we were giddy. Any thoughts of low carb went out the window! This was something worth splurging on. We all ate our entire jumbo popover and wanted more. The rest of the meal was just as delicious.

The icing on the cake was the simple popover recipe that BLT hands out to all its patrons. I couldn't believe I was going home with this treasure. We have enjoyed them several times since then. They do work in a muffin pan, but if you want to wow your guests, serve them jumbo size from a popover pan with creamy butter and salt. The presentation alone says that your guests are worth the extra effort. Little do they know that there are only five simple ingredients. If you really want to lavish love on your guests, print out or write out the recipe on a plain note card, punch a hole in the corner, tie it to a ribbon and attach it to a popover pan, and give it to each guest on the way out the door. Most people do not own a popover pan, so it is a delightful surprise. It would also be a great way to encourage your guests to do the same for someone else. Here are some of our favorite popover varieties that we have come up with, inspired by our experience at BLT. These puffy hollow delights are always best served straight out of the oven with butter. We like to make cinnamon sugar butter with sweet popovers and maple butter with savory.

Each recipe makes twelve popovers.

Cinnamon Sugar Popovers

INGREDIENTS:
   3 cups milk
   3 cups all-purpose flour
   1 tablespoon kosher salt
   6 eggs
   ¼ cup sugar
   1 tablespoon cinnamon

TOPPING:
Mix and sprinkle on top before placing in oven
   1 tablespoon sugar
   1 teaspoon cinnamon

CINNAMON SUGAR BUTTER:
Combine ingredients and stir with a fork
    ¼ cup softened unsalted butter
    1 tablespoon sugar
    2 teaspoons cinnamon

Bacon Cheddar Popovers

INGREDIENTS:
    3 cups milk
    3 cups all-purpose flour
    6 eggs
    6 strips maple bacon, precooked and chopped
    1 cup sharp cheddar cheese, shredded
    ¼ cup Parmesan or Gruyère, shredded

MAPLE BUTTER:
    ¼ cup softened unsalted butter
    2 tablespoons brown sugar

INSTRUCTIONS:
Place a six-cup popover pan or a standard or jumbo muffin pan in the bottom third of the oven. Place a baking sheet on the rack underneath to catch any drips. Preheat oven to 400 degrees.

In a small saucepan over medium-high heat, warm the milk until small bubbles form around the edges. Sift the flour and salt onto a sheet of waxed paper. In a large bowl, whisk the eggs until frothy, about 2 minutes. Slowly whisk in the hot milk, whisking constantly so the eggs don't cook, then gradually whisk in the flour mixture until almost smooth. Depending on what recipe you chose, add the cinnamon and sugar or the bacon and cheese.

Remove the popover pan from the oven and coat the cups with butter. Nonstick vegetable spray works, but butter allows the popovers to come out of the pan more easily. Fill the prepared cups about ¾ full with batter. If doing a topping, sprinkle on top at this point.

Return the pan to the oven and bake for 15 minutes, then rotate the pan 180 degrees. Continue baking until the popovers are browned and puffed (25 minutes more); do not open the oven after rotating the pan.

Invert the pan and remove the popovers. Serve immediately. Using a paper towel, wipe out the excess fat from the popover cups. Heat the pan in the oven for 5 to 10 minutes. Repeat to bake the remaining batter. Makes 12 popovers in a popover pan or 20–24 in a standard muffin pan.

If you are using a standard muffin pan, reduce the second baking time from 25 minutes to 10–12 minutes.

The "Lifestyles of the Rich and Famous" Quiz

If you grew up in the eighties, you remember the television show *Lifestyles of the Rich and Famous*. Who can forget Robin Leach signing off each episode with his signature, "Champagne wishes and caviar dreams"? The show allowed viewers to glimpse into the high-end homes of actors, athletes, and the business elite.

COME TO THE FAMILY TABLE

Here are some multiple-choice questions to share with your family tonight. Everyone is guaranteed to learn something.

1. How much is the most expensive house in America?
   A. $50 million
   B. $100 million
   C. $140 million
   D. $190 million

   Answer: D. $190 million—a fifteen-thousand-square-foot home on fifty acres in Greenwich, Connecticut

2. How big is the largest house in America?
   A. 60,000 square feet
   B. 90,000 square feet
   C. 120,000 square feet
   D. 150,000 square feet

   Answer: B. 90,000 square feet. According to Luxuryhomes.com, Versailles is a 90,000-square-foot mansion, which includes a grand ballroom, three swimming pools, ten kitchens, a roller rink, two tennis courts, bowling lanes, and a thirty-car garage.[2] For your information, the third-largest home in the United States is 72,000 square feet and is located twenty miles from where we live in

Branson, Missouri.[3] If you're ever heading south
on Highway 65 to Branson, Missouri, look to
your east and you will see it sitting a mile or two
off the road.

3. The most expensive caviar comes from the eggs of
a rare albino sturgeon between sixty and a hundred
years old. How much does one pound of this caviar
cost?
A. $1,000
B. $5,000
C. $15,000
D. $25,000

Answer: C. $15,000. According to the Guinness
Book of World Records, "the most expensive
of all caviar, and indeed the world's most
expensive food is 'Almas', from the Iranian
Beluga fish—1 kg (2 lb 3 oz) of this 'black gold'
is regularly sold for £20,000 (then $34,500).
Almas is produced from the eggs of a rare albino
sturgeon between sixty and one hundred years
old, which swims in the southern Caspian Sea
where there is apparently less pollution. Caviar is
traditionally eaten directly from the skin between
the index finger and the thumb. The eggs are
rolled slowly around the mouth and pop to
release the flavour."[4]

Devotional

> See what great love the Father has lavished on us,
> that we should be called children of God! And that
> is what we are!
>
> I JOHN 3:1

Pastor Rick Warren once said, "God is love. He didn't need us. But he wanted us. And that is the most amazing thing."[5] When we think about the extent to which God lavished His love on us, our hearts are filled with song. We all relate to love songs. Some songs speak of our sadness over a broken heart. Others fill us with joy as they remind us of the refreshing love of a new relationship. Over the centuries, writers of hymns and worship music have stretched our imaginations to sing of the exceedingly great love of our Father in heaven.

Hymn writer Kurt Kaiser penned, "O, how He loves you and me; He gave His life, what more could He give? O, how He loves you; O, how He loves me; O, how He loves you and me."[6]

A century ago, Frederick M. Lehman wrote:

> *Could we with ink the ocean fill,*
> *And were the skies of parchment made,*
> *Were every stalk on earth a quill,*
> *And every man a scribe by trade;*
> *To write the love of God above*
> *Would drain the ocean dry;*
> *Nor could the scroll contain the whole,*
> *Though stretched from sky to sky.*[7]

More recently, the David Crowder Band led us in worship with these contemporary thoughts:

He is jealous for me, loves like a hurricane, I am a tree
Bending beneath the weight of His wind and mercy[8]

A love language is the way a person gives and receives love, and God gives and receives love through His Son, Jesus Christ. In John 3:16 we read how God gives His love: "For God so loved the world that he gave his one and only Son, that whoever believes in him shall not perish but have eternal life." How does God receive love? Jesus said, "No one comes to the Father except through me" (John 14:6) and "Whoever has my commands and keeps them is the one who loves me. The one who loves me will be loved by my Father, and I too will love them and show myself to them" (John 14:21).

Discuss
- Using your own words, describe God's love for you.
- What is your favorite song that describes God's lavish love for us?
- How does God give and receive love?

Prayer
Father, we love You. Your love for us is so high it is hard to imagine. According to the Scripture, "we are more than conquerors" through You because of Your love (Romans 8:37). There is nothing we can say or do to make You love us any more than You

already do. There is nothing we can say or do to make You love us any less. Nothing keeps us from Your love. Nothing—not death, angels, demons, heights, depths—will ever "separate us from the love of God that is in Christ Jesus our Lord" (verses 38-39). Words fall short in describing our gratefulness for You and Your love. In Jesus' name, amen.

CHAPTER 9

HONORING MARRIAGE AT THE TABLE

The family table pours into the marriages and families around us.

TED

Sarah is an elementary teacher, an avid foodie, and a dear family friend. She takes care of our chickens when we are out of town. She is also a caregiver who loves children and advocates for the marriages of her friends.

Now, when it comes to marriage issues, Amy and I usually get the calls that go something like this:

"My sister is getting a divorce. She is devastated. We have talked several times this week, and I don't have a clue how to encourage her. Where can I send her to get help?"

That comes from the heart of a sibling who loves her sister deeply. No doubt. But what if a pastor or counselor is not the only answer? What if every follower of Christ was equipped to do the work of marriage ministry?

That's what made Sarah's request so refreshing. Recently, she asked us to help her find ways to bless a friend who was struggling in marriage. Sarah asked us what to do and say to help her friend honor marriage by staying true to her marriage vows. All we needed to do was cheer her on as she did this most important work of ministry: save a marriage and family.

We invited her over to dinner to come up with a plan of action. Sarah's love of cooking was our first line of defense. We see her regular posts on Facebook about recipes she tries and cookware she is saving up for. The week before she came to our house for dinner, she posted a question: "How many quarts should I consider as I am buying my first Le Creuset French oven?"

When I read that post, I looked at Amy and said, "It's time to invest in Sarah as she invests in her friend." Amy agreed and bought the 4.5-quart yellow Le Creuset French oven. We were all giddy to surprise Sarah. Our kids were the most excited. Our daughter is the gift giver in our family, so we let her do the honors.

Dinner that night was more than memorable. We talked about Sarah's friend and ways she could encourage and support her. We even discussed specific talking points she could share. When we gave her the gift, we could tell she knew how she would use it.

The very first meal she prepared was a Julia Child chicken recipe. And yes, her friend joined her for the meal. Friends gathered around the table, advocating for marriage. Your family table can be a place where many couples and families gather not just for physical nourishment but for emotional, relational, and marital support as well.

Helping a Friend or Family Member through a Marriage Crisis

What do you say and what do you do when a family member or friend tells you, "We're getting a divorce"? Most parents have no clue what to say when they hear that from their son or daughter. Most moms and dads just freeze. What if a brother or sister calls you? What if a coworker shares that something is going on?

Every spouse needs family and friends advocating for both spouses in the marriage. If it's your son calling, don't let it be a bashing session on your daughter-in-law. If it's your brother calling, don't let it be a bashing session on your sister-in-law. No bashing allowed. We are for marriage.

The emotional continuum of a marriage crisis looks like this:

Shock → Confusion → Anger → Disconnection → Divorce

First comes shock. Your friend or family member says, "I don't know how we got here, and I don't know what to do." If you ever come upon the scene of an auto accident and see a bystander taking charge, you know they are helping someone who is unable to process everything going on. I saw this when Amy's grandfather died in 2012. Although his death was not sudden, Amy's grandma was in shock. I'll never forget the chaplain taking Lorraine by the hand and sitting her down in the waiting room. He said, "Lorraine, I am so sorry for your loss. I know you are hurting right now. It is important that we get you something to eat. You will need to rest over the next couple of days. Allow your family to take care of you."

Those words were simple. Yet as a pastor I had never before considered the physical needs of someone mourning. My focus has always been on helping someone emotionally and spiritually at that moment. So when a friend or family member is in shock, even if they saw the divorce coming, your family table needs to be a place of emotional and physical restoration.

After shock, they move into stage 2: confusion. Questions like "Where did this come from?" "How did this happen?" "Am I not good enough for him?" "Is there someone else?" "Was she never in love with me?" Many of the questions at this stage will have no answers. Some will find answers but not good ones.

When someone finds no healthy answers to the confusing questions, they move to stage 3: anger. Questions turn to statements: "This shouldn't be happening." "He made a vow before God and gathered witnesses." "She needs to get some professional help." "You don't end a twenty-year marriage overnight." "He's lost his mind." Unresolved anger is like drinking poison and expecting the other person to get sick. Some merely sip this toxic poison, while others drink it by the gallon. We never bury anger dead; we always bury it alive. It resurfaces when we least expect it.

Be very careful at this stage not to jump in with the

hurting person and join in with the toxicity. "I never wanted you to marry him anyway! Honey, I just want you to be happy. No one should have to put up with this. You've tried everything. You've been dealing with this for this long. Come on; it's time enough. You didn't see this coming?"

Encourage a spirit of forgiveness when your friend or family member hits this stage. Remind them that they can't expect the offender to be their source of forgiveness. They must forgive as God forgave them in Christ Jesus.

If they don't resolve the anger, they will move into stage 4: disconnection. "I want nothing to do with him." "I need to move out and get my own place." As a pastor, I am called in most often at this stage. As a parent, sibling, or friend, you may see the signs of anger and disconnection, but the point of separation is the first time you begin to discuss the marriage with your family member or friend. This stage has brought many to our table. It may bring many to yours as well. Last Christmas, your daughter or son came with the whole family. This Christmas it will be just your child because your daughter-in-law or son-in-law is going to her or his parents with your grandchildren. Don't lose hope at this stage. We have developed reconciliation plans for many separated couples.

If you don't intervene in the disconnection and separation, the last stage is divorce. A friend of mine called me a few months ago from outside a lawyer's office. When I asked what he was doing, he said, "I'm meeting with an attorney to figure out next steps. I need to know how you determine custody and division of assets."

My friends had recently separated, but I had not given up hope. I encouraged my friend to stay in the car, call the attorney, and cancel the appointment. I told him, "We are not giving up just yet. Go home and tell your wife that you plan to work on and fight for your marriage." He did. After a brief separation, they reconciled and were both under one roof again.

Be a Backup Singer

In the Song of Songs, we learn that every marriage is a duet in need of great backup singers. In this romantic book of our Bible, we read the song of King Solomon and the Shulammite woman. They sing lyrics of love to each other in the greatest duet of all time. As you read this beautiful Hebrew poetry, you see a man and a woman building exclusivity in marriage. And throughout the book, we hear from the daughters of Jerusalem. They are the backup singers to Solomon and the Shulammite. Every time we hear them, they are celebrating the budding love of this couple. The first time we read their words, they sing, "We rejoice and delight in you, we will praise your love more than wine" (Song of Songs 1:4).

This should be the heart of every follower of Christ. We should pour into and back up the marriages all around us. As you advocate for the struggling marriages around you, guard your heart. Do not add toxicity to a bad marriage, thus becoming an off-key backup singer. Don't bring discord to the marriage. Instead, rejoice, delight, and praise what God can do in their marriage. The tone of a marriage advocate is, "I want to bless what God is doing. I want to bless what God can do."

In Song of Songs chapters 1 and 2, the duet is focused on dating and courtship. In chapter 3, we see their wedding. Chapter 4 gives a detailed description of the honeymoon. By the time we get to chapter 5, you would think this couple has it going on. However, it is in chapter 5 that we read about their first fight. Their conflict is as common today as it was over three thousand years ago. The husband comes home late at night from a long day and wants to enjoy physical intimacy with his new bride:

> I slept but my heart was awake.
>   Listen! My beloved is knocking:
> "Open to me, my sister, my darling,
>   my dove, my flawless one.
> My head is drenched with dew,
>   my hair with the dampness of the night."
> I have taken off my robe—
>   must I put it on again?
> I have washed my feet—
>   must I soil them again?
> My beloved thrust his hand through the latch-opening;
>   my heart began to pound for him.
> I arose to open for my beloved,
>   and my hands dripped with myrrh,
> my fingers with flowing myrrh,
>   on the handles of the bolt.

I opened for my beloved,
  but my beloved had left; he was gone.
My heart sank at his departure.
I looked for him but did not find him.
  I called him but he did not answer.

SONG OF SONGS 5:2-6

The Shulammite bride is ready for bed. She's in bed. Solomon has been at work as a busy shepherd king. "Open to me, my sister, my darling, my dove, my flawless one," is what we would call today "pet talk"—"Hey, baby," "Hey, sweetie." He desires her physically. To paraphrase him, "I've been out, but now I'm home and I want to be with you."

At first, she does not want to be with him and tells him no. So he gently leaves—and she has second thoughts. She says, "I arose to open for my beloved . . . but my beloved had left; he was gone. My heart sank at his departure." Ever wish you could take something back? We all have. With this, she goes looking for Solomon.

As she searches for him, she finds the daughters of Jerusalem, her backup singers. Watch how they advocate for this couple:

Where has your beloved gone,
  most beautiful of women?
Which way did your beloved turn,
  that we may look for him with you?

SONG OF SONGS 6:1

In other words: "Where is he? What happened? Tell us what's going on. Why are you crying? Why are you emotional? What happened tonight?" This is spot on. Just like the daughters of Jerusalem, a good backup singer asks more questions than they give answers. They want to know what is going on.

Backup Singers for Hurting Marriages

Let's get practical. How can you be a backup singer for crisis or struggling marriages around your family table? We recommend a three-course meal. As the meal progresses, each course builds off of the one before. Work through the emotions as you work through the meal.

FIRST COURSE: ADVOCATE AND VALIDATE

Advocate for both spouses. You have one simple goal. Make it very clear: "I know I'm talking to you right now, but I am for both of you." Yes, even if it's your son-in-law and he has treated your daughter poorly for a long time. People can change. For example, don't define your son-in-law by things he said and did when he was in his twenties. (Does anybody here want to be judged by things they said and did in their twenties? No.) Instead, reassure your family member that you want both of them to win.

Focus on feelings, not issues. If you focus on issues, lines will be drawn and you will be asked to pick a side, even if you don't want to. Money, sex, in-laws, jobs, careers are not what's driving the marriage conflict. It's what's going on inside, not external circumstances, that destroys the marriage. Focus on the heart. Find out how each spouse feels. Feeling words include *disconnected, cheated, controlled, judged, abandoned, worthless,* and *devalued.* Listen to what they say. Understand it the best you can from their perspective. Validate what they feel.

Now, you may be wondering, *What if validating makes them think I am siding with them?* Make sure you validate feelings, not choices. This is tricky. If you tell someone, "I get what you are feeling," they may hear you say, "I agree with you, and you have every right to end this marriage." Validation of emotions does not mean you are supporting a person's wrong choices. For the same reason you shouldn't make major life decisions late at night when you are exhausted, you shouldn't make drastic marital choices when emotions are high. Remind the one in crisis of this fact. We decide based on what is right, not what we feel is right.

I was recently challenged by a friend who interpreted my validation of his feelings as an endorsement of his bad decisions. He thought he should suppress his feelings and live in a rotten marriage for the rest of his life. I validated his frustration, and then I followed up with the following encouragement:

You should never suppress your feelings. Feelings are not a right or wrong issue. We want to listen, understand, and validate your feelings, not suppress them. A key relationship principle for healthy living says, "Do the right thing always and allow your feelings to catch up." You never can go wrong doing the right thing. But boy oh boy, I have made a lot of mistakes in life following my feelings as the chief guide or source. So I always want to do what is right, and then my feelings can follow. The happiness of others is not my source of life. I want to pour into the people around me with no expectation of them pouring back into me. If I look to people as my source of life, I am codependent. Amy and I remind ourselves on a regular basis: Jesus is my source of life, not you.

Never ignore feelings. But remind your friend or family member that decisions rooted in truth lead to long-term happiness. Decisions based on feelings provide happiness up front but not for the long haul. Help your friend or family member find a way to validate and tend to their feelings while fulfilling the responsibilities of their marriage and family. They do not need to choose. They can do both at the same time.

During this course, say less, accomplish more. The less you say, the better. Proverbs 10:19 says, "Sin is not ended by multiplying words, but the prudent hold their tongues." Post a guard at your mouth. May your son, your daughter, your brother, your sister, or your friend know you love them and care for them by your mere presence.

Make the goal of the first course a second course. As the meal progresses, you want the person in a marriage crisis to think, *My friend understands. My parent is showing a lot of compassion right now.* If you handle the first course well, your friend or family member will open up more to you during the second course. You want your family table to be a warm, inviting, and safe place that guests want to return to.

SECOND COURSE: ASK QUESTIONS, ANSWER QUESTIONS

Wait for questions. If you're having dinner, this is the entrée. You showed safety, and now you get to answer questions. A safe person is trusted with personal and incriminating details of life and marriage.

As parents, we do this with our kids. This is why we play video games we don't comprehend. We engage our children in their play world to create opportunities for questions. Whether we're playing with them on the Wii or the trampoline out back, our kids will ask us anything when we are engaged and safe. You wait for it. You hope for it. When it comes, you are ready. "Dad, why do you and Mom date each other every week?" "Mom, will you and Dad ever get a divorce?" Profound questions with a wide-open door for discussion. That's what the first course sets you up for with a couple around your table. They will seek your advice and wisdom when they trust you. When you dig into their world and show interest, they will seek your help.

The worst thing you can do during any course is start preaching with a pointed finger. Nothing shuts a person down faster than a judgmental spirit accompanied by a condescending tone. Resist instruction on the first and second course.

Focus on what is true and avoid rewriting history. Watch for statements like, "He says he doesn't love me. He's never loved me." Caution the person in crisis against taking the last couple of months or maybe the last couple of years of marriage and painting the entire marriage with that brush. Great backup singers remind couples of the truth.

If the person sitting at your table is feeling beat down and worthless, look them right in the eyes and say, "I want to remind you of something. You were created in the image of God. You have worth and value. You need to understand that." Remind them of your love for them. Say it. They need to hear it. They need to feel it.

A stressed-out spouse likely has a negative narrative in their head. They have been lied to for so long, they now believe the lies. Backup singers are truth tellers. You will blow major wind in their sails when you speak truth over them. Bless them with your words.

As I told a friend who divorced and believed he screwed up his life and would never amount to anything, "Not true. God has big plans for you. This is part of your story, but it does not define your future. No way." Picture a special future for the hurting spouse.

Keep in mind that you never know the whole story. You don't know everything going on, so you have to do the best with the information you have before you. Probing for more information is not always necessary. Focus on truth in what you know and move on to the third and final course.

THIRD COURSE: HOPE IN JESUS

Pour the coffee and serve the dessert. It's time to deliver the Good News, and it's fitting that we share it with something sweet.

Our hope is not in our husband or wife.

Ever hear statements like these?

"He's never going to change."

"She's changed."

"We're not compatible."

"I want to be happy, and we can't be happy together."

"We've tried everything."

Our hope can't be in our spouses. We fail. We fall. We are a limited supply. We must turn to a power that is not of us but can be in us. What is this power, and how do we get it?

Share with your hurting friend the resurrection of Jesus from the dead. Drop the name of Jesus into the conversation and watch what happens. Jesus is still the name above all names, and there is power in His name. Jesus was raised from the dead, and according to the Scripture, the power that God used to raise Jesus from the dead is the same power available to you today to raise your lifeless soul and your dead marriage.

Ask the spouse, "Do you believe in the resurrection of Jesus Christ from the dead?" If they believe that, remind them of the resurrection power available to them. Jesus breathes life into dead marriages. Hold out that hope for your friends.

The happiness we might look for outside marriage is more than possible and even better inside marriage. If you are the one struggling in marriage, recruit some backup singers and receive their love and support. Don't isolate yourself from those who can help. Lean into them. Let them be part of your marriage miracle. You can experience a marriage you never dreamed possible.

Backup Singing for Young Duets

AMY

My husband has a passion to see young people fall in love, marry, and grow up together. He encourages young people at our church and all over the country to pursue relationships and eradicate prolonged adolescence. He has set up couples on dates in the middle of sermons. Together, we spot couples all the time. They just don't know they're a couple yet.

Angela was smitten with Jonathan. He served in student ministries and was the servant of all. His love for the Lord and desire to invest in others attracted her to him. The only problem was that she was so infatuated, she couldn't function around him. To her close friends, she called him "The Jonathan." It was a term of deep affection.

After months of discussions, I couldn't take it anymore. Everyone but "The Jonathan" knew of her young budding love. Enough was enough. Ted and I invited Jonathan to a Thai restaurant, where I planned to lay it all on the line.

We started by asking the "What's your five-year goal?"

type questions, but quickly escalated to "What do you think of Angela?" Ted looked at me as if to say, *Wow, that was fast.*

Jonathan explained their friendship and how much he enjoyed serving with her, but there were no tingles. As he talked, we leaned in and said, "Sounds like she would make a great wife." He had a lightbulb moment and decided to ask her on an official date that night. He was excited, but I think Ted was more excited. He started texting Angela.

You are in for the best night of your life, he wrote.

What do you mean? she asked.

I can't tell you, it's a surprise, but I promise you it is something you have wanted for a very long time, he hinted. I had to stop him from stealing Jonathan's thunder.

The rest, as they say, is history. The next year at Christmas Jonathan and Angela became Mr. and Mrs. Hill at the Dogwood Canyon Chapel in Southwest Missouri. (If you are single, and Ted and I invite you to lunch, beware. It may be a setup.)

Who are you thinking about right now? Single friends who need encouragement? Newlyweds no one has talked to about marriage since their premarital counseling? Maybe you have a family member who is waiting for someone to validate the pain of separation or divorce. You are not being a busybody if you call them with a desire to help. Just the opposite is true. Your heart for their physical, emotional, and marital wellness needs to be shared with them. The reward is worth the risk. Take initiative and reach out. You are responsible for your effort. They are responsible for how they respond.

⋗Your Family Table

Recipe: Sarah's One-Pot Pumpkin Salsa Soup

Our friend Sarah loves to spend time in the kitchen. We are blessed to enjoy everything from her ice cream creations to her homemade granola. This soup is one of my favorites. Both healthy and hearty, it is one of my go-to dinner recipes when I need something quick or I want to make lunch for the week ahead of time. I am all about pumpkin, especially in the fall. This soup gives you a reason to enjoy pumpkin all year round. Not to mention you'll have to clean up fewer dishes because it can be prepared in one pot! In my opinion, this soup is even better the second time around. I usually double the recipe so our family can enjoy several meals throughout the week!

Recipe serves 6–8.

INGREDIENTS:

- 1 teaspoon minced garlic
- 1 large white onion, chopped
- 1 pound ground turkey (ground chicken or beef works well also)
- salt and pepper to taste
- 1 teaspoon chili powder
- 1 teaspoon cumin
- 4 cups vegetable broth
- 15-ounce can pumpkin puree

15-ounce can whole-kernel sweet corn or hominy
2 15-ounce cans black beans, rinsed and drained
1 cup Rotel
¾ cup your favorite salsa (we prefer fresh salsa from
produce section)

TOPPINGS:
Shredded cheese
Sour cream
Chopped green onions
Avocado

INSTRUCTIONS:
Spray a medium to large pot with nonstick spray or heat
2 tablespoons oil in it. Place garlic and diced onion in the
pot. Once onion is transparent, remove the onion and garlic
and set aside. Place ground meat in the pot and cook over
medium heat. Season with salt and pepper. When this is
cooked through, add the onions and garlic and cook together
for 2 minutes. Add the spices and bring to a simmer. Stir in
remaining ingredients and bring to a boil and then reduce
heat. Simmer for at least 10 minutes. The longer this soup
simmers, the more flavor it will have. Serve with shredded
cheese, sour cream, chopped green onions, and avocado.

The Guess-Who Game
This is a fun game you can enjoy with family and close friends.
A good knowledge of each person around the table is important.

1. Give each person a notecard.
2. Ask them to write their name on top of the card.
3. Turn all cards in to the hosts.
4. Shuffle the cards and pass them out facedown. Each person gets one card.
5. Ask each person to write five honoring words describing the person on the card.
6. Turn all cards back in to the hosts.
7. The hosts read the descriptions on each card, and everyone guesses who the card is describing.

Devotional

My dove in the clefts of the rock, in the hiding places on the mountainside, show me your face, let me hear your voice; for your voice is sweet, and your face is lovely.

SONG OF SONGS 2:14

When Solomon and the Shulammite were dating, he had a strong desire to find out more about her. He likened her to a dove hidden in the mountainside. He was curious and wanted to spend time getting to know her. Going beneath the surface and into the heart requires commitment and time. The ability to stay in a relationship when conflict arises and times get tough flows from your character, not your compatibility. Faith, purity, integrity, and commitment trump the pursuit of chemistry and compatibility every time. Finding the right match is less complicated than we like to make it.

A good match is a good start, but it will never sustain a thriving marriage. Dating websites are advertised everywhere. There are sites for singles at large like Match.com and eHarmony.com, sites for singles over fifty, and even sites for single farmers and ranchers. The common theme with all of these sites is that chemistry and compatibility are the keys to great relationships.

But marriages fall apart because of deep character issues, not because of surface issues such as likes and dislikes. Compatibility is not something you discover, test for, or stumble into. You build compatibility over a long time. It is something you negotiate through tough times. Early in a relationship, chemistry focuses on similarities and downplays differences. When conflict and differences surface, so does a person's character.

Conflict is a pathway to compatibility, and it requires commitment from your character to stay the course. You may like the way he or she looks and behaves in public, but if that person has no character or integrity, you're in trouble. Character is everything.

Discuss

Note: Even young children can benefit from early conversations about relationship formation.

- Share with your family the most recent online dating advertisement you have seen. What was the main message? What did the couples say about each other?
- Why do you think opposites attract?

- If you marry someone who has a different personality than yours, what will some of the challenges be?

Prayer

Father, it's in the name of Jesus that we thank You for our lives. We thank You for marriage. We thank You for Your heart for marriage. Equip us to bless the marriages in our family. May we be ready and willing to help marriages that are hurting. I ask that You cover people in hurting marriages in the blood of Jesus and protect them from evil and fulfill Your purpose in their lives. It's in the name of Jesus that we ask all of this, amen.

CHAPTER 10

THE LOVE JUG

The family table points us to the True and Only Source of Life.

*Above all else, guard your heart, for everything
you do flows from it.*

PROVERBS 4:23

TED

Everything we say and do flows from our hearts. Our mouths are a reflection of our hearts. Our behavior is a barometer of our emotions. It all comes from within.

At the center of our family table sits the love jug. It is a clear plastic pitcher that is a necessary part of our family table. Why? In our home, we refer to the heart as a love jug, and part of caring for our hearts means eradicating codependency from our home. The textbook definition of codependency is "excessive emotional reliance." Whenever we sense excessive emotional reliance creeping into our family, we pull out the love jug. Each individual member of the family is responsible for his or her own love jug. We each are 100 percent responsible for what is going on inside of us. This means we do not blame others for how we think or feel and what we say and do.

Jesus is our source of life, not any other member of our family. In 1 John 4 we read, "If anyone acknowledges that Jesus is the Son of God, God lives in them and they in God. And so we know and rely on the love God has for us. God is love. Whoever lives in love lives in God, and God in them. . . . We love because he first loved us" (15-16, 19). Jesus is an unlimited supply, and He will overflow our love jug if we let Him. He gives us what no other person ever can. When we rely on Him and His Word, we stay connected to the unlimited supply of love, life, forgiveness, joy, patience, kindness, and gentleness.

To teach your family that Jesus, not others, is the true and only source of life, designate a clear plastic jug as a teaching tool in your home. Then go to the cupboard or china cabinet and retrieve several glasses of all shapes and sizes to represent the people we pour into. Each glass or vessel represents someone else's love jug.

In our home, a champagne glass represents my wife. This wouldn't have been an approved glass in the independent Baptist church I grew up in but works great for this illustration. The average woman speaks twenty thousand words a day, and the average man speaks seven thousand words a day, so I want to make sure I save my words to pour into her. She is a priority in my life, and I want to serve her.

The medium-sized drinking glass represents my daughter. She is the most social person in our family. She comes to life at night. Pouring into her means we share in her love of animals and the great outdoors. Pouring into her hobbies brings me great joy.

The second medium-sized drinking glass is for my son. He is my mighty warrior and has a passion for weapons and surviving in the great outdoors. Bear Grylls's *Man vs. Wild* is his passion. He asked me a couple of years ago to take him out into the woods for a weekend with nothing but a knife and a canteen. (What he didn't know was that my plan was to take him to the woods right behind Cracker Barrel.)

The tall drinking glass represents my parents. I love my mom and dad dearly. They retired fifteen years ago and now live two streets over. My dad loves watching Fox News, and he keeps us posted on the latest developments around the country and world. I joke with him regularly that he needs to mix in a little Joel Osteen—"Dad, you can't watch the news cycle repeating every thirty minutes and be healthy emotionally. You need to mix in a little happy every now and then." My mom is easy to pour into because all she wants is for her family to be connected. She is the social organizer and grand connector of our extended family. My parents don't need any more stuff. They prioritize time with family and friends over everything else.

The little shot glass represents my mother-in-law (family inside joke). Linda Freitag is the best mother-in-law a guy can ask for. She cares for her children and her husband in a way that inspires her family. Pouring into her brings both Amy and me great joy.

After you've poured into your family, your love jug is half empty and you haven't been to work yet! When you put in a full day, your love jug is running on fumes. This is when I use coffee mugs to represent my coworkers.

So you've reached the end of your day, and your love jug is empty. Codependency is holding that empty love jug and waiting for all the people you poured into to pour back into you.

Who Is Your Source?
We must be on guard and aware of who we are plugged into as a source of life. When my spouse is my source, I blame her for our problems. This is the ultimate definition of stuckness, because when your spouse is the source of your problem, he or she automatically becomes the solution as well. You sit and wait for that person to make a change so you can be happy. Not good.

Amy and I spent the first several years of our marriage plugged into each other as the source of life. We would disagree over issues and not be happy unless the other conformed to our way of thinking.

When we were plugged into each other as the source of life, parking lots were a serious source of conflict. She'd point to a parking space three spots in, and I would drive past it to park in a spot twenty spaces down. Filled with pride, I would say, "I did this all by myself. I provided this for my family. Amy, there's not a lot of adventure left for us men in the world anymore, so please let me find my own parking space." She didn't say anything, but her nonverbals screamed, *You are so stubborn!*

About ten years ago, we decided to unplug from each other as the source of life. The blame game and escalated arguments ended almost immediately. We still have times where we get under each other's skin, but we quickly recognize in those times that we have plugged into each other again.

Now when we pull into a parking lot, everything is different. I still want to find my own spot, but we have fun with it. When I pull past the spot she finds and into my distant space, she leans over and starts massaging my bicep and says, "You did this all by yourself!" One time she reached into her purse and pulled out a mint. As I unwrapped it, I realized, *My wife just handed me a treat. She is rewarding my good behavior. I am a dog.*

For years at marriage conferences, Gary Smalley asked me to end my session by asking spouses to fire each other as the source of life. I asked all spouses to raise their right hand and repeat after me: "I, (state your name), do hereby resign as general manager of the universe and my spouse." Then each person would point to their spouse and say, "You're fired!"

You can't plug into Jesus as the source until you unplug from the wrong source. Marriage is at its worst when spouses plug into each other and give to each other out of a limited, toxic supply. Marriage is at its best when a husband and wife unplug from each other as sources, plug into the true and only source, and spend their days giving each other the overflow.

COME TO THE FAMILY TABLE

When my children are my source of life, I use them to impress other people. It doesn't take long to see this one on social media. The faulty input/output theory of parenting teaches, "Whatever you pour into your child is what you will get out of your child." In this equation, a successful child equals a successful parent, and an out-of-control child equals an out-of-control parent.

Parents of generations past did not struggle with this like parents today do. If I pitched a fit in the store, my parents had no problem disciplining me in front of God and gathered witnesses. Today, parents are too concerned with what others think of them as a parent, so they will forego the discipline in exchange for appeasement. Get the child to calm down quickly so people think your family has its act together.

When your child is your source of life, you use their attributes and accomplishments to impress other people. You raise the bar of success high so the world will know you know how to raise successful children. Maybe you compare the strengths of one child to the weaknesses of another. You seek extra special opportunities for your children because you truly believe they stand head and shoulders above the rest of the field. And you try to protect them from all pain, loss, and trials so you do not have to go through it with them.

The goal of parenting is not to hold on to our kids forever. Children will one day leave their father and mother (Genesis 2:24). We are their primary influence, not their primary source. Good parenting points children to Jesus as the primary source of life. I want Jesus to be Corynn and Carson's priority relationship.

When parents are children's source of life, the kids make decisions based on how the parents think and feel. One of the fastest ways we teach our children to be codependent is when we tell them, "You are making me mad." With that one simple statement we teach our children that they can hijack our emotions.

Enmeshed families rely on each other for fulfillment and happiness. In healthy families you will never hear, "If momma ain't happy, ain't nobody happy." Mom can have a bad day but should have the emotional intelligence not to take it out on the rest of the family.

Adult children struggle with this unhealthy attachment to home when they make decisions in life based on how mom and dad will respond. The Scripture calls us to separate (though not isolate) from our parents after we leave home. That means we disconnect physically, financially, and emotionally from their home to thrive in our new home. Feel free to seek advice from your parents, but remember, adult decision making means you think and act on your own. Mom and dad have their opinions, but so do you. You no longer obey them, but you never stop honoring them.

Here is the formula for a healthy family of love jugs:

Parent is 100 percent responsible for his/her love jug
Child is 0 percent responsible for parent's love jug
Child is 100 percent responsible for his/her love jug

When we correctly model having Christ as our source of life, we teach our children that their future spouse is not their source of life. Relationship formation is a regular part of our family table conversations. Character trumps chemistry. We want their future marriages to thrive, and that process begins now by teaching healthy relationship formation.

The love jug illustration works for all people, places, and things. Here are a few more to consider as you fill in the blank:

When your boyfriend or girlfriend is your source of life,

_____ .

When your coworker is your source of life,

_____ .

When your career is your source of life,

_____ .

When your 401k is your source of life,

_____ .

When your church is your source of life,

_____ .

When sports are your source of life,

_____ .

When academics are your source of life,

_____ .

The Unlimited Supply

I still remember waking up to the news that Twinkies went bankrupt. It's been twenty years since I enjoyed a Twinkie, but for some reason that news made me crave Twinkies. I told Amy we needed to rush off to the store to buy a lifetime supply. Why? It's because a limited supply makes people desperate. The key to eliminating codependency is understanding that people, places, and things will never fill you up. They're a limited supply.

My pastor friend Joel Thomas uses Skittles to illustrate the limited supply of people and the unlimited supply of God. On a table you have five glasses filled with Skittles. Each glass contains only one color. The red Skittles represent how your parents gave you life. You pour those into the love jug. The yellow Skittles were the words of high value your parents spoke over you. Green were provision. Orange represented your parents picturing a special future, and purple were all the other good gifts your parents gave you. At the end of the pouring, you have a rainbow of the good that your parents poured into you . . . but still, the love jug is only half full.

In Joel's illustration, there's a two-foot-tall cylinder of Skittles hiding behind the table. That's when the real pour begins. It takes only a little bit to fill the love jug, but he keeps pouring anyway. Thousands of Skittles overflow the love jug and bounce off the table and all over the floor. God's love is unlimited and overflows in our lives when we know and rely on Him. Why would we want to plug into the limited supplies of people when we have access to that kind of love?

On a trip to Target to buy the supplies for that Skittles sermon illustration, I scared some people into thinking Skittles went bankrupt. In a rush, I grabbed a cart and raced back to the candy aisle. Frantically, I started throwing one-pound bags of Skittles into the cart until the shelf was empty. There were senior couples at either end of the aisle watching the entire episode. One couple looked at each other as if to say, *What don't we know? There must be a shortage of Skittles and this guy is stocking up.* The other couple walked over and looked in my cart. I guess they had never seen a shopping cart full of Skittles before.

The man looked in my cart, then looked at me and said, "Well, it's a good thing I don't want any Skittles."

"Oh sir, I'm sorry—if you would like some, help yourself," I responded.

"No, I don't want any Skittles. I'm just saying it's a good thing I don't want any Skittles because you are taking them all," he said.

When people rely on limited supplies, they get jealous of what others get and begin thinking, *I want some of that too.* Maybe you've seen this with your kids. If you spend time with one child, another child gets jealous and wants their fair share. But with an unlimited supply, there is plenty to go around.

Pouring into the love jugs of others is at its best when we pour with no expectation of them pouring back into us. Pouring with expectations leads to manipulation. Pouring without expectations leads to pure ministry.

Free

Pouring into others is fun when it is free of expectations. My family loves a little sandwich shop in our town called Sugar

Leaf. Everything is made from scratch, and their pastries are to die for.

One day in the fall of 2013, the place was packed. On my way to the restroom I noticed a senior couple who seemed quite frustrated. I don't know why I did it, but I stopped at their table and asked, "How was everything?"

"To be honest, we're frustrated," he said.

"What seems to be the problem?" I asked.

He continued, "Your sign out front advertised bratwurst, so we stood in line for twenty minutes. When we got to the register, we were told you were out of bratwurst."

"Sir, what can we do to make this right?" I asked. He looked at his wife but said nothing.

I smiled. "What if I get you a piece of pie?" That seemed to brighten their day. So I stood in line, bought a piece of pie, and brought it to their table. They lit up.

He started asking me questions about the restaurant, and I stopped him to say, "Oh sir, I do not work here. That's my family seated over there, and we are here enjoying lunch ourselves." This, shall we say, threw him for a loop. He didn't know where to go from there.

This is my new hobby. I love finding ways to engage strangers in shocking ways. For example, sometimes when I'm on my way to the restroom at a restaurant, I'll grab the water pitcher and walk around filling empty water glasses. At first, the wait staff will show signs of confusion, but within a few minutes, they'll be saying, "Smoke break," and be out the back door.

Amy challenged me with this a few months back. She said, "Ted, you love engaging Branson tourists in conversation." (She's right. I love leading with, "Where y'all from?") Then she said, "But when you see a church member you're not as quick to engage." She's right on that one too. I searched my soul for a bit on that and came to the conclusion that expectations are the drainer in those relationships. I engage tourists because it is easy to be fully present in the conversation without setting up another time for dinner or coffee. Not true with family and friends.

Unmet expectations drain the life out of relationships. When a wonderful first conversation with a guest to our church is followed up with an e-mail requesting that I be their mentor, that's tough. When the potential for a refreshing meet and greet is sabotaged by the thoughts of "We need to do this more often," a person becomes reluctant to engage in the future. Are you able to engage in conversation today without developing unhealthy or unrealistic expectations?

Pouring into others means you are fully present in conversation and free from expectations. May you each come to the family table with full hearts ready to pour into those gathered. When Jesus is the Source of Life around your table, pour into each other out of the overflow. Unplugged from each other and pouring into each other, your table will be forever changed. With Jesus as your Source, your children will want to return to the family table long after they leave home. They will desire similar tables for their families. With Jesus as your Source, guests will leave refreshed and live with anticipation for return visits. Your family table will inspire other family tables, where we all gather to enjoy food, each other, and Jesus.

⇒Your Family Table

Recipe: Grandma Erliss's Puffy Skillet Corn Fritters

AMY

Shortly after Ted and I moved to Branson, my grandparents visited from Minnesota. They stayed at a fishing resort and spent the week fishing and cooking for us. On the first day, after several hours of fishing from the dock, we caught nothing. So they invited us into their little cabin for lunch. A meal with Roland and Erliss Kelzenberg was always a treat. I couldn't wait to see what we were having for lunch, especially now that we were not having fish. Grandpa went straight to the kitchen, washed his hands, and joined my grandma as she prepped our lunch. My grandparents always prepared meals in the kitchen together.

When we decided to do recipes in this book, my grandparents were the first to come to mind. I always enjoyed their cooking. They lived on a farm for many years and knew how to use fresh ingredients to make delicious meals.

Grandma passed away recently. We are grateful that my mom found her recipe box. Going through her old recipes is a trip down memory lane. There is a story and a memory in each recipe. I have been able to share many of them with my daughter, Corynn. She loves to look through old memorabilia and try new things. We have cooked and baked several of Grandma's recipes since receiving the box. There is something really special about knowing that Corynn will probably be cooking Grandma's recipes for her kids and telling the stories I told her.

I've decided to share the meal they made for us that day in the fishing cabin: Puffy Skillet Corn Fritters. If you have not ever had a corn fritter, you are in for a treat. Serve them as an appetizer, side dish, or main entrée. When I serve it as an entree, sometimes I add bacon or maybe a little chorizo. Serve with sour cream and salsa, and enjoy!

Recipe makes 7–8 fritters.

INGREDIENTS:

    2 cups of corn (about 4 ears of corn; fresh off the cob is best, but frozen or canned also works well)

    2 eggs, beaten

    ¼ cup chopped green or red pepper or both

    ¼ cup chopped onion

    ¼ cup flour

    ½ teaspoon baking powder

    ½ teaspoon salt

    ¼ teaspoon pepper

    2 tablespoons milk

    2 tablespoons canola oil

    1 tablespoon melted butter

INSTRUCTIONS:

Mix together all ingredients except canola oil and butter in a medium-sized mixing bowl. Heat oil and butter in a cast-iron griddle or nonstick pan over medium heat. Use ⅓ cup measuring cup to scoop batter onto greased pan and spread out batter like a pancake. Cook for 2–3 minutes on each side. Serve immediately.

Guess the Object Game

Have the children select random items from around the house and place them in a paper bag. You can establish the rules up front as a family. (Establishing rules is a game all by itself. For example: "Nothing alive." "Nothing gross." "Nothing that is easily broken.") Ask one family member at a time to close their eyes. Place one item from the bag in their hands and ask them to guess what it is. If they struggle, give hints.

Devotional

> Above all else, guard your heart, for everything
> you do flows from it.
>
> PROVERBS 4:23

Jesus said, "Don't you see that whatever enters the mouth goes into the stomach and then out of the body? But the things that come out of a person's mouth come from the heart" (Matthew 15:17-18). If you want to change your behavior or the way you treat others, then start by changing your heart.

Imagine that your heart is a clear empty jug and God's love is water. The goal is to have a heart that is full of God's love. The desire is for a jug full of clear, fresh water. We fill the jug by spending time with God in His Word and prayer.

With a full jug, we pour into family, friends, coworkers, and strangers. When our jug is empty, we are abrupt, unkind, rude, and impatient with others. Spending time with God fills our jug. People are not our source of life. They may fill us for a short time, but they can never fully satisfy.

The good news is that God's love and power are unlimited. The best relationships are when two people are both connected to the true and only source of life and then give each other the overflow. Never look to people to do what only God can do.

Discuss

- What happens to our hearts when we allow people, places, or things to be the source of life?
- How do you respond to others when your heart (jug) is empty?
- Can you think of a time when you went on empty for a long time? What did that season of your life look like?
- When we feel drained, what must we do to be filled up with the unlimited supply of God's love?

Prayer

Father, You are the Source of Life. Today, we unplug from other people as the source and look to You as the only source. We will not blame others for how we feel. Others are limited supplies. You are unlimited. We will serve, love, and give to each other with zero expectations of anything coming back to us in return. Fill us up with Your love and power. We rely on You from this day forward. In Jesus' name, amen.

Notes

CHAPTER 1: SPACE AROUND THE TABLE

1. "A Delicious Revolution: How Grandma's Pasta Changed the World," Slow Food USA, http://www.slowfoodusa.org/history.
2. "The Slow Food Manifesto," Slow Food USA, http://www.slowfoodusa.org/manifesto, italics in the original.
3. "Tim Hawkins on Farm Dances/Real Quick/Balance Bracelet," YouTube video, 1:36, posted by "lovemykidz316," October 4, 2010, https://www.youtube.com/watch?v=VsM_5rRPxt4.
4. Richard Swenson, *Margin: Restoring Emotional, Physical, Financial, and Time Reserves to Overloaded Lives* (Colorado Springs: NavPress, 2004), 42.
5. Swenson, *Margin*, back cover.
6. Gary Chapman, *The Five Love Languages: The Secret to Love that Lasts* (Chicago: Northfield Publishing, 1992, 2015).
7. Dr. Kevin Leman, "How Birth Order Affects Personality" (accessed November 3, 2015), http://www.birthorderguy.com/parenting/how-birth-order-affects-personality/.
8. "Tripp and Tyler Laughing," YouTube video, 1:54, posted by "Tripp and Tyler," August 1, 2013, https://www.youtube.com/watch?v=rPY4yOmNw7w.
9. Adapted from Kat Hobza, "5 Games to Play at the Dinner Table," SheKnows, January 11, 2013, http://www.sheknows.com/parenting/articles/824467/5-games-to-play-at-the-dinner-table.

CHAPTER 2: A PLACE FOR MEMORIES

1. Mark Batterson and Richard Foth, *A Trip around the Sun* (Grand Rapids: Baker Books, 2015), 32.

CHAPTER 3: FOOD, WINE, AND GOD'S FAVOR

1. Jim Gaffigan, *Food: A Love Story* (New York: Crown Publishing Group, 2014), 22.
2. J. R. R. Tolkien, *The Hobbit* (New York: Houghton Mifflin Company, 2001), 312.

CHAPTER 6: HOSPITALITY AT THE TABLE

1. Max Lucado, *Outlive Your Life* (Nashville: Thomas Nelson, 2010), 55–56.

CHAPTER 7: A SIMPLE TABLE

1. "North Platte Canteen," Cru Military, YouTube video, 7:04, October 7, 2007, http://www.youtube.com/watch?v=07DGeLvDw8I&sns=em.
2. Used with permission.
3. David Friedlander, "What Would Our Homes Look Like If Designed around How We Use Them?," Treehugger, September 2, 2014, http://www.treehugger.com/green-architecture/what-would-our-homes -look-if-designed-around-how-we-use-them.html.
4. Abbreviated list adapted from The Family Dinner Project. For a complete list see http://thefamilydinnerproject.org/fun/would-you-rather/.

CHAPTER 8: A LAVISH TABLE

1. *Oxford Dictionary*, s.v. "trust."
2. "The Today Show Goes Inside Florida's Versailles," Pricey Pads, February 22, 2013, http://www.priceypads.com/the-today-show -goes-inside-floridas-versailles/.
3. Jan Peterson, "Chateau Pensmore Being Built to Last," *Springfield News-Leader*, April 29, 2015, http://www.news-leader.com/story/life /home-garden/2015/04/29/chateau-pensmore-built-last/26564541/.
4. "Most Expensive Caviar," Guinness World Records, http://www .guinnessworldrecords.com/world-records/most-expensive-caviar/ (accessed November 18, 2015).
5. Rick Warren, "God Didn't Need Us, He Wanted Us," interview by David Kuo, October 2005, www.beliefnet.com/Faiths/Christianity/2005/10 /Rick-Warren-God-Didnt-Need-Us-He-Wanted-Us.
6. Kurt Kaiser, "O, How He Loves You and Me," © 1975 Word Music, LLC.
7. Frederick M. Lehman, "The Love of God," 1917, public domain.
8. David Crowder, "How He Loves," *Church Music*, © 2009 sixstepsrecords.

Recipe Index

BATTLE GROUP!

BATTLE GROUP!

GERMAN KAMPFGRUPPEN ACTION OF WORLD WAR TWO

JAMES LUCAS

RIGEL

Rigel Publications
A division of the Orion Publishing Group Ltd.
5 Upper St Martin's Lane
London WC2H 9EA

First published by Arms and Armour 1993
This Cassell Military Paperbacks edition 2000
Reprinted 2002
This edition published in 2004

British Library Cataloguing-in-Publication Data
A catalogue record for this book is available from the British Library

ISBN 1-898-80008-1

Printed and bound within the European Union

CONTENTS

CONTENTS

Acknowledgements

It is with very grateful thanks that I acknowledge the help of friends and institutions in the research, writing and production of this book. I wish to express my gratitude for the expert advice and assistance given to me by the officers of the Imperial War Museum's Department of Printed Books and to Julie Robertshaw in particular; the Department of Documents, and in particular Philip Reed. Marion Harding of the National Army Museum also afforded me great help; so, too, did the officials of the Militaer Archiv in Freiburg, Germany; the National Archive in Washington, USA; and the ex-Service associations of the divisions and regiments whose exploits form the text of this book.

At a personal level, thanks go also to former soldiers of the German Armed Forces who supplied me with information on, or accounts of, their active service experiences, as well as to those who carried out research on my behalf or who supplied the background details which are essential to a book of this nature. Of those many men there are four comrades whose help I particularly acknowledge: Adi Strauch, Hans Teske, Jupp Klein and Mark Yerger.

To the editorial staff of Arms and Armour Press, to the dust jacket designer and layout team of DAG Publications, as well as to my agents for the active support and advice they have always given, I am particularly indebted. It is, however, to my dear wife, Traude, that the warmest expression of my thanks goes in gratitude for her unfailing love and encouragement.

James Lucas, London, 1993

INTRODUCTION

Helmuth von Moltke, the famous German military commander of the 19th century, wrote "...no plan of operations will ever extend, with any sort of certainty, beyond the first encounter with the hostile main force", and also stated that success in battle was gained through the commander's ability "...to recognise the changed situation, to order its foreseeable course and to execute this energetically...".

These and similar dicta by one of Germany's greatest soldiers, stressing that victory is won by the flexibly minded leader capable of adapting to the rapidly changing circumstances on the field of battle, were principal factors in the training of officers for General Staff and High Command positions. Von Moltke's maxims were reappraised by Hans von Seeckt, a German military commander and philosopher of the 1920s and 30s, in his book "Thoughts of a Soldier". He wrote, "The essential thing is motion. It has three stages: the decision, the preparation and the execution...". Although half-a-century separated those two men they agreed on basic concepts and both emphasised the need for flexibility and will at all levels of command.

The principles laid down by von Moltke and by von Seeckt, define precisely those governing the employment of battle groups — the subject of this book — those pragmatic creations of the German Army at war. The creation of battle groups and the skill in using them gained for the Wehrmacht victories throughout the Second World War. Not just in the first dynamic years when its forces swept the armies of one European country after another to defeat in fast campaigns, but also in the years after Stalingrad and Africa when Germany was going down into defeat. The operations which this book describes are not great strategic movements by infantry and Panzer armies in the East and in the West, but tactical missions at a much lower echelon of command.

Battle groups can be defined as the bringing together of miscellaneous, and often disparate, military units to undertake a specific and local operation. It was usual, but not always the case, that once the mission had been completed the battle group was broken up and its components returned to their parent formations. As we shall discover in the text one battle group, created in 1945, was enlarged to become a division. In a politico-military sense battle groups were an essential element in German strategy. The leaders of Nazi Germany knew that given the Reich's poor economic situation it could not wage a long, economically-based war, but must fight and win swift, decisive victories in a succession of short, land-based campaigns. Out of that economic imperative was born the idea of "Blitzkrieg" — the "lightning war" — the essence of the principles of Moltke and Seeckt; flexibility and the will to win. Battle groups were a logical development of the Blitzkrieg concept.

Although the Blitzkrieg concept and its application on the battlefield were neither new nor German — Allied leaders had propounded and used them in the final offensives of the Great War — it was the German Army's skill in combining mass and aggressive tactics, in conjunction with the battle group commander's ability to exploit the changing situation, which brought success on every battlefield. The commander's mental alertness and drive were essential factors, for the force of his personality affected the whole. It is small wonder, therefore, that some men who had led battle groups in the first years of the war were commanding armies or even army groups at the end of that conflict. The resolution, planning ability and the gift to see what lay on the "other side of the hill", abilities which they had demonstrated as junior commanders, were vital when they rose to senior posts in the Army.

German Army training in the pre-war years employed another of von Seeckt's proposals: that every soldier should be capable of taking over the post of the man above him. As a consequence the German Army in the immediate pre-war years was made up of potential leaders, individually selected and intensively trained to be pragmatic and aggressive. That system produced men who, as already stated, rose to prominence in the years of that conflict — men such as Model, Kumm, Langkeit, Harmel and Weidinger. Because Germany's military leaders and men had entered the war imbued with the dynamics of Blitzkrieg, that Army enjoyed a distinct advantage over its opponents whose military thinking was still restricted to conventional, linear warfare and who were, thus, at a disadvantage vis-a-vis the Wehrmacht until they, too, adopted and used German methods.

Battle groups — which will be described in the text either by that name, by the German noun "Kampfgruppe" or its abbreviation "KG" — were usually given the name of the men who led them or less frequently, the name of the parent formations from whose sub-units they were composed. For example, KG Marcks was the battle group in Libya commanded by Colonel Marcks; or KG "Reich", was the battle group composed of units of the SS Division "Reich" on the Eastern Front. The actions covered in this book are taken from each Theatre of Operations and cover all the war years. The groups range in size from a small detachment of bicycle-riding SS tank-busters who, in 1945, fought Russian armour at close quarters, up to the miscellany of units which in the autumn of 1944 were flung across northern Belgium and southern Holland to halt the Allied advance. Due to the pedantry of German administrative procedures some units mentioned in the text of this book did not begin life described as "Kampfgruppe" but attained that distinction during their lifetime. In such cases I have anticipated the event and described them as "Kampfgruppe" in the text.

It will be appreciated that in a war which ranged across six years, out of the vast numbers of battle groups which were created, my text can include only a small selection but these include, in my opinion, those which are especially interesting. In every case the account of the Kampfgruppe action has an introductory section which describes the theatre of war and the military situation obtaining when the KG was created, before going on to describe the actions which it fought. Battle groups were employed chiefly in a "shock troop" capacity, to smash a breach in the enemy line or to seal off a penetration which he had made. The accounts included in my text range from those KGs closely controlled by the divisional commander as, for example, by Reinhardt over his Panzer division's Kampfgruppen in Poland, or Rommel's firm grip over the 7th Panzer Division battle groups in France in 1940, down to the independent actions by the desert KGs or that of Peiper's battle group south of Kharkov during February 1943. What many of those accounts demonstrate is the degree of autonomy given to a commander of quite low rank and the use he made of those powers.

Because they had only a brief life, Kampfgruppen have been, generally, overlooked in the writing of military history and this book is intended to acknowledge the particular contribution they made to German military operations of the Second World War.

Battle groups of General Reinhardt's Panzer Division in the campaign in Poland, Autumn. 1939

The Second World War began on 1 September 1939. At dawn on that bright autumn day the German Army, covered by an umbrella of Luftwaffe aircraft, attacked the Republic of Poland, although the Third Reich had made no declaration of war.

In this, the first campaign of the Second World War, one and a quarter million German soldiers, organised into 60 divisions, nine of which were armoured, invaded Poland from the north, the west and the south. The battle plan drawn up by the Armed Forces High Command (Oberkommando der Wehrmacht -OKW) was for the enemy armies to be caught in two separate encirclements. The jaws of the first, or western encirclement, would close along the line of the River Vistula. The jaws of the second, or eastern encirclement, would meet along the River Bug.

The disposition of the six armies which Poland fielded aided OKW's strategic plan. In the west Poland's borders projected as a blunt-headed salient into the eastern provinces of Germany and the four armies which the Polish High Command crammed into that salient had orders to open an offensive, to carry this through into Silesia and then on to Berlin. It was a plan without any hope of fulfilment for that western salient was outflanked in the north by East Prussia and to the south by Slovakia. Once the Blitzkrieg was in full swing the Polish forces in the salient, far from attacking would not even be able to maintain a long defence. When they were forced to retire eastwards towards Warsaw, as they undoubtedly would be, they would find themselves caught in a ring of steel - the first German encirclement - and would be crushed between the Panzer divisions along the eastern bank of the Vistula and by the German formations advancing towards that river. Along the Vistula the great mass of the Polish Armies would be destroyed. Those units which formed the eastern group of Polish armies behind Warsaw, would then find themselves trapped between the German forces advancing towards them after the victorious Vistula battle and those which were now lining the River Bug.

To carry out OKW's plan the German host was divided into von Bock's northern and von Rundstedt's southern Army Group. In Bock's Group, the 3rd and 4th Armies would form the northern pair of pincers. The 4th would attack out of Silesia, cross the Vistula and drive south-eastwards down that river towards Warsaw, while the 3rd, striking southwards out of East Prussia, would head down the Bug. In the south von Rundstedt's Army Group was to advance eastwards and north-eastwards across Upper Silesia and Galicia. The left flank 8th Army would thrust for Kutno where it would join hands with the pincer of Bock's 4th Army and together they would bar the way to the retreating Poles. Rundstedt's central Army, the 10th, would advance in two groups. The left towards Kutno to support the 8th and the right one directly towards the Vistula and Warsaw. On the right, the 14th was to advance towards Lemberg and would then strike northwards up the Bug to meet 3rd Army's pincer coming down from the north.

The OKW plan, given the shape of Poland, was a very obvious one but the campaign was not, as many Nazi propagandists claimed, easily-won. There were times when it seemed as if the Polish forces retreating eastwards would crush the German formations seeking to contain them. In this account of the first campaign of the Second World War we shall follow the exploits of the battle groups of 4th Panzer Division (10th Army) and then that of the 1st Mountain Troops Division (14th Army.) It is necessary to explain that at that time 4th Panzer Division was known by the name of its commander, General Reinhardt, and not by its number. In addition, the battle groups created by the 4th were known as "Gefechtsgruppen" and not by the term "Kampfgruppen", although the two terms are synonymous. Finally, the infantry component of a Panzer division was known as a Rifle regiment until 1942, when there was a change of name from Rifles to Panzergrenadiers.

The 4th Panzer Division formed part of Hoepner's 16th Corps and on the penultimate evening of peace received orders that upon the outbreak of war it was to advance and capture Krzepice, to carry the attack towards Ostrowy and then to gain bridgeheads across the River Kocinka. The thrust line was to be north-eastwards.

Reinhardt, one of Germany's leading Panzer theorists, divided his division into three Kampfgruppen (KG). That on the left flank was made up of 12th Rifle Regiment, 1st Battalion of 36th Panzer Regiment, artillery, reconnaissance, pioneer and construction units. The righthand battle group consisted of 12th Infantry Regiment, minus its 1st Battalion, 2nd Battalion of 36th Panzer Regiment, artillery, reconnaissance and pioneer detachments. The division's remaining armoured component - its second Panzer regiment - formed the third battlegroup. For the opening attack, the infantry KGs on either flank were to have the support of an entire artillery regiment supplemented by additional gun batteries. Once the frontier river had been crossed the Panzer Kampfgruppe was to advance at top speed to cross the River Kochinka before the Poles could set up a strong defence.

At 04.45hrs on the first day of the war the divisional artillery opened up and at 05.00hrs, both infantry battle groups moved across the frontier - ghostly figures shrouded in a morning mist. A great many unit war diaries contain entries stressing the poor condition of Polish roads and mentioning that along even the main ones the ground on either side of the hard surface was made up of a deep, scouring dust. That is reported as not only causing difficulties for the wheeled vehicles but is mentioned as being particularly tiring for the marching troops. Those terrain conditions required the employment of the divisional pioneers who, as early as 07.45hrs, had needed to lay corduroy roads while the infantry, whose battle groups were moving steadily forward, had met and had beaten down the first Polish cavalry attacks.

The divisional history candidly admits that there were difficulties encountered on the first day of campaigning; difficulties which had not been anticipated and, even more honestly, accepts that at one place German troops of a supply unit retreated in panic at the cry "enemy tank!" - an alarm which proved to be false. The divisional history records that as a result of the difficulties on that first day none of the Kampfgruppen reached their given objectives.

During the morning of 2 September, an attack by the group on the left wing, the 12th Rifle Regiment, drove the Poles out of Ostrowy but then the advance came to a halt under a hail of shells. On its sector, 12th Infantry Regiment had also been forced to abort its attack. Then the Rifles battalions regrouped and, covered by a strong barrage, opened a new assault which made good ground until the battalions reached the final stage of the operation. That last bound was a flat, open expanse of ground swept by enemy artillery and machine gun fire which halted the Rifles' advance. On that sector no further advance was possible but, by early afternoon, 12th Infantry Regiment on the right had carried its assault into the great woods at Debnik. At 17.00hrs the Rifles resumed their stalled attack and this time fought their way across the "killing ground" and into the woods. That attack had cost them dear. One of 2nd Battalion's companies, for example, lost 10 killed and 20 wounded in the short fire-fight to clear the edge of the forest. Ignoring sniper and machine gun fire and accepting the steady drain of losses which it was suffering, 2nd Battalion pushed on, flung back a Polish Uhlan attack, captured Kocin and began preparations to cross the River Kocinka. Later that evening the leading companies of the battle group on the right wing also reached the river's banks and linked up with the Rifles. Both infantry Kampfgruppen laagered for the night but sent out patrols, one of which brought in a prisoner who stated that the enemy formation facing 4th Panzer was the Wolhynska Cavalry Brigade. German Intelligence identified this as an elite unit equipped with modern anti-tank weapons and supported by another first class formation, an assault battalion.

During 3 September, the right flank Kampfgruppe, 12th Infantry Regiment, was broken up and was returned to 31st Division from which it had been seconded for the opening operation. In the evening Reinhardt ordered four new Kampfgruppen to be created and directed that they were to move out at 06.00hrs on the 4th.

An interesting light on first days of the war is given in an anthology of letters published by the Propaganda Ministry in Berlin, one of the many works which were published on the Polish campaign. The authors of the letters in the anthology are not completely identified by name or unit but from remarks in the text of several letters by the same author, parts of which are quoted below, it is almost certain that the author was in 10th Army and probably in 16th Corps. His letters read:

"Let me give you my impressions of the campaign so far. Firstly, the filth and dirt that we met even in the first villages cannot be believed unless one sees it for oneself. Houses uncared for and falling into ruin with no attempt made to repair anything or to put a coat of paint onto house fronts. The conditions we met with were as primitive as one imagines them to be in darkest Africa - but these people here are Europeans.

"Secondly, their country roads are little more than tracks with a hardened surface. On either side of the hard surface there is a layer of dust or sand centimetres deep. In some places so deep that it reaches as high as the hubs on our lorry wheels. Half an hour of driving in such conditions and our faces are covered by a mask of red dust with narrow lines where rivulets of sweat have rolled down our faces. The third thing is the terrible heat here and the chronic shortage of water. The hours of sunshine have produced very high temperatures. It is as hot as an oven.

"The Polish civilians are franc-tireurs and very good snipers. The regiment has lost several officers and NCOs to their unlawful activity.... Polish infantry attacks are made in mass formation and although they are absolutely suicidal in the face of our fast firing machine guns I must admit that to stand and watch as those long lines of infantry come storming forward is quite unnerving. Before any attack the Poles give three cheers - each one a long drawn out cry that sounds like animals baying for blood. A Panzerman told me how his unit was attacked by enemy cavalry. Imagine it, sabres against steel plate. A prisoner taken after one such charge is said to have told the interrogating officer that his regiment had been assured the German tanks were made either of cardboard or of wood and sacking. My Panzer informant recalled seeing one officer charge up to one of the vehicles in his squadron, rise up in the stirrups and give a vicious downward stroke with his sabre. This shattered in his hand and the Pole looked dumbfounded. Immediately he pulled out a pistol and fired several rounds at the Panzer, finally shooting himself, determined to die rather than surrender.

"After a week of campaigning it was clear that the enemy to our front was pulling back towards Warsaw. You cannot imagine the scene of desolation on the road along which the Poles had retreated. Burnt out houses and ruined farms, weapons, vehicles and horse-drawn carts abandoned by the roadside. And everywhere the dead. The horses and other animals, their bellies distended by the gases of putrefaction, lie stiff legged and fly-blown. The dead men, too, are grossly inflated and their faces have a mottled blue/grey colour. We tried to find local civilians to bury the fallen Polish soldiers but the villages were deserted. The civilians had all fled and it fell to our battalion to put the enemy fallen into mass graves. The stench was terrible and we really earned the spirit ration which the CO ordered for us. Thank Heaven, we were quartered near a stream so that we could wash off the slime which covers dead bodies and try to wash out of our noses the terrible stink which had enveloped us all. We washed our uniforms, too, and sat all day in the nude while our clothing dried. The mosquitoes here are voracious, blood sucking beasts which bit us all over while we waited for the sun to dry out our wet clothes.

"We know very little about the way in which the war started, but it is clear that the intention of Mr Chamberlain [the British Prime Minister] and Marshal Ridz-Smygly [the Polish Head of State] to encircle our Reich has not succeeded. They have failed, but we have not. Warsaw is only 130km distant and the victorious outcome of the campaign seems to have been already determined."

The 4th Panzer Division resumed its advance on 4 September, and during the evening divisional headquarters ordered the existing KGs to be broken up and new ones to be created. These would each be similar in size and were to contain an infantry battalion from 12th Rifle Regiment, artillery and anti-tank detachments. The infantry battle groups were to force a crossing of the swamp between Laski and Borono, whereupon the Panzer battle group would pass through them and head towards Warsaw. After long and inexplicable delays, which could only have served to give the Poles time to prepare a defence, the infantry moved off. The group on the right wing, 1st Rifles Battalion, struck enemy resistance near Laski which took several hours to break. The first stages of 2nd Battalion's thrust also made good ground but en route to its second objective, the eastern flank of the Borowa mountain, it encountered fanatical resistance. The subsequent pace of the advance was slow and at last light 2nd Battalion was ordered to disengage from the enemy and to consolidate on the positions which had been won. The Polish commanders seeing the Rifles' withdrawal flung their infantry into a fierce, heavy counter-attack which caused the battalion severe losses.

During the night the main elements of Reinhardt's Division moved northwards to close up with the battle groups, but the advance was slow and frequently halted. The reason was soon clear. Prisoner interrogation indicated that in addition to the units opposing 4th Division's advance, there was in the woods to the north-east of Petrikau, a Polish infantry regiment preparing to fight its way past the battle groups so as to escape northwards. Despite the slowness of the advance divisional headquarters was able to report to corps that on 5 September its units had achieved an advance of 30km. Shortly before 07.00hrs, on 6 September, heavy firing was heard coming from 1st Panzer Division's sector and that unit reported itself as being under pressure from an enemy who was determined to recapture Petrikau. The Rifles battle groups were halted to meet this new and seemingly dangerous situation, but then the Petrikau garrison reported the situation as quiet and both KGs resumed their stalled advance. Just before midday, 2nd Battalion was halted again to meet the threat of a Polish thrust which was said to be coming from the direction of Lodz. Luftwaffe reconnaissance aircraft reported enemy columns moving from that city towards Petrikau and the 2nd Battalion battle group was deployed to meet that likely threat. From their actions it was clear that the Poles considered the thrust by 16th Corps towards their capital to be a very serious threat and by employing the Lodz troops to strike at corps' flank, were taking active measures to oppose it.

The first indication that Polish resistance was growing came with an increase in enemy patrolling, in which some groups worked their way through the extensive woods and opened fire on the division's artillery positions. This increase in Polish opposition, together with intelligence reports that a Polish mountain division was moving into the area, influenced Reinhardt's decision to postpone a new attack, but corps overruled his decision and ordered 4th Panzer to maintain its advance. The infantry battle groups then moved forward into an unclear and potentially dangerous situation for, although they did not know what lay ahead of them, they were certainly aware that a great many Polish groups which had been bypassed over the past days had withdrawn into the forests. The danger now was that they would regroup and come out of the woods to attack the divisional supply and service convoys moving up towards the Front.

Despite the awareness of growing resistance, corps' orders for 7 September predicated on 10th Army's claim that the Poles were in full retreat to the Vistula, and ordered 4th Panzer to continue its forward movement. In order to to exploit the situation which he had been assured was favourable, Reinhardt created two Panzer battle groups. The righthand one, 36th Panzer Regiment and a battery of artillery, was to drive northwards towards Lubochnia to intercept the enemy forces which it was anticipated would be retreating eastwards under the pressure of the left-hand column made up of 35th Panzer Regiment, 12th Rifle Regiment, artillery, anti-tank and a pioneer company. That leftwing KG opened its assault shortly after 05.00hrs on the morning of 7 September, smashed through the enemy's front and thrust through the burning village of Uyazd to reach the woods east of that place. From prisoner statements it was clear that the fresh troops brought into the area by Polish High Command had been overrun before they could prepare strong defensive positions. The rightwing battle group, too, encountered only weak opposition as it moved towards Lubochnia. Both battle groups reported the taking of a great many prisoners.

As a result of its operations from 5-7 September, the 4th Panzer Division had not only fought its way through the Polish forces holding the ground between Petrikau and Lodz, but had also reached the highway which led to Warsaw. It was Warsaw, the capital of Poland, which was the magnet that now attracted both German Army Groups. Reichenau's 10th Army [Army Group South], was the formation which von Rundstedt directed towards the enemy capital. But there was in Army Group South's order a certain reservation. The Luftwaffe had ruled the skies over Poland since the first hours of the war and that superiority meant that any enemy formations moving in the open were identified, bombed and machine gunned. To avoid such attacks Polish units hid up during the day in the deep forests of central Poland and used the cover of night to reach new positions or to deploy for an attack against the advancing Germans. There was little positive intelligence information coming to division from ground sources and the results of aerial reconnaissance showed little troop movement. Thus the German High Command had very little idea of the strength of the enemy forces, their exact location or whether these could be brought to battle and destroyed west of the Vistula. OKW decided, therefore, to carry out a wide encircling movement to the south of Warsaw to trawl the enemy forces, to compress them into a huge pocket and then to crush them. Tenth Army, which had an important part to play in that operation, began its advance although Army Group could not state with any certainty what level of resistance it would meet. Despite OKW's lack of intelligence details and the reports of their own formations detailing increased Polish pressure, High Command was confident that the enemy army was beaten and in full retreat. What OKW did not know was that the Polish commander, General Kutzreba, had grouped the forces of Kutno Group with those from Lodz Group and that that mass of 12 divisions was preparing to strike into the flank of 10th Army, determined to force a way through to Warsaw. OKW ordered 10th Army to conduct "a vigorous pursuit" and to race for the Vistula in order to prevent the Poles, whom they thought were retreating, from escaping across that river. Reichenau, the Army Commander, selected Hoepner's 16th Corps to form the lefthand pursuit group which was to make for the Vistula bridges at Gora Kolwarya. Corps' order to 4th Panzer Division was that it was to capture Warsaw on the 8th.

Reinhardt created two new infantry battle groups as well as a third, armoured, battle group which was to be put into action once the town of Rawa on the Warsaw highway had been captured by the infantry groups. The General rode with the leading units, determined to have close control of the battle and to deploy his Kampfgruppen as the situation developed. The first KG of 4th Panzer, commanded by General von Hartlieb, was made up of 5th Panzer Brigade Headquarters Group, 35th Panzer Regiment and 12th Rifles Regiment with artillery, anti-tank and pioneer detachments. Hartlieb's battle group crossed its start line at 06.00 hrs in fine autumnal weather and made good progress until Babsk where the first check came. That opposition was beaten down and the advance brought forward so quickly that the town of Mszcoznow was reached by 08.00hrs, after which Hartlieb Group moved in a north-easterly direction toward Nadarzyn. The result of that group's swift advance convinced the Corps commander that Polish resistance was diminishing and that 4th Division's groups now had a clear run-up to Warsaw. Hoepner ordered the pace of the advance to be quickened so as to capture the Vistula bridges before they could be destroyed.

Following Reinhardt's 4th Division, the 1st Panzer Division began its advance and took the same road route until it reached Radziejovice. There the road forked. The 4th had taken the right fork leading to Hadarzyn and Rasazyn. The 1st Panzer Division took the lefthand road to Pruszkow. By midday the spearheads of 16th Corps were only 20km from Warsaw but the speed of that advance carried with it the danger that Polish formations, bypassed by the Kampfgruppen, would recapture the towns and villages through which Hoepner's groups had passed and would cut off the spearhead corps from the main body of 10th Army. Reconnaissance aircraft reported that the Poles had, indeed, infiltrated back into the towns and that, in addition, large bodies of enemy troops were marching eastwards from Tarczyn. Then reports came in of Polish motorised formations heading eastwards from Sochaczev towards the capital which lay only 45km distant. There was a very real threat that the Western Polish Army was about to destroy 16th Corps. The fighting in which detachments of the recce battalion had been involved in their battle to protect Division's northern flank, grew in intensity but by contrast the recce units on the southern flank met less opposition and were able to gain a great deal of ground. Throughout the day every German column moving on Warsaw met resistance of some sort ranging from staunch Polish defence to isolated bursts of sniper fire.

The aim of 4th Division's 35th Panzer Regiment, to capture the bridges at Raszyn to the south-west of Warsaw, could not be realised. A gallant attempt by two Polish light tanks held the 35th long enough for the enemy to blow the bridges while the tank battle was being fought. But the action of the Polish tank men was brief and ended with their vehicles broken and burning. Within minutes of the Panzer duel ending, a patrol from 35th Panzer had located a ford through which the armoured fighting vehicles advanced, while behind them a pioneer company worked hard to repair the damage to the bridge and thus re-open the road which was now jammed with a mass of vehicles from "follow-up" units.

During the afternoon of 8 September, division issued orders for the entry into Warsaw, which OKW was convinced would soon be declared an "open" city. Two new Kampfgruppen were set up. The left-hand one contained elements seconded from 1st Panzer Division and was to enter Warsaw via the south-western suburb of Pruszkow with the northern Vistula bridge as its objective. The righthand battle group was to advance up the main road via Falenty and enter the capital after having captured the southern two Vistula bridges. The leader of this latter KG had under his command the whole of 5th Panzer Brigade as well as 12th Rifles Regiment and anti-tank detachments. By 16.00hrs the engineers had repaired the Raszyn bridges, the point units were being regularly rotated and the advance was moving swiftly. The destruction of the bridge at Pruszkow, however, retarded the advance of the lefthand battle group and this was slowed even farther by being continually attacked by Polish units firing from the cover of the woods. At 17.15hrs the righthand battle group approaching Mokotow airfield, to the south of Warsaw, was struck by a storm of fire, demonstrating that Warsaw would not be an "open" city but one which its civilian and military defenders were determined to hold. The road leading towards the city centre was heavily barricaded. Small groups of Panzers attempting to bypass that obstruction by filtering through side streets and gardens were quickly driven back. Reinhardt was well aware that it was a misuse of armour to employ it in what was urban warfare and halted 35th Panzer Regiment ordering its forward units to pull back to the outer suburbs.

The divisional commander issued orders for the following day that both battle groups were to advance into Warsaw covered by a short barrage and stressed that the Panzers were to reach the city centre without halting. For so unusual a situation as warfare in a built-up area - unusual for Panzer men, that is - the vehicle crews were given brief instructions on fighting in towns. Dawn of 9 September brought reports from reconnaissance aircraft that most of Warsaw's streets were barricaded. At 07.00hrs both battle groups moved off and soon met such determined resistance that the companies of 12th Rifles which had been riding on the outside of the Panzers were forced to dismount. The men of a second rifles battalion, meanwhile, continued with their attack on foot. In a bitter battle the pioneers and a Panzer company fought their way forward and destroyed the first barricade, but then the armoured vehicles ran onto a chain of mines laid in the cobbles of the road. The advance halted. Immediately, from behind the barricade defenders came out to attack the Panzers with explosive charges and hand grenades. Their action stalled the armour but the infantry continued to make ground despite machine gun fire coming from blocks of flats and snipers firing from trees. Polish artillery guns dominated the long, straight roads which are a feature of Warsaw's western suburbs, halting every forward movement. On the German side the divisional artillery gave close support fire which brought the battle group's assaults slowly forward, but the closer these came to the city centre the more fanatical grew the Polish resistance and although a vedette of three Panzers reached the main station it was clear that the city would not fall unless 4th Panzer Division received infantry reinforcements. Street fighting is part of an infantryman's war and Reinhardt soon became concerned that his three Rifles battalions would be absorbed and vanish in the city's network of streets, parks and squares. By this time resistance to his division's advance was so severe that each attempt by the KGs to make ground was struck by a storm of fire which drove them back or, in the case of one Panzer battalion, was halted by another minefield near the suburb of Ochota. At 09.45hrs Reinhardt, accepting that his division could not take out the capital, ordered a withdrawal to the the city boundary where the units were to prepare defensive positions. To disengage from an enemy who is determined to hold fast is a time-consuming task and one costly in lives. During the operations of that day 35th Panzer Regiment lost eight men killed and 15 wounded as well a 30 Panzers totally destroyed. From a total of 120 armoured fighting vehicles (AFVs) with which the regiment had begun the day's battle, by nightfall only 57 were still "runners". Despite the workshop companies' efforts, that total could only be brought up to 90. Losses to the rifles regiment were, of course, considerably higher.

Reinhardt stressed to corps that without strong infantry and artillery reinforcement he could not capture the Polish capital; that fighting to take the city would result in heavy casualties and that the capital had, in any case, little military significance. It was, he claimed, more important for 10th Army to prevent the tidal wave of enemy units sweeping towards Warsaw, from reinforcing the capital's garrison. But even a blocking mission such as Reinhardt proposed was beyond the capability of his division which stood on a highway that the eastward-flooding Poles would try their hardest to recapture and use. As if to confirm the commander's fears, aerial reconnaissance reports confirmed that enemy columns, estimated to be five to six divisions in strength, were advancing towards Warsaw from the direction of Socaczew and had reached the town of Blonie, only 24km west of the capital. Between the huge mass of Polish units determined to break through there stood only the lefthand battle group and the divisional reconnaissance battalion. The other units of 4th Division were facing Warsaw. With ammunition running low and under growing pressure, the recce battalion was forced off the highway and the way now seemed clear for the Poles to strike into the back of 4th Panzer. The pressure which the enemy hosts were exerting on other sectors had forced apart 8th and 10th Armies and there was no contact between the units of 16th Corps. Detachments of Reinhardt's Division stood isolated on the Warsaw road and corps had very few units which it could send forward to support them.

Determined to relieve the critical situation on Reinhardt's western flank, Hoepner ordered the battle group in position there to hold out and moved the motorised SS Regiment "Leibstandarte SS Adolf Hitler" forward into the threatened area. To resolve the desperate situation, Reinhardt broke up his existing Kampfgruppen and regrouped division so that its units now stood facing east and west fighting, in effect, back to back. In the west stood the "Leibstandarte", the divisional recce battalion and an artillery battalion. In Warsaw's southern and south-western suburbs, was the 33rd Infantry Regiment, two battalions of artillery and the anti-tank battalion. Aware of the danger both in the east and the west and also that he would need to switch units quickly between the threatened sectors, Reinhardt created a strong mobile counter-attack battle group. This was made up of the divisional Panzer Brigade, 12th Rifle Regiment and the pioneer battalion and was located in Warsaw's south-western suburbs. The divisional commander, advised that Polish units were filtering through an unguarded sector north of his divisional area, sent 5th Panzer Brigade to cover the open gap and to dominate the Modlin-Warsaw road. The remaining units of his group facing Warsaw were ordered to hold any Polish sortie out of the city while his west-facing groups, now further reinforced by a Panzer battalion and an artillery battalion, were ordered to attack at 12.30hrs on 10 September. The purpose of that operation was to gain ground to the west and thereby enlarge the divisional area. Within the present perimeter, units were so compressed that artillery batteries in one battalion were firing on targets in Warsaw while other batteries of the same battalion were engaging the enemy in the west.

Between 10-14 September, 4th Panzer Division fought that defensive battle on two fronts against a numerically superior enemy force whose formations battled with unparalleled fury to break through and reinforce the capital city. On the first day (the 10th) the Germans achieved two minor victories. First, the northwards advance of 5th Panzer Brigade was carried out successfully and the "Leibstandarte's" westward attack gained its objectives. The outcome of the day was, so far as Reinhardt was concerned, a successful one although his division still stood isolated from the rest of 10th Army and was bearing an undue burden of the fighting. He was assured that other units were advancing to support his hard-pressed KGs but when it became clear that his men would hold fast, most of those promised support groups were switched away to plug gaps on other sectors. The course of the fighting was described in an article in another Propaganda Ministry work which was apparently based on post-battle reports.

"The crisis began to boil up before dawn on 11 September, when reports came in of Polish infantry attacks being made in regimental strength and supported by artillery. Heavy fighting continued until well in the afternoon and enemy resistance was not broken until the armoured cars of the divisional recce battalion were put into action. The main Polish effort then swung towards Kutno in a move which brought pressure upon 8th Army. During the early morning of the 12th, Polish forces in Mokotow, in the south-eastern sector of Warsaw, launched an infantry attack supported by two companies of tanks. That enemy attack gained a great deal of ground and 33rd (Motorised) Infantry Regiment had to be taken from reserve and committed. The 'Leibstandarte', too, came under attack and was forced back by enemy infantry pressure supported by heavy artillery. The enemy's assaults were met by 4th Panzer Division's own counter-attack although the recce battalion had to be put in at Blonie to restore the situation and at Pruszkow the pioneer battalion had to be committed. This was the last divisional unit which Reinhardt had to hand. With that battalion now in action there was nothing else the General could commit.

"Fighting at that high level of intensity continued throughout the whole morning with division unable to give support to its hard-pressed battlegroups, or to carry out the tasks which corps continued to demand. Under the pressure of enemy attacks along its whole battle line 4th Panzer Division made no ground at all and was, indeed, forced to pull back. Polish prisoners reported that this day's attacks were the first of a series which would be made against both the eastern and western Kampfgrup-

21

pen. During the night, to shorten the line and to create a reserve, the Leibstandarte was withdrawn to its original positions. At 17.50hrs on 12th, Army Group South ordered 16th Corps to undertake an attack in the direction of Sochaczew. Reinhardt pulled his group facing Warsaw back behind a safety line when he learned that the city was to be massively bombed at 13.00 hrs on 13th, and opened an attack with his western group to capture Leszno and thereby to encircle the enemy around Blonie. That attack made good progress against only moderate resistance but it was clear that although the roads and woodland tracks were littered with destroyed and abandoned war material, the enemy forces were not yet in a state of dissolution. Corps then ordered for 14 September that part of 4th Panzer was to advance and to gain the line of the River Bzura, a tributary of the Vistula and that the division's remaining formations were to hold themselves in readiness to clear the woods north of Kampinos. Those units of the 4th which were facing Warsaw were relieved from the Line by 31st Division which then assumed command over all the units which had been subordinate to the 4th except the 'Leibstandarte' and some heavy artillery units. These remained under Reinhardt's control. During the night of 13-14 September, the General regrouped his forces and ordered Kazmapfgruppe Hartlieb to advance at 08.00 hrs on 14th to block the River Bzura between Brochow and Sochaczew. The KG moved off formed into two columns. That on the left of the Blonie-Suchaczev road was made up of HQ 5th Panzer Brigade, 2nd Panzer Battalion, 1st Battalion of the 'Leibstandarte', two battalions of artillery and a pioneer battalion. The right hand column, on the Leszno-Brochow road, held the mass of 36th Panzer Regiment, the 'Leibstandarte', minus its 1st Battalion, an artillery battalion, an anti-tank battalion and a light flak detachment.

"The right flank KG made good progress to begin with but, late in the morning, met increasingly strong opposition from infantry and armour in the Brochow and other areas. Nevertheless, the righthand column eventually reached the River Bzura. The lefthand battle group was first held up by a mine field outside Sochaczew but eventually entered the town and came under such pressure that it had to fall back and was then so strongly attacked that it was only with difficulty that it could hold the ground it had captured. It was the held opinion at divisional headquarters that the staunch defence put up by the Poles as well as their well-led and spirited attacks were the prelude to a mass break-out attempt from the Bzura towards Warsaw. That opinion was confirmed when Polish 26th and 27th Divisions made a general assault along the fronts of both battle group, and which overran the Leibstandarte positions. That, in turn, brought pressure upon other units of 4th Division. Those divisional units which were not embattled stood to arms at 10-minute readiness to move, but hard fighting by the SS and by the Panzer detachments eventually restored the situation."

"On 15 September Reinhardt received orders to take his division across the Bzura in conjunction with the rest of 16th Corps. It was 10th Army's intention to use that corps' two Panzer divisions to fragment the enemy along the Bzura. The creation by Reinhardt of three new battle groups produced a rifle regiment and Panzer battalion on the left, a Panzer regiment and the "Leibstandarte" on the right and a strong Panzer battle group reserve, which would be put in to exploit the situation. At 07.00hrs under a short, intense barrage the battle groups of the 4th waded across the shallow river and into action against determined Polish opposition.

The Poles fought in the open, in woods and coppices in the countryside, in farms and barns and from room to room in the houses of the villages and little towns to the west of the Bzura. In the battles which ranged between the river and the town of Ruszki and during which attack was succeeded by counter-attack, the battle groups lost heavily. But the suicidal attacks of their enemies were more wasteful. So furious were those Polish assaults that in some places corps units were surrounded and cut off from each other. The critical situation was not helped when corps issued orders and later countermanded them. To add to the problems the battle groups then reported they had fired off nearly all their ammunition. Despite the various crises which arose with the isolated and cut-off units of the 4th fighting desperately, General von Hoepner issued a directive to his subordinate formations that they were to surround and destroy the enemy to their front. Then the General changed his mind and ordered the Kampfgruppen to strike northwards up the eastern bank of the Bzura and to seal the area to the north through which the Poles were infiltrating. The west bank bridgehead which the 4th had been holding was then handed over to a relieving division.

"At 05.00hrs on 17 September, the battle groups moved up the Bzura while the other units of corps struck first westwards and then northwards. By this stage of the battle the enemy formation were no longer conducting attacks as divisions or as corps, but were coming in in regimental groups or in even smaller sub-units. Because the Polish Command structure had now begun to break down, enemy resistance to 4th Panzer was un-coordinated and Reinhardt's battle groups were forcing the troops trying to escape back into the encircling ring which had been cast around them.

"The end of the battle of the Bzura was in sight but the Polish troops still attacked in a most gallant fashion, seeking to force a way through to Warsaw. Those assaults needed the employment of all the division's units to defeat. For two days the final battle rolled, by day and by night, by Polish units to destroy the German units they had encircled and by the Kampfgruppen to relieve the trapped detachments. But the efforts of 16th Corps and, particularly those of 4th Panzer Division were having their effect and once the divisional units had been relieved and a firm front had been established, the collapse of the Polish army was only a matter of hours. Such efforts as the Poles did make were only the death throes of a dying army."

To conduct those final bitter battles the Polish fighting troops abandoned their heavy equipment and advanced into mass attacks. The berseker fury with which they charged tore open 4th Division's western flank and the Poles poured through the breach to attack the artillery batteries holding post there. The gunners firing over open sights destroyed whole groups of the enemy, but as fast as those charging men fell, others stormed forward to take their place. In the confusion of the fighting senior officers fought as common soldiers and on the Polish side, Cavalry General Skotnicki led a bayonet charge with a pistol in his hand, encouraging his men until he fell mortally wounded. Reinhardt could only repeat his injunction for his men to hold on, that the enemy was weakening. He was correct. Polish efforts suddenly began to weaken and the enemy's last major effort was easily beaten off. Now the time had come for Reinhardt's men to open their own operations to destroy the enemy.

At first light on 19 September, a battle group of the "Leibstandarte" and 35th Panzer Regiment fought their way through to relieve the last of the cut-off German units.

At 11.00hrs on that day the Poles began to surrender en masse and, as they moved down into captivity, the units of 4th Panzer began to advance into the ground held until only recently by the enemy forces. Both banks of the River Bzura were covered with the fallen. On the southern bank of the Vistula the Polish dead lay four or five deep, cut down as they attempted to cross to the northern bank and unaware that German 2nd Corps was in position there. In the bend of the River Bzura the Polish Army died and on that killing ground stood Reinhardt's men, exhausted by the strain of combat and horrified at the scale of the destruction they were viewing.

Battle Groups of 1st Gebirgs Division in the advance to Lemberg and the fighting for that City. Poland, Autumn 1939

The role of German 14th Army in the Polish campaign was a two-fold one. Primarily, it had to guard the right flank of 10th Army as that formation drove towards Warsaw. Its secondary, but no less important task, was to reach the River Bug in eastern Poland. It would then be forming one of the jaws of the second, or eastern, encirclement and was to strike northwards up that river. The 18th (Gebirgs) Corps of 14th Army was placed on the extreme right of Army Group South and had, therefore, the greatest distance to cover of any formation of that Army, in order to reach the Bug.

At the start of the Polish campaign the task of 2nd Gebirgs (ie, Mountain) Division of 18th Corps was to advance out of Slovakia and to invade southern Poland. It was then to thrust for and capture Novy Sandec, whereupon 1st Gebirgs Division, in its turn, would advance out of Slovakia and gain touch with its sister Division to the east of that town. Both formations would then wheel and march, side by side, eastwards towards Lemberg, the capital of the province of Galicia. That city had to be taken before 18th Corps could resume its advance to the Bug and the northwards thrust up that river.

Both Gebirgs Divisions gained touch east of Novy Sandec and went into the second stage of the High Command battle plan. The OKW communique of 13 September stated, "...advancing on either side of Przemysl, [the towns of] Sambor and Javorov were captured and Lemberg reached by our spearhead units...". Behind the last, bland seven words of that announcement lies the story of battle group operations, opening with the storming charge to Lemberg by Schoerner's Kampfgruppe of Kubler's 1st Gebirgs Division and the unsuccessful battle by other divisional KGs to capture the city. In essence what the 1st had been ordered to carry out was to thrust, like a lance, through the Polish Carpathian Army and to seize a large and well garrisoned city. That such a bold enterprise was fraught with danger was obvious. Kubler's Division would be totally surrounded by Polish forces. To the north of the Carpathian Army stood the Tarnov Group and to the west the Cracow Group. Either or both of those major formations might be called in to assist the Carpathian Army in cutting off 1st Gebirgs Division as it stormed across the plains of southern Poland, "bounced" the River Dniestr and raced to Lemberg. But the risks confronting 1st Gebirgs were as nothing compared to the glittering victory which would be gained were the Polish operations to be brought to naught by a successful lance thrust. The eastern encirclement would have been accomplished and enemy resistance along the Bug crushed. The factor of determined, even fanatical Polish opposition to the German assault was certainly an important consideration but more worrying to Beyer, commanding 18th Corps, was the problem of the distances which his troops would have to cover in order to reach Lemberg. Beyer's corps took Sambor, only 80km from Lemberg on 11 September, and it soon became apparent that the enemy armies in the western half of Poland had begun to withdraw eastwards and that the possibility existed they would reach and escape across the Bug before the German pincers closed and trapped them. Fourteenth Army must be first to reach the Bug, but to achieve this 18th Corps would have to move rapidly, accepting the risk of being cut off and having to battle against overwhelming odds.

The successful outcome of the eastern encirclement thus depended on the speed with which Beyer's 18th Corps covered the distance to the Bug. Because of the poor state of the very few Polish roads, corps' advance was restricted to the width of one main highway - that along which 1st Division was already advancing. Beyer ordered that division to head the corps' thrust. Kubler, the divisional commander, created a Kampfgruppe around four companies of Jaeger or infantry, artillery, flak, anti-tank and pioneer detachments. Behind that battle group the remainder of the division would follow as a shaft follows the spearpoint.

The Kampfgruppe's advance along the Lemberg road opened and made good ground against only minimal opposition. The daring of the German operation and the tempo of its advance had, perhaps, confounded the enemy's reactions and Kubler hoped that the enemy's slowness would last until Malovanaka had been reached and taken. That place, a land bridge between two lakes, was the last major natural, defensive obstacle before Lemberg. It was a naturally strong position which the Poles would try to hold at all costs but it was also one which the divisional commander thought might be stormed using a combination of speed and audacity. The battle group raced towards the narrow land bridge and entered Malovanaka, which stands at its neck. The tempo of the assault brought the Kampfgruppe almost to the town centre before it was halted by a storm of fire. The Jaeger leaped from the lorries and opened an attack against the Polish defences sited behind a pair of anti-tank ditches, each more than two metres wide and filled with water. A company of the battle group waded slowly and under fire through the chest-high water, captured both ditches and then raced across open parkland towards the land bridge. The battle to seize that strip of ground between the lakes lasted for over one and a half hours, but the Jaeger attack proved irresistible and not only were the Polish trenches stormed and taken but each enemy counter-attack was beaten down.

While pockets of the enemy were still fighting courageously - and indeed while the main battle still raged – small detachments of Jaeger were pulled out of the fight, embussed and ordered to drive towards the objective. Part of the instructions the truck drivers were given were to "... make as much dust as you can...". Kubler reasoned that a huge dust cloud hanging over the column might deceive the Poles into thinking the Kampfgruppe to be a stronger force that it really was. The spearhead group moved fast and as each Jaeger detachment finished its own small battle it boarded trucks and set off following the point unit, now rapidly approaching the Galician capital. Nothing was allowed to halt the lorried charge - neither Polish opposition, nor the tiredness of the Jaeger drivers. The given task was to reach the day's objective and where the press of traffic caused jams these were sorted out by senior NCOs and officers whose orders were to keep the advance rolling. "The storming race to Lemberg", drove on and by 15.00hrs the first trucks of the battle group were in the city's western outskirts where Polish resistance hardened dramatically, halting the forward movement and forcing the Kampfgruppe onto the defensive. As has been stated, the width of front along which 1st Gebirgs Division was advancing was restricted to one road, which left the defenders free to concentrate their whole opposition upon the single German vehicle column.

Throughout the day sub-units of 1st Gebirgs Division reached the battle group and took their places in the ring which Kubler was trying to cast around the city. The length of front held by the units of the division was over 10km long, and so loose that Polish detachments were able to filter through and reach the beleaguered city. Lemberg was almost, but not completely, encircled. One small sector in the east could not be closed and preparations began for an assault to block that eastern loophole. Then came alarming news. Three Polish infantry divisions, the 11th, 21st and 38th, which had been fighting in the west around Przemysl, were being driven back eastwards by 14th Army's advance. Their retreat brought them crashing into the back of the Jaeger units holding the western sector of the perimeter and the battles which both sides fought were long, bitter and often decided by hand to hand combat. The Poles tried desperately, but unsuccessfully, to smash a way through and the Jaeger fought no less hard to prevent this. An indication of the intensity of the struggles in the wooded hills around Lemberg can be gained from an entry in a battalion war diary which recorded that its company in the Reszna-Ruska area had fought off the attacks of four enemy battalions. While the Kampfgruppe of 1st Gebirgs Division, 120km deep in enemy-held territory and cut off from the other formations of 18th Corps, was holding off the assaults of the Polish Przemysl group coming in from the west, a fresh crisis developed when the Lemberg garrison opened an offensive striking in from the east. Kubler decided that the threat coming out of Przemysl was the more serious one and to reinforce his western flank ordered that every Jaeger detachment coming into the area was to be halted, formed into a battle group and put in the line on that sector. Kampfgruppen Kress, Zimmer and Pemsel were created in this way but the fierceness of the fighting drained their strength so quickly and they lost men in such alarming numbers to the continuous assaults of the enemy that fragments of their groups were amalgamated to form other Kampfgruppen. In another effort to reinforce the firing line Jaeger were brought, by lorried convoy, as far forward as possible to the positions held by the battle groups. Units for which there were no trucks force-marched to reach their embattled comrades. Those efforts brought up the 98th and 99th Jaeger regiments during the night of 12-13 September, to reinforce Schoerner's 100th Regiment and with that force to hand Kubler moved to cut off the city. That offensive opened a nine-day long struggle during which the weight, number and fury of the Polish attacks coming down from Przemysl and those of the garrison of Lemberg, smashed 1st Division's regiments and battalions. The remnants of established formations amalgamated to form other battle groups, most of which had a life measured in hours only.

Fresh attacks coming out of Przemysl tore a 5km-wide gap in the northwestern sector of the perimeter and to close that breach every man, even the lightly wounded, was kept in the firing line. Schoerner's Kampfgruppen from 100th Regiment, in the northern sector of the perimeter, were under constant and intense pressure; on one wasteful day of battle five separate attacks were launched against it, each covered by heavy barrages and on one occasion supported by tanks. Schoerner was a very big man, well known for his courage. In this desperate situation he repeated the uncompromising message to his men during the daily inspection of their trenches: "The battle group will hold its positions". On 19 September, the struggle rose to a crescendo of fury during which his group lost 21 men killed in action and 35 wounded, but slowly the gap that had yawned between Kampfgruppe Schoerner and 3rd Battalion of 99th Regiment was closed. With the arrival in the perimeter of fresh German regiments, Kuebler regrouped his division and planned for the final all-out assault to go in on the 20th. That frontal and potentially wasteful assault by the exhausted Jaeger did not need to be launched. The Russian invasion of Poland made it redundant. The battle for Lemberg was at an end and the Polish garrison insisted upon surrendering their uncaptured city to the Gebirgsjaeger who had fought so hard, but unsuccessfully, to take it. The battle group of 1st Gebirgs Division was stood down; its work completed. It had lost 11 officers and 232 other ranks killed and over 400 of all ranks wounded; that is to say, one-third of its men had been killed or wounded. Even if the ultimate objective had been denied them, the Jaeger could still be proud of what they had achieved in the race to Lemberg.

Battle Groups of Rommel's 7th Panzer Division in the fighting in the West. France, May–June 1940

The declaration of war by Great Britain and France in September 1939, caused Hitler to decide to extend hostilities into Western Europe. He was determined to subdue France and in Directive No 6 stated his intention to carry out offensive operations with minimum delay. OKH, the Army High Command, prepared "Operation Yellow" – an attack by three Army Groups through Holland, Belgium and France. Army Group A would form the main thrust with B and C covering the north and south flanks.

In this account we are concerned with 7th Panzer Division of Hoth's 15th Panzer Corps, 4th Army, Army Group A. It was the task of that Army Group, carrying the main burden of "Operation Yellow", to drive through the Allied forces in northern France and southern Belgium and to cut them off from those south of the Seine. The Order of Battle of 7th Panzer Division was a tank regiment with 218 vehicles, two infantry (rifle) regiments, an artillery regiment, three battalions strong and a battalion each of reconnaissance vehicles, machine gunners and anti-tank weapons. The divisional commander, Erwin Rommel, had formerly commanded Hitler's Escort Battalion and had only taken over the 7th in February 1940. The campaign in France and Flanders was to be his first active service command as a senior officer, and so well did he succeed in this new position that he raised his division's role from that of acting as a flank guard to become part of the armoured spearhead which helped decide the outcome of the war in the West.

The 7th's operations began conventionally enough with a standard attack on 10 May, but Rommel had soon created the first of the many battle groups he was to raise during the campaign. By last light on that first day of operations, there was a Panzer and artillery KG in the western end of the divisional salient, supported by another infantry battle group, 6th Rifle Regiment, the motor cycle battalion and pioneers. In the centre of the salient the divisional headquarters group was protected by the recce battalion and, finally, a long way to the east were 7th Rifles, Flak units and the main body of the divisional Panzer regiment. The 7th Panzer had already thrust deep into Belgium, "bounced" the River Ourthe, and had laagered for the night. On the morrow it was to face its first major test, the crossing of the River Maas, but a foretaste of the resistance that the Division was to meet came west of the River Ourthe during the night of 10-11 May.

The divisional advance guard was carrying out a reconnaissance as far as the Maas when its left flank came under attack. Rommel, who was with the leading detachment, created a small battle group of Panzer companies and led them into a counter attack. The French riposted with an assault made up of two waves of tanks. In the growing light of dawn Rommel ordered forward some batteries of his artillery regiment and formed them into a single line. The gunners were told to load with high explosive and not armour piercing ammunition and to aim so that the shells landed between the first and the second armoured wave. This was a psychological ploy and a calculated risk. He reasoned that the tank commanders of the second wave would see fountains of explosions from the German barrage rising in front of them. They would not know what was happening to the first wave vehicles but would reason they were being struck by even heavier fire. Rommel's reading of the enemy mind was correct. The second line unwilling to brave the German shells turned away. The barrage then loaded with armour piercing rounds and switched to the AFVs of the first line, now very close to the German guns. The 88s fired and dense smoke clouds rose from five machines hit and burning on the battlefield. The surviving tanks pulled back under a smoke screen. It was the first of a series of armoured attacks that came in during the day but despite those assaults the 7th Panzer Division continued its advance: it was less a case of French opposition than a shortage of petrol which affected the pace of the division's movement. To keep his Panzer companies moving Rommel ordered them to fill up at civilian garages but the amounts obtained were too small to do more than supply a few machines. It was not until the Luftwaffe air-dropped fuel containers that the advance rolled strongly again. During the afternoon of 12 May, a quick thrust by a combined infantry and armour KG stormed and seized Dinant while the leading elements of a Panzer battle group pushed to within a few kilometres of the Maas. To defend the river line against 7th Panzer Division the French High Command fielded two divisions, massively supported by artillery which, according to German reports and war diaries, fired almost continuous barrages. An example of a small but successful Kampfgruppe was that created by the divisional commander to fight down snipers whose activity was delaying the construction of a bridge. Rommel lined up a few AFVs along the river's eastern bank which poured fire upon sniper posts which could be identified. Soon there was no more opposition from the French snipers. At 04.30hrs on the 13th, the leading battalions of 7th Rifles began to cross the river, created a bridgehead and within a matter of hours had burst out of its confines. The war diary records that the 13th was a day of bitter fighting, but for the relatively small cost of 60 killed and 200 wounded, 7th Panzer had crossed a major water obstacle and had, thereby, confounded the expectations of the French High Command which had expected to hold the Germans there for at least a week.

Throughout the following days the fighting was a bewildering mix of attack, counter-attack and defence with small battle groups being switched between the two major Kampfgruppen, either to reinforce an assault or to strengthen a wavering defence. Corps, aware that Rommel's Division was achieving a succession of military successes, reinforced it temporarily with those elements of 5th Panzer which had crossed the Maas. Rommel's formation was in urgent need of reinforcement. It was strung out east and west of the Maas and was under attack from French heavy tanks whose armour could not be penetrated by the shells of standard German anti-tank guns. The excellent German wireless system helped convert a likely reverse into a success. Rommel's demands for Stuka attacks against the French "heavies" soon brought Junkers Ju 87 dive-bombers into action and under their bombardment the armoured assault collapsed. The French vehicles scattered but, found again by Luftwaffe reconnaissance aircraft, their positions were radioed back to the 7th, whose Panzer battle group closed in for the "kill", engaged the enemy vehicles at point-blank range and destroyed them.

Operations after 14 May demonstrated Blitzkrieg techniques being applied by a master. The Panzer and infantry KGs thrust through the country west of the Maas and a brief but difficult battle for Phillipville was fought, during 14-15 May which was only resolved when the Stukas came winging, once again, to the aid of 7th's left flank Kampfgruppe. The Division's next test was the attack made against the extension of the French fortifications system, the Maginot Line. The weight and fury of the French artillery barrage which crashed down upon the German advance was indicative of the enemy's determination to fight hard to hold those fortifications. The Panzer KG led by Rommel crossed the start line at 18.00 hrs, shrouded in a dense smoke screen. Individual forts were targeted. Assault pioneers cut their way through belts of barbed wire and the Panzers rolled through the gaps which had been created, moving closer and closer until they could fire into the gun ports and embrasures. Collaborating with the AFVs, other pioneers thrust explosive charges into loopholes from which fire was still coming, or sprayed the interior of pillboxes with machine gun fire. By late evening the leading vehicles of the Panzer KG were pushing relentlessly forward and the defenders, confused by the noise of the air and ground bombardments, streamed in to surrender. At 23.00hrs a battle group made up of the machine gun battalion and the recce battalion, with Rommel once again leading the advance, opened the final assault. Following closely behind the screen of light vehicles came the Panzer battle group, each vehicle firing its main armament while on the move; not a standard tactic of those days. When the armour reached the Avesnes-Solre le Chateau road the exultant crews knew that they had smashed through the supposedly impregnable Maginot Line. Their columns then opened a fast advance — the pursuit stage of the battle — shooting to pieces French columns heading towards the forts and overrunning others marching away in the direction of Avesnes. The streets of that town were filled with French soldiers whose low spirits were raised, temporarily, when their heavy tanks rolled into battle and forced the German armour to withdraw. Then a single Panzer IV came into action and its powerful main armament, firing into the backs of the French "heavies" destroyed them. Rommel, determined not to be delayed by fighting inside the town, directed the Panzer Kampfgruppe to bypass Avesnes and to leave the mopping up to follow-up units. Throughout the day the divisonal commander had created and broken up battle groups to meet fast changing situations. Von Bismarck, the commander of one Kampfgruppe, led his vehicles in a fast advance which captured Landrecies and the bridge there by 06.00hrs on 17 May and had gone on to reach the heights of Le Cateau, intending to continue with the attack. The 7th was far ahead of the other Panzer Divisions and Rommel, aware that his units were over extended, ordered Bismarck's group to halt but did send out an infantry and artillery battle group which captured the bridge at Berlimont across the Sambre and, thereby, aided the advance of 5th Panzer. It was as well that the advance of Rommel's Division had been halted, for the French High Command put in a series of attacks to smash the vulnerable salient, more than 50km long, in which it was contained. The Division's units closed up for mutual protection and launched their own attacks by all-arms battle groups which dominated their French opponents.

Cambrai was taken during the morning of the 18th, and the advance was pressed towards the Escaut canal and the bridges at Morenchies. To seize these before they could be blown Rommel created a strong sub-battle group, detached it from the main body and sent it into action. That KG took the objectives but a French infantry counter-attack found the boundary between 5th and 7th Panzer and temporarily created a tense situation. The French were driven back before they could exploit that weakness and 7th Panzer Division spent the remainder of the 19th consolidating the gains it had made by wiping out pockets of French troops.

The campaign in the West was only days old but the whole country between the Scarpe and the Somme was in German hands and Army Group A already had bridgeheads across the latter river. The Allied forces in northern France, cut off from those below the Somme, were being compressed into a perimeter around Dunkirk. At 01.40hrs on 20 May, Rommel created two new battle groups which burst out of the Canal du Nord bridgehead and with the divisional commander riding with the righthand KG, advanced to the north of Cambrai, found the bridge across the canal at Marquien destroyed but quickly crossed the canal in rubber boats. That crossing was followed at 05.00hrs by one at Vis en Artois made by the Panzer KG.

Arras was held by the British Expeditionary Force and Rommel directed his Division to bypass the town to the south. Concerned that the Panzer Kampfgruppe lacked infantry he set off down the Vis en Artois road to urge the Rifles to speed their advance. En route his vehicle and escort came under attack by French tanks and he was out of contact for several hours until the infantry group roared up the road and brought about his release. It was an operation typical of the confused fighting, in which attacks were met with counter-attacks with which the Allies sought to slow 7th Panzer's forward movement.

The Corps commander offered Rommel the opportunity to give his exhausted soldiers the rest they so desperately needed, but instead the General asked that his Division's offensive be allowed to continue until the Scarpe had been crossed and the high ground south-east of Arras had been taken. To accomplish this two main battle groups attacked and the Panzer KG made such good progress across excellent tank country that it soon held the area around Warlus. The infantry battle group hit the stronger opposition of British 4th Royal Tank Regiment (RTR), which took it in flank and not only dispersed 6th Rifles, but overwhelmed the guns of several anti-tank units. The German gunners found that the shells of their Pak were as useless against British armour plate as they had been against the French and it seemed that the RTR thrust might crumple the whole divisional salient. Then a battery of 10.5cm guns roared up, deployed and went into action. Within minutes 20 of the British machines had been destroyed.

Meanwhile, on the Mercatel sector 7th RTR smashed an anti-tank gun screen and killed four Panzers, but the fraught situation was restored by the division's 88mm guns. Both battle groups fought their way forward and although they reached the day's objectives by 23.00hrs, that first clash with the British had cost them dear. Six Panzer III and three Panzer IV machines had been destroyed together with a great number of unarmoured vehicles and nearly 400 soldiers of the Division had been killed or wounded.

The British armoured regiments renewed their attacks throughout 22 May, and although these were heavy and costly, Rommel did not allow them to deflect him from launching his attack across the Scarpe. At 10.15hrs he led a combined infantry and Panzer battle group across the river but heavy Allied counter-attacks brought on a crisis which began in the early evening and endured until the following afternoon. In bitter fighting 7th Panzer was able to hold the ground it had taken although Allied probes once again found the seam between the inner wings of 7th and 5th Panzer Divisions. A battle group of infantry and recce units created by Rommel held the attacks and prevented an exploitation of that potentially dangerous situation.

At about this time the Allies withdrew behind the La Bassee canal and except for persistent British sniping, there was little opposition to the division's advance. Then came Hitler's order for the Panzer divisions to halt and for the next two days there was only infantry activity. When that ban was lifted on the 27th, the Division's battle groups forced bridgeheads across the canal between La Bassee and Le Preclan, intending to continue the attack on the following day. That operation was cancelled by Corps and 7th Panzer, taken out of the Line for rest, did not return until 3 June. A few days later it went into the battle of France. The set-piece attack which opened that offensive began at 10.00hrs on the 6th and was almost classic in execution. As usual, Rommel was up with the leading vehicles of the Panzer regiment, with the motor-cycle battalion forming the right flank and the armoured-recce battalion the left. Behind that group came 7th Rifles, with some battalions mounted in personnel carriers and others marching into the attack. Following the extended lines of infantry came Flak and anti-tank units, the lorry-borne 6th Rifles and field artillery. Wherever they were met the French counter-attacks were halted and flung back. Thiennloy l'Abbaye was cleared by 7th Rifles and the anti-tank battalion broke up enemy tank thrusts. The French divisions on this sector had suffered appalling losses and no fewer than 1,500 of their soldiers were taken prisoner, 18 tanks destroyed and guns captured; all for the loss to 7th Panzer of 21 killed and 56 wounded.

The sitrep (situation report) from Division to Corps, dated 7 June and outlining the previous day's operations, recorded that its two Kampfgruppen had crossed their start lines at 10.00hrs. Von Bismarck's on the right, was made up of a Panzer company, 7th Rifles (Bismarck's own regiment), artillery, light and heavy Flak and an anti-tank detachment. Rommel was with the lefthand column, Kampfgruppe Luck, comprising 25th Panzer Regiment, the recce battalion and 6th Rifles, supported by light and heavy calibre field and Flak artillery.

By this stage of the campaign the Blitzkrieg dynamic was for units not to capture villages and small towns but to bypass the Allied soldiers who sought to hold the German advance by defending them. That Allied tactic was a vain hope. The armoured vehicles of Rommel's division with the rifle companies bouncing uncomfortably in their troop transport trucks, flooded like waves around the villages which were intended to be the rocks of Allied resistance, leaving them isolated and ready to be taken out by follow-up units.

Another fast-paced drive brought the Kampfgruppen so deep into the French Army's rear areas that in Saumont, 7th Rifles captured two goods trains, took prisoner the troops riding on them and seized the supplies which they carried. Although the day's objectives had been taken Rommel ordered the advance to continue. The enemy was to be given no rest. KG Bismarck reached and gained the main road between Dieppe and Paris meeting only light opposition, but the resistance which KG Luck encountered grew until, by 21.30hrs, it was under attack from a mass of enemy AFVs. Also during that first evening of the new offensive, the anti-tank battalion brushed an enemy column and was also quickly involved in fierce fighting.

During 8-9 June, the Division began its assault upon Rouen. Reveille on the 8th had been early but Corps' battle orders did not arrive until 09.00hrs and confirmed that 7th Panzer was to move on the city. Rommel, annoyed at how much time had been lost, held a verbal "O" Group, then mounted up and rode with the point group. By 10.30hrs that spearhead body comprising the recce battalion, the motor cycle battalion, a Panzer company, a battery of howitzers and Flak, was on the road. Despite enemy air attacks it reached Ancelle and there fought against British rearguard units which blew up the Sigy bridge as the point unit came into sight. The Kampfgruppe halted and prepared to undertake an assault crossing of the river, using a new battle group which Rommel had created. That KG, the recce battalion and the motor cyclists, covered by a short barrage, swung into the attack and with that assault rolling Rommel sent out patrols to locate fords. One was found south of Sigy through which a Panzer detachment crossed and where it set up a bridgehead.

While the fighting on the Sigy sector was still at its height a report was received that the Mormanville bridge had been taken intact. Immediately, Rommel ordered the KG in Sigy to break off its attack and switched the Division's axis of advance towards the bridge and the high ground of La Chapelle. The objectives were captured and at 18.00hrs the battle groups opened their assault upon Rouen. The main thrust of the attack was with the left column, led by the Panzer regiment, which went well until the road junction at La Vacherie, 7km east of the city. There the main body, strung out behind the point units, was suddenly struck by enemy columns which had blundered across the 7th's thrust line. The situation, already unclear, deteriorated when other enemy units which had been bypassed, opened fire upon both Kampfgruppen. As a consequence their assaults gained little ground until Rommel arrived, and directed the Panzer KG to seize the bridges at Elbouef and for the righthand battle group to capture those at Tourville. In order to "beef up" the attack of the Panzer battle group, the divisional commander switched 7th Rifles from KG Luck to the armoured column.

A propaganda account reported the events:

"The night was dark but our advance was pressed forward. The objective, we had been told, was Rouen. Suddenly the dark of the summer night was split by gun flashes. At ranges below 100 metres, enemy guns began to fire into the flank of the Panzer column. It could not be determined at first whether that gun fire came from enemy artillery pieces or whether it was from the main armament of his heavy tanks. With a few crisp orders our Panzer commandants order their 3.72cm guns to retaliate. The turrets swing towards the gun flashes. More orders follow and then flames leap from the barrels of our tank guns; our reply to the enemy's assault. Within minutes those guns are silent. Our Panzers have crushed this attempt to surprise us and to halt the advance."

Shortly after midnight 25th Panzer Regiment reached the valley of the Seine and three hours later the motor cycle battalion had captured the Elbouef bridges, but KG Bismarck had the misfortune of seeing the Tourville bridges blown as they roared up. There was a compensation for that disappointment when the rifles battle group stormed and captured the heights of Mont St Eignan. According to the divisional war diary, 10 June was a dramatic day in an offensive which was filled with drama. The battle groups left the laagering area at 04.30hrs, and had passed through the northern suburbs of Rouen in the direction of the Channel, when the right flank KG saw, struck and dispersed French formations. At Auainville the recce battalion also engaged the enemy when it collided with the 31st French Division. Luck, leaving a few armoured cars to dominate the enemy with machine gun fire, pressed on with the rest of his KG and at about 14.15hrs, reached the sea at Veulettes. Bismarck's group did not reach the Channel coast until later that afternoon. Enemy columns which attempted to break through the German line to reach their own Army, were shot to ruin leaving their survivors to flee in disarray or to be taken prisoner.

The fighting in the afternoon of that day was as successful as had been that of the morning. The heights of Fecamp were taken and from them the division's artillery bombarded the harbour and ships onto which enemy units were embarking. A battery of heavy coastal guns which KG Luck captured near Fecamp, were turned against enemy shipping hitting an auxiliary cruiser and damaging a destroyer. Luck's battle group then encountered serious opposition. Rommel formed a sub-battle group made up of the motor cycle battalion and two companies of Panzer and put this in to aid Luck's group. Late in the evening of the 10th, a suburb of

Fecamp was captured after a short battle against British and French troops. During the following afternoon, in an operation which lasted throughout most of the day, Bismarck's battle group opened an attack to seize the heights west of St Valery and a hard battle forced the surrender of over 1,000 Allied soldiers.

For a second time enemy troops on the mole, waiting to be evacuated by ship, were attacked and the barrage fired by the divisional artillery used 2,500 rounds. A new battle group, KG Kenter, units of the Panzer regiment, the recce battalion and 1st Battalion of 7th Rifles, began to tighten the ring around St Valery. The 12 June brought 7th Panzer Division a glowing victory with the surrender of part of 51st Highland Division, following which a new battle group, Rothenburg, the division's Panzer regiment and 1st Battalion of 7th Rifles, attacked St Valery with such determination that by the afternoon it had forced the surrender of the Allied troops in the town, among whom were the GOCs of French 20th Corps, the 2nd and 3rd Light Divisions, 30th Mountain Division and the British 51st Highland. For a loss of 28 men killed in action and 40 wounded, Rommel's Division had captured St Valery and had taken 12,000 prisoners, 328 machine guns and 95 artillery pieces.

The request from Marshal Petain for an armistice produced the hope that the war would soon be over but this was not the case as 7th Panzer soon found out. Kampfgruppe Luck, moving through Normandy, met such determined enemy resistance at Les Fosses that Rommel halted the advance, with the intention of bringing forward the rest of his Division and of launching a full scale attack on the morrow. Throughout the 18th and 19th, the Division was involved in hard fighting against French troops seeking to break through the German forces to reach Cherbourg. Both battle groups were involved in bitter struggles up the length of the Cotentin peninsula but by late night the Kampfgruppen had fought their way into the town of Cherbourg and had captured most of its fortifications.

The dawn attack on 19 June against the remaining forts brought the surrender of the garrison at 14.00hrs. With the end of the campaign in the West a sort of peace descended upon Europe. Less than a year later Rommel was to achieve prominence again, this time as commander of the German Afrika Korps in Libya.

The Group of SS and SD Detachments created to take part in Operation "Sealion", the plan to invade Great Britain in the Summer of 1940

At the end of the war in the West in June 1940, Great Britain faced the possibility of a German invasion. Among the very first units which were to land when Operation "Sealion" was launched, was a special, political, commando force. Those men of the SS and the Sicherheitsdienst (SD) were to form part — a secret part — of a large battle group made up of Army and Brandenburg detachments. That political group had its own codenames: to begin with "England Operation", later "Great Britain Kommando".

In those threatening days of 1940, the invasion and possible subjugation of Great Britain was a very potent threat, for poised across the Channel was the strongest army and air force in Europe. It seemed only a matter of days before the Wehrmacht's forces would strike. Their power, their awful power, was a terrible threat. Now, half a century later, one reads with bewilderment of the SS and SD "experts" who were brought together for the "England Operation" and who would form part of that terrifying German military machine. From a reading of the files which are held in the Department of Documents in the Imperial War Museum, the men of the political SS/SD group and the things that obsessed them have an Alice in Wonderland air.

Although "Unternehmen Seeloewe", the invasion of Great Britain, was never launched and, therefore, the need to activate the Army/Brandenburg/SS/SD Kampfgruppe did not arise, I felt that an account of the "Great Britain Kommando", the political faction, should be included in the text of this book.

The first and most bizarre element was that Gruppenführer Heydrich, Head of the SD, was besotted with the British Secret Service. Upon learning that the Head of MI5 was identified by a single initial, Heydrich insisted that he, too, had to be identified in the same way. A great many papers in the mass of documents which passed, either as letters or memoranda, between the several branches of the SS Intelligence Departments refer to Heydrich by the initial "C".

There was a remarkable lack of liaison — a striving for pre-eminence and Empire building is perhaps a better description – between the SS, the SD and the Gestapo. That fierce competition led to clumsy bureaucratic tangles and more bizarre happenings. An internal memorandum dated 8 August 1940, is evidence of the lunatic world into which the "England" group had plunged. According to the note from Hauptsturm-fuhrer Braune to Untersturmfuhrer Schubert, the need to make out identity documents for certain men of No II Section — the invasion was thought to be so imminent that he requested those men be issued with temporary Gestapo documents. There was, apparently, no general identity card in use throughout the whole security service and each department had its own. Another memorandum to Hauptscharfuhrer Liedtke requested that each man of the spearhead group be supplied with an attache case, a pocket torch, a map case and a field dressing. One man, Wolf, also needed to be issued with a gas mask.

The decision to form the "GB Kommando" was made within a week of the armistice with France coming into operation. The principal and political concern of Heinrich Himmler, Head of the SS, seemed to have been the need for him to be the first of the Nazi leaders to get his hands on the riches of the Church of England and the Roman Catholic church in Great Britain. To ensure this he needed a suitable and confidential man to be in charge of the confiscation of Church property. To conceal the iden-tity of the whole "GB Kommando" he proposed that SD men, who were members of the Allgemeine SS and who would have the task of carrying out the confiscations, should be taken onto the strength of the Waffen SS and hidden among the SS Divisions which would take part in the invasion. Thus their activities would not become common knowledge among the other Nazi leaders who may have had their own men looking for the spoils of war and invasion. Himmler's proposal led to a top level meeting and an aide memoire dated 11 July, reported the progress of that meeting between the author, Sturmbannfuhrer Suhr and Juttner the Head of the SS Person-nel Department. Juttner declared his willingness to allow between 10 and 12 SD men to be transferred, temporarily, from the Allgemeine SS and the SD to the the Waffen SS for the duration of the operation. It was his belief that the SS Verfugungstruppen and the Totenkopf Divisions would be used in the assault with, possibly, the employment of just one special battalion of the "Leibstandarte" SS Adolf Hitler. The selected 12 undercover men of the spearhead unit would be posted to and distributed among the battal-ions of those Waffen SS units.

Further discussion made the point that there was a shortage of space on the assault landing ships. The SD group would not be able to take vehi-cles with them on the sea crossing but would have to commandeer trans-port once they had landed in England. Therein lay a problem. No one in the group of 12 could drive, nor could drivers be posted from the SD to act as chauffeurs. It would become necessary to co-opt and to post to the unit civilian members of the Nazi Party's own motoring organisation, the

NSKK. The letter ordering the recruitment of these civilians stressed that the men chosen must have a soldierly appearance. Competence in driving seems to have been a lesser consideration. Those NSKK men, too, would be accepted as temporary members of the Waffen SS, but would neither join their unit nor use their new-found rank until shortly before D-Day for the operation. They would then be taken by truck to their respective battalions, armed with their new — and very brief — authority. Juttner proposed that all the SD men named on one list and described as liaison personnel were to hold the rank of Waffen SS Leutnant. The other men of the Kommando would be given ranks corresponding to the civilian posts they had held in their parent formations. That piffling piece of time-wasting nonsense was actually sent to "C" for his attention and decision.

The next interesting document laid out the names and functions of some of the SD men. Dr Levin would deal with the questions of Freemasonry, Richter would have the Jewish problem, Stiller and Hucke would handle the question of the political church, Marxism would be the province of Dr Mahnke, Liberalism that of Kunze, press and authorship would be covered by Jonas while Dr Mahnke, doubling up his work on Marxism, would also deal with matters relating to culture. In that area he would be assisted by Dr Wolf, the man who had needed a gas mask.

Dr Wolf seems to have been an interesting character who, according to the letter dated 24 August, had spent some time in England and had the necessary experience and practical knowledge of British political life to equip him for the post. He did not get it. A letter dated 26 August, names a senior SS officer, Prof Dr Six, as the man chosen by "C" to lead the GB group. From the correspondence one cannot escape the feeling that Prof Dr Six was a particularly difficult person, whether one worked with him as an equal or as a subordinate. It is also clear he was empire building by selecting for his chums of Department II, vacancies on the GB gravy train. The letter of 26 August requests the immediate transfer to the GB group of a number of Prof Dr Six's Department II colleagues. They were to be seconded from their posts in Metz, Brussels and Paris. The reaction and comments of those officers and men to that request is not recorded in the files, but I doubt they were complimentary or their recipients grateful. They were undoubtedly living very well indeed in the fleshpots of France and Belgium. Now, as a result of Prof Dr Six's demand they were being taken away to undertake a perilous voyage across the Channel in order to carry out an assault landing upon a country which, according to German accepted thought, was perpetually covered by thick fog and where, again according to held opinions, the food was appalling. The Germans subscribed to the continental belief that the English had 100 different religions but only one sauce.

The energetic and academic Prof Dr Six, who was in later years to be tried and sentenced to 20 years imprisonment as a war criminal, lost no time in carrying out research work for his kommando group. A telegram sent to Kiel University stated that he and a Dr Prinzing would be making a visit to inspect material covering British persons, organisations and institutions. Kiel held, at that time, the most complete coverage of such material.

Things moved a little faster in the second week of September. A letter dated 10 September, ordered that the men of Section II who had been selected for the special mission were to parade at 10.00hrs on the 11th in the SD headquarters conference hall. The dress of the day was laid down as grey uniform and greatcoat. Civilian clothes were to be brought as well as a passport photograph. It seemed to the group that D-Day was imminent. It was not. Although they did not know it and, indeed, it was a fact unknown even at fairly senior military levels, Hitler had called off the invasion. Prof Dr Six's group, together with all the Wehrmacht units, continued to go, unknowingly, through elaborate charades connected with preparing for an aborted invasion — embarking or disembarking from barges and running up beaches carrying heavy weapons. The SD were fortunate in that they were spared the more vigorous exercises. As substitutes for embarkation and disembarkation and trudging through shingle they had education periods and exercised their minds with vexatious problems concerning rank.

The thorny preoccupation with who was primus inter pares is shown in a letter dated 17 September, which raised again the question of inequality of rank between the SS and the SD. The problem was, according to the memo writer, that disciplinary complications might arise among the group members. To resolve which it was, therefore, proposed that all members of the SD who held honorary rank in that organisation were to become Second Lieutenants in the Waffen SS unless, of course, they already held a higher honorary rank, in which case they would use that. All SD specialists were to become Senior Lieutenants of the Waffen SS and all Departmental Heads were to receive the rank of Hauptsturmfuhrer or Captains. The ranks would be held for only as long as the operation continued.

With such delicate matters as rank priority dealt with, attention turned to the composition of the units which were to make the landings. There was to be a spearhead group of SD men and that advance unit would be followed by the main body. In London, which the minute writer assumed would also be the seat of the military governor, that SD group would set up its headquarters where it would be joined by the main kommando group. From SD headquarters in London small groups would go out to West and Central England and to Scotland to recover any evacuated files.

A discussion with "C" concluded that the whole SS/SD political group would be made up of 300 men, 50 of whom would be drivers. The most important detachment within that main body would be Prof Dr Six and his spearhead group of 12 men belonging to Section II. The main body would supply 20 men for London, Bristol, Birmingham, Liverpool and Manchester. Outstations would have up to 15 men, and there would be flying groups who would set out from London to pursue any likely leads. There was then a great deal of discussion as to what name the central organisation should carry before talk turned to what buildings would be occupied by the SD. It was determined that the Secret Field Police (GFP), would be billeted in the Strand Palace Hotel and in the Dorchester in Park Lane. Departmental offices would be set up in two clubs in St James but there would be no need to commandeer private houses in central London.

It was accepted that in the thrust from the beachhead to London, Prof Dr Six's advance-guard group would have no time to search all the archives in all the palaces occupied by bishops and archbishops. Those premises would be sealed and the prelates confined to their palaces under house arrest. A list of suspects had been compiled by the SD and that list would be the basis of the search and arrest operation. Those named in the list who were to be put into camps were almost exclusively emigrants from Germany or Austria, converted Jews, Anglican or Roman Catholic priests and laymen who had spoken out against the German government.

It must have occurred even to Prof Dr Six and his group of 12 that the onset of autumn would make an invasion in 1940 very unlikely, but they still continued with the belief that it would go in during that year. By now, to pass the endless hours of waiting, they clutched at political straws. The problem which absorbed them, according to a memorandum dated 20 September, was which things in Great Britain had to be paid for in cash, what did not have to be paid for and what could be taken upon the issue of a receipt. Of particular interest was a decision on how one was to pay for the confiscation of supplies, the occupation of billets or the requisitioning of motor vehicles. Weighty problems to be sure, but ones which would not, one feels, have concerned them had they gone in with an assault wave in late July. The rough and ready rule of military necessity would have provided the answer to any requisitions and confiscations. With D-Day continually postponed the concerns of the SD group then centred more and more around the type of piping which was to be worn on the epaulettes of their tunics. Green piping had been worn during the Norway campaign and had been worn also in Paris, but some members had taken to removing the SD diamond from their sleeves while others had taken down their cuff title bands. It was all very worrying and "C" would have to decide on these sartorial niceties.

Still convinced that the invasion would take place in 1940, another worry was that civilian clothes could not be taken as part of the luggage during the assault crossing. There would be no space to take mufti. A decision was sought on whether civilian clothing was to be commandeered or paid for upon arrival in England. By this time the group had set up instructional courses for the SD personnel. The principal practical subjects were language and pistol shooting while lecture courses were given on England, the country and its geography. Those last subjects are interesting because a list of those who had been in England shows that one man had spent just a few days in London in 1937, two had been in the German Embassy in London, one man had spent 10 months in southern England in 1934, one man was in Liverpool in 1930, another man had been in England 38 years earlier and one man had spent several years in America. The greatest amount of English spoken by one SD man was "Good morning. How do you do ?", while others were only a little more fluent in the language of the people whom they expected to control.

To summarise, then, a group of characters led by a man who demanded to be addressed as if he were the Head of MI5, was to be launched on an invasion, against a country of which they knew almost nothing. The picture conjured up is of a small and mysterious group of politicals intermingled WITH the fighting men of the Waffen SS, but not being part OF those units. The panorama unfolds to show that as soon as the politicals landed upon a shingle beach in southern England their immediate concern would be to find a tailor from whom they would be able to obtain, either with cash or military vouchers, a reach-me-down suit that would have to last them until they reached London. En route to the Imperial capital members of the group, not one of whom was fluent in reading ecclesiastic documents, were to stop off at archbishops' palaces either to confiscate what they could see or else to seal what they cannot. Upon entering London they would lodge in the Strand Palace Hotel or the Dorchester and work from gentlemens' clubs in St James — and all this with just a smattering of English, limited in the case of one man to simple conventional greetings. The concluding mental image produced from a reading of the files in the Department of Documents in the Imperial War Museum, is of Prof Dr Six and his sinister 12 from Section II, dressed by the Fifty Shilling Tailors and bumping towards London in their commandeered motor vehicles with their little attache cases on their knees earnestly discussing the frightening hold of Liberalism, Marxism and the Freemasons upon the fog-bound, sauce-deprived inhabitants of Great Britain. Thank God, this was one battle group which did not go into operation.

Battle Groups of 2nd Fallschirmjaeger Regiment in Operation "Mercury", the German airborne assault on Crete, May 1941

In June 1940, after France had been defeated, the German Army had no other enemies to fight on the mainland of Europe although in Africa a war was being waged in the Libyan desert. There Axis troops, Italian and German, were battling against a British and Imperial force. Then, on 28 October 1940, a new campaign opened on the European continent when Italy attacked Greece in what Mussolini, the Italian fascist leader, expected to be a short, victorious campaign. It was not and his Army was held in the mountains of Greece. The Italian leader's action had been both a snub and a military embarrassment to Hitler. It was a snub because Mussolini had acted without consulting Germany and a military embarrassment because Britain, anxious to help the Greeks, had sent an expeditionary force. A British presence in the Balkans would affect Hitler's plan to attack the Soviet Union and he decided to secure Germany's south-eastern flank by aiding his Italian ally. The Fuehrer ordered a plan to defeat the Greek Army, to drive the British out of Greece and thereby take the burden of Mussolini's Balkan blunder from the shoulders of his hard-pressed army.

In a move to protect Germany's southern boundary Hitler offered a non-aggression pact to the government of Jugoslavia which was accepted by the Regent, Prince Paul. A coup overthrew the Regent and the young King Peter abrogated the Treaty. Hitler, enraged at this insult, ordered OKW to extend its plans for the campaign in Greece and to include in them an operation which would crush Jugoslavia. German Army and Luftwaffe staffs produced the revised plan and although Hitler knew that to implement it would involve a complete regrouping of Field Marshal List's forces in the Balkans he insisted that the campaign against both countries open on the original D Day, 6 April. On that day advances by German forces out of Austria into Croatia and Serbia gained touch with Panzer units striking westwards into Serbia out of Bulgaria. Other German formations which were concentrated in that latter country, broke through the Metaxas Line defending northern Greece and advanced into her central and southern provinces and into Corinth, from whose harbours the remnant of the British expeditionary force took ship back to North Africa and the Libyan desert. Other British units, also evacuated from Corinth, were taken to Crete there to form part of the Greek/British/Dominion garrison on that island.

With the campaigns in Jugoslavia and Greece successfully concluded and the major new war against the Soviet Union not yet begun, Hitler determined to strengthen Germany's hold in the Mediterranean area. By capturing Crete he would bestride the great inland sea and thus dominate the approaches to the Middle East. The campaign in Crete was to be a short one — 10 days' duration and 11th Flieger Korps was ordered to capture the objective by airborne assault. Little time was given to General Student, the corps commander, to prepare and to mount Operation "Mercury" but his staff was equal to the task despite several serious setbacks. The chief of these was that 22nd Airlanding Division, corps' support component, was not available for the operation but that 5th Alpine Division had been substituted. This was a crack formation certainly, but not one trained in airlanding techniques nor one which had collaborated with the Paras in past campaigns. The task of an airlanding Division was to land on captured airfields and to take over the burden of the fighting from the lightly-armed Paras. Student would have under his command, the entire 7th Fallschirmjaeger Division plus Corps troops. The 5th Gebirgs Division, much of which would be brought to Crete by ship, would take over direction of the operations on Crete once the main body had landed. The mission to capture the island was, thus, a combined Services operation.

The mountainous island of Crete lies in the eastern Mediterranean. A narrow, fertile strip running along the island's northern side between the sea and the mountains, was the area upon which the 7th Division was to make its airlandings. That choice of area was determined by the fact that on the northern side ran the single main road connecting Crete's principal towns and that three of those — Maleme in the west, Retimo in the centre and Heraklion in the east — were served by small, primitive aerodromes. Perilously short and dusty the airstrips of those fields may have been, but they would have to serve Student's purpose. His men would carry out the initial assaults by parachute or by glider and, once the landing zones had been taken, Luftwaffe transport aircraft would bring in the heavy weapons. The operation would then move into its second phase — the capture of the rest of the island by 5th Alpine Division. A second factor which adversely affected the planning of "Mercury" was that the Luftwaffe had too few transport aircraft to airlift the paratroop contingents in one single operation. There would have to be more than one "lift" and this would increase substantially the risks for those who would have to fly in the second, or in any subsequent "waves".

For the initial — that is to say, airborne — part of the Crete operation, Student decided to "field" the division's three Fallschirmjaeger regiments, the Sturm (or assault) regiment, and all corps' troops detachments. The opening assault would be carried out in the West by three major groupings. That first wave would be made up of the bulk of Meindl's Sturm Regiment which would drop or glider-land at Maleme and Heidrich's 3rd Regiment which would land by parachute and make for Canea. The second wave of the assault, to be carried out in the afternoon of D-Day, would be made by the central and eastern groups. The central group, the bulk of Sturm's 2nd Regiment, would drop around Retimo while the eastern task force, Brauer's 1st Regiment, reinforced by 2nd Battalion of 2nd Regiment, would take out Heraklion. D-Day was set for 20 May 1941. All flights were to take off from airfields on the mainland of Greece during that day but the 5th Alpine's sea-borne component and the the heavy weapons units, being carried in slow vessels, would have to sail from the Greek ports a day or two earlier than the airborne "lifts".

The following account deals with the battle groups employed only by 2nd Regiment and I am indebted to Adi Strauch and to other comrades of that regiment for supplying the details and anecdotes which furnish the basis of my text. Official war diaries show that Oberst Sturm's 2nd Regiment formed four battle groups, three of which served with the regiment while the fourth, Kampfgruppe Schirmer, (2nd Battalion of 2nd Regiment), acted as a support group to Oberst Brauer's 1st Regiment. The three Kampfgruppen serving with 2nd Regiment were, firstly, that one built around Major Kroh's 1st Jaeger Battalion and including No 2 Company of the divisional machine gun company, a half-company of the divisional Flak battalion and a platoon each from Nos 13 and 14 Companies. The second battle group was that of Hauptmann Wiedemann made up of 3rd Jaeger Battalion, No 2 Company of the divisional artillery battalion, No 1 Company of the divisional machine gun battalion, a half-company of Flak and a platoon each of Nos 13 and 14 Companies. Major Schulz's Kampfgruppe was to form 2nd Regiment's reserve and comprised regimental headquarters, a signals platoon, the HQ of the divisional machine gun battalion, No 2 Company of 2nd Battalion, and a platoon each of Nos 13 and 14 Companies. The task of the three Kampfgruppen was to capture the town of Retimo and the aerodrome outside the town. KG Kroh was to paradrop on either side of the airfield, to capture it and to make it ready to receive support landings. Wiedemann group was to jump between the River Platinas and Retimo, to capture the town and to hold it. KG Schulz was to land between Kroh and Wiedemann would hold the drop zone and be available for use as Oberst Sturm directed, either to "beef-up" an attack or to support a defence.

The battle plan produced by Sturm and his officers was an excellent one, and given optimum conditions might have succeeded. But as we have seen in other accounts, no plan survives past the first shock of battle. In the case of 2nd Regiment the plan did not even need that shock before it went awry. It began to go wrong as the Jaeger were still falling through the air. It will be understood that it was vitally important for the pilot of the aircraft to drop his "stick" of men OVER the objective. Two seconds too soon and the Jaeger would have to march or, under the worst possible conditions, fight their way to reach the drop zone. Two seconds too late and they would overshoot the drop zone and would have to march or fight to return to it. In the case of 2nd Regiment, the pilots were told to look out for a rocky cape to the east of Retimo. Once identified it was the despatchers who took over command and gave the orders that would keep the aircraft at its correct height and speed and who told the pilot when to sound the klaxon which signalled the first man of the stick to jump. A few seconds would decide whether the group landed on target or whether they would be faced with a tiring march to the objective, probably under enemy fire. Success would be decided by a second or two.

On the night before Operation "Mercury" there was little sleep for anybody. The officers and senior NCOs had their "O" Groups to attend, while the rank and file had their own preparations to make. Then, when these were all finished the Paras sat round camp fires, singing in the way that soldiers throughout the ages have sung on the eve of a battle which they knew would cost them dear in casualties. To spend the last night in a farewell sing song was as good a way as any to build confidence for the coming day. And the Fallschirmjaeger would need all the confidence they could muster.

During the mid-morning of D-Day, the engine noise of approaching aircraft alerted the Jaeger of 2nd Regiment and they gathered round the airfield perimeter to watch the return of the transports which had carried the first wave. Most of the machines were the old tri-motor Junkers Ju 52s, corrugated metal, dark green in colour, slow but so reliable that they were known throughout the German Services as "Auntie Ju". They came flying in from the south, swooped low and touched down, taxi-ing slowly through the dust clouds which their landings had created, to refuel at the petrol bowsers. From the appearance of many of the planes it was clear that they had met severe opposition. Rips and tears in fuselages and wings told the story of the heavy anti-aircraft fire throught which they had flown. Noting those scars, the thought must have passed through the minds of many of the waiting paras. These aircraft had been the first over the target and the Tommies would not have been expecting them and would not have been ready to put up a strong AA defence. And yet the Ju's had suffered damage from anti-aircraft fire. Now we, the second wave, are about to go in and the Tommies will be waiting and will be prepared to meet us. But there was little time to dwell upon such morbid thoughts. Already whistles were blowing. It was time to dress and to prepare for the mission. A great deal of time had already been lost, most of it taken up with refuelling the aircraft. The Greek 'dromes lacked the mechanical pumping equipment which was standard on German airfields and the fuel had to be pumped by hand, a time-wasting operation on a mission where time was the most important factor. Refuelling took a couple of hours, time which the paras filled with cleaning and checking weapons, and then loading them in the containers.

One check followed another but then came the order: "An die Maschine" and in single file the Fallschirmjaeger stick marched to a Ju52 whose scars had been roughly patched up. A final check was made by the sergeant dispatcher and then came the order to board. Each man held in his mouth the metal clip of the static line so that his hands were free to pull himself into the aircraft. Inside the Ju one end of that static line would be clip-fastened to the jump wire shortly before the time came to jump. The other end of the static line fastened onto the flap of the para pack. When the Jaeger leapt from the aircraft the static line pulled open the flap, automatically releasing the parachute canopy. But that was yet to come. Ahead lay the two-hour flight to the objective

On the Greek airfields, in a long procession, one after the other, the Ju52s made their run up and took off, partially enshrouded in billowing clouds of fine sand blown up from the airfield's dusty surface and which all but obscured them from the onlookers around the perimeter. Airborne at last and flying low over the sea the aerial armada of nearly 200 aircraft took up formation and flew southwards. Ahead lay Crete. Inside the machines the men sat uncomfortably. According to Adi Strauch, who served with KG Schirmer, some men actually played cards during the flight, others read and some dozed. In the minds of all of them were the aerial photographs of the target areas around Retimo they had been shown. They all knew the objectives and they were all kitted up and ready. Each man had been handed an extra 120 rounds of small-arms ammunition in the aircraft and had somehow stowed that extra amount into pockets already bulging with supplies and ammunition. Each man ran over in his mind the design and markings on the red, white and yellow containers which the Ju carried. Ring markings identified the contents of each container. Some carried rifles, others the familiar MG34, the standard machine gun of the German forces, or else light mortars, while the remainder held ammunition and essential supplies. Food was not carried. Each man was expected to survive and fight on the hard tack with which he was issued before the mission.

It was vital that the colour and designs on the containers be familiar to all ranks. The first and most vital task on landing was to retrieve them, to open the containers and distribute the arms they contained. Until the containers were retrieved, opened and the weapons issued to the Jaeger, the paras were not able to fight. The height at which most drops were made was only 100m and the German chute, designed to open after the man had fallen 60m gave the Jaeger only five or six seconds in the air before he reached the ground. After touchdown he had to release himself from his chute, orientate himself and then make for the containers. Only then did he become an armed fighting man. The first excited cries "Crete ahead" woke the sleepers, broke up the card games and brought them all to full alert. The order was given to "link up" and each man hooked his clip onto the jump wire. The door of the Ju52 was opened and already the first man of the stick stood in the low doorway waiting for the signal. Rushing fast below the aircraft he could see the tawny coloured ground of Crete. The klaxon roared and one after the other the Jaeger jumped, each experiencing the breath-taking thwack as the canopy opened and each, looking down, saw the ground rushing up to meet him.

The Allied troops in and around Retimo were very well aware that a new airborne drop was on its way. Two hours before the paras were due to land, Luftwaffe bomber aircraft had attacked the area around the central and eastern drop zones. Those attacks were a very clear indication that an airborne drop, similar to that morning's drop around Maleme in the western part of Crete, would soon be made. Once the Stukas, the Heinkels and Ju88s had finished that first mission and flown away the British and Dominion troops began to prepare a reception for the Jaeger of the 1st and 2nd Regiments, whose aircraft were now closing in upon the island.

The drop by 2nd Regiment was a disaster. In order to achieve a smooth, quick departure and, thus, a compact grouping of their Para sticks, the aircraft on the run-in had to fly, throttled back to just above stalling speed at a precise height and maintaining a dead straight course, until the last man had left the plane. Against an unsuspecting enemy the element of surprise might possibly allow a smooth run-in and a fast drop, but at Retimo in the afternoon of 20 May, the Australians and New Zealanders were waiting. More than that they were aroused, angry and determined to wreak revenge on the German aircraft now flying in an undeviating line, only 100m above them. The heavy barrage of anti-aircraft fire which met the incoming Ju52s was unexpected because it was believed that the Stukas had wiped out the gun positions. That curtain of fire caused many pilots to take evasive action, an automatic reaction but one which caused the Jaeger sticks to be dispersed over a wide area instead of narrow one.

As an example, Major Schulz's HQ group of the machine gun battalion was very widely dispersed as were the other sticks of his Kampfgruppe. The men of the signals detachment of HQ 2nd Regiment were dropped 8km east of their designated landing zone. Colonel Sturm, who had jumped with the battle group somehow lost contact with the rest of his headquarters stick and was posted missing. He did not reach the regimental sector until the evening of D-Day plus 1, and when he came in he had with him 10 prisoners of war. No 3 Company HQ and its signals group were also wrongly placed but No 2 Company, which by contrast was correctly dropped over Retimo airfield, met such severe fire during the time the paras were in the air that all its officers were casualties. The remnants of Nos 1 and 4 Companies also overshot the airfield which was their objective, came under heavy fire and were pinned down, east of the drome.

The situation immediately after 2nd Regiment had made its drops was one of total confusion as the sticks which had been landed on the wrong zones criss-crossed the area trying to reach the correct ones. In such a situation it was not possible for the Kampfgruppen to fight their battles in their original composition but this narrative will relate their experiences as if they were the original battle groups. Major Kroh's group, made up chiefly of three of the four companies of 1st Battalion, was scattered but he acted quickly, collected together as many men as be could find and led them from the drop zone towards a vine-covered hill named in German post-battle reports as the "Weinberg". That hill was crowned by the three stubby chimneys of a small olive oil refinery, identified by the Germans as the "oil factory". Those chimneys on the low hill were a landmark and the Jaeger of 2nd Regiment had been given the oil factory as a rallying point. Not only was that the regimental concentration area but the Weinberg was the highest piece of ground in the area and dominated the airfield. Possession of that feature was essential for the development of 2nd Regiment's battle plan.

During its advance towards the Weinberg, Kroh's small group picked up detachments from his own battalion as well as Jaeger from No 12 Company (KG Wiedemann) who had been dropped incorrectly in his area and whose advance had been halted by heavy enemy fire. Kroh carried out a swift regrouping and led his men in an attack to capture the Weinberg. How well he succeeded can be seen from the fact that starting from a small foothold gained at 18.00hrs on the northern side of the hill, in less than 90mins the whole feature was in German hands. An attempt to carry the advance from the hill and towards the airfield had to be broken off at last light. Fallschirmjaeger who fought in the battle are convinced that had the Kampfgruppe been dropped correctly the airfield could have been taken and the German hold upon it consolidated well before dark. To compound the confusion in 2nd Regiment's area there was uncertainty about who was in command in the absence of Oberst Sturm. Major Schulz, the CO of the divisional machine gun battalion, took over and began to issue orders, many of which had either not been discussed or agreed with the battle group commanders and some of which were, indeed, contrary to the regiment's battle plan.

Kroh group, which had quickly identified the rallying point and had gone on to capture it, was counter-attacked by New Zealand troops. During the fighting the paras had one slight advantage. Among the weapons which had been air-landed was a 2cm Flak gun which was used to destroy an enemy dug out dominating the road around the airfield. Fresh but unsuccessful attacks by New Zealand units continued throughout the night but these had one positive result: Jaeger, cut off and isolated in the drops, marched towards the sound of German machine gun fire, worked their way through to Kroh group and reinforced it. With those few but welcome additions to his detachments' strength, the battle group commander decided that the time had now come to pass from the defensive back again to the offensive and to try and gain touch with the other battle groups.

The first moves of this began with a battle patrol which he sent out during the night of the 21st. This had as its aim to unsettle the enemy units lying all around. The battle patrol not only achieved that objective but also returned with 56 paras who had been captured during the first landings. This was a useful but qualified reinforcement to KG Kroh, for none of the released men was armed. What that increase in numbers did mean, however, was that those fresh men could release from the firing line the Jaeger who had now been fighting for over two days without rest. During 22 May, there were two developments. The first was the unsuccessful night attack by British troops supported by a couple of tanks. The two vehicles rolled through the darkness with the first one firing its machine guns into the Jaeger positions. The KG had neither anti-tank weapons nor explosive charges but a small group of men decided to take action on their own, raced up to the first vehicle, sprang onto its forward and rear decks and dropped a couple of hand grenades into the open turret. The tank stopped and the wounded crew members surrendered. The second machine swung on its tracks and vanished into the dark of the night. The next development was the appearance in front of the German lines just after sun-up of an Australian waving a white cloth on the end of a stick. That officer brought a request from the local Dominion commander for a temporary truce in order that the wounded of both sides who were lying out in No Man's Land could be brought in. Over 50 wounded men were carried into the German lines. Another 71 soldiers were handed over to the Australians because the battle group had no medical facilities to treat the seriously wounded. KG Kroh's proposal that their opponents surrender to them was turned down.

The battle raged to and fro for the next three days with an attack by one side being followed by a counter-attack by the other. Slowly KG Kroh began to gain small but important successes. First, another hill, then a village and finally a piece of ground to the east of the oil factory which the Jaeger cleared as a sort of makeshift airfield onto which Ju52s might land with supplies of food, water and ammunition. The battle group had no radio contact with any unit on Crete, so the ground-clearing detachment went out onto the nearby beach and laid out a message in stones. A piane flew over, waggled its wings in acknowledgement and three hours later a flight of Ju52s dropped the supplies which the battle group needed.

On the following day a single Ju52 flew over and released a message from corps HQ ordering the battle group to fight its way through to Heraklion and to gain touch with 1st Regiment. Kroh's men pulled out on the 26th, heading eastwards and leaving behind in the oil factory 17 Jaeger too badly wounded to be evacuated together with 11 Australians who had been taken prisoners of war. The battle group had scarcely begun its march when an aircraft dropped a fresh message. Corps now directed it to hold the oil factory — the factory from which it had just marched out. KG Kroh, now numbering only nine officers and 450 other ranks including the lightly wounded, regrouped and within two days was ready to try and recapture the high ground and the oil factory. As the weary Jaeger opened their attack, soldiers were seen in the distance on the plain and, as they came closer, they were seen to be German troops. Ringel's Gebirgsjaeger had broken through and linked up with the paras after 10 days of isolation and danger. Almost by reflex action as soon as the tension was broken the Jaeger realised just how tired they were and dropped to the ground where they stood to sleep for hours.

By contrast with the experience of Kroh's battle group, KG Wiedemann landed well. Nos 9 and 11 Companies opened an attack upon Retimo but halted this when opposition grew, mindful of the orders issued before the drop not to allow themselves to be drawn into house-to-house fighting. There were too few men and too little ammunition to fight such a battle. Although they had been dropped in the correct area there were several minor crises. Chief of these was the difficulty of locating the weapons containers in the thick undergrowth of the drop zone. The Dominion soldiers, each of whom was, according to German reports, a first class shot, not only kept the paras of KG Wiedemann from retrieving some of the containers but destroyed others on the ground with well aimed, small arms fire.

Another crisis was when Wiedemann's Jaeger, whose own attack had been halted at the outskirts of Retimo, were attacked by New Zealand infantry advancing under a heavy artillery barrage. Wiedemann, lacking any sort of reserve or counter attack group which he could commit to action, was forced to pull back his force into the tiny village of Perivolia where it took up all-round defence. The Dominion troops, sensing that they had gained the upper hand, mounted fresh attacks supported, according to German post-battle reports, by tanks although it is more likely that those machines were Bren carriers They were driven off by Jaeger fire.

During 21 May, the second day of Operation "Mercury", Luftwaffe aircraft flew bombing missions to support the hard-pressed paras although one raid had a fateful outcome when bombs from a Dornier Do17 fell on the Jaeger positions and caused casualties. Fighting continued, rising and falling in intensity over the following days. The battle report of KG Wiedemann recorded that a 3.7cm Pak gun which had been air-dropped, destroyed a British tank and then on 27 May, a further three tanks. That post-battle account also reported that during the fighting two officers were killed and that Wiedemann, the battle group commander, had been shot through the throat and badly wounded. Those losses left the group with only three officers still in action.

Throughout 29 May, the battle group which had now been isolated and cut off since the 20th, fought off a fresh wave of attacks by British and Dominion troops and were nearly at the end of their strength and endurance. But early in the morning of 30 May, came the promise of relief. Far away in the west could be heard the sounds of battle and, very reassuringly, the distinctive noise of German machine guns. It was the Gebirgsjaeger of Ringel's 5th Mountain Division fighting their way through. At this point mention should be made of the sufferings which all the paras had undergone — not just the men of KG Wiedemann, but those hardships which were endured by all the men of 7th Airborne Division which fought on Crete. Firstly, there was little water on the island and the soldiers who had access to it did not only have enough to drink but were able to keep themselves clean. Those who did not soon became verminous as German post-battle reports showed. German para rations included Perivitin tablets which were taken to ward off tiredness but those tablets had a terrible side effect — they produced acute thirst. The tablets to quench thirst and which also formed part of the rations were largely ineffective and there was no food to be had from civilian sources. One post-battle report records how a goat was caught, slaughtered, dressed and cooked in German Army ammunition boxes. The resultant stew, tasting strongly of rifle oil produced sufficient meat for a matchbox-sized piece for each man. As one Jaeger wrote, "I did not realise how small a goat was without its fur skin. It was really only about the size of a very large rabbit". One can well imagine the condition of the paras at the end of the nine days of isolation during which they had fought and endured. One can picture the haggard faces, the cheeks sunken with hunger, the eyes deep set in their sockets, glazed with exhaustion and strain. That exhaustion was so total in one group that it was the officers and NCOs who had to set up the machine guns on their tripods because the rank and file were sunk in apathy. Only when the officer/NCO gun teams fired the first belts to beat off a fresh British attack did the Jaeger react, rouse themselves from their tired stupor and come back into action. The course of the Second World War is rich with examples of airborne soldiers cut off and subsisting for days aware that they are surrounded, that food and ammunition are scarce and that relief which should have reached them quickly has not arrived.

The 2nd Battalion of 2nd Regiment formed KG Schirmer, but it did not serve with its parent regiment in the Crete operation but with Brauer's 1st Regiment, the eastern task force. That regiment's task was to capture the town of Heraklion and its airfield. During the time that Brauer's 3rd Battalion was engaged in fighting for the town, KG Schirmer was to cover its advance and to protect 1st Regiment's left flank. When the sticks of Brauer's regiment jumped the British and Dominion forces, like those in the Retimo sector, were ready and waiting. The drop was marred by a number of tragic incidents. The approach flight was not made from the northern — or sea — direction, but from the south — or inland — side. As the machines flew low over the island and came under anti-aircraft fire, pilots either took evasive action or increased speed. Thus, when the time came for the sticks to jump, although evacuation was swift not all the Jaeger left the planes while they were over land and some fell into the sea, where they were dragged down by their heavy equipment and drowned.

Schirmer group having landed then concentrated and, by the evening of D-Day, had managed to fight a foothold onto its drop zone and there gained touch with 3rd Battalion of 1st Regiment, on the western and southern sides of the town. The first attack of Brauer's regiment to capture Heraklion did not succeed. The 3rd Battalion fought its way from house to house and reached the centre of the town but was then driven back. Two days later, on the 22nd a second attack was made by a combined force using 3rd Battalion and KG Schirmer, but the assault met such fierce opposition that it was not even able to gain a foothold in the town.

When that attack opened the main body of KG Schirmer had moved forward and was making good progress when it came under sniper fire and was pinned down. The Jaeger tactic in such a situation was to thin their line and while a few men kept up a rapid fire the others moved to a flank position. Schirmer's men managed to work their way forward and reach a piece of high ground on which they formed a defensive line. In the afternoon of the 22nd that perimeter came under attack from a large group of infantry and from six AFVs. That first assault as well as the second which came in on the following day were both driven back with heavy loss to the enemy. The New Zealanders were seen to be forming up for a

55

new attack but, a few hours before that came in, a German aircraft which
flew over alerted a squadron of transports and bomber aircraft to the critical position facing Schirmer's Jaegers. A bomber attack preceded an air-
drop of supplies and there is little doubt that that air-raid inhibited the
Allied troops for not until the early morning of the 24th did a new attack
come in. This was mounted by two companies of 2nd Battalion The Black
Watch and although the Highlanders came in with great courage they
lacked the numbers to break into the German perimeter. Their attack collapsed. As the Highlanders pulled back under fire a wave of German aircraft swept low over the battlefield and dropped a battalion of Jaeger reinforcements who grouped quickly and pursued the Scots, capturing 31 of
them. KG Schirmer, now reinforced with the newly dropped men, was
ordered to take part in a fresh attack upon Heraklion. This was beaten
back by strong Allied machine gun and rifle fire and it was clear that any
attempt to capture the town from the west would fail. A new plan, a new
regrouping and a fresh attack being made from a different direction might
succeed. To carry out that regrouping required the troops on the western
side of Heraklion to undertake a long night march which had to be a silent
one in order not to alert the Dominion troops to the fact that that the German troops were disengaging and leaving the western sector.

The column set out led by the heavy machine gun platoon of No 18
Company commanded by Lieutenant Kirsten. Adi Strauch was one of
Kirsten's men who made that long, tiring march and related how the file
of men came under fire at about 04.30hrs on the morning of the 26th. Two
Companies of KG Schirmer opened an immediate attack and not only
drove the British from their positions on a hill marked Point 296, but also
took 28 prisoners. A New Zealand counter-attack was launched at
09.00hrs but the weary men of Schirmer's battle group, summoning up
their last reserves of energy, managed to beat off that assault. Strauch
recalled a wireless message from the British suggesting a temporary
ceasefire in order to bring in the wounded. His diary records: "The offer is
accepted and the badly wounded are handed over. Those Jaeger who can
still walk do not go over but stay with the unit."

During 28 May the British evacuated Heraklion and in the early
hours of the 29th German troops entered the town. KG Schirmer's task
was now completed and it received orders that its secondment to 1st
Jaeger Regiment was at an end and that it was to march westwards to gain
touch with the other groups of 2nd Regiment. The weary Jaeger began
their march but en route met the leading companies of Ringel's Gebirgsjaeger. With that link-up of the Fallschirmjaeger and Ringel's mountain
troops the campaign, so far as 2nd Regiment was concerned, was over.

Battle Groups of 3rd Panzer Division in the advance to Tula, Operation "Typhoon", the Offensive to capture Moscow, October–November 1941

On 22 June 1941 the armed forces of Nazi Germany invaded the Soviet Union and in the first months of a campaign codenamed "Barbarossa", scored a series of successes, gaining not only a vast area of territory but also capturing or killing millions of Red Army soldiers.

As early as 3 July, Halder, Chief of the General Staff of the Army, wrote in his diary "...It would be no exaggeration to say that the war has been won in less than fourteen days". It was a terrible miscalculation. The war which that senior commander had considered won was to endure for nearly four more years and was to end in a Russian victory and a German defeat.

On 26 August, despite the resounding successes which the German Army had already achieved, despite those which were to be gained in coming battles and only a scant few weeks removed from Halder's confident prediction of a Russian defeat, OKW accepted that the war against the Soviet Union could not be brought to a successful conclusion in the year 1941. One reason for that failure had been Hitler's initial decision not to make the capture of Moscow the primary objective of the campaign. Late in August, soon after he realised the enormity of his strategic blunder, he issued orders for an immediate offensive, codenamed "Typhoon", to retrieve the situation and to capture the Russian capital. Army Group Centre, commanded by Fedor von Bock, was nominated to execute the operation.

Von Bock's plan was for a massive blow to be made on either side of the Smolensk-Moscow highway. This would tear a gap in the Russian front through which two Panzer groups, or armies, would flood and create a pair of pincer jaws. These would thrust deep into the Red Army's rear areas and would then begin to close at Vyasma, some 150km to the northeast of Smolensk. Within that ring of steel the encircled Russian hosts would be destroyed. The German planners then considered that with that first part of the ambitious Operation "Typhoon" successfully completed the Red forces defending Moscow would be either dead or captive and the way to the Russian capital would be open.

The Eastern Front was one where superlatives were not the exception but the norm. To begin with there was the vast battle line which extended from way above the Arctic Circle down to the Black Sea. Across that huge length of front masses of men and machines advanced or retreated in the mightiest military operation of all time. As an example of distances involved in the first stages of "Typhoon", when the two pincer arms of Army Group South were widest apart, there would be a gap of 250km between them; then, too, the distance from the start line of "Typhoon" to the objective, Moscow, was over 320km. That the operation was an enterprise which stood on brittle glass could not be denied. The period of campaigning weather was coming to an end. Soon the autumn rains would begin and it needed no staff-trained mind to know that heavy rain falling upon soil produces mud. There were very few all-weather highways in Russia so that the great mass of vehicles which would be employed in "Typhoon" would have to drive along so-called second- and third-class roads which were often little more than rural tracks. When the rains came the tanks and lorries of the German vehicle columns would turn those second- and third-class roads into mud slicks which would hold the lorries fast, resulting in immobility at a time when speed was the most essential factor in the battle plan. The German Army was soon to become depressingly familiar with a phenomenon hitherto unknown — the Rasputitsa, a type of mud so deep and clinging that even tracked vehicles were frequently trapped in it.

And then, behind the autumn rains and the resultant mud, loomed winter, the bitter cold Russian winter for which the Wehrmacht was totally unprepared. Hitler must have been aware of the risks he was taking in ordering Operation "Typhoon" to begin so late in the year, but the words of his Order of the Day were confident enough and declared that this was "...the opening of the final decisive battle of the War...".

Army Group Centre, the force which was to carry out "Typhoon", although already quite powerful was massively reinforced for the operation with formations taken from Army Groups North and South. When all the moves connected with those secondments had been completed, von Bock's Army Group contained the 2nd, 4th and 9th Infantry armies as well as the 2nd, 3rd and 4th Panzer Groups. The whole made up a host of 70 divisions, 14 of which were Panzer and eight of which were motorised.

On the right wing of Army Group Centre was Guderian's Panzer Group 2, which had the task of protecting Army Group's right wing and, in particular, the flanks of 4th Army and 4th Panzer Army as those formations made the main thrust towards Moscow. The establishment of 2nd Panzer Group included 24th Motorised (later Panzer) Corps, made up of 3rd and 4th Panzer and 10th Infantry Divisions. It is with the Kampfgruppen of General Walther Model's 3rd Panzer Division and those of 24th Corps, from the start of Operation "Typhoon" to 13 November 1941, that the following account will deal.

Throughout the brief period during which the units of Army Group Centre were being reshuffled, reinforcements of men and equipment came in. In the case of 3rd Panzer Division sufficient AFVs were received to bring its 6th Panzer Regiment up to a full establishment of three battalions and to outfit them with updated versions of the Panzer III and IV. Under the leadership of General Model the 3rd Panzer Division had gained, very early in the campaign against the Soviet Union, a reputation for combat efficiency, the product of the aggressive driving force and tactical brilliance of its Commanding General. Model was not only a charismatic leader but one whose degree of self confidence was matched by his pragmatic approach to battlefield problems. He created a great many battle groups — forming almost by instinct the right combination of arms to achieve a certain objective. He had demonstrated this ability in the great encirclement battle of Kiev and was to further exhibit it during that preliminary stage of Operation "Typhoon" — the advance to Tula. Model was a soldiers' soldier and had so impressed the power of his personality upon his men that they were confident of a swift and overwhelming victory in the now imminent offensive.

Army Group set D-Day for "Typhoon" as 2 October. Aware that some parts of 2nd Panzer Group, in particular 3rd Panzer Division, were still engaged in combat and had great distances to cover to reach the new battlefield, it ordered that those units were to move towards the "Typhoon" start line two days earlier than the mass of Army Group — that is to say, on Sunday 30 September. Another reason for advancing 24th Corps' D-Day was to secure for it full Luftwaffe dive-bomber support. The 24th Corps was to form the main point of 2nd Panzer Group's effort. Guderian's plan was for 24th and 47th Corps to smash through the front of Russian 13th Army, to advance deep through that formation's rear areas and then for his whole Panzer Group to wheel and take the town of Briansk and the industrial complex surrounding it. The drive by 24th and 47th Corps would then be taken up by 48th Motorised Corps which, together with the 34th and 35th Infantry Corps, would flood through the gap which had been created.

Before the new offensive opened, Guderian appreciated that terrain difficulties would affect the flow of supplies to his spearhead Corps and ordered that every one of its vehicles was to carry an additional three and-a-half issues of fuel. As an emergency measure this was an excellent precaution but the long-term problem remained of what would happen when as a consequence of poor road conditions, insufficient supplies of fuel came forward to the Panzer regiments. The matter of maintaining supplies was, however, not just a shortage of adequate roads. Army Group had noted, with concern, an increase in partisan activity in its area and a steep rise in attacks against supply columns. A shortage of proper roads and guerilla attacks were only two factors which were likely to slow the Panzers' onward rush. A third condition, soon to be met with, was the climatic, which more than the other two was to starve the Panzer divisions of fuel and supplies.

The objectives of 24th Corps were, first, to cut the Orel-Briansk road and to go on to capture Tula to the south of Moscow. For the opening of the assault General Metz, the Corps commander, put his 3rd and 4th Panzer Divisions in the first line and placed his 10th Infantry Division in the second. Corps opened its offensive at 05.30hrs on 30 September, and under an artillery barrage, the two Rifles regiments of 3rd Panzer Division went over the top. Under the weight of a double blow by 3rd and 4th Panzer Divisions, the left wing of Russian 13th Army crumbled and the units which composed it retreated in disorder. Corps had gained an initial victory despite terrible difficulties. During the night on which the offensive opened a downpour of torrential rain had turned the ground in corps' concentration area into a swamp. The only way of creating a firm surface was to lay corduroy roads and soon every available pioneer unit and Reichs Arbeits Dienst (RAD) detachment was working on this urgent task. Across tree-trunk roads covering the worst patches of ground the advance to battle stage of the operation opened and was maintained although the pace of that advance was frustratingly slow.

Even before Metz's Corps reached its start line and opened the offensive Model, whose 3rd Panzer Division was positioned on the right flank, to the south and south-west of Glukov, created the first Kampfgruppe of the new operation. Colonel von Manteuffel's battle group was a combined infantry-artillery force given the dual task of acting as link between 3rd Panzer and its left flank neighbour 28th Corps, and also of clearing the enemy from the divisional advanced concentration area located between the form-up line and the start lines of the opening attack. Manteuffel's infantry group set out to capture the village of Savarkov which dominated the concentration area but in order to capture that objective the leading companies had to advance uphill and across completely open ground. To hold down the enemy during that stage of the infantry advance the whole area was smothered by an artillery barrage. The operation began to roll and showed signs of success. At a given point vehicles bringing up two lorry-borne companies passed through the companies attacking on foot, drove through the Soviet defensive fire and up to the Russian trenches outside the village. Even before the APCs had halted, riflemen from the battalions had leaped out and in a series of short rushes had advanced, bombing and machine-gunning their way across the enemy trenches and into the streets of Savarkov. Behind them, coming in at a jog trot the companies which had made the attack on foot moved forward to reinforce the battle line.

Russian resistance hardened as the rifles companies fought their way through the narrow, rutted streets of Savarkov. Some houses the Red Army soldiers had found the time to fortify and these houses had to be fought for room by room. Eventually, 1st Battalion's point company had fought its way into the village square. It had been planned that from that point the riflemen would go into the pursuit stage of the attack. The personnel carriers were ordered forward, drew up in the square and parked almost nose to tail. A cry of alarm was raised. Rushing towards the vehicles from a group of houses only 40 to 50m away was a pack of dogs. They were not the usual timid, village mongrels which would attach themselves to any friendly soldier, but instead were clearly a trained and determined group which was heading for the personnel carriers. Each of the racing beasts was seen to be wearing a sort of thick body belt and projecting upright from that corset was a long, thick stick. The significance of stick and corset could not be guessed at but the riflemen had learned that against the Russians it was best to take no chances. Machine gun and automatic pistol fire cut down the racing animals and when their corpses were examined it was found that each belly band contained a 2kg explosive charge and that the upright stick was a detonator. The dogs were live mines which Soviet dog handlers had trained by throwing meat under the bellies of armoured vehicles so that the animals associated armoured machines with food. It was later learned that before a mission the dogs were starved for days and then brought into the front line where the explosive corset and detonator were fitted. Once released they raced towards the German AFVs expecting to find food. As they wriggled underneath the Panzers the stick would foul part of the vehicle's chassis and break off, activating an instantaneous fuse which would then set off the explosive charge. As a tactic "exploding dogs" had a brief life. The animals could not differentiate between German and Russian vehicles and when Red Army tanks were blown up STAVKA ordered that "exploding dogs" no longer be used. In Savarkov German pressure coupled with the failure of the mine-carrying beasts brought about a Russian retreat from the village but the death-bringing hounds were not the only unpleasant surprise to be met with that day. The infantry group mounted in their APCs were driving from the village square to its eastern exit when the vehicles were smothered by a Russian artillery barrage — a bombardment which contained unusual elements. In addition to the standard whistling sound of incoming fire there was an eerie howling noise and among the crash of bursting shells it was noted that some other sort of projectiles were falling in groups and exploding in set patterns of detonation. Manteuffel's battle group was meeting, for the first time, Katyusha or the "Stalin Organ", the multi-barrelled rocket projector. At midday and quite abruptly the Russian barrage stopped and the infantry battalion which had been halted by its fury was preparing to resume its advance when orders were received for one of its companies to stand fast and to consolidate its grip on the village and for its other companies to withdraw to their start lines.

The other components of 3rd Division, and particularly the armoured regiment had experienced a difficult day. Not only had they had to struggle through mud but their advance had been halted by blown bridges and on one of the rifle battalion's sectors extensive fields of wooden mines were found. These small, green painted wooden boxes could not be located by conventional detectors. It was necessary for the Pioneers to prod the ground with their bayonets, knowing that any careless move would trigger off an explosion which could rip off a hand or a foot. Despite those obstructions 3rd Panzer's battle groups reached the village of Chinel, its first day's objective. At first light on 1 October, the second day of the offensive, the advance continued against growing resistance which increased from rock hard to fanatical with frequent, heavy Soviet counter-attacks. Kampfgruppe Kleemann, which formed the Panzer core of Model's division, came under such persistent attack that it had to radio for help and Model reinforced it with Manteuffel's group. Although the Red Army was now fighting with terrible desperation its strongest efforts could not prevent the combined Manteuffel/Kleeman groups from reaching the second day's given objectives. Then, quite suddenly, the enemy's resistance broke and it became clear that the furious opposition of the past days had been put up by Russian rearguards which had sacrificed themselves to cover the retreat of 13th Army. The Commander of 24th Corps, responding to Model's message that although enemy resistance was diminishing the ground conditions on his front made a further advance almost impossible, ordered 3rd Division to move into 4th's area where the going was better and then further directed that Model was to lead a vigorous pursuit of the enemy forces in the direction of Ssversk. The 2 October was a day of hot sunshine which dried the top crust of the ground enabling good advances to be made and on that day the main body of Army Group Centre opened its offensive as OKH war diary noted "...in beautiful Autumn weather". Among the substantial gains recorded in the High Command war diary was that 24th Corps had not only penetrated 130km into the Soviet lines but had torn Russian 13th Army apart, forcing 183rd Infantry Division, the 21st and 55th Cavalry Brigades and two tank brigades to retreat northwards.

On 3 October Model formed KG von Lewinski, an all-arms combination of infantry, armour, artillery and engineers and directed this to form the divisional spearhead. At first light KG Lewinski was under way and by 16.00hrs had reached the small town of Kamarisha-Lobatovo where it laagered for the night. During the hours of darkness one of its Panzer patrols on a roving mission, met and destroyed a Cossack cavalry unit. During 4 October, Division advanced on a broad front headed by battle groups Manteuffel, Lewinski and Kleemann, each of them struggling through thick mud or across long stretches of sandy soil in which vehicles sank above their axles. Lessening enemy resistance allowed Model to move his Division at a pace whose speed was regulated only by ground conditions. Close to Dmitrovsk the columns halted to take on fuel and ammunition and in those few hours of rest the front line soldiers realised how exhausted they were. Although the strain of combat in the terrible weather and ground conditions were exhausting for the fighting troops, the divisional history acknowledged that its soldiers in the supply services had had no less tiring a task. The fuel and ammunition columns of 6th Panzer Regiment, for example, took six hours to cross a 7km-wide strip of land, with the drivers and the crews stopping frequently to dig their bogged down lorries out of the clinging mud.

On 6 October, OKH recorded that Briansk fell but the High Command war diary also recorded the return of heavy rain to the battle area and increased Soviet resistance. The Russian news agency, Tass, reported on that day that snow had fallen on the battlefield. It was the shape of things to come. The 3rd Panzer divisional history described 6 October as "an eventful one for the German Army on the Eastern Front". From early in the morning of that day low-flying clouds driven before a strong west wind brought icy rain and snow flurries. The German Army had already experienced heavy rain during Operation "Typhoon" but that which fell during 6 October had the nature of a monsoon. It marked the end of the summer period of dry weather. The time of the autumn downpours producing even deeper mud was there — and behind the rain would come the snow storms and the ice of winter. It was already clear from the chaos produced by those first snow and rainfalls that the German vehicles — and particularly the wheeled units — would encounter such difficult ground conditions that they might find it impossible to reach an objective which had been set them. With the capture of Briansk, Corps had not only closed part of the eastern side of the ring around the Russian forces but more importantly had reached its first given objective, the Orel-Briansk road. The next stage of the operation was the advance upon Tula. But in order to gain the springboard positions and to carry out that part of the offensive, Metz's Corps would first have to fight its way across the River Susha.

The first part of "Typhoon" had already produced the shocks of explosive dogs and the Stalin Organ. On 6 October, 3rd Panzer Division encountered yet another and this meeting produced almost a sense of total despair when its Panzer regiments met for the first time the Russian T34 tank which made its debut appearance. That AFV was superior in every way to the standard machines in German service and was one which the German tank guns could not destroy except in close-range, tank-to-tank battles. To compound the misery, the weather, already bad grew worse and war diaries for the 7th all mention a hurricane-like snow storm which covered the ground to a significant depth. Behind the blizzard came a warm wind bringing a thaw which deepened the mud. The situation for the wheeled vehicles deteriorated to the extent that a heavy tank had to winch each individual truck out of the clinging slime in which it was trapped.

On one stretch of the road between Dmitrovsk and Kromy, more than 2,000 of 3rd Panzer Division's wheeled trucks lay immobile. As a great many of those stranded lorries were divisional supply columns, it needs no words of the author's to describe the misery of the fighting men who huddled in muddy slit trenches, soaked through, cold and hungry, waiting for food which would not reach them because it was carried in trucks which were stuck fast in the Rasputitsa. For the armoured regiments the situation was even more serious as the petrol-bowsers could not reach the Panzers and their fuel tanks had again run dry.

Despite those difficulties the advance still inched its way forward until the jaws of the great encirclement finally closed at Vyasma on 7 October, and with that meeting 2nd Panzer Army had sealed fast the pocket. Weather and terrain conditions notwithstanding, the forces of von Bock's Army Group Centre had gained their first main objective and the opening part of Operation "Typhoon" had been successfully concluded. The OKW communique issued during 8 October, reported that Army Group Centre's operations had resulted in massive battles of destruction. In the Vyasma area alone a number of Russian armies had been surrounded while the communique of the 9th reported that on the Briansk sector three Red Armies were cut off. According to German reports Marshal Timonshenko had sacrificed his last remaining active armies. The logical deduction from that claim was that the advance towards Moscow, the second part of "Typhoon", could expect to meet little opposition.

Seen from Command level the situation was thus very satisfactory. At troop level it was less so. Each division in the field needed a daily total of 900 tons of supplies to sustain it. The effects of bad weather and terrible ground conditions had reduced the amounts actually reaching the front line to 20 tons per division. Such a state of affairs could not long continue otherwise 2nd Panzer Army would starve to death on the steppes, trapped in the Rasputitsa without having reached the final objective, Moscow, only 100km distant. On 10 October, 3rd Panzer Division made its own

Above: One of the most frequent complaints about conditions in Poland was the state of the roads. The dust track seen here was classed as a major road.

Below: The advance to Warsaw by Reinhardt's 4th Panzer Division was halted by Polish attacks coming from both East and West. The "Leibstandarte" Regiment was rushed up to support Reinhardt's western flank, and here men of its motor cycle platoon are seen in street fighting in Sorcharzow. The battle was so intense that the town changed hands three times before finally falling.

Above: On 21 September 1939 the Polish city of Lemberg, which 1st Gerbirgs Division had failed to capture, offered to surrender. The German plenipotentiary, Major Schlank, is here seen in negotiations with the Polish emissaries. The Poles insisted on surrendering only to the 1st Gebirgs Division.

Left: Colonel-General Heinz Guderian was one of the pre-war architects of the German Panzer force. During the war he produced numerous victories and led Panzer Group 2 in the early stages of the Russian campaign before becoming Inspector-General of Panzer Troops in 1943. He was chief of the General Staff of the Army in 1944 before Hitler retired him.

Top right: Units of a Panzer Division advancing through France during the campaign in the West in May 1940.

Right: The famous 88mm gun, probably from 7th Panzer Division's artillery component, seen in action near Arras in May 1940.

Above: A Panzer II of Rommel's 7th Division on the Channel coast.

Right: Erwin Rommel, commanding 7th Panzer Division and Herman Hoth, commanding 13th Panzer Corps, seen in France during the Blitzkrieg there in May-June 1940.

Reichssicherheitshauptamt   Berlin, den 26.8.40.
Amt II B.Nr. *1670* /40.

𝕬𝖒𝖙 II	Nr.:*1670/40*
2 6. 8. 40.	*D*

An
I c (b) 4
ℋ-Sturmbannführer Braune
im H a u s e

Betr.: England-Einsatz.

                    ℋ-Standartenführer Dr. Six ist von C mit der
Aufstellung eines England-Sonderkommandos für das Amt II
beauftragt worden. Um ein reibungsloses Arbeiten dieses
Kommandos zu gewährleisten, ist es erforderlich, eine An-
zahl vom Amt II abgestellter Führer und Unterführer zurück-
zurufen.
                    Mit sofortiger Wirkung wären zurückzukommandieren:

            ℋ-H'Stuf. Burmester, Metz
            ℋ-O'Scharf. Gürtler, Paris
            ℋ-O'Scharf. Tieke, Paris
            ℋ-O'Scharf. Rudolf, Brüssel
            ℋ-O'Scharf. Flemming, Brüssel.

Mit Wirkung vom 1.9.40 wären zurückzukommandieren:

            ℋ-H'Stuf. Dittel, Paris
            ℋ-O'Stuf. Mehringer, Paris
            ℋ-O'Stuf. Reissmann, Paris

                    Von der Verbindungsstelle Leipzig wären mit so-
fortiger Wirkung bis auf weiteres ins Hauptamt zu komman-
dieren:
            ℋ-O'Stuf. Nitzsche
            ℋ-U'Stuf. Focke.

These documents show that SS General Heydrich insisted upon being known by the single letter "C", thus imitating the head of British MI5. The second document gives instructions for
the Secret Field Police to take up quarters in the Strand Palace Hotel and the Dorchester in
London.

Betr.: Besprechung C.

1.) Kommandoeinteilung- und Stärke:

   3oo Mann insgesamt und 5o Fahrer
   2o Mann Vorkommando London

   Kommando 2 - Bristol
   Kommando 3 - Birmingham
   Kommando 4 - Liverpool
   Kommando 5 - Manchester

   Aufteilung der Grafschaften
   Offenstehende Kommando: Schottland und Nord-Irland.

2.) Kleine Aussenstellen:

   Maximalstärke: 15 Mann
   Fliegende Kommandos von London aus.

3.) Dienstbezeichnung:

   Befehlshaber der Sicherheitspolizei und des SD
   für Gross-Britannien, oder

   Der Beauftragte des Chefs der Sicherheitspolizei und
   des SD für Gross-Britannien.

4.) Wehrmilitärbefehlshaber:
   Kommt Chef der Zivilverwaltung, rückt GFP mit ein
   Wohnort: Hotel Strand, London WC 2
            Hotel Dorchester, Park Lane.
   Arbeitsräume: 2 Clubs.

   London zentral keine Privatkäufe.

Above: SS General Heydrich, the Chief of the SS Security Service, and the officer in charge of the planned invasion of Great Britain - Operation "Sealion". When he learned that the Head of MI5 was known only by a single initial, he insisted that he, too, should be similarly identified.

Right and below: British troops killed in action to the west of Heraklion during the battle for Crete, after an unsuccessful attack upon battle group Schirmer.

Left: Soldiers of battle group Schirmer in Crete. These men are part of Strauch's company moving up after the capture of Heraklion.

Bottom left: Members of battle group Schirmer advance prior to a new attack during the fighting for Crete.

Below: Hauptmann Schirmer (wearing a white peaked cap) and men of his Fallschirmjaeger battle group after the fall of Heraklion, 29 May 1941.

Above: The first elements of the Afrika Korps parading in Libya in February 1941.

Top right: General Rommel enjoying an *al fresco* meal during the 1942 offensives in the Libyan desert.

Right: Rommel and his senior commanders planning operations in the summer of 1942.

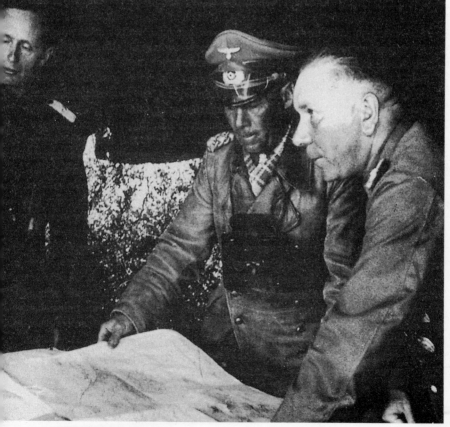

Above: General Walther Nehring who commanded the Afrika Korps during the May 1942 offensive, and who was nearly run down and killed by vehicles of a Panzer division retreating from the battlefield.

Right: Major Georg Briel, leader of a battle group whose task it was to break through the British positions at El Alamein and capture Alexandria, summer 1942.

Above: General Field Marshal Walther Model who commanded 3rd Panzer Division in the advance towards Moscow - Operation "Typhoon". He later rose to become Supreme Commander West and commanded Army Group B in North West Europe in 1944. He committed suicide on 17 April 1945 rather than surrender.

effort to keep the advance rolling by creating a special column group to supply the leading troops with fuel, ammunition and food. War diaries do not mention the composition of that column but in view of the ground conditions it must have been made up of tracked and not wheeled vehicles. Another method of supplying the forward troops was by air-drop. This was not a method which was widely practised by the Luftwaffe whose machines were not designed for such a purpose and each of which could, in any case, carry only two tons of supplies. The Ju52s also burned a great amount of aviation fuel in their flight from distant airfields to the front line. Logistically the flight in and out was hardly worth the effort to carry just two tons of supplies, but those flights were seen as essential to maintain troop morale.

OKW may have believed that Timoshenko had lost all his fighting troops, but that was not the experience of the men in the front line. On 13 October, 29th Infantry Division were so severely attacked by 3rd Red Army that it asked for help. Model created KG Schmidt-Ott, a company of Panzer, one of riflemen, a battery of artillery and a detachment of anti-tank guns. The KG moved out that night and struggled through deep mud only to find when it reached the crisis area that it was no longer required as the 29th Division had mastered the situation. Then came a cry for help from the sister division, 4th Panzer, which had been held at the approaches to Mzensk. Once again the 3rd responded and sent a new battle group.

On 14 October, OKH issued detailed orders for Army Group Centre to capture Moscow. Guderian's Panzer Army was directed to cut off the Russian capital from the south, south-east and east and the Commanding General selected 24th Corps to act as the spearhead which was to carve its way through the Soviet defence and reach Tula, which was to be its final objective.

The start line for the second part of "Typhoon" was the River Susha and Corps intended to have both Panzer divisions "up". On the 14th, too, 3rd Division was strengthened by the infantry regiment "Grossdeutschland". The following days were taken up with conferences and reconnaissances preparing for the offensive. Shortly before the second part of "Typhoon" opened, OKW communiques announced the results of the fighting in the Briansk and Vyasma pockets. Those operations, the communiques claimed, had followed their planned course and had fragmented the enemy units. The number of prisoners taken was first claimed to be 350,000 but by 15 October, that figure had risen to half-a-million. The soldiers of Army Group Centre could be well pleased with the successes that they had helped to achieve and in that confident spirit looked forward to the opening of the new offensive that would carry them out of the cold, wet steppes of western Russia and into the warm houses of Moscow.

Corps' plan for the next stage of the operation was for its divisions to capture the strongly defended town of Mzensk. The 4th Panzer had already carried out a series of attacks but had been unable to take the town. The 3rd now moved forward to line up with its sister division on the banks of the Susha. Corps would then have to seize Mzensk and cross that 40m-wide river before undertaking the advance to Tula. Metz divided his force into two main Kampfgruppen and the following account will deal first of all with those battle groups created by 3rd Panzer, and then go on to detail the actions of Kampfgruppe Eberbach — a colonel who had been seconded from 4th Panzer to lead Corps' specially created battle group North. For the forthcoming operation Model disbanded the existing battle groups of his division and created two new ones designed to carry out the assault crossing of the Susha. The right flank one, an infantry battle group made up out of the rifle regiments, was to advance from Glasunova, while the left flank one, consisting of two Panzer regiments, was to strike out and at a given point was to wheel towards the main highway where the enemy artillery was thought to be concentrated. It would destroy those regiments and thereby not only cover the infantry's open flank but bring its advance forward. Several important changes occurred just before the offensive opened. Model, the General Commanding 3rd Panzer was promoted and handed over the leadership of the division to Major-General Breith. Model had, however, worked out the plan of the stages of the campaign up to Tula and entrusted the execution of this to Breith. Another important change was the return of Colonel Lewinski to Germany on health grounds.

The first objective of 3rd Division's lefthand Panzer KG lay only 25km from the start line — that is 25km as the crow flies, but a far greater distance in terms of Panzer operations. Because the terrible ground conditions might run the fuel tanks of the AFVs dry before the Panzers reached the day's objective, Model ordered that each armoured battalion was to be accompanied by a tracked vehicle carrying 1,500 litres of fuel in jerricans. Another tracked vehicle towing several low-loaders and portering 6,000 litres of fuel was to march with each Panzer regiment. By the evening of 22 October, 3rd Panzer Division, positioned on Corps' lefthand side, reached its concentration area. At this point we must take temporary leave of 3rd Panzer Division and move back to the first days of October and to 4th Panzer Division. The reason for this is to introduce Colonel Heinrich Eberbach of that division who was to lead a strong battle group in the advance to Tula. The Kampfgruppe he commanded in the opening stages of that operation was a Corps' creation and was the battle group North. In order for him to undertake this operation in which the greatest number of units would be provided by 3rd Panzer Division, he had to be seconded from 4th Panzer Division and posted to Model's formation.

Eberbach had already achieved a splendid reputation. His brigade in 4th Division had captured Ssversk and had taken Dimitrovsk at a run before being directed to seize Orel, the cornerstone of 13th Red Army's defensive system. During the night of 3-4 October, Eberbach's brigade seized the town in a swift advance and with it vast amounts of war material. The next objective was Mzensk and as we have learned that heavily defended town lay on the River Susha. The advance of Eberbach's brigade towards Mzensk was intercepted by a Russian armoured formation superior in numbers and equipped with the new T34s and heavy KVI tanks. The German Panzermen suffered from four disadvantages: they were outnumbered, their enemy had better vehicles, the Russian armour was thicker and the Soviet tank guns had greater penetrating power. The German main armament was a gun of such low velocity that the Panzermen had to fight their heavily armoured opponents at very close quarters instead of picking them off at long range as they had been taught. Thanks to superior German battle training, greater front line experience and more sophisticated tactics, the Soviet tanks attempting to halt the advance of Eberbach's brigade were driven from the field. Brigade laagered and on the morning of 10 October, a day of thick fog, wet snow and deep mud, Eberbach led his group upon the final bound that would take it into the town of Mzensk. Ground conditions halted one Panzer after another and to such effect that only one vehicle of the entire point unit actually reached the river bridge at Mzensk. That single Panzer thundered forward and in a quick but furious fire-fight destroyed four Russian tanks guarding the western approach to the bridge, smashed its way into and crushed a Soviet Pak front then stormed across the River Susha followed by German infantry carried in troop transporters. That infantry group met and fought down strong enemy resistance so quickly that by nightfall Eberbach could report the capture of the town of Mzensk.

Panzer Group's next objective was Chern on the Tula road and to strengthen his brigade for the capture of the town Eberbach was given both 6th Panzer Regiment and a battalion of 18th Panzer Regiment. With that reinforced armoured group he struck and destroyed a Russian tank brigade north of Mzensk, leaving more than 30 Soviet tanks burning and the Soviet commander dead on the battlefield — an officer who shot himself when the depth of the disaster became apparent. Chern fell to Eberbach's Panzer and infantry Kampfgruppe on 25 October. The way to Tula, it seemed, was open.

The commander of 24th Corps, determined to give his formation a strong spearhead to carry out its task and added to Eberbach's reinforced battle group, which numbered over 220 AFVs, the 3rd Rifle Regiment, a battalion of 394th Rifle Regiment, the whole of "Grossdeutschland" Infantry Regiment, four battalions of artillery, a pioneer battalion and Flak detachments. KG Eberbach then received from Guderian, commander of 2nd Panzer Army, the brief signal: "Conduct an all-out advance and capture Tula", and in the night of 27-28 October the battle group commander set out, accompanied for part of the journey towards the new objective, by the Army commander.

To return to 3rd Panzer Division, by the evening of 22 October it had reached the River Susha and assault squads from 3rd Rifle Regiment went into action even before next morning's H Hour. It had soon established a small bridgehead and had dug in on the eastern bank to protect the crossing points from which the pioneers had begun to ferry across other companies of 3rd Battalion. At H Hour, 06.00hrs on the morning of 23 October, the artillery group comprising field guns, Nebelwerfer and the close-support infantry guns opened fire upon Russian villages and suspected artillery positions. Under that barrage both 1st and 2nd Battalions of the rifles crossed the river, entered the 3rd Battalion bridgehead, regrouped and then burst out of the constricting perimeter to advance towards their objectives. The companies of 1st Battalion soon broke into the Russian defensive positions around the village of Bobenkovo and, within 45mins of the opening of the Susha river battle, had reached and had cut the main road south of Nikolskaya. The 2nd Battalion closed up to that town fighting its way through a blanket of Soviet shellfire. A divisional order then halted the advance of both battalions since, according to Model's battle plan, they had reached the point at which the AFVs were to gain touch. Hours passed with the two battalions enduring the fury of the Russian guns while they waited for the Panzers to arrive.

There were two reasons for that delay by the armour. Not only deep mud which held the vehicles fast in its grip, but also a tenacious Russian defence had combined to slow the German advance. All along the River Susha a continuous stream of German infantry detachments was now being ferried to the east bank and at certain places pioneer companies had begun to construct bridges. The river had, as we have learned, only one permanent bridge, that at Mzensk, which lay in 4th Panzer Division's area. For the heavy armoured vehicles of the 3rd to cross the river it would be necessary for the pioneers to construct bridges in the divisional area. It was already clear from the hail of shellfire falling around the bridging sites that the Red Army artillery was determined to halt construction and to smash any bridges that were completed. This, Model could not allow to happen. The future of the second stage of Operation "Typhoon" by his 3rd Panzer, would depend upon the courage of the pioneers in constructing bridges, upon the flow of the armour across those bridges and, finally, upon the speed of the Panzer Kampfgruppen to advance upon Tula. Heavy and accurate Russian shelling had its effect upon the progress of the work so that it was not until 09.30hrs on the morning of the 23rd, four hours after it should have been completed, that the first 18m-long bridge was ready. Even so, it was not a solid construction. Only parts of it had a firm, wooden roadway. The other sections rested on pontoons. But solid or not, the vehicles of 6th Panzer Regiment were ordered to cross the shaky, unfirm construction and these were closely followed by empty infantry personnel carriers. But the problem of bringing the vehicles from the west to the east bank did not end with the completion of the bridge. The press of vehicles moving towards the bridge churned the river banks on both sides of the Susha into deep mud and the eastern bank, particularly, had been turned into a cliff of liquid mud. It required great skill on the part of the vehicle drivers to bring their lorries from the swaying, bridge roadway up the slippery eastern bank and up to the top of that bank.

Inside the bridgehead, Eberbach's KG North was reinforced and was then ordered to move out and to link up with the southern, infantry battle group. During that move 6th Panzer Regiment came under such a storm of shellfire that it was forced to change its thrust line and to find an alternative route to its objective. The Panzers did not in fact gain touch with the rifles until early afternoon but once regrouped the combined infantry/armoured Corps' North and South Kampfgruppen, began to drive south-eastwards towards Tula. The advance was brief and the point battalion was halted by a heavy barrage, resulting in yet another change of direction. The vehicles of that Panzer battalion flowed over a low ridge disposed in battle formation, cut the Mzensk-Belev road and on that road came under attack from a group of T34s which involved it in a wasteful battle. The Panzer battalion mastered the enemy, forced him to retreat and then took off in pursuit of the remaining Red tanks until last light. It then laagered in the area of Shalyamova and was reinforced there as additional Panzer battalions arrived. Eberbach ordered that the advance was to resume at dawn on the following morning.

On their sectors the infantry had experienced little success. An attack mounted by the Rifles 2nd Battalion made no ground until each company was supported by five Panzers. With that "beefing-up" the infantry opened up a new attack and captured the town of Malaye-Bersenki. The lorry-borne 1st Rifles Battalion had been given as its objective a strongly defended Russian trench system but an enemy artillery barrage pinned down the riflemen and held them fast until the battalion commander grouped his heavy weapons companies. The fire of those weapons blew gaps in the first Russian defence line and, eager to exploit the situation, the rifles companies then went in with the bayonet so that by midday they had taken all the enemy field fortifications lying between Krestshovo and Malaye-Bersenki. Eberbach's KG had still not moved from its positions near Shalyamova, where its advance had been halted by fanatical Russian resistance. Eberbach would not tolerate any delay and ordered a fresh attack to be made. This one was to go in under cover of a Stuka raid. The dive-bombers whose support had been promised for 10.00hrs did not arrive and the impatient Eberbach, rather than wait until the Luftwaffe did turn up, committed his battle group to action without that support. Two Panzer battalions rolled forward, one on each side of the Shalyamova road, advancing steadily under moderate artillery fire until they reached the hilltop village of Malaye-Bersenki. There they were forced to halt and laager, not by Russian resistance but because the fuel tanks had run dry and all the ammunition they carried had been fired off. During the following afternoon supplies were rushed forward, brought up by 18th Panzer Regiment whose AFVs were draped with jerricans of fuel and loaded with racks of ammunition. As a result of such improvisations Eberbach's battalions were refuelled and the Kampfgruppe made ready to force its advance in the face of growing Soviet resistance.

The Stukas which should have supported the attack at 10.00hrs, finally arrived at midday. Now with Luftwaffe support and having adequate supplies of fuel and ammunition KG Eberbach went immediately into action. Too much time had been lost already. The Stukas made their attack and even before they climbed away the riflemen had climbed out of their slit trenches and moved into the attack following the Panzers, forcing their way through the thick woods which dominate the area to capture the village of Katushishtsha and the nearby height, Point 118. Although his units had reached their given objectives, Eberbach would not halt the advance but directed a Rifle battalion and a Panzer Company to reach Shomovo, leaving a second Rifle battalion to consolidate its hold on the village, while 3rd Rifles battalion was switched towards Saroshtsha. Its orders were to force a bridgehead aver the Butyrki river and to gain touch with the "Grossdeutschland" infantry.

During the early afternoon 6th Panzer Regiment captured Mezneva against strong enemy armoured counter-attacks and Eberbach, determined not to let the enemy recover, decided to carry on with the attack throughout the night, to cut the Mzensk-Tula road and thereby the Red Army's line of retreat. Shortly before last light the vehicles of 3rd Panzer Battalion refuelled and carrying the rifles' 1st Battalion moved off through the darkness. Relying upon compass bearings and the vehicles' mileage counters to tell off the distance covered, the panzer/infantry group closed in upon its objective, a road junction and a collective farm to the north-west of Mzensk. The German column was surprised to find the Kolkhoz was a Russian supply depot and were unpleasantly surprised by the speed of Soviet reaction to their presence. Then was fought a battle at close quarters in the farm courtyard — German rifleman against Russian infantryman and Panzers against the mass of T34s. Shortly before midnight the Soviets retreated and drove off leaving Eberbach's KG to laager for what remained of the night.

Just after dawn of 25 October, a column of fuel and ammunition trucks reached Eberbach who had planned to begin a battle of pursuit. Corps cancelled the operation. By breaching the Red Army front the objective had been gained and he could halt. That order was countermanded only a little later and the battle group was directed to begin the advance upon Tula. On that day, too, 3rd Panzer Division created KG Schneider-Kostalski, made up of a Panzer battalion, a rifle battalion, an SP detachment and artillery, and sent it on a special raiding mission. That group opened a swift advance which brought it as far as the railway station at Chern. One of Eberbach's Panzer battalions and part of "Grossdeutschland" regiment opened an attack which, although it was carried out in pouring rain, quickly reached Chern only to find that companies of "Grossdeutschland" were already in the town and preparing a further advance. Eberbach ordered the tired "Grossdeutschland" Grenadiers to climb onto the outsides of the armoured vehicles and the attack rolled on through Gorbatchevo to reach and capture Plavsk by last light. With the taking of that town 24th Corps had broken the last Soviet defensive lines based on the River Susha and had forced the Red forces, including 6th Guards Division, 41st Cavalry Division and 4th Panzer Brigade, to retreat north-east and eastwards.

Any further advance on 26 October was out of the question. The days and nights of unceasing rain had produced mud so deep and thick that even the division's tracked vehicles could not master it. The 3rd Division nevertheless issued orders for the advance upon Tula to resume on the 27th and broke up the existing battle groups only to recreate new Kampfgruppen. The first of these was KG Cuno (39th Panzer Regiment), KG Hoernlein ("Grossdeutschland" Regiment), KG Eberbach, (now reduced to 6th and 35th Panzer Regiments) and KG Kleeman (3rd Rifles Regiment, 2nd Battalion 394th Rifles Regiment, 75th Artillery Regiment and 39th Pioneer Battalion.) The morning of 27 October found the vehicles of the several battle groups still held fast in the mud. Nevertheless, Division ordered the advance to begin and the battle groups sought to comply. Indeed, by the evening of 28 October, KG Cuno had reached a point only 26km south of Tula. Orders for a resumption of the advance were issued for the 29th and frost which came in during the night of the 28th/29th gave hope that it would be strong enough to harden the ground sufficiently for the advance to roll. It did and at 05.30hrs the first vehicles of the battle groups moved out for the advance towards the final objective.

For this final part of the Tula operation, Stuka squadrons were brought in to smash the Red Army's ground-support fire, allowing the 2nd Panzer Battalion and the 2nd Battalion of "Grossdeutschland" to capture Kunaki. Outside that place the Russian units which had regrouped after retreating during the shattering dive-bomber attacks, bombarded the battle groups with heavy artillery fire from the flank and from the front. The battle group's Panzer vehicles moved into the great forest which extends on both sides of the Tula road while "Grossdeutschland" 2nd Battalion attacked through the woods and reached the enemy's artillery positions after hard fighting during which the gun crews and their infantry defenders were all killed. Once again it was clear that the Russian resistance had been put up by determined rearguards and their efforts had been so successful that, although Tula was only 5km distant, the onset of darkness caused Corps to halt the attack. Eberbach proposed to Corps that his KG carry on with the attack, particularly since "Grossdeutschland" Grenadiers were already in the suburbs of the town. Corps rejected his proposal and ordered that the attack was to go in at 05.30hrs on the 30th. Through that decision the opportunity to take the industrial complex of Tula by coup de main was lost. Eberbach's attack went in on the following morning but the Soviets had so massively reinforced the Tula garrison with infantry, armour and artillery, that when the battle was ended, once again at last light, Kampfgruppe Eberbach had gained only 500m. During the night of 30-31 October the Soviets were able, once again, to reinforce the Tula defenders and in the morning of the 31st, regiments of Red Army tanks passed from the defensive to the offensive, drove through their own Pak fronts and marched out to engage those Panzers which had survived the wasteful battles of the previous days. Fighting between the armoured vehicles of both sides endured for the whole day but it was clear that the German battle groups lacked the strength to take the city. The 3rd Panzer Division spent the next few days fighting against Soviet tank and infantry attacks which slowly, but very surely, drove it back out of the villages which it and the "Grossdeutschland" Regiment had gained in the past weeks. Then on 9 November, Division issued the order that its units were to pull back from Tula so as to create a shorter battle line and to go over to a wholly defensive posture.

In order that the divisional units could disengage without interference from the enemy, Division formed three battle groups: KG Kleeman was made up of infantry, artillery, Flak and SPs; KG Audoersoh, which was similarly constructed; and KG Ziervogel which was the divisional recce battalion. The "Grossdeutschland" Regiment was held as a divisional counter-attack reserve. The disengagement from the enemy was carried out swiftly, efficiently and without any trouble.

For the Division's front line infantry, the bad conditions which it was suffering had become almost unbearable. The temperature dropped until it registered 16 degrees of frost and for the soldiers there was no winter clothing. The riflemen and the Grenadiers of "Grossdeutschland" were still dressed in the uniforms they had worn at the beginning of Operation "Typhoon". As the days passed temperatures fell further and on 13 November, reached 34 degrees below zero. Despite its best efforts it was the end for the German Army on the Eastern Front. Within a few weeks OKW would be compelled to break off Operation "Typhoon", the Red Army would then open a general attack and as a result of that counter-offensive Army Group Centre was to suffer a catastrophe at the gates of Moscow, the capital it had set out so confidently to capture.

Battle Group Scherer, which held out in Cholm for 105 days and nights, December 1941 to March 1942

In an earlier chapter of this book mention was made of the great battles of encirclement and destruction which had marked the German Army's advance through Russia in the autumn of 1941. In the Kiev encirclement the Red Army lost 665,000 men taken prisoner and in the Vyasma-Briansk pocket another 663,000 soldiers were captured. Yet these were only two of the many encirclement battles fought throughout the autumn of 1941.

During the first week of December Operation "Typhoon", the German offensive to capture Moscow, was brought to a halt by a combination of winter weather and Siberian troops, men accustomed to the bitter climatic conditions, who had been brought out of the Far East by Supreme STAVKA and deployed on the Western Front. The German operation came to an end and immediately the Red Army opened its counter-offensive. In that massive operation Soviet soldiers advanced, overran and destroyed German formations caught on the open steppe, but STAVKA was less concerned with killing enemy troops than with regaining lost territory and especially those areas which would be of strategic or tactical importance to the conduct of future offensives —road junctions, communications centres and land bridges.

Russian tanks and cavalry flooding westwards bypassed retreating German units and surrounded them. Now it was not Red Army formations that were trapped in encirclements, but the regiments, divisions and even corps of the German Army. Those formations pulled back from the gates of Moscow and their withdrawal soon became a retreat which might very easily have degenerated into a panic rout. That it did not deteriorate was due to Hitler's uncompromising order for his soldiers to stand fast and for units to form "hedgehogs" around strategic areas and towns. That order had a three-fold intent: first, the creation of hedgehog strongpoints would bring the German westward retreat to a halt; second, by holding areas of strategic or tactical importance these would be denied to the Red Army; and, third, following on from the two previous considerations, the Soviet advance would thereby be slowed. Although Hitler's order to stand fast cost the German Army dear in dead and wounded, there can be no doubt that it was the correct one to have made, given the circumstances. His concept of a chess board pattern of defended localities did play a significant part in slowing the Russian advance, even though the effect was only a temporary one. That respite may have been only brief but it enabled

Hitler to pull the Eastern Front together again so that the renewed Soviet winter offensive did gain initial successes but lost the impetus that had gained it such great victories in the first December days.

When, during the second week of January 1942, that revived Russian offensive reopened, 3rd Shock Army, a major grouping of the Kalinin Front, struck and drove back 39th Corps on the right wing of Army Group North. The Shock Army's objective was the small town of Cholm standing at the confluence of two rivers, the Lovat and the Kunya. The terrain around Cholm was marshland, except for a small piece of firm ground on which the town stood. That solid area was not only a land bridge across the marsh but was also a junction of a north-south and an east-west road. The land bridge and the roads which crossed it would form a spring board for any future offensives which the Germans or the Russians would make. Cholm was, therefore, important to the battle plans of both sides.

As von Arnim's 39th Corps fell back before the hammer blows of 3rd Shock Army, it dropped off a small garrison whose task was to hold Cholm. Corps accepted the inevitability of the town being cut off but believed it would be isolated for only a week or two. The reason for that optimistic belief was the corps commander's knowledge that at Army Group level plans for a massive German counter-stroke were well advanced. In view of what von Arnim anticipated would be but a brief encirclement, it was considered that the units dropped off to form the garrison of Cholm, some 3,500 men, would be sufficient to hold it. Command of that garrison, which was first titled "Fortress Group" and then retitled "Battle Group", was invested in Major-General Scherer who had formerly commanded 281st Security Division.

In compliance with the Fuehrer Directive the main body of von Arnim's Corps formed a hedgehog position, locating this a few kilometres south-west of Cholm and intending to maintain a physical link with Scherer's group by keeping open the road between itself and the Kampfgruppe. Then corps learned that the Cholm garrison was not, as had been believed, a homogenous force, but was made up of remnants of units from two infantry divisions, a Luftwaffe field regiment, some policemen and a handful of drivers from the German Navy. Staff officers at corps planned to run a regular series of convoys carrying supplies of food, ammunition, clothing and fodder for the horses but only the first column was able to reach the group, deliver its cargo and return. Within an hour of the first convoy making its way back into 39th Corps' hedgehog, Russian ski-troops had cut the road between it and Cholm. The garrison in the town was now isolated. Despite that early setback, but determined to support Scherer and his men, the Corps commander next planned attacks by an all-arms group to take off the pressure from the beleaguered garrison. Neither armoured nor soft-skinned vehicles could operate on the ice-bound roads and the German infantry, who waded through waist-deep snow to attack their objectives, gained little ground. Von Arnim accepted the bitter truth that the garrison in Cholm was cut off, although he still believed this to be only a temporary isolation. That siege was to last for 105 days and nights, the battle group's only link with the outside world being wireless telegraphy and air-drops.

Inside the town, Major-General Scherer took stock of his position. The greatest area which his few men could hold was a 2km-square perimeter. Since there was no longer a land-link between his group and corps, he would have to be reliant upon air-dropped supplies although air-drops were inaccurate and it had to be accepted that much material which the Luftwaffe would despatch was certain to fall into Russian hands. As an alternative to air-drops he ordered the construction of a runway whose maximum length of 70m and width of 25m was sufficient as a landing strip for Ju52s. The Luftwaffe accepted the challenge of flying in supplies to the Scherer group and of evacuating the seriously wounded. That well-meaning intention was short-lived. Losses of transport planes became too high to accept —25 aircraft in the course of the siege —and gliders had to be substituted. These were towed by a powered aircraft to a point above Cholm and there released to skid-land on the short runway. It goes without saying that each glider operation was a one-off, one-way mission with the machine being a total write-off and that, therefore, it was no longer possible to fly out the badly wounded. The ruins of the peasant houses of Cholm became hospital wards in which the wounded shivered, suffered and endured throughout the bitter weeks of January and February.

The town was cut off on 21 January and the first heavy assaults of the enemy came in two days later. Earlier than those there had been probes to establish the garrison's determination to resist and also to count the defenders' firepower, but the first major efforts were made on 23 January. The Soviets made aware through those initial probes that the garrison, although small, would fight to the end to destroy KG Scherer, using heavy artillery and tank attacks to achieve its goal. The first of the armoured assaults came in from the western edge of the perimeter. It failed. The assault then swung to the eastern side, changed direction again and came in from the north before, finally, striking from the south. The massive concentration of shell fire which the Russian artillery brought down had another purpose. The Germans needed the houses of Cholm to shelter and protect them against the bitter weather and the Soviet commander was determined to destroy the houses, reasoning that the enemy denied their shelter must soon be forced to surrender.

A check by one of Scherer's officers showed that there was not a single anti-tank gun in the defenders' arsenal. Without adequate defence it must, therefore, be only a matter of time before the enemy armour crushed the KG's last resistance. Barricades would have to serve as deterrents and two were erected across the top of one street. A pioneer laid a simple explosive device as a line of Soviet tanks rolled towards the first obstruction. The lead vehicle struck the barrier and began to push it aside. The pioneer lit a long fuse. Fire ran quickly along the cable and detonated the primitive mine with such violence that it destroyed the lead tank. The other vehicles turned away. Kampfgruppe Scherer had gained its first small victory.

A few days later the defenders heard the sound of German machine guns being fired from outside the perimeter. This was not the relief force which they were expecting but was welcome just the same. The men firing the MG34s belonged to a machine gun battalion which, itself cut off, had fought its way through the Russian ring to join up with KG Scherer. Those reinforcements carried out an attack on the day after their arrival and drove the Soviet soldiers out of that part of the town in which they had managed to establish a foothold.

Day followed day with Russian attacks made all round the perimeter. Men, frozen from an hour of sentry duty and hoping to warm out in the cellar of a destroyed house, would be alerted as Red Army infantry advanced in long, unbroken lines towards them. Then the freezing German Landser would take up positions behind a snow wall which served as a parapet and would aim into the brown of the oncoming enemy. The unchanging pattern of those attacks and their very rigidity actually assisted Scherer to overcome them. The Red Army's assaults were launched at precise times on predictable sectors, so that when an attack had been repulsed at one place, the defenders knew that there would not be another made in that area for a couple of hours. That knowledge allowed the commander to move the men of his Kampfgruppe from the place in which one assault had just been crushed to that sector on which he knew from experience fresh attacks would soon be made.

However staunch the defence, and Scherer held his men's morale high, the 2km perimeter shrank under continual attack to an area of only 1km. Gliders could no longer land and air-drops — inaccurate or not — had to take their place as the only source of supply. And when air-drops were made and the containers fell into No Man's Land, German sentries watched the boxes with keen eyes. Any Soviet attempt to seize them was met with a hail of machine gun fire or a barrage of rifle grenades. Then in the darkest hours of the night a kommando of Scherer's men would slide out across the snow to retrieve the containers and drag back the supplies they held. Although drops were made regularly and although the numbers in the garrison were few, there was never sufficient food for a proper meal to be issued. Indeed from the very first day of encirclement the battle group had been on reduced rations.

Von Arnim, the corps commander, made aware by radio of the privations which the garrison was suffering, prepared a new, major relief operation and created a battle group which he planned to be strong enough to fight its way through to the isolated defenders. Scherer, advised by radio of the relief attempt, created two small sub-battle groups which he located on the west side of his perimeter. The plan was that when von Arnim's corps made its attack his two groups would storm forward and gain touch with the relief column.

Sherer selected as the form-up area for his sub-battle group detachments a low but dominant hill on the perimeter's western side. There was a problem connected with the choice of that hill — it was in Soviet hands. A battle patrol of mountain troops was put in to capture it and using their specialist abilities had soon driven the Red Army soldiers from the height. With the feature now in German hands, a short column of porters brought up the supplies and ammunition that the attacking companies would need when they made their link-up attempt. It was during the portering stage of the operation that the weather, already bad, deteriorated rapidly. Snow blew in hour-long blizzards and the bitter, east wind carried small slivers of ice which cut into the faces of the porters. To add to their misery they had to wade through drifts of snow that were sometimes thigh deep. On the peak of the hill a small garrison of soldiers took up position and built defensive positions and igloos out of the frozen snow. Those conditions which were causing such misery to Scherer and his men also affected the Corps relief column. Although the distance between its forward positions and Cholm was only 15km, corps' trucks, AFVs and Panzers could not gain a purchase on the icy road so that the attempts at raising the siege had to be borne by the infantry.

The first objective to be taken was a hill, Point 72.7, and von Arnim's Grenadiers launched attack after attack to wrest this from its Russian defenders who were well aware of its tactical importance and were determined to hold it. The snow on this sector of the front was not just waist-deep but was, in places, chest-high. To force a way through only 100m of so deep a drift was an exhausting torture for the Grenadiers who had, in addition, also to hold their rifles and machine guns above their heads so that the bolt action would not be fouled by snow and freeze into immobility.

Each Grenadier attack gained a little more ground and in the course of days brought the leading companies closer to the crest of the hill.

Finally there remained only the last bound. But this obstacle, a natural "killing ground", was a flat and open space 300m wide. The first attempt to cross it was made behind a barrage whose fire was largely ineffective because the shells sank deep into the snow before exploding and this lessened their effect. The barrage stopped. The Grenadiers stood up, formed line and began to wade in. That attack failed; so did the second, the third and each subsequent one. The German infantry pulled back to the start line and lay exhausted and desperately tired on the snowy slopes of Point 72.7. Then from the crest came the sound of cheering. The Soviet infantry was about to make a counter-attack.

Through the clear, cold air sounded the Russian battle cry, the long drawn out, terrifying "Oooooray". Then the Red Army men came downhill to destroy the surviving Germans. The Russians, too, had to wade through the snow and their first line moved slowly, but inexorably and menacingly, forward. At the news that the enemy was closing in the spirits of the exhausted Grenadiers rose. Now they could exact revenge for all the misery, pain and tribulation they had suffered. Aware that they would have no field of fire lying prone in the snow the German soldiers stood up to engage their adversaries.

Then was fought the type of battle that belonged to the past of military history as the two lines of standing men clashed. The MG34s, with one man loading the belts, one man operating the gun and with a third man acting as a human mount, opened fire upon the Russian soldiers floundering through the snow. Slowly, the MGs traversed along the enemy line, backwards and forwards until there were no longer any Red soldiers still standing.

Breathing hard, the Grenadiers took their first drag on a cigarette; one that would have to be shared with three other comrades because cigarettes, the soldier's most immediate comfort, were in short supply and one had to comfort several men. There was no elation among the experienced Grenadiers; no joy that they had crushed one Red attack. They knew from past battles and with terrible certainty that it would be the first of many. And already the long-drawn out "Ooooray" was sounding again from the crest as a new line of Soviet infantry trudged downhill, was struck by the fury of the German fire and was destroyed. Each attack, and there were many, died in the fire of machine guns and machine pistols, in the fire of the Gewehr 98 and in the crashing detonation of stick grenades. As a last resort the Soviet commanders committed their whole reserve in one concentrated mass attack and under that blow the Grenadier line recoiled and the German soldiers were forced back to the base of Point 72.7. That the Grenadiers had experienced a defeat could not be denied, but their efforts and sacrifices had gained 39th Corps one advantage. A shallow salient now penetrated into the Russian line from whose easternmost point German guns were now able to fire barrages in support of Scherer and his men.

The disappointment of the garrison that corps had failed to break through can well be imagined, although the artillery support which was now immediate and massive was welcome. In view of corps' failure, Scherer stood down his attack companies but still garrisoned the hill commanding the perimeter. The physical and mental strain upon the men who had to hold that peak was an unimaginable hell of sleeplessness. Red Army attacks could come at any time so that they were on watch throughout the day and night. Any relief column ordered to the crest could only march by night and its accompanying porters were given as much rest as possible before they began to move out into the total darkness, trusting to compass bearings to bring them to the peak and hoping that they would not be intercepted and attacked by Siberian ski patrols which roamed the area. The ascent from the last houses in Cholm to the summit took the greater part of an entire night and the under-nourished, ill-clad troops of KG Scherer reached the objective in a state of total exhaustion.

As day succeeded day the strain upon the Cholm garrison began to tell. Siberian snipers, who lay out in the snow for unending freezing hours, picked off the unwary or the uncautious adding to the losses brought about by sickness and illnesses, by deprivation and poor food. That constant drain upon the numbers of soldiers manning the firing line forced Scherer to make the difficult decision to pull back to a shorter perimeter. This meant, of course, that the new line could be more strongly manned but it also meant that the Russians, too, had a shorter line —and they had superiority in numbers. Their infantry attacks continued to come in —successive waves of men presenting easy targets which were shot down by the desperate garrison. But there were times when attackers and defenders fought hand to hand in the ruins. Then, one night, the sound of a great many tank engines was heard by the German sentries. It was a sure indication that the Soviets were preparing to undertake a major armoured assault.

Its opening moves were made by Soviet artillery regiments equipped with 17.2cm howitzers. The Red Army commander was determined to crush the defenders under a deluge of those heavy calibre shells. The destructive path of explosion and fire did not in fact clear a way for the follow-up Red infantry and the Russian General on that sector then brought into action every artillery piece he could collect together. The following days and nights were filled with the thunder of explosions, but the garrison knew that this was only a preparation for what was to come. When the barrage finally stopped Red tanks and infantry would swarm in.

Another search through the cellars of the ruined houses unearthed a German anti-tank gun, a 3.7cm weapon of such limited penetrating power as to be useless against Russian AFVs except at very close range. There was yet another reason why the gunners would have to fire at pointblank range: the gun had no optical sighting system. To fire this almost useless weapon over open sights was in the nature of a suicide mission, but there was never any shortage of volunteers to form the gun crew. The 3.7 was set up to contest the advance of one column of three vehicles and at short range engaged the enemy. The first of four rounds destroyed the lead vehicle and the second shot knocked out the middle one, but two other rounds failed to destroy the third tank in the column. Nevertheless, it turned away, unwilling to face the fire of such determined gunners. As explained earlier in this chapter Red Army attacks were made to a rigid timetable. That inflexibility allowed the defenders to move the gun from the spot on which it had been in action and rush it to a sector on which they knew the next attack would soon come in.

Radio contact between the beleaguered force and corps was excellent, and so proficient were the gunnery officers of the garrison in forward observation duties that they could select a target and know that within a minute German guns would pour down shells upon it. So precise were the details they passed and so accurate was the gunnery that corps artillery could —and did —act in the role of long-range Pak, actually picking off individual AFVs. The repeated failure of the Soviet armoured, artillery and infantry forces to crush the Cholm defenders brought a slowing-down of the enemy's effort. Confidence began to grow among the garrison and morale was raised to a high pitch when, under cover of a Stuka raid, three Ju52s landed within the shrunken perimeter and unloaded three anti-tank guns, an 81mm mortar and vitally needed medical supplies. Cellars were strengthened in anticipation of fresh Russian attacks and in the course of that work six anti-tank mines were found. They, like everything that could be converted to a military purpose, were restored and put back into service. In this way Russian weapons were employed to increase the garrison's firepower and even one of the immobilised T34s was repaired and entered the battle as a fixed strongpoint.

On most long freezing nights Siberian snipers would crawl forward infiltrating the German positions. Life became a grim contest between the Siberians, who often lay partly buried in the snow, and the garrison whose soldiers tried to camouflage themselves with bed linen taken from the peasant houses or with overalls made from the white parachutes used in air-drops. By the middle of February the most bitter weather was past and, although the cold was still intense, there were days when the sun shone from a cloudless sky and its weak warmth brought a promise of spring.

There were days and even nights when it was so quiet that it seemed to the defenders as if the encircling Soviet units had given up the siege and had voided the field. On such days there would be a total silence —no artillery fire, no crack of rifle, no machine gun burst to break the almost-Sabbath stillness. But by comparison there were days and nights on which every hour was filled with the sound and fury of battle; of wounded men with gaping wounds inflicted by exploding bullets which the Russian snipers fired; and the pallid dead, released at last from the agony of hunger, cold and the awful sense of isolation which the living members of the garrison felt.

On such nights when the long drawn-out Russian battle cry heralded yet another Red Army infantry attack, the exhausted soldiers of the garrison would take up their positions, unscrew caps from stick grenades, lay the bombs close to hand and then feed belts of ammunition into the MG34s. They would then look out into the darkness waiting for the harsh light of a Very flare to illuminate the ground in front of their icy trenches. First a dull red light tracing the path of the signal cartridge would rise swiftly into the air and would burst exposing in an incandescent, magnesium light perhaps a battalion of Red infantry trudging, menacingly, towards the German lines. Under the machine guns' fire the first ranks would fall but the remainder would continue to march unflinchingly over the bodies of their comrades and into the fire. Then more and more would fall, their bodies adding to the numbers of dead from earlier attacks. Some of those unburied dead, the greatest number of them Russian, had lain out there since the beginning of the siege. In December and January snow had covered them in a deep white shroud, but now in mid-February the occasional thaw unveiled them until a fresh snowfall covered the bodies and hid them from sight once again.

A young officer, not in the Cholm garrison but fighting with Army Group North, wrote about the first battlefield he saw. He had been hurried up the line as part of a hastily composed Kampfgruppe to relieve a unit on the Leningrad sector. He and his few men carried out the relief and then he tried to orientate himself and to identify the noises of the night. It was cold and cloudless. Moonrise was at midnight and when the light of that full moon flooded the battlefield it revealed a shocking sight. The Kampfgruppe seemed to be the only living humans in a sea of dead men — German as well as Russian. A helmeted head projecting from the snow served to identify the nationality of its wearer, otherwise they were all anonymous. Arms raised out of the snow showed where another man was lying and in the bright moonlight it seemed as if the upraised arms of the dead were beckoning, inviting the living to join their company. Most bodies seemed to be complete but here and there on the snow lay unmentionable and indescribable horrors — fragments of corpses, headless torsoes and single, severed limbs. It was the young officer's first day in the line.

In Cholm, too, there was not only the horror of an uncleared battlefield, but also the enduring fear of death or mutilation. Even though by the middle of February the snow was no longer as tight-packed nor as deep as it had been in the earlier months, Siberian troops still exploited its cover to bring themselves close to the German slit trenches. An enemy raiding party would wait until the night frost hardened the snow and would then dig a tunnel. Into this the men would be packed and when it was long enough an exit hole would be cut and the concealed Siberians would erupt from this hoping to catch the German sentries off guard.

Although front line conditions for the Red Army troops were poor they were infinitely better than those endured by the German garrison. The Russians were relieved from the line at frequent intervals, their rations came up regularly and they were warmly clad. And yet, throughout the siege, a trickle of Soviet soldiers came into the German lines to surrender themselves. Two who walked into the garrison's forward positions late in February, reported that a major Soviet offensive was to be launched on 23 February — Red Army Day. They spoke the truth. On that day of commemoration an entire Soviet infantry division marched into the attack preceded by a wave of tanks. Tensely the garrison waited and then realised that the Soviets were still using the familiar tactic of attacking on only one sector of the perimeter at a time. Men were taken from less threatened areas to thicken the German line that would meet the Red challenge. The garrison had already learned certain battlefield tactics — kill the officers and commissars in the infantry waves and the rank and file lost heart and retreated. Then, once the Red infantry had begun to flood back the armour was isolated. The next important step was to destroy the Russian command tank, the only vehicle fitted with both a transmitter and receiver. Only he could give orders; the others could only receive them. Kill that command vehicle and the other tanks were leaderless and confused. Tank-busting teams could then move in among the undirected armour to exploit that confusion, using explosive charges to destroy the T34s and KVIs.

On this Red Army Day, Kampfgruppe Scherer waited for the opportunity to use those tactics. The Soviet infantry were still not within killing range, that distance when every shot was certain to kill its target. After their first burst of "Ooooray" the enemy troops were silent. The strain of forcing a way through the snow left them with little breath to continue with the battle cry. There was, all at once, a deep silence overhanging the field, as if both sides knew that this was the testing time. Then the Russian infantry division opened its front to let the tank columns pass through. The armour formed into line abreast in front of the infantry. Scherer's snipers then opened fire, each of them a first-class marksman. Soviet infantry officers were picked off one after the other and under that selective destruction the great, brown-overcoated mass of the enemy began to waver. Immediately the German machine guns opened up and that waver became a move back, then a retreat and, finally, a flight. The Red armour still continued to rumble forward although tank-busting teams were already in action and had gained some victims. The AFVs that those close-quarter fighters did not destroy were "killed" by the single Pak. Despite those losses the tank armada rolled forward and a few vehicles managed to enter the streets on the eastern side of Cholm. The others stayed outside using their main armament and their on-board machine guns to beat down German resistance.

Away to the east of Cholm the Red infantry regrouped and advanced once again. That fresh assault was broken in its turn. The enemy battalions were reformed and came on again. They were driven back again. At intervals they made other attacks and these were destroyed in succession. But each attack gained the Russians more and more ground until Scherer's outpost line had been driven in. The next assault brought the Red Army infantry into the eastern streets where they would be able to support their armour. The battle reached its climax. It seemed as if the enemy soldiers needed to make one last effort and the weight of that assault MUST carry them through the ruined town. One thing aided the German defence. The streets of Cholm were narrow and the press of Soviet troops could not take up any sort of tactical formation. They were squeezed together shoulder to shoulder and came in at the charge. At the western end of each narrow street German machine guns, sometimes in pairs, sometimes in groups of three, opened fire upon the masses of men charging towards them. It was not, in the words of one German survivor, a battle but a slaughter. So great was the number of enemy soldiers storming through the broken streets and so closely were they compressed that in some places dead men of the first ranks, held erect and unable to fall through the crush of their comrades, were carried along with the living. Under that enormous pressure the garrison was forced to undertake a fighting withdrawal. Behind the hard-pressed men fighting in the streets Scherer brought to readiness the alarm companies of his Kampfgruppe. These stood fast while the rest of the garrison pulled back through their ranks. The alarm companies stood waiting and then went into action. A shower of hand and rifle grenades burst among the leading files of Russians, and then with machine pistols and machine guns firing the alarm companies strode steadily up the streets. For the Red troops the appearance of these implacable and unshaken men was the last straw.

To their front there advanced short lines of German soldiers armed with fast-firing automatic weapons. They themselves could make no reply to that fire; the crush of men around them made it impossible to bring their weapons into action. Almost defenceless, they were shot down in batches. No soldiers can stand that sort of punishment. Sullenly, the front groups of Russians began to push back against those behind them until step by step, still taking fearful losses, the Soviet host withdrew. Then the time came when they broke in panic and ran. The alarm companies had restored the situation.

This was not the end of the Soviet division's efforts to capture the town. For more than two days and nights they came on again and again, advancing across the bodies of their fallen comrades, across a carpet of dead men which grew thicker with every unsuccessful assault. No fewer than 18 major attacks came in, some with — but most without — tank support. Each and every one, whether major or minor, came in under an artillery barrage of crushing weight and, as an added element, the improving weather allowed the Red Air Force to carry out low-level ground attacks in support of their ground troops. The appearance over Cholm of Soviet aircraft attracted the Luftwaffe to the scene and under cover of the Messerschmitt fighters, Stukas strafed Soviet targets and Ju52s flew in with supplies or with infantry replacements and took off again loaded with the badly wounded men of the garrison.

The assaults on Red Army Day and those succeeding it had shown Scherer how precarious still was the garrison's hold on Cholm. Another major Red offensive might capture the town. His solution was to construct a sort of fort or redoubt, made out of the wrecked vehicles which littered the area. In that bastion he proposed to fight the final battle, but no sooner had that redoubt been built than it was found to have a defect. Russian snipers could infiltrate into it and hide in the ruined trucks. On other sectors Soviet patrols filtered through gaps in the perimeter, hoping to establish a bridgehead on the bank of the River Lovat to the west of Cholm. Such an outpost would isolate the garrison even more and, more significantly, would set up a Soviet springboard for a new offensive. The garrison commander saw with dismay his perimeter shrink under fresh enemy attack, to an area only 200 by 500m in extent and he accepted that the town would certainly fall unless help came. His casualties had been many and the replacements he had received, although welcome, had been too few to make good the losses which had been suffered since the beginning of the siege. The Russian enemy, by comparison, was as strong as ever and was now so firmly established in the eastern part of the town that he could not be driven out, even though the alarm companies were committed to battle time after time. An indication of the fury of the fighting was shown in General Scherer's post-battle report which stated that more than

900 hand grenades were used in a few hours fighting to win back the GPU (secret police) house which the Reds had captured.

The warm weather at the end of February and the beginning of March, produced thick fog and the onset of Typhus among the louse-ridden soldiers of the Cholm garrison. At a personal and individual level, lice were considered the worse of the two phenomena but the fog had a more sinister significance from the military viewpoint for it meant that winter was nearly over and that spring would bring back campaigning weather. The strategic importance of the land bridge on which Cholm stood was understood by both sides. It was expected that the Reds would open a massive offensive to take this military springboard, but it was the Germans who made the first move. During March von Arnim's corps formed relief columns which fought their way eastwards towards Cholm. Ground conditions and tenacious Russian resistance slowed their progress. The men inside Cholm were well aware that relief operations were in progress but were concerned that a link-up might not succeed before STAVKA opened the expected all-out assault on May Day. To the surprise of KG Scherer, the first Soviet attack on that day was a weak one which was quickly driven off with a loss to the enemy of five tanks. On 2 May, a new and equally weak thrust was made and on that day four more Russian tanks were destroyed.

On 3 May, at 04.50hrs, 39th Corps' column made up of Panzers and Colonel Trumm's 411th Infantry Regiment, set out to raise the siege but was held and then repulsed. The column, reinforced this time by SPs, went in on the following day. That attempt, too, failed to get through although the leading infantry companies reached to within 1km of the town. At dawn on 5 May the Panzer, infantry and SP group moved off once again and, as the units opened their advance Stukas opened an air assault, bombing the Soviet formations west of Cholm. Under the double blow of an artillery barrage and dive-bombing, the Soviets broke and fled and within an hour the garrison of Cholm welcomed the lead vehicles of the relief group. Scherer's tired soldiers were taken out of the line, proud of what they had achieved. They, fewer than 4,000 men in all, had withstood 100 separate major Soviet assaults launched by a total of six infantry divisions, six independent infantry brigades and two tank brigades. The garrison had brought down two enemy aircraft and had destroyed 42 tanks. They, themselves, had carried out 10 major infantry attacks and 43 counter-attacks. The garrison had lost 1,550 killed in action and 2,200 wounded and on 5 May, the number of men still fit for action had numbered only 1,200. Scherer and his battle group had held the vital land bridge. The reward for their effort was a metal arm badge bearing the name of the place where they had endured for 105 days and nights.

Battle Group "Reich" in the winter battles of 1941-42, west of Rzhev and in the bend of the River Volga

On 2 October 1941, too late in the year in the opinion of many of his military commanders, Hitler launched an offensive — "...the last great decisive battle of this year..." — which was to capture Moscow and lead to the destruction of the will of the Soviet people to prosecute the war. On that same day the Russian Press agency Tass reported the first falls of snow. These were the early warnings of a bitter winter to come and one which would turn the Eastern Front into a frozen hell for the soldiers of the German Army. Hitler's offensive, Operation "Typhoon", died in the blinding snowstorms of the coldest winter for decades.

The failed Operation "Typhoon" was succeeded by a Russian counter-offensive against whose severe blows the German Army on the Eastern Front, dramatically weakened by the losses and privations it had suffered, was not able to stand. The attacks of Stalin's first strategic offensive struck at every sector of the far-flung battle line and fierce though the fighting was everywhere along that vast front, nowhere was the battle more intense than at Rzhev on the approaches to the Russian capital.

Stalin planned the main blow of his offensive to go in along a thrust line Rzhev-Smolensk. If that blow breached the German front and reached Smolensk, then a northern pincer arm would have been flung around Army Group Centre. For Stalin's plan to succeed, the capture of Rzhev was an imperative and the formations of Koniev's Kalinin Front were launched to seize that first objective as a prelude to the breakthrough to Smolensk. The importance of Rzhev to the strategic plans of both sides cannot be overemphasised. The Germans had to retain their hold on it because the railway line which ran through the town was the principal supply route for their 9th Army and also because, when campaigning weather came back, Rzhev would be the launching pad for a fresh advance upon Moscow. The importance of Rzhev to the development of the Red Army's northern pincer, has already been stated.

SS Division "Reich" had taken a major part in the German autumn offensive. Spearheading the final assaults of Operation "Typhoon", its regiments had reached as close to Moscow as Stalino, west north-west of the capital from where, so it was claimed, observers could see the domes of the Kremlin churches shining in the sun. When Operation "Typhoon" finally ground to a halt in December 1941, there was a very brief period of relative quiet before Stalin's counter-offensive opened. When it did its weight and fury forced back all the formations of Army Group Centre, but 9th Army was especially hard hit. That the 9th reeled under the assault of Koniev's Kalinin Front is not to be wondered at for the Russian commander employed a total of 30 rifle divisions, five cavalry divisions and three armoured brigades to strike the initial blow against it. "Reich" Division, at that time serving with 57th Panzer Corps, conformed to 9th Army's retrograde movement and pulled back, first, from its forward attack positions at Stalino and then from defensive positions at Istra.

Every infantry soldier in the line lives a life compounded of fear, boredom, hunger, thirst, tiredness and cold. The needs of an infantryman must be carried on his back. His home is a slit trench, which he has dug for himself and which will be his ready-made grave if he is killed. In that short, shallow trench he spends his time either waiting to go over the top into an attack or defending himself against enemy assaults. Sentry duty comes round all too frequently and when it does the infantryman will look out into the darkness of the night trying to determine whether the shadows he sees moving about are shrubbery or the figures of an enemy patrol. Food reaches him erratically and hot food scarcely at all. In some places, to man-porter the food from where it is cooked into the front line means hour-long marches for the carriers. For water the infantryman relies upon local sources or the infrequent — and by God how infrequent — visits of the water truck.

Tank men carry their bedding and supplies with them in or on their vehicle. There was even space for a few comforts — such things as primus stoves and thermos flasks. In winter the tank men are warm inside their steel skin and in summer there are cooling fans. Units of the artillery and engineers have sufficient transport to carry all the wordly goods of their soldiers, so that the roughest edges are taken off their discomfort. And all those other units sleep sound in their sleeping bags or warm blankets, knowing that the front line is manned by vigilant infantrymen looking out over the parapet of a trench while at the bottom of other slit trenches their mates try to sleep, wrapped in a single thin blanket.

Life for an infantryman is a misery. The suffering when he has to carry out attacks in blizzard conditions is only surpassed when the Army is no longer advancing, but has been forced into a withdrawal which then becomes a retreat. In Russia in the winter of 1941-42, the columns of foot-slogging German infantry, stumbling through drifts of waist-high snow, were kept moving chiefly by the fearful knowledge that Russian tanks were in pursuit and that AFVs could move more quickly across snow than they could. Although the German soldiers were citizens of a highly industrialised state, there were many who still retained a primitive fear of mounted horsemen. When, out of the blinding curtain of a snow storm Russian cavalry suddenly erupted, the cry was raised that had alarmed Napoleon's Grande Armee 13 decades earlier: "The Cossacks, the Cossacks!" It was a cry which could create panic among the freezing, lousy, sodden, German infantry. But woe betide those units which did break and scatter. To disperse meant that they could could be more easily cut down by the pitiless riders of the steppes. Where the German soldiers stood at bay, and this was more usually the case, they fought with the desperation of men faced with the terrible alternatives of kill or be killed; win or die. To surrender gained them nothing. Cossack sotnias on harry and pursuit missions had neither the men nor the facilities to take prisoners and a bullet was the standard Cossack response to an offer to surrender. Such a quick death could, under certain circumstances, be a mercy. Each soldier who went through those long and freezing days and nights, trod his own personal Via Dolorosa, but it was an agony out of which he might, as most did, emerge alive. To be badly wounded was, however, a virtual sentence of death. Where frost penetrated into a serious wound almost invariably it became gangrenous. To save the body often meant losing the limb in an operation carried out under the primitive conditions of a casualty clearing station. With so many sick and wounded, doctors had to make quick decisions and when faced with a gangrenous limb the decision usually was to amputate it. In view of the suffering and privations which they had had to endure it is small wonder that the German Landser bestowed upon the East Front medal, which each was awarded, the nickname of "The Order of the Frozen Meat".

But it was not all retreat and rout on the German side. Most units kept military discipline, withdrew in proper order and when the Russians pressed too hard, turned and demonstrated an unshaken ability to fight. Then, too, there were commanders who launched counter-attacks and even local offensives, necessarily limited in scope and size, but able to raise morale which had been diminished by a seemingly unending retreat. SS Division "Reich", pulling back with morale intact, often formed the rearguard. It carried out that task at Istra and then along the line of the River Rusa, shielding the other divisions as they pulled back westwards. "Reich" Division eventually reached and took up positions above Sychevka, a town to the south of Rzhev, where Koniev's attacking armies had managed to achieve a slight breakthrough and had set up a shallow perimeter. But the Soviets had not been able to capture Rzhev. There the German defenders held out against the assaults of 39th Red Army and the 11th Red Cavalry Corps, the undaunted garrison being an unbreakable rock in a Soviet sea. Repeated assaults by Soviet infantry, cavalry and armour backed by divisions of artillery could not take the town. Their persistent assaults did succeed, however, in tearing open a gap, 16km wide, to the west of Rzhev. Through that breach in 9th Army's front poured Koniev's soldiers driving southwards to meet up with the units which had breached the line and had formed the shallow Sychevka perimeter.

In the weeks of retreat and confusion the German senior commanders had not been idle but had planned counter-blows. The plans of 9th Army suffered a setback when the Army commander fell ill and had to be replaced. His successor was General Model, not only a very confident leader but also one unafraid of his superiors. When he was asked by the staff officers of 9th Army after he took post on 17 January, what he had brought to restore the broken front, his confident reply was "Myself". On 20 January, three days after taking up his new appointment, he flew to Hitler's headquarters to discuss the situation in the Rzhev area. Model stated that it was his intention to employ 46th Panzer Corps in the Sychevka sector to which Hitler replied that he had selected that Corps to take part in operations around Gshatsk. Model bluntly demanded, "Who commands 9th Army, my Fuehrer. You or I ?", and was given permission to employ the Panzer Corps in the operation which he had already planned. The offensive opened on 22 January and within a day his formations had not only sealed the breach in the line to the west of Rzhev, but had also cut off 29th and 39th Red Armies from the main body of the Kalinin Front and had partially encircled them. Model then called for a concerted effort by 9th Army to destroy the Soviet forces.

The role of 46th Panzer Corps in that operation in the Sychevka sector was to push the Russian formations northwards towards the Volga and onto the guns of 6th Corps which was positioned along the line of that river. It is the course of those operations which are the burden of the following account and specifically the actions carried out by Kampfgruppe "Reich", which was a component of the Panzer Corps.

Aware of the division's grievous losses during and after Operation "Typhoon", and particularly those which "Deutschland" regiment had suffered, Kleinheisterkamp, the divisional commander, decided to reform that regiment as a battle group. The need to regroup became urgent when the Commanding General was advised that Model's offensive was imminent and that "Reich" Division was to play a prominent part in it. Orders were issued on 25 January 1942 to create Kampfgruppe "Reich" and these laid down that this would be achieved by amalgamating four of the rifle companies of "Deutschland" Regiment to form just two, and for No 15 Company to be placed under the command of No 1 Company. In addition the regiment's 2nd Battalion was to be placed temporarily in suspended animation. All "Deutschland's" infantry units were to be concentrated into Harmel Group which would be controlled by regimental HQ. That HQ would also have under command four heavy weapons companies and three smaller groups: Tost, also known as 1st Battalion of "Deutschland" Regiment; Tychsen, or the motor cycle battalion; and Kment, the reconnaissance battalion. The last two named groups were to be outfitted with a larger than usual establishment of machines and both were to be supported by AFVs. Command of Kampfgruppe "Reich" was invested in Standartenfuehrer Ostendorff. The other infantry component of "Reich" Division, "Der Fuehrer" Regiment, was not affected by conversions or amalgamations. In the battles described below "Der Fuehrer" played equally as prominent a part as Kampfgruppe "Reich", but is not the subject of this account.

The Soviet forces which had broken through to the north of Sychevka formed a perimeter roughly triangular in shape, with its point facing southwards towards the town which the Soviet forces were still making determined efforts to capture. A succession of villages in the area, strung out along the main road to Rzhev, were strongly garrisoned and were believed to be fortified for defence. The most southerly of those villages was Karabanovo and some 10km to the north of that place was Lubany. Then, running north through the heavily wooded terrain, were Alexino, Borshovka, Svinoroyka and Maximova. The strategic road and railway passed through Sychevka to Rzhev.

Many of those former soldiers who contributed to my book on the 2nd SS Panzer Division "Das Reich", supplied details on the battle on the Sychevka sector which, through lack of space I could not, at that time, use. Several letters repeated the same or similar details and to avoid repetition, I have amalgamated all those individual memories into a single narrative. Little did the men of KG "Reich" know when they went into battle for the village of Lubany on 28 January, that the battle group to which they belonged would still be in existence five months hence — five months which they were to spend in almost continuous fighting.

At 06.00hrs on the morning of 28 January 1942, the attack by 46th Panzer Corps rolled forward out of its form-up areas on a north-westerly/westerly thrust line. Weather conditions were appalling. Snow showers which had been falling for days past suddenly degenerated into a violent snow storm driven by the Buran, the bitter east wind from Siberia.

The task of Harmel Group was to drive the Russians out of two villages, Lubany and Karabonovo, and to hold those places. The German military tactic of concentration of maximum force on a narrow front was applied here when, in view of the estimated strength of the Red Army units defending the two villages, Harmel demanded and was given both armoured and aircraft support. A Stuka squadron was allocated as long range artillery and Panzer Company "Albrecht", a detachment of 11 vehicles from 1st Panzer Division, was placed at the SS commander's disposal. The successes obtained from this limited attack were the result of close collaboration between the SS infantry and the armour, as well as from that between the Army and the SS units. Harmel made special mention of those factors in an Order of the Day when "Albrecht" Company left his Command. One telling passage in that "thank-you" note was, "...the infantry enjoyed not just the moral support of the armour but also active support [in the form of] tank gun fire. As a result it was spared losses [which it might otherwise have suffered]."

The first SS attack, on that opening morning of the new offensive, was not due to begin until after Corps reconnaissance detachments had moved forward. In preparation for their own move, at 06.45hrs the Grenadiers laid out aircraft recognition flags and pots of coloured smoke to mark their front line trenches; and when the Stukas flew in they fired flares in the direction of Lubany and the other targets which they were to dive-bomb. For more than half an hour the aircraft fell in screaming dives over the collection of miserable huts which constituted the village, then rose and dived again, machine gunning anything that moved. At 07.30hrs the aircraft regrouped, waggled their wings to show their part in the operation was ended and flew off westwards. The Stukas had carried out their long-range artillery task of softening up the enemy. Now it was up to the ground troops to finish the task.

A final "O" Group was held at 07.30hrs and, as the dive-bombers flew away, the SS climbed onto the armoured fighting vehicles and saw from their handholds on the turrets, clouds of smoke and gouts of flame rising from the burning houses of Lubany. At 07.45hrs the tank company commander gave the signal "Panzer marsch". The operation had begun and the armour roared forward on either side of the Sychevka/Rzhev road. The Grenadiers, draped around the turrets and on the rear decks of the vehicles, sat huddled, snow covered and freezing in the blizzard. They could see little. The Panzer drivers could see even less, blinded as they were by an opaque curtain of falling snow. The Panzer company commander, standing upright in the turret of his Panzer IV, sensed rather than saw movement on the right flank of the advance. "Panzer halt" and then through his binoculars he made out, dimly seen through the blizzard, masses of brown-coated Red Army soldiers marching out of Karabanovo and up the road to Lubany. The Soviet commanders, reacting to the direction of the Panzer advance, were concentrating their forces to meet the threat and had decided to reinforce the garrison of that village.

The tank man tapped the SS company commander on the shoulder and handed over an intercom through which he explained his battle plan. He proposed to swing his 11 Panzers in a right wheel that would intercept and destroy the Russians moving towards Lubany. The Grenadiers were to dismount and were to carry out a standard infantry assault on that village. Once the Panzers had completed the interception and destruction mission, they would continue with the attack on Lubany where they would join the Grenadiers in fighting down any remaining enemy resistance. Both groups would then turn back and attack Karabanovo.

The freezing SS infantry jumped from the vehicles and took up tactical formation. Machine gun detachments set up their weapons at each end of the short infantry line and opened fire. Covered by a hail of bullets from the MG34s, the Grenadiers struggled through the snow. Soon, where formerly they had clung frozen to the outside of the Panzer turrets, now the SS men were sweating with the effort of wading through deep drifts. They knew that the Ivans could see their short line closing in upon the village, but metre after metre was covered and Soviet reaction was weak and lacking in determination. It was clear that the Russians saw the Panzer company's outflanking movement as a more dangerous threat than a line of trudging Grenadiers.

"Albrecht" Company swung into the attack and at the southern end of Lubany a vedettte of two Panzers blocked the road and sent a hail of tank-gun and machine gun fire into the mass of the Bolsheviks coming up the road out of Karabanovo. The Red infantry broke and fled. A second vedette of two vehicles, positioned at the northern end of the village, began systematically bombarding those hovels which the Stuka attack had failed to destroy. The remaining seven tanks swept through the burning, narrow side streets and split up as they entered the village square. Three turned towards the vedette at the northern exit and the others cruised southwards towards the vedette facing Karabanovo. By 08.10hrs the sweating Grenadiers and the powder-blackened Panzer crews had gained touch in Lubany and within a quarter of an hour had beaten down all resistance inside the village.

"Grenadiers mount up." The infantrymen clambered onto the outsides of the vehicles and held fast. "Panzer marsch" and the combined group struck towards Karabonovo. At its northern end the Panzer halted, the Grenadiers dismounted and their machine gun teams moved to positions on either side of the village to fire at Red Army troops who might seek to escape into the open country. Slowly the Panzers rolled down the main street firing HE into any place which looked as if it might conceal a group of determined Red Army defenders. Then tank machine guns sprayed the suspect area. The SS men, nerves taut, kept pace with the armour, flinging hand grenades and spraying the ruins with bursts of fire from Schmeisser machine pistols. Little Russian opposition was encountered and where it was met the Panzers and the Grenadiers wiped it out.

By 09.45hrs the Grenadier and Panzer groups could report to their respective headquarters that Lubany and Karabanovo were both in German hands.

That first day of the new offensive had been a great success but, tragically, among the casualties were several Grenadier machine gunners who had frozen to death while lying in the snow. The first villages in the defensive triangle north of Sychevka had been taken and breach made in the Russian perimeter. Ahead lay the remaining villages and then the area in the bend of the Volga where the two Red Armies were fighting desperately.

Day after freezing day the fighting continued on the Sychevka sector with Kampfgruppe "Reich" protecting the western flank of 46th Panzer Corps and exerting pressure on the Red forces. On 8 February a crisis developed along the perimeter of the German ring when a build-up of Russian pressure threatened to smash open the encirclement. To surmount that crisis battle group HQ and Tost Group were ordered to leave the Sychevka sector of the line and to march at best possible speed to the area under threat in the bend of the Volga. For those units to disengage from the enemy was no simple task. Their soldiers were locked in furious battle, often with both sides fighting in the same houses. If there was danger inside those houses there was more outside them. In the open any careless action by day drew immediate and accurate sniper fire while every movement by night brought danger from fixed line machine guns, from mortar barrages or from the battle patrols which roved across the combat zone. These were chiefly Red Army groups for the SS were too few in number to patrol as vigorously as usual and were often able only to react to Soviet movements.

The other units of the battle group remained in position around Sychevka where the task of containing the attacking Soviet attacks had become harder with the loss of battle group HQ and of Tost. Then came the order for all the SS units in the Sychevka sector to move forward to new positions in the bend of the Volga and to reinforce the groups already there. During the period from 10-18 March, those Sychevka formations marched from their positions in the south and west of the encircling ring to new ones just below the river. March is the operative word, for there was insufficient transport to carry all the battle group across the distance of over 100km and into the new area of operations. The Grenadiers footmarched the whole way.

One hundred kilometres does not seem too far a distance until it is remembered that the surface on which the columns trudged was either deep snow or ruts of frozen ice carved out by vehicle and tank tracks. One hundred kilometres seems not too long a march until it is recalled that these men were so tired that when the column halted many fell down and were asleep before their exhausted bodies had even hit the snow. One hundred kilometres is not so far until one thinks that the men in the marching columns had been embattled for weeks without proper rest or adequate food. Supply lorries running the gauntlet of Cossack and partisan attacks to bring forward munitions and food were loaded with a 75%:25% ratio. Soldiers could live — just — on starvation rations but without ammunition they had no future.

Nor did the marching columns trudge forward unmolested. Like the truck convoys they were under frequent threat of attacks by bands of marauding cavalry or from guerilla groups who who lay in wait to cut off stragglers or to ambush any unit whose security was seen to be lax. One hundred kilometres — and on a good day 20km was an achievement — does not seem so great a distance, but for the exhausted SS Grenadiers each step represented a triumph of the human spirit over adversity. Each kilometre marched, every Cossack attack beaten off, each night spent in the sub-zero temperatures was a vindication of the training these men had undergone on the barrack squares of Germany and demonstrated the inspiration which each soldier drew from the awareness that he was a member of an elite force.

The Grenadiers spent most nights sleeping in the open, denied even the comfort of warming fires and with nothing to keep out the numbing night cold which often dropped to 30 degrees below zero. They slept out in the open because the area across which they were marching and across which the tide of battle ebbed and flowed was a sparsely populated, rural one. Villages in which units might find shelter were small in size and widely separated. The countryside of rural Russia was only lightly sprinkled with small settlements and these were separated from each other by vast prairies of steppe, or by forests of such depth as to be almost impenetrable and of such age as to be considered primaeval. In winter weather, with its freezing temperatures, to be out of doors was to risk death from exposure and the villages past which the marching columns of SS men trudged, en route to the bend of the Volga, were already occupied by other German units who had no room for the freezing Grenadiers. It should be stressed at this point that there were so few villages in rural Russia that a great many operations in winter were carried out to gain or to retain possession of them, or even of their houses and barns. Fighting was for any building that would give shelter from temperatures which already below zero, sank still further when the Buran blew — the icy eastern wind from Siberia which brought death to the unwary or the unprotected. The history of any formation which fought in Russia during winter will be found to contain details of a number of small unit actions fought to gain shelter.

The account by Ewald Ehm of an attack made by his company to rescue a cut-off detachment of the battle group is typical of just such a small
unit operation. On 6 March, Ehm's Company was ordered to smash
through a Russian group which was surrounding an isolated house at the
edge of a large wood at Skurly, some 5km south of the Rzhev-Olinin railway line. That house was garrisoned by No 3 Company of the divisional
pioneer battalion which was completely cut off and whose food and
ammunition were both running low. It was a desperate situation. The
house was held by 12 men, the last survivors of No 3 Company, and
because it offered warmth and shelter against the freezing cold, it was the
target for attacks by Soviet infantry. For four days and nights they had
launched one assault after the other. They had come over in waves, not
dressed in camouflage clothing and, as they waded slowly forward, their
brown overcoated figures had been silhouetted against the knee-deep
snow. That depth of snow slowed the pace of the Russian soldiers and as
they slogged forward they were shot down without compassion. Their
attacks had been made in platoon and sometimes in company strength, but
had not even gained a foothold in the house. For four days and nights the
Reds had battled in vain but that situation was unlikely to continue.
Losses, shortages of food and ammunition and, above all, lack of sleep
were diminishing the ability of the SS pioneers to hold out. The young
officer commanding the remnants sent out a request for help. Battle group
responded quickly and soon men of 16 Company, in which Ehm was serving, mounted in a half-track vehicle were en route to the isolated house.
The half-track rolled over the Red positions near the house, firing machine
pistols at enemy soldiers offering resistance or at others trying to escape,
and blowing up Red machine gun posts with explosive charges. By such
aggressive action the men of 16 Company Group smashed the Russian
encirclement and relieved their pioneer comrades. It had been an operation typical of everyday life on the Eastern Front.

By mid-March the whole battle group was holding a roughly semi-
circular line — if one could dignify the scattered and isolated machine
guns posts as a battle line -around the Red forces in the bend of the Volga.
Other units of corps formed part of that ring. It must not be thought that
the trapped Russian armies were defenceless or defeated. On the contrary,
Koniev's orders were to continue with the offensive and his armies sought
to carry out the orders of their commander. They had first struck northwards towards the Volga hoping to force a way through German 6th Corps
and to escape across the river. Frustrated in that endeavour their commanders had then changed the direction of the main thrust and driven south,
intending to escape from the ring by filtering through the densely wooded
areas which are a feature of the terrain in that region. A massive concen-

tration of Soviet strength struck, and seemed likely to smash through, at Reschatalovo, where battle group's right flank touched the left flank of 251st Infantry Division.

On that sector Russian attacks had already created a wide salient and their persistent assaults were intended to deepen this. Their formations had sheltered and rested throughout the eve of their new offensive in a number of villages, chiefly Kishkino, Chernovo and Lyschchevo, places strung out along a lateral east-west country road. Early in the morning those units began their southward advance led by the formations which had sheltered in Chernovo. Those detachments advanced through Sticfel wood — so-called from its jackboot shape on maps and aerial reconnaissance photographs — and then through Riegel wood before emerging onto the open ground which runs up towards the small town of Ovskanskovo. There in the open below Riegel wood they lay down, a solid brown mass on the white snow, waiting until the formations which had sheltered in the other villages reached them. The whole line then made a general advance, a mass attack, designed to crash its way through the flimsy German ring by sheer weight of numbers. The offensive planned by the commanders of Kampfgruppe "Reich" was designed to collapse the salient behind the attacking Soviet forces through the capture, first, of Riegel and then of Stiefel wood.

The battle opened with the great mass of Red Army formations moving upon Ovskanskovo. Their advance lacked subtlety or finesse and was little more than a huge movement of lightly armed men advancing in blocks into the fire of machine guns. Otto Kumm described the outcome of one assault upon "Der Fuehrer" Regiment — and although "DF" is not the subject of this account, the General's words illustrate the intensity of the blood-letting which was to become the norm in the battles around Stiefel wood. Kumm wrote "The enemy dead formed walls of corpses in front of our Company positions...".

It was such suicidal assaults which now came in against the men of battle group "Reich". They were used to Soviet officers wasting their men in bravura charges and had become accustomed to facing overwhelming odds in the savage battles peculiar to the Russian Front, but everything that they had experienced to that time paled when compared to the frenzied assaults which now came in upon them. The Red infantry tramped up the long slope towards Reshetalovo where Harmel and Kment Groups held the ground and without making any attempt to deploy into a battle formation. They were unwieldy blocks of soldiers incapable of carrying out even simple manoeuvres and that slow-moving, brown-coated mass soon came under the massed, accurate and destructive fire of the men and machines of the SS. The day had opened clear and without the snow storms which had fogged earlier mornings. In the dove grey light the men of Kment and Harmel groups saw great numbers of the enemy moving over the snowy plain. Some of the younger SS men, new to battle, were awed by the masses being put in against them. Others were aware of how few they were and how many were the hosts of the enemy. The veterans merely saw the oncoming Reds as new targets. It would be more easy for them to kill the masses of enemy soldiers who seemed to cover all the ground to their front, to their right and to their left. And, far away, in the distance fresh contingents of the enemy could be seen debouching from Riegel wood. Today would be a day of slaughter. And so it was. And so was the following day. On the third day of this, relatively minor battle on a very small part of the Eastern Front, the SS commanders sensed with relief that the enemy effort was slackening on their sector.

Now was the time for the German counter-blow to go in. In order to gain a clear understanding of that operation the position of units in the battle line as well as tactically important pieces of woodland are described below. On the left flank of 251st Infantry Division stood Kment and Harmel Groups. The line then swung north-westwards up towards Komorokovo and to the area held by the SS pioneers. In front of that village there extended the large expanse of Birnen wood. Holding the ground on the left of the pioneers was Tost Group which had first captured Y wood and had then gone on to take Hantel wood. Battle group HQ was in Ashevo. Along the narrow east-west country road mentioned earlier lay the village of Dorogino and east of that place the small — small by Russian standards — Riegel wood. North-east of Riegel lay Stiefel wood, an objective which should have been taken in the first week of the offensive, but which still remained uncaptured when Kampfgruppe "Reich" left the line in June. It was the measure of the importance of that piece of woodland that both sides fought so long and so hard to possess it.

The German counter-blow on the sector held by KG "Reich" began on 21 March, when Standartenfuehrer Ostendorff issued his battle orders. Harmel Group, reinforced by the ski company, was to advance from Ovsyanikolovo, on a northerly thrust line through Riegel wood, was then to change direction and thrust north-east towards the final objective — Stiefel wood. The left flank of Harmel's advance would be covered by the SS pioneers who were to capture Birnen wood. On their left Tost Group was also to support Harmel's advance with heavy machine gun and mortar fire from positions along the eastern edge of Hantel wood.

Ostendorff's battle plan did not expect Harmel's Grenadiers to meet serious opposition until they had passed through Riegel wood and, although that wood was not yet in German hands, a strong platoon-sized group from Tost battalion was to "comb it out" and to hold it. The flank of that platoon would be covered by another of Tost's platoons. As soon as those two units advanced into battle the rest of Tost Group were to follow. Once the whole battalion was on its objective in Riegel wood, all-round defences were to be dúg and contact gained with the ski company. In Ostendorff's opinion the success of the combing-out and consolidation operations would so ease the Harem Group's advance that it would meet only minimal opposition. The events of that day were to show that Harmel's appreciation of the situation was over-confident and that he had badly underestimated the determination of the Soviet commanders to retain their hold on this important area.

As was now standard operational procedure a Stuka squadron bombed and machine gunned the enemy's positions in Stiefel wood. The dive-bombers finished their work and half an hour later, at 13.40hrs, the guns of the battle group fired a barrage. The Soviet artillery response was not long in coming and when it did, it was a crushing counter-barrage which fell along the entire length of the SS perimeter. That hurricane of fire brought with it heavy losses and the battle patrol of Tost Battalion which was grouped for a briefing, was wiped out by a cascade of heavy mortar bombs. Losses among commanders were also high and so intense and accurate was the Russian gunfire that a Panzer company on Tost's right flank was forced to withdraw. Each attack by the pioneers towards Birnen wood was smothered by intense Russian artillery fire which drove the pioneers back and the battle group's only success was that gained by the ski company which had managed to penetrate into Stiefel wood. On the piece of high ground which was their objective the ski troops dug in to await further developments. It was soon very clear that they were surrounded and a night operation by Tost Battalion was mounted to bring them out. This had barely got under way when the point unit saw figures coming down a forest path and as these drew near they were recognised as being from the ski company's heavy weapons detachment. The company commander had been among those wounded during the operation and, with the strength of his company reduced to five NCOs and 26 men, had ordered those survivors to pull out of the wood.

There was now no purpose in Tost continuing with its relief operation and it pulled back to the positions it had earlier left on the eastern edge of Hantel wood. One fact was very clear: the enemy was determined fight to hold Stiefel wood. Another fact was that it was vital for the development of future operations that the SS capture it. A standard infantry attack having failed, the next attempt would have to be made using armour. It does not need to be stressed that the employment of AFVs in urban or wooded areas leaves them at a grave disadvantage vis a vis a determined defender armed with a Molotov cocktail or explosive charges.

But the orders were that Stiefel wood had to be taken and the Panzermen would have to risk themselves and their vehicles to take it.

During the late afternoon of 22 March, battle group HQ issued orders for a fresh and stronger attack to take place on the following day. The main burden of that new operation was to be carried by Tost Battalion whose effort would be supported by SP Battery Malachovski and Panzer Company Hummel. That mixed infantry and Panzer group was to advance from a point to the south-west of Unova and to pass through Stiefel wood, destroying the enemy there as well as those to the west of the woods. This would be, in effect, a thrust into the back of the enemy and would unsettle him. As soon as it became clear that the infantry/SP/Panzer attack had achieved that unsettling effect, then Harmel and Kment Groups were to carry out a frontal attack and were to pursue the enemy closely if he pulled out of Kishkino.

Aware that the exhausted condition of his men jeopardised the success of the new attack, Harmel requested and received a 24hr postponement. In the morning of 23 March there was a conference with the commanders of the recce battalion, of the battle group and of Tost Group and during the afternoon Harmel and Tost went to inspect the wooded area to the east of Ovsyanikoivo, the ground across which the attack would be made. The ski company, now under the command of recce battalion, was given orders to reconnoitre the southern edge of Stiefel wood. While the ski detachments were carrying out that task a message from battle group HQ announced that the Stuka strike arranged for the following morning had been postponed. Without that bombing, essential to "lift" his men onto the objective, Harmel knew that the operation stood no chance of success and would result in unacceptable losses. Once again he requested a further postponement of 24hrs. His appreciation of the enemy's strength and resolution was confirmed by the ski company whose recce patrol was driven off with heavy fire. Once again the request for a postponement was authorised. The attack, when it did go in, and even though it was made with SP and Panzer support, could not take the wood and it remained in Russian hands.

Any attack by one side was followed by an immediate counter-attack by the other. The fighting took on more and more the character of the battles of the Western Front in the First World War. Where it was possible the SS collected the German and Russian fallen and buried them with respect. The Red Army did not bother to gather the bodies of their dead soldiers which lay uncollected among the trees. As the snow melted and the bodies corrupted the smell of decaying flesh, excrement and other stinks poisoned the air. Spring came in and with the rise in temperatures the Rasputitsa returned -the thick glutinous, seemingly bottomless mud that covers rural Russia during the spring thaw and in the autumn rainy period. Two incidents from the fighting in Stiefel wood recall its horror:

"After the Stukas flew away there was a deathly quiet. Here and there one could hear cries of pain or the crackling sound of fires burning. A few of us survivors stood up and rubbed our eyes. Then we heard the distant sound of armoured fighting vehicles — but coming from behind us. German Panzers and infantry were coming forward. The advance was led by a couple of SPs roaring along and running over everything in their way. Luckily, they recognised us as friendly troops.

"Everything that could move joined in the attack against the Russians in the wood. During the fighting we overran a Russian slaughterhouse. Dead horses lay all over the area and there was a strong smell of blood in the air. Some animals which had not yet been slaughtered had their lives saved by our advance. It was odd. We had never thought of slaughtering our horses, even when we were starving. Horses, so far as we were concerned, were mates and we would have considered ourselves to be cannibals had we eaten them..."

The events of 7 April were remembered by another veteran:

"In the morning of that day Russian tanks came in against one of the heavy machine gun posts manned by No 3 Company of Tost Battalion. A T34 carrying Red infantry on its outside broke through into the German positions and swung its main armament around towards an MG34. The tank opened fire and its second shot hit the machine gun, knocked it out of action killing two of the crew. The tank lumbered on crushing beneath its tracks the machine gun tripod and ammunition cases. Red infantry jumped down to finish off the job and rushed towards the two surviving men of the machine gun team. These pulled out their Walther pistols and opened fire upon the advancing Russians. Some time later another Company of Tost put in a counter-attack and recaptured the lost position. The two SS gun numbers were found still holding their pistols and with a half-circle of dead Red Army men around them. Both were dead, killed by a shot in the head. Model's order of the day dated 22 May, praised the exemplary bravery of the two men who had done their duty to the end."

An incident from the struggle for Hantel wood shows the intensity with which that, too, was conducted. This shortened account of a Russian attack against a Company of Tost battalion has been graphically described by W.R.Lerner, one of those who fought and was wounded there:

"Losses to No 2 Platoon had reduced it in strength to 10 men manning an Infantry gun under the command Unterscharfuehrer Hitzelberger. We took post in the extreme north-eastern corner of Hantel wood. The losses from wounds and frost bite had not only reduced our numbers, but had also lowered our morale. On top of everything else the daily temperatures often went below minus 40, we were all hungry and were crawling with lice.

"Our infantry gun was aimed along a forest ride with an OP looking towards Stiefel wood. In front of us and not 500 metres away there was a small group of enemy-held houses with smoke rising from their chimneys. Where there was smoke we knew there was warmth and cooked food. We of No 2 Platoon had nothing to shelter us except a large, single standing, fir tree. We grouped ourselves round its base, covered the snow with branches, lay on these and tried to snatch some sleep. Unfortunately, Regiment did not issue the order to capture that little hamlet whose houses would have given us warmth and cover. But we had one little luxury. One of our group had 'liberated' an empty petrol drum which we had turned into a sort of stove. Over this we melted snow in our mess tins so that we could make some sort of hot drink.

"The enemy's artillery barrages did not really worry us. The deep snow usually absorbed much of the blast from the explosions but one shell which did explode destroyed the stable we had made out of blocks of snow to shelter the Panje horses which pulled our little gun. The death of those two beasts meant that in future we would have to tow the gun ourselves. On 24th March, we were given some good news. Rations were coming up. They did. Each man received a tin of sardines and there was rum in our tea. Those lucky ones, of whom I was one, also had post from home. Since it was night time I could not read my letter and stuck in into my map case. Neither could I eat my tin of sardines — they were frozen solid and I put them into my map case as well. I took off my belt on which hung the map case and settled down to rest. We did not sleep very long. In the early hours the Russians fired a barrage on our positions but there were no casualties.

"We manned the gun and moved towards the OP only to find that it was already under direct attack from enemy tanks and infantry. Some of the Russian infantrymen rode on the outside of the T34s; others were brought into action on sledges pulled by the tanks. The infantry soon overran our OP but before they could reach the gun position we had removed the optical sights and part of the breech mechanism. Unterscharfuehrer Hitzelberger told us to strike out in a south-westerly direction where we would gain touch with our own troops. We were all surprised at how quickly everything had happened and in the confusion I lost my belt, map case, sardines and letter from my mother.

"An officer of 11th Infantry Regiment joined us and then an SS captain of our own Division. It was decided that we would make an immediate counter-attack and our group of eight men went in against a Russian tank Company and two companies of infantry. We moved forward, half hidden by a gulley in the snow, but when that cover ran out saw ahead of us an open space which we would have to cross to reach the enemy. It was then we realised that we were practically surrounded. A flurry of shells fired by our own artillery flew over us but fell too short to have any effect upon the Russians. I saw one of my comrades lying on the snow and went across to see if he was alright. In a loud voice he warned me to keep away as there was a sniper in a tree. Then I was hit...shot through the stomach. My comrade dragged me into a shell hole and practically undressing me to get at the wound applied a field dressing. Strangely, I felt no pain... He crawled out of the shell hole to fetch a stretcher bearer then fell over, shot dead. By this time the rest of the group had pulled back. I was alone and expecting any minute that the first people to reach me would be Russians who would club me to death.

"However, it was Hitzelberger who reached me first. He had noticed that I was missing and had returned to find me. He raised me to my feet and pointed in the direction I had to go. Then he left me to deal with the others in the group. I found that I was able to walk and moved slowly with Russian explosive bullets whizzing round my head until I met another one of our platoon. He told me to lie down on his shelter half and he would drag me across the snow. There was a sudden explosion and he, too, fell dead. I staggered to my feet and walked on alone. Then I saw in front of me, and only a hundred metres away, a T34 whose gun was aimed directly at me. The gun fired but the shot fell short and so much of the force of the explosion was absorbed by the snow that the blast did not even knock me over. But I was not wearing a steel helmet and was wounded on the crown of the head and on the cheekbone. Those wounds bled heavily. Then my left arm went numb. I was now completely helpless. My left arm was useless and I needed my right hand to hold up my trousers. I decided to end it all and deliberately walked towards the tank, looking neither left nor right but straight to the front. But nothing happened... Some way past the T34 I saw some of my platoon and realised that I was safe at last. I fell to the ground unconscious and came round in the dressing station of Harmel group."

On 30 May the war diary recorded the last offensive operation carried out in Stiefel wood by the men of "Reich" battle group. A barrage was fired between 17.00 and 21.50hrs by all the batteries which had been brought together to support the attack. While the artillery was firing, a small assault group consisting of a few Grenadiers, a heavy machine gun team, a demolition squad and two flame-thrower detachments was briefed on the operation. At 22.00hrs the assault group went out and struck enemy opposition only 18mins later. Despite that resistance within 5mins the group had broken into Stiefel wood and at 22.30hrs had reached its objective. An immediate Soviet counter-attack was smashed and flung back. The regimental artillery then opened fire on the northern sector of the wood to cover the group's withdrawal and as it pulled back it came under heavy Russian machine gun and mortar fire. Shortly after 23.00hrs the assault group was back in German lines having suffered three casualties — one pioneer badly wounded, and one pioneer and one Grenadier lightly wounded. A prisoner was taken, 25 of the enemy were killed and a number of installations were destroyed.

On 1 June, Kampfgruppe "Reich" was relieved from the line by 53rd Infantry Regiment and a few days later left Rzhev railway station en route to Germany. The hard and bitter mission was at an end.

There is a German Army song that runs, "We buried so many of our best in foreign soil". Among the great number of men of Kampfgruppe "Reich" who were buried in foreign soil was Hauptsturmfueher Tost, the commanding officer of 1st Battalion "Deutschland" Regiment. He was mortally wounded by mortar bomb shrapnel and died in the regimental aid post in Stiefel wood.

Battle Group Marcks, which led the advance of the Italo–German Army during the 1942 spring offensive in Libya

A desert is by definition a bare and hostile region which cannot sustain human life much above a primitive level. A desert is a treeless wilderness whether it be the wastes of ice at the North and South Poles, or the hot, barren sand seas of Africa, Asia and Australia.

The Libyan desert in North Africa was a theatre of war in which German soldiers fought from March 1941 until the surrender of the Axis armies in May 1943. That Libyan desert, more than 1,000km from west to east, was described by one German commander, General von Ravenstein, as a tactician's paradise but a quartermaster's hell. It was crossed by only one, single, all-weather road, the Via Balbia, which ran from the provincial capital, Tripoli, to the frontier with Egypt where it met a British military road leading to the Canal Zone and Palestine. To supplement that road's freight and passenger carrying capacity on their side of the frontier the British had built a railway line to the Nile delta, but there was no comparable railway system in the Italian colony. This meant that a land journey from from one side of Libya to the other could only be made by motor transport or by animal. In addition to the permanent Via Balbia there were the Trigh, impermanent tracks tramped out by the feet of generations of Arab desert dwellers. The Trigh surface could be destroyed by a strong downpour of rain but in dry weather it was often the only firm surface in a sea of shifting sand into which vehicles could be — and frequently were — bogged down to their axles. Although desert covered most of Libya's land area there was a narrow fertile strip which ran along the Mediterranean coast. Deep in the southernmost region of Libya was the impassable, vast Qattara Depression. Below the narrow, fertile area the desert began. Only seldom was this made up of the golden dunes of popular imagination. More often the desert surface was a gritty grey dust which had been scoured over millenia from solid base rock and which blanketed the vast and empty wasteland. A sand desert is an arid region but even in the great Libyan desert there were native water wells which were identified on military maps by the Arabic term "Bir", as for example, Bir Hachim, a place which we shall meet in the account of Kampfgruppe Briel.

As aids to navigation in the Egyptian section of the great desert, the British Army had set up trigonometrical points, piles of stones surmounted by an empty petrol drum on which the trig bearing was painted. These vital aids to orientation were carefully marked on British maps, yet even with such information it was possible to lose one's way. The compass and the vehicle mileage counter were two indispensables in a wasteland that could be as featureless as the sea, or nearly so. Rock hills or Djebels rose abruptly out of the desert's surface, but it was often so difficult to distinguish between individual pieces of high ground that during the battle of El Alamein, for example, officers of the Highland Division could not agree on which was the hill they had been ordered to capture. The surface of the desert was also cut by steep and wide wadis or dried up river beds, which restricted vehicle movement.

In short, the desert was a grim, forbidding and hostile environment in which to have to fight and it was to this barren land that the German Army came. Its soldiers were unaccustomed to desert conditions, unlike their Italian allies and their British opponents whose armies had soldiered for decades in hot colonial territories. The Germans had no recent experience of tropical colonies nor, did it seem, had OKW undertaken much preparation before sending its troops to these stony wastes. High Command had assumed perhaps, that because the German force would be conducting purely defensive operations at the end of a short and assured supply line, neither special food nor equipment were necessary. As a consequence the rations issued to the German soldier in Africa did not give him a balanced diet and were completely wrong for the climate. This may have been due to the fact that the German dietary experts knew little of conditions in Libya. They printed leaflets containing precise and detailed descriptions of how to dress and prepare gazelle for cooking, overlooking or not knowing that there were few gazelle in the fertile strip and none at all deep in the desert. Nor had the experts given thought to how food was to be cooked. The German Army field cooker was solid-fuelled, an excellent method of cooking in continental Europe with its ample supplies of wood but of limited use in a treeless desert. Wood for fuel had to be brought over by ship from Italy and if those ships had to be loaded with firewood, then there was no space to carry more important cargoes such as ammunition, supplies or petrol, the absolute essentials of mobile, motorised warfare.

The Germans may have come unprepared to Africa but they adapted so quickly that they achieved great successes in offensives which they launched within weeks of arriving in this totally alien theatre of war. Being without recent colonial experience the Germans came to the tropics with no preconceived ideas. Thus they went about in the sun without shirts or hats and seemed to need no acclimatisation period. This led to stories circulated by English language newspapers that the men of the Afrika Korps had trained for war in the desert by being marched to and fro in monster glass houses set up on the sands of the Baltic coast. How else, British newspapers asked, was it possible for Rommel and his men to inflict frequent and humiliating defeats upon a succession of British veterans?

A more likely explanation was that the Afrika Korps had a flexibility which was found at every level of command from senior officers down to the squad leaders. The Germans also had complete trust in, and were absolutely familiar with, their equipment. They knew that their weapons and vehicles were well built, well designed, robust and powerful. Another factor which made for German success was confidence in their commanders and in themselves. But battles are not won simply through flexibility and confidence. Victory is on the side of the big battalions. Although it is certainly possible for skilled and able commanders of smaller battalions to delay or sometimes diminish the victory of the big battalions, size or strength usually prevail. The Western Allies were to demonstrate this factor in the final months of the war in Africa.

But before the Western Allies gained their maximum strength, their opponents, the German commanders, conducted operations in the unfamiliar terrain and extraordinary conditions with consummate skill and gained many victories through the use of Kampfgruppen. Almost from the earliest days in Libya and right through to the mountains and hills of Tunisia, the employment of such groups was a significant campaign factor, irrespective of whether the German forces were conducting defensive or offensive operations. Time and again groups were created to meet some particular situation and were broken up once the object of the mission had been accomplished. From the great number of Kampfgruppen which were created during the war in Africa, I have made a small selection. These will demonstrate the skill with which battle group leaders used the men and resources placed under their command, as well as illustrating their ability to overcome terrain conditions to gain the objectives which had been set them.

In February 1941, the advance parties of those units which were to win fame and glory as the German Afrika Korps, landed in the port of Tripoli. They had been sent by Hitler to support Mussolini's all-but-defeated "Army of Libya" and, thus, to keep Italy in the war. Military operations in the vast expanse of territory consisting of Libya and Egypt had opened the previous year. On 10 June 1940, at a time when the war in Western Europe was drawing to a close, the Italian fascist dictator had declared war on France and Britain and opened, thereby, a new theatre of operations in North Africa and specifically in Libya, a country lying between Tunisia and Egypt. As a consequence of the Franco-German armistice of June 1940, the French colony of Tunisia had become neutral but Egypt, although nominally an independent country was, in effect, a British protectorate. It was garrisoned by troops of Middle East Command and was, consequently, the nearest objective of Mussolini's military ambitions.

He acted promptly and shortly after he had declared war ordered his Commander-in-Chief in Africa, Marshal Graziani, to lead the Army of Libya into Egypt and capture Alexandria and the Suez Canal. Graziani, acutely aware that the weapons and vehicles on issue to his army were obsolescent and also concerned at the difficulties he would encounter in supplying and maintaining his force of 300,000 men, demanded modern AFVs before he would advance. Mussolini, impatient for military victory, issued a direct order. Graziani was forced to obey but marched the Army of Libya less than 90km into Egypt before he halted the advance and made camp on the acres of arid sand which his Army had captured. The prize of that shallow penetration into Egypt was the capture of Sidi Barrani in whose streets, according to Italian radio, "...trams were still running when it was captured...", a statement which would have surprised the inhabitants of the small Egyptian town which had no tram system.

During the months that the Army of Libya rested after the strain of its 90km advance, the British Commander, Wavell, planned a counterthrust. This opened on 6 December 1940, and not only flung the Italians out of Egypt but pursued them across the eastern Libyan province of Cyrenaica and into Libya's westernmost province of Tripolitania. It was at this time, when it seemed as if Mussolini's African Empire would fall to Wavell's 30,000 warriors, that the leaders of Britain and Germany issued orders which brought about a dramatic change in the military situation in Africa. Churchill, the British Prime Minister directed Wavell to send the bulk of his army to Greece, a country already under assault from the Italians and which now faced an all-out German attack. The loss of those two veteran divisions left the British forces in Libya understrength and incapable of capturing Tripoli and bringing the war in the desert to a victorious conclusion. For his part the German leader, Hitler, alarmed by the Italian military collapse and aware that the loss of Mussolini's empire would take Italy out of the war and, thereby, change the balance of power in the Mediterranean, ordered a blocking force to be sent to Africa, a force strong enough to bolster the Italians and keep them in the war as Germany's ally.

The General to whom Hitler gave command of that blocking force, Erwin Rommel, was not the type of man to be content with conducting a defence. He had won Germany's highest award for bravery during the Great War and in the 1940 campaign in France, had handled his 7th Panzer Division so effectively that its role changed from a support one to becoming the spearhead of the Panzer thrust to the Channel. Rommel was an aggressive commander and on 31 March 1941, within six weeks of landing in Tripolitania, opened his first offensive. Such was the pace of the German advance that much of the Libyan territory which had been taken by the British was quickly recaptured from them. Only the important port of Tobruk did not fall at that time, but it was cut off from the main body of the British desert force — soon to be known as 8th Army. That first and very successful German operation brought the name of Rommel and his Afrika Korps to the attention of the world and when that first offensive was halted, the Axis army was on the Halfaya Pass, almost within sight of the Egyptian frontier. During that first offensive a great many battle groups had been created and disbanded. The 21st Panzer Division, for example, formed three: Kampfgruppe Stephan, around 5th Panzer Regiment; Kampgruppe Schutte, a machine gun group; and Kampfgruppe Panzerhagen, a battalion-sized unit of 90th Light Division's 347th Regiment. But it is not those groups which will be described below nor even those formed during "Crusader", the British counter-offensive of November-December 1941. Instead the first account of this section is that of Kampfgruppe Marcks, created by Rommel for his January 1942 offensive, and the second account that of Kampfgruppe Briel, which was to spearhead the German thrust through the Alamein line in June 1942. Then we shall leave Libya and the desert and deal with battle groups which went into action in the hills of Tunisia between November 1942 and May 1943.

To introduce Kampfgruppe Marcks we go back to the conclusion of 8th Army's "Crusader" offensive. One result of the British operation was that the Axis armies had been driven back almost to Agedabia, from where they had begun their first offensive. But although Panzer Army Africa had lost ground it had not lost heart and by 12 January, was preparing to go over to the offensive once again. Axis supply ships had reached Tripoli and the increase in Panzer strength, together with abundant fuel supplies which he now possessed gave the German commander the confidence to undertake new operations. The opening attack had been planned as a pre-emptive blow to spoil 8th Army's anticipated offensive, but it quickly developed into a rolling and thundering storm which reached the Gazala area during May 1942 and as far as the Alamein line by June. That offensive marked the high tide of Axis hopes in North Africa. Thereafter came Montgomery's victory at El Alamein in October 1942, followed by the Anglo-American landings in Algeria and Tunisia, leading inevitably towards the surrender of the Italo-German forces in May 1943.

In the late autumn of 1941, Lieutenant-Colonel Werner Marcks was posted from the Eastern Front to Libya where he took over command of 155th Infantry Regiment, a component of 90th Light Division. His handling of that regiment during the November fighting attracted Rommel's attention and he selected Marcks to create and to lead a special Kampfgruppe, composed of detachments taken from the 155th Regiment, the 21st Panzer Division, the 90th Light Division and a tank group from the Italian Armoured Division "Ariete".

That battle group, as the spearhead of Rommel's new offensive in the spring of 1942, was to drive up the Via Balbia and to smash through the Guards Brigade which was blocking the road to Agedabia. Once KG Marcks had breached the British line a follow-up group, consisting of Italian 20th Corps and the main of 90th Light Division, was to pour through the gap, race eastwards and create the northern arm of a pincer operation. That pincer would strike downwards to meet a southern one made up of the Panzer divisions of Afrika Korps which would be striking through the Wadi el Faregh. At a given point the pincer jaws would meet and the British forces in the Agedabia sector, principally 1st Armoured Division, would be encircled. Rommel arrived at Kampfgruppe HQ shortly after sun-up on 21 January 1942 and during the pre-battle discussion repeatedly emphasised that the successful outcome of the new offensive would depend upon the speed with which Kampfgruppe Marcks operated.

Over the radio of his command vehicle Marcks named Agedabia as the day's objective and then gave the order, "Kampfgruppe marsch". The armoured cars of the point unit bounced across the uneven surface of the desert, their faster speed allowing them to outdistance the slower vehicles of the Panzer detachments. Behind the armour came lorries carrying the infantry component and half-tracks towing Flak guns, while on either side of the racing columns motor cyclists of the battle group's reconnaissance formation protected the flanks. At this stage of the operation, the advance to contact phase, the Kampfgruppe drove tightly closed-up for better tactical control. There was little need for it yet to spread out into open formation. At that time the Luftwaffe held air superiority in North Africa and ruled the skies over the battlefield. The vehicles raced eastwards and then far away on the distant horizon small plumes of dust could be seen rising in the cold, still January air. Through field glasses the German Panzer commandants studied the silhouettes of the vehicles at the base of those dust clouds and identified them as British armoured cars. The 8th Army's patrols had Marcks' group under observation and it would not be long before battle was joined. The British armoured car patrols pulled back in

the face of the German superior numbers and over their radio sets opera-
tors in the Panzers picked up messages being passed by their British opponents reporting the movements of the German force. Any hope that there
might have been of gaining the tactical advantage of surprise had gone.
Over the air the armoured cars called the tank regiments to battle and very
soon the familiar outlines of the main British tank types — Matildas, Cru-
saders and Valentines — could be distinguished in the bright, sunny morning, forming up behind the field defences to the west of Agedabia.

Marcks watched the British armour deploy and took careful note of
the lanes through which the tanks were advancing; those lanes were, he
knew, channels through the enemy's minefields. On both sides of those
minefield gaps he could make out sandbagged defences — anti-tank gun
positions and a larger number of infantry slit trenches. The battle group's
advance to contact had been but a brief journey. Now had come the time
for his KG to fight its first battle under his command. Marcks decided to
use his artillery to bring down a barrage of shells and to dominate the
British. Under that rain of gunfire the Panzers would work their way forward and close in for the kill. It was not standard German armoured policy
to engage in tank-versus-tank duels. The held opinion was that this was a
misuse of the function of armour, but in this situation where he had to
smash a way through prepared defences, speed was the most important
factor. Speed to dominate the enemy by smothering him with fire, speed to
close with him, speed to create a gap in his defences and speed to exploit
the breach made so that the follow-up corps could sweep through and create the northern pincer.

Circumstances had dictated the situation and, wasteful or not, Marcks ordered his Panzers to stand off and fight duels with their opponents.
While the armour of both sides fought their long-range actions, the motor
cycle reconnaissance battalion was brought forward, ordered to dismount
and was put into an infantry attack which went in covered by concentrated
mortar and machine gun fire. Soon the motor cyclists had gained a
foothold in the British infantry positions. Radio communication was
excellent on this occasion and as the motor cyclists reported over their
wireless sets the exact location of the anti-tank gun positions surrounding
them, German mortar teams switched to those targets and smothered them
in a storm of bombs. Soon the small gap which the motor cyclists had created had been widened and then extended again as more and more anti-
tank gun positions were knocked out and infantry positions taken out.

Colonel Marcks supported the infantry battle by continually pushing
his Flak guns forward to give close and direct fire to the motor cyclists.
Then he sensed that it was the moment for the Panzers to charge the
enemy positions and to create the breach. Over the radio he gave the order

"Follow me" and led them towards the gap which his motor cyclists were fighting hard to hold open. At top speed the tracked and half-tracked AFVs roared over and through the British defences and thrust towards the day's objective, leaving the motor cyclists to mount up and follow in their tracks. Left behind on the desert were knocked out Matildas and Valentines and the dead of both sides. The wave of German armour raced on, meeting no opposition until west of Giofia where a British artillery regiment reacted swiftly to the approaching Panzer columns and opened fire. The KG had no time to halt for a set-piece attack. Agedabia was still some way ahead so this troublesome artillery obstacle would have to be attacked on the run and without proper planning. German organisation and flexibility were equal to the task. Weaving their way through the explosions of 25pdr shells the Panzers charged at and overran the defiant gunners. With that obstacle cleared the battle group had shattered the hard crust of the British defence and was now in 8th Army's rear areas meeting only tail units — lorry columns of the supply services, most of which turned and fled to avoid destruction or capture. The way to Agedabia was now wide open. Less that four hours had passed since the battle group had begun this operation and it was already close to the target.

Marcks' columns drove through the short winter afternoon deeper into the British rear areas, but then the deeper they penetrated the stronger grew the opposition. Wireless messages had gone out warning 8th Army that a rogue Panzer column was on the loose and units were taking appropriate action to destroy it. Out in "the blue" units were being brought together to attack the flanks of the battle group, but those formations in its path which could not take evasive action, were ordered to stand fast and open fire to destroy or at least delay it. One after the other those flickers of resistance were smothered but the Kampfgruppe had no opportunity to take and guard prisoners. In such circumstances prisoners were an encumbrance. Under the unwritten rules of desert warfare, captured transport which could not be used was destroyed and the disarmed enemy soldiers left with supplies and water and given the choice of marching across the desert to find the main body of their own army, or of waiting to be put "in the bag" of the forces following closely behind the spearhead.

An hour before last light the columns halted. Darkness comes quickly in the desert. Within minutes of sunset the night is a black and obscuring cloak. Everything which needs to be done has to be done in that single, last hour of daylight. Food prepared, positions allocated and taken up, vehicles tanked up and serviced ready for the move out at dawn. The intense dark of that January night was deepened by thick cloud and in total darkness the men of KG Marcks slept immediately and soundly despite the numbing cold.

An early start on the 22nd and a swift drive soon brought them close to Agedabia. Through the breach which KG Marcks had created, Rommel had already begun to sluice Italian 20th Corps and the rest of 90th Light Division and those formations flooded across the desert in a vast assaulting armoured wave. The battle for the town was neither as hard nor as long as Marcks had feared. Agedabia fell within an hour. The given objective had been reached and taken but the battle group was given no opportunity to rest. A new objective was assigned it — Antelat, 60km away to the north-east. Marcks set out but then Rommel changed the battle plan. KG was not to advance upon Antelat. That objective would be taken by the newly created Kampfgruppe Warrelmann. Marcks was to move southeastwards to reach Abd el Giara from where it was to drive along the Wadi Faregh and now, forming part of the southern pincer, it was to close the ring around 1st Armoured Division in the Agedabia-Giaf el Natar sector.

At dawn on 24 January, the Kampfgruppe moved forward and with all his formations now in position Rommel began to destroy 1st Armoured Division. The tactic he proposed to employ was a simple one — a wall of 88mm guns and a line of tanks whose less powerful main armament would form an auxiliary gun line. It would have to be a short wall of 88s, the others were dispersed across the desert. But despite that shortage of guns the situation favoured the Germans. First, they had a prepared plan while the British could only react to the Afrika Korps' initiatives; second, the Germans, being more flexible, could switch their point of maximum effort to meet any developing crisis before it became serious; and, third, the main armament of British tanks, the 2pdr, was outranged by the standard German tank guns — the 5cm and 7.5cm backed by the fearsome 88s in the gun line. It was an uneven contest. Wherever 8th Army's armour sought to create a breach, Marcks was soon on the spot leading forward a small group of men, a battle group within a battle group, to hold and to fling back any break-out attempt. British infantry attacks were driven to ground by heavy machine gun fire and, while pinned down, were smothered by 88mm airbursts.

The fading light of day brought the fighting of 24 January to an end. It had been a success for Afrika Korps and particularly for Colonel Marcks and his men. More than 1,000 prisoners had been taken and 117 tanks had been knocked out. Much of 1st Armoured Division had been destroyed but a sizeable remnant was withdrawing through the desert towards the fort at Msus. Rommel laid out his plan to destroy that remnant by pincer attack. Kampfgruppe Marcks was to come in from the west and the combined strength of Afrika Korps and the Italian 20th Corps was to strike in from the east.

The German units moved to their assigned positions and fighting began at first light, but before it had developed Rommel arrived at Marcks' HQ with an amendment to the plan. It was essential to weaken 1st Armoured further still before the coup de grace could be given. To achieve this he proposed to draw the British armour into a trap — the sort of trap that he had set successfully in France during 1940. He sent out officers to bring in every available anti-tank and 88mm gun, formed these into a Pak front and set this up behind Kampfgruppe Marcks. The battle group was ordered to drive towards Msus as if seeking battle, but at a given signal it was to turn and withdraw westwards as if in panic flight. Rommel knew that the British commanders would take the bait and pursue what they saw as fleeing vehicles.

Marcks, knowing that his KG was the bait and that bait is often chewed up, unhesitatingly led his Panzers forward into the line of the British armoured Division's fire. A Panzer formation attacking in open order across the desert looked, according to a British soldier who experienced several of them, just like a naval operation. The churning tracks of the Panzers and the turning wheels of the lorries threw up behind each vehicle a plume of dust that looked like smoke rising from ships' funnels. Theoretically, the British had the advantage. They were firing from stable platforms at the advancing Panzers which, bumping and lurching across the desert, were not able to aim their guns with any accuracy. In theory, the British had only to fire at a point just in front of the dust plume to hit and destroy an onrushing Panzer. In practice, however, the 2pdr gun lacked the power to cut through the thick frontal armour of the Panzers and to knock out the enemy vehicles.

Over the radio came Rommel's order for the group to turn about. Each commandant ordered his driver "Hard lock" and the heavy Panzers swung on one track, skidded through an 180-degree turn, then as the track was unlocked the AFV raced away westwards. The lorries needed more space to wheel but soon the whole battle group was streaming back across the desert. Whether any 8th Army tank commander issued the excited pursuit call "Tally ho", is not known but the sight of the "fleeing" Germans roused the hunting instincts of the cavalry-minded British commanders and they set out in pursuit. Skilfully the vehicles of Kampfgruppe Marcks drove back passing through the gaps between the German guns, the racing Panzer tracks flinging up clouds of dust which obscured the 88s and their crews and which hid the gun line from the sight of the charging tank squadrons. Then, as the opaque dust screen blew away the German gunners saw before them a dream target — tanks whose main armament was short-ranged and ineffective. The gun line fired its first salvo, then reloaded but before the smoke of the second salvo had cleared seven tanks lay burning and the others were fleeing back towards Msus.

Rommel created yet another Kampfgruppe and sent this in to reach the Trigh junction at Msus, then changed its orders again and directed it to reinforce Marcks. Rommel had a new plan: a swift drive to capture Benghasi. To strengthen Marcks' group still further the German commander posted to it a number of units including 33rd Reconnaissance Battalion. Rommel knew that such reinforcement was necessary. Benghasi would be no easy objective. It was defended by three brigades of Indian infantry.

The attack opened in the evening of 26 January. While the main body of Kampfgruppe Marcks formed a tight formation — a mailed fist — some of the reinforcement groups were sent out to secure the Kampfgruppe's open, eastern flank and to protect it against 8th Army's armoured thrusts. Less than an hour after the operation began a khamseen enveloped the battle group. Thick swirling clouds of sand and dust blinded the drivers and forced them to reduce speed to a crawl. This waste of time and failure to exploit a climatic opportunity infuriated Rommel who was riding with Marcks. The General ordered his driver to the head of the column where, acting in the role of a ship's pilot, he led the battle group forward through the choking sand storm. Then it began to rain and had soon degenerated into a torrential downpour which washed out the surface of the Trigh and trapped the lorries driving along a wadi, in a thick and clinging slime. A few vehicles were manhandled out of the swamp and brought to high ground where they winched out others and soon Kampfgruppe Marcks was mobile again.

During the morning of 28 January, it reached Ridotto and late that afternoon Benina. Benghasi airfield was taken but as the battle group drew closer to the town, the Indian Brigades' defence stiffened, halting the German advance. Marcks, determined to force the attack forward, took post at the head of the Panzer group and led the charge towards the city. His command vehicle was knocked out but he climbed immediately into an armoured car and continued to lead the attack. Fires and detonations showed that the Indian troops were destroying ration stores and ammunition dumps before they evacuated the town. Benghasi fell and Marcks set out in pursuit of the Indians seeking to escape captivity by forced marches across the desert. An armoured car patrol backed by Panzers, intercepted the retreating troops, took many prisoner and sent them back to Benghasi.

Without pause or let-up Marcks thrust on, capturing town after town along the Via Balbia — Tocra, Barce, Marau and then his KG headed across Cyrenaica, meeting and overcoming British and Indian opposition wherever this was met. By the end of the first week of February, within 16 days of the new offensive opening, Cyrenaica had been recaptured and

Rommel's offensive to pre-empt a British attack had been successfully concluded. The advance then had to be halted. Afrika Korps had outrun its supplies. The front hardened in the Gazala area and both sides then lay behind extensive mine fields and prepared defences which they were to hold until Rommel's new offensive in the last week of May brought back to the desert those highly mobile operations which characterised it, and the static front "rommelled" again.

But even before the Gazala line was reached Kampfgruppe Marcks had been disbanded, its work completed. On 5 February Rommel had decorated its commander with the Knight's Cross of the Iron Cross and on 1 May was able to announce his promotion to the rank of colonel. These were fitting rewards for work well done.

It was stated above that the front "rommelled" again in May 1942. For that operation Kampfgruppe Marcks was reformed. It is not, however, the actions of that battle group which we follow in the story of the May-June battles but the operations of other groups and, principally, that of Kampfgruppe Briel.

Battle Group Briel created by Rommel to drive through the Alamein positions and capture Alexandria, summer 1942

In the spring of 1942, the plans of General Rommel and those of OKW coincided. The German commander in Africa proposed to mount a pre-emptive strike to diminish the growing strength of British 8th Army. German intelligence sources had advised him that his enemy's tank strength had risen to 742 machines and would continue to grow, whereas his own tank strength, including obsolescent Italian machines, was less than 600. His proposal for a new offensive met with sympathetic consideration at OKW for it accorded with Supreme Command's grand strategy. This was for a southern pincer arm striking through Egypt and the countries of the Middle East to link up with a northern pincer driving via Bulgaria and the Caucasus region of southern Russia. Those pincer arms would meet in Iran and would drive on towards India.

Rommel's plan and OKW's strategy also had a common link — the port of Tobruk. Rommel needed it to nourish his offensive and OKW to supply the southern pincer arm. Supreme Command's agreement to Rommel's plan for an offensive was however, conditional upon Tobruk being captured swiftly. If that happened then his advance was to halt on the Egyptian frontier, but if the town held out then his forces were to withdraw to Gazala.

The shape of Rommel's battle plan was dictated by vast and deep minefields which ran southwards from Gazala for a distance of about 60km into the desert. The obvious option for the new offensive would be to mount a frontal assault through those mine fields, but that would lose the element of surprise and be costly in men and material. A second option was to turn the southern flank of the British defence line by passing the bulk of the Axis army at night, round that desert flank at Bir Hacheim. That mobile force would then drive northwards towards the Via Balbia and the Mediterranean, would come up behind 8th Army's fixed positions, known as "boxes" and attack these from the west and from the east. With those boxes destroyed and his western flank now secure, Rommel would lead his armoured forces eastwards, would capture Tobruk and then, conveniently forgetting OKW's instruction to halt at the frontier, would press on towards Alexandria, the Suez Canal and the Middle East. He and Afrika Korps would have created the southern pincer before the northern one had even begun its opening moves.

Rommel was aware of the difficulties which would face him during that stage of the offensive when his forces were making their northward march to the sea. On his right would be the great mass of 8th Army's tanks and on his left the line of British boxes, each garrisoned by an infantry brigade, each of which would have to be taken out. While one part of his army attacked and destroyed those boxes another part would hold off the British armour until he could turn upon this and destroy it. He would, in effect, have to fight two battles at the same time — one infantry and the other armour. It would be a difficult operation and one requiring swift planning, flexible command decisions and immediate action. Battle groups would provide the answer as they had already done in earlier offensives.

At this point it is time to introduce Major Georg Briel whose battle group is the subject of this account. Among the first formations of Afrika Korps to debark in Tripoli was Briel's 606 Flak Battalion; and of the man himself, it would be true to say that he was one of a handful of unit commanders who fought without a break from the first German offensive in March 1941, to the battle of El Alamein in October 1942. He was also the first soldier of the Army in Africa to win the German Cross in Gold.

Briel, like Rommel, grasped the principles of desert warfare almost by instinct. It was a sort of sixth sense, an ability to utilise whatever facilities were available and the skill to exploit any weakness which the enemy showed. As early as the battles of March 1941, Briel had demonstrated his flexibility. He had gone on to show further evidence of command ability in May 1942, during the unsuccessful British counter-offensive Operation "Brevity", undertaken to raise the siege of Tobruk. He was the ideal battle group commander.

Rommel's offensive to pass round the British flank opened during the afternoon of 26 May 1942, with a feint by a regiment of 90th Light Division spearheading an Italian infantry division. Shortly after dawn on the morning of 27 May, the mass of Axis vehicles which formed the strike group and which had made a long night drive, halted to refuel. The columns had by that time reached a point some 15-20km south of Bir Hacheim, sufficiently deep in the desert, so it was believed, for them to have passed round the British flank. Unknown to the Axis commanders a box garrisoned by Indian troops had recently moved into an area below Bir Hacheim and the Italian "Ariete" Armoured Division stumbled into that Indian position. The first attacks of the "Ariete" were driven off by the resolute Indian soldiers but Rommel, conscious that he needed to destroy that troublesome position quickly, created battle group Briel and committed it to action. The battle group was made up of Briel's own 606 Flak Battalion, Captain Kayser's 2nd Battalion Panzergrenadier Regiment

155, and Captain Schulz's 605 Panzerjaeger Battalion. The battle group had soon destroyed the Indian box and was then put in against the aggressive Free French in the Bir Hacheim box. By the time that that position fell after more than a week of bitter fighting, the bulk of the Afrika Korps had already swung north towards the Via Balbia while 90th Light was striking along a northeasterly thrust line where its duty was to protect the eastern flank of the armoured divisions of Afrika Korps.

Battle group Briel had had scant time to celebrate its part in the fall of the Bir Hacheim box when Rommel arrived at its HQ. The orders he gave to the commander were that his group was to overtake the 90th Light, to spearhead its drive and at a given map reference was to strike out alone and to smash the British box at El Adem. The battle group set out and quickly fulfilled the first two parts of Rommel's orders. It then went over to its independent role and its ranging columns struck into what 8th Army thought of as its safe, rear area. The the KG created confusion, particularly when it overran and dispersed the TAC HQ of both 7th Armoured Division and 30 Corps. To all intents both the British armoured division and 8th Army's principal corps were leaderless at a crucial stage of the battle. But although the battle group had the power to create confusion, it was too weak to capture the El Adem box and after several vain attempts was deflected southwards, destroying in its careering advance a number of British ration dumps.

At the track crossing at Sidi Mammut, an unpleasant surprise awaited Briel's columns. A British 6pdr anti-tank gun, one of the first of that new weapon to be used in Africa, opened fire and with its opening shot knocked out one of the battle group's two 88's. The other gun was brought forward, went into action and in an exchange of shots soon destroyed the British gun position. The deeper that KG Briel drove into 8th Army's rear areas and the closer that it advanced towards Trigh Capuzzo, the stronger grew the resistance for by now the British force was taking action against the Axis operation. After heavy fighting the battle group reached the El Adem airfield, captured this and then thrust towards Point 162, the Hagiag el Adem. By 14 June, Briel's group had cut the road and the whole El Adem area was in German hands, once again.

The direction of the advance then turned due east as battle group spearheaded the advance of Afrika Korps' armour towards Bardia. Just east of that town a supply dump was captured which held the whisky ration for 8th Army as well as other useful and very desirable things. The first of the supplies to be distributed were English cigarettes and each man was issued with 1,000.

The advance bypassed Tobruk and raced eastwards. Resistance at Tobruk was heavier than Rommel had anticipated and a signal sent from

Afrika Korps HQ halted the advance of both 15th and 21st Panzer Divisions and directed them to return to the Tobruk area. That order left 90th Light as the only division still pursuing the retreating 8th Army; and a long way ahead of 90th Light was battle group Briel thrusting towards Sidi Barrani. When that place fell the Axis forces were, once again, back in Egypt. Ahead lay Mersah Matruh. Tobruk fell to the Afrika Korps armoured assault and without delay Rommel turned 15th and 21st Panzer Divisions round and sent them hurtling forward in support of 90th Light. The German commander's intention was to now surround and capture the slower moving British infantry forces retreating from the Gazala positions. If Rommel's plan succeeded there would be insufficient British troops to dig defences or to man any positions in front of Alexandria.

Afrika Korps changed KG Briel's thrust line to a south-easterly one, straight across the desert. The coast road was choked with the transport and vehicles of Italian 20th Corps and Rommel was insistent that his German units lose no time tied up in traffic jams. The battle group's advance across the desert was an exhausting and agonising one. Temperatures rose to well over 55 degrees and summer Khamseens often shrouded the columns in clouds of grit and sand. Affected by these wearing conditions the first signs of physical and mental exhaustion showed themselves. Some soldiers collapsed with stomach colic, others saw mirages, while many drivers fell asleep at the steering wheels of their vehicles. Briel's firmness and personality held the group together through this difficult period. Then the KG's advance took it through the minefields which enclosed Mersah Matruh to the south and swung up to capture that place on 28 June.

There was a lightening of spirits on the following day when another supply dump was found. This one, according to German reports, held a cold store. The battle group concentrated round the dump to refuel, to take on supplies and to rest but before the exhausted soldiers could relax Rommel appeared, led Briel away from his men and gave the commander the most astounding order he had ever received: "You are to drive on and are to capture Alexandria. You and I will drink coffee together in Shepheard's hotel in Cairo." The Field Marshal then drove away leaving Briel to tell his exhausted soldiers of the new plan. He knew them and they knew him and they all knew Rommel. If the Field Marshal had come to issue their commander with special orders then it was clear that another effort was to be asked of them. This one, Briel told them, was the big prize which only they could pull off. They were a great distance ahead of the rest of the Afrika Korps and were the only German unit in a position to "bounce" the British line and reach the objective for which they had been fighting for over a year. Alexandria was within spitting distance in the terms of desert

fighting. Up the "blue", advances or retreats of 150km were not excep-
tional. Alexandria was only a day and-a-half's drive away and all that
stood between the battle group and its final objective were the shattered
remnants of 8th Army.

Briel called an "O" Group and divided the battle group into three
small columns, each of equal strength and composition. Kayser commanded the first group, Briel the second and Schulz the third. Rommel's
orders had been clear and precise and had laid down three bounds. The
first was Point 216 (Alam Halvig), the second was Point 128, just to the
west of the Fuka Pass and the third bound was south of Ras Abu Giras,
some 25km to the east of the pass. At 11.30 on the morning of 29 June,
within 5mins of the "O" Group breaking up, the battle group set out to
race the British into Alexandria.

The three columns were all fighting units. There was no "tail" as
such and battle group's only reserve was a few soft-skinned vehicles carrying fuel, water and supplies together with an escort of a few 2cm cannon.

The German columns raced on, scattering the British forces withdrawing from the Gazala battlefield. Less than three hours after the battle
group had begun its mission the first objective had been reached and
taken. With no pause or halt the colums raced on to reach the second
bound. Up to that point there had been no opposition but, shortly after the
group had consolidated on the second bound, a group of British armoured
cars came bouncing across the desert. The German guns opened up and
destroyed three enemy vehicles for the loss of a pair of 2cm cannon.

With the British recce vehicles driven off, Briel's battle group rolled
on once more, drove through the Fuka Pass and was on the third bound by
18.00hrs. That objective should have been the day's final objective and
the weary men disposed themselves for rest and began to unwind from the
rigours of the day. Briel sent off a sitrep to Afrika Korps HQ reporting that
he had gained the third objective. The signal acknowledging receipt of
that report included the order for his group to push on to El Daba, a place
some 25km farther eastwards.

The weary men mounted up and set out. At 22.10hrs Briel wirelessed
another report. El Daba had been taken and his battle group was driving
on with the aim of reaching Trigh Abd el Rahman. Driving through the
short summer night the German columns bypassed British units camped in
the desert, thinking themselves to be safe being so far in the rear and
assuming that the vehicle columns passing along the coast road must be
ones of their own army.

At midnight Briel sent out another message. He had reached the Abd
el Rahman track and was consolidating around the mosque from which

the trigh received its name. The men of the battle group went into the now familiar routine of posting sentries, siting headquarters and cooking a meal. On checking his map Briel realised that his columns had covered a distance of 120km in less than 12hrs. If he continued at that speed they would be in Alexandria some time during the following afternoon. During the first hour of the night Briel held an "O" Group and gave orders that the minimum number of soldiers were to be on guard at any one time. He stressed the importance of the men resting themselves as much as possible for he intended that the columns break laager shortly after sun up. They were to head towards the railway station at El Alamein and only 80km beyond that lay Alexandria. Captain Kayser took a more pessimistic view of the battle group's situation. That day's march, climaxing all the other days of movement and fighting, had totally exhausted the troops. They could do no more. This present position on the Abd el Rahman trigh MUST be seen as the final objective. The present physical condition of the men ruled out any further advance. The battle group, Kayser stressed, was isolated, more than 120km ahead of the nearest German troops. Ammunition was running low and so was fuel. In fact, there was not enough to carry the group the 80 or so kilometres to Alexandria.

At first light on 30 June 1942, a signaller woke Briel with a short message from Afrika Korps HQ. It read: "Halt the advance. Return and rejoin the 90th Light Division. Await further orders."

What had caused Rommel to recall the battle group cannot be known, but one consideration must have been that a body of troops, so few in number as KG Briel, could have had little hope of reaching and holding such a major objective as Alexandria. Although it was clear that 8th Army was in disarray, it was equally obvious that the British must have set up defences to delay any further Axis advance. Although battle group Briel was too weak to force a decision, the 15th and 21st Panzer Divisions which would arrive in the Abd el Rahman area during the 30th, would give Rommel the strength he needed to open a major assault which would drive through the bottleneck at El Alamein. It was a terrain bottleneck. Between the railway station at Abd el Rahman and Alexandria the wide expanse of "good going" of the Libyan plateau narrowed until it reached the railway station of El Alamein. Beyond that place the ground opened out again to become a wide expanse of "good going" once more. El Alamein was the important place. Take it and the road to Alexandria and the delta was open. Rommel ordered the main body of 90th Light to continue its attacks throughout 30 June and to give the British no respite. On the following day, the mass of Afrika Korps armour would open the final assault — an operation which even the German commander knew would be in the nature of a gamble. A strength return on 30 June, showed that the Panzer strength of Afrika Korps had shrunk to only 55 "runners" and that 90th Light had a strength of just over 2,000 men. The attempt to "bounce" the Alamein line must, therefore, be a last throw attempt — a calculated risk that his force, weak in numbers but high in morale with the prospect of winning the final battle, could overcome and defeat the retreating British 8th Army.

It may also be the case that Rommel had decided to withdraw battle group Briel in order to keep the battle zone clear for the attack on 1 July, but whatever the reason and however much Briel disagreed with the order it had to be obeyed. On 1 July, the battle group was broken up and the constituent units returned to their parent formations.

On 22 July, Briel took over command of 200th Panzer Grenadier Regiment and six days later received the Ritterkreuz in recognition of his work as the leader of a battle group which had operated with considerable success ahead of the main body of Afrika Korps.

Before leaving the desert battle groups to move into the hills of Tunisia, we return to the opening of the Gazala offensive when, at 16.00hrs in the afternoon of 27 May, a British armoured formation opened fire upon the soft-skinned vehicles of 15th Panzer Division's supply columns.

General Nehring, commanding Afrika Korps, was forward with the leading troops when the tank attack came in. With him was Colonel Wolz, commanding 135 Flak Regiment. Both commanders were observing the course of the battle and discussing the action to take when they were surprised by a column of 15th Panzer's soft-skinned vehicles streaming in retreat across the desert. In their haste the trucks of the Panzer Division's "tail" units ran over Afrika Korps' TAC HQ which had accompanied General Nehring. The lorried column raced away shrouded in clouds of dust. Only Nehring, Wolz and their aides were left in the area. At that moment Rommel arrived leading a Flak battery from Corps HQ's battalion, whose retreat he had managed to halt. The General's first question was why Wolz's 88s were not in action and he then he went on to condemn the Flak as solely responsible for the debacle because the guns were not engaging the enemy. Wolz halted another three 88mm guns and had soon added three more from his own regiment's 1st battalion. The British tanks, some 40 in number, now only 1,500m distant, had begun to fire ranging shots. Nehring formed the seven 88s into a battle group and ordered Wolz to take command of the unit. The Colonel positioned the guns 150m apart and lined them into a short "Pakfront". In such situations there was a simple question: which had the superiority — the armour or the guns? In the situation facing Wolz, it seemed that the tanks had an overwhelming advantage in numbers: a 6:1 superiority, but that imbalance was redressed by the fact that the range of the 88 was far greater than that of the main armament of British tanks. The German weapon's high velocity shells could penetrate the enemy armour plate before the tank guns could effectively engage the Pakfront.

Rommel and Nehring had both sent out parties to search for 88mm gun batteries and these were led back to be placed in Wolz's battle group. Soon a wall of guns, 3km wide, stretched across the desert. During the time that the Pakfront was being created, British artillery had been brought into position behind the wall of tanks and had opened a destructive fire upon the line of 88s standing, uncamouflaged, on the surface of the desert. For battle group Wolz it was a matter of enduring the British bombardment. If the gun line collapsed then a wave of 8th Army's armour would sweep across the desert and cut a wide swathe of destruction through the German rear echelon units and go on to strike into the back of Afrika Korps. The barrage stopped and then the regiments of British tanks moved forward in a sort of Balaclava charge, rolling over the desert in beautiful tactical formation, advancing, then halting to fire before coming on again. As soon as the range had decreased to 1,200m, 16 of the 88's opened fire. The British tanks turned away, regrouped and advanced again. At last light 24 British AFVs were lying in front of the Pak line, and the smoke rising from them and into the desert sky indicated where most had "brewed up". The first operation of Kampfgruppe Wolz, an extensive Flak front against tanks, had proved its value. Wolz was ordered to return to his regiment and handed over command of the battle group to Major Guerke, the commanding officer of 1st Battalion of the Flak regiment.

At a later stage of the Gazala operation, Rommel ordered Wolz to form a new battle group out of detachments fighting around Bir Hacheim and chiefly, 33rd Reconnaissance Battalion, 33rd Anti-tank Battalion and 2nd Battalion of 25th Flak Regiment. Rommel ordered KG Wolz to position itself to intercept the British forces which would be forced to withdraw by the advance of 15th and 21st Panzer Divisions. On 5 June, east of Bir Harmat, KG Wolz encountered a unit of 8th Army withdrawing from the battlefield at a fast speed and for this battle Wolz employed a new tactic — a mobile Pakfront. Half of his 88s halted and opened fire while the other half carried on with the advance. That moving group then halted and opened fire until the first group had come through their positions. In this leapfrogging, fire and movement method Wolz brought the advance forward.

The following day, 6 June, was recorded by KG Wolz as its hardest day of battle. The battle group which, together with 15th Panzer Division, had driven into the back of 8th Army's forces in the "Knightsbridge" area, had created a shallow salient which was under fire from three sides of the perimeter. British tank regiments mounted attack after attack to crush the German penetration but each assault was driven off by the 88s of Wolz's battle group, extending in 4km-long line across the desert.

As each tank regiment pulled back after its unsuccessful charge, its withdrawal was covered by a massive barrage fired by the 8th Army's artillery regiments. At the end of that terrible day the battle group's 88s could muster between them only nine armour-piercing rounds, but lying strewn across the desert, smashed or burning, lay 50 British tanks, most of which had fallen to Wolz's gunners. The 8th Army's attacks had been repulsed and the battle group was ordered back to Bir Hacheim where, despite days of attack, French resistance had still not broken. Wolz was ordered to place his unit under the command of KG Briel and later, as sub-units were withdrawn, suggested to Rommel that he should hand over command to Major Dittrich, commanding 2nd Battalion of 25th Flak Regiment. Rommel agreed and with that agreement the short life of KG Wolz in the Gazala battle came to an end.

Colonel Wolz did not remain long at Afrika Korps HQ and was soon called upon by Rommel to lead his Flak regiment in the battle for Tobruk. When, on 10 July 1942, Rommel's offensive rolled in the direction of El Alamein, Wolz created another battle group and led this until, in September, he was named as Flakfuehrer Afrika, a post which took him away from active operations.

Battle Group Peiper in the mission to rescue 320th Infantry Division, surrounded and cut off south of Kharkov, February 1943

The second winter in Russia, that of 1942-43, was coming to an end. It had not been as bitter as that of the previous year and the German Army had been better prepared to meet this second cold weather period than it had been in 1941, but the military situation had changed. The Wehrmacht's summer offensive died in the ruins of Stalingrad and in November 1942, long before the last flickers of German resistance had been extinguished, the Red Army's winter offensive had already swung into action, driving westwards with the aim of capturing Kharkov. The power of the Soviet counter-offensive had torn through the miscellany of foreign divisions which had been fielded to help Army Group South and those non-German units had broken creating a gap 100km wide in the battle line. The Red Army's drive which had begun in November 1942 was still running in February 1943, although the early elan which had carried the Soviet forces forward had begun to flag by February. Nevertheless, the advance still moved westwards against opposition maintained chiefly by German formations standing like rocks around which the Red Army flooded.

In such a fluid situation there could be no such thing as a firm front line and by the same token, if there could be no firm front line then there could be no rear area with its guarantee of safety. None could be sure of the identity of the units on the flanks. None knew whether out of the dark night a Panzer battalion might attack or a Cossack sotnia sweep from the cover of a snow storm, sabring to death any unit which broke. No formation could be certain whether during a march it might not encounter a pocket of enemy infantry, desperate men cut off but determined to fight a way through to reach their own army. The front line was everywhere. Under the heavy blows which the Red Army rained down upon the formations of von Manstein's Army Group Don in those first days of February 1943, the German front began to fragment. Army Groups B and Don were ordered to hold fast in order to prevent the Soviet military advantage turning into a German rout. Those corps and divisions still fighting as organised bodies also had the task of closing gaps in the battle line, particularly that one, now over 200km wide, which yawned between Army Group B and Army Group Don.

To bolster up the wavering Eastern Front Hitler ordered the transfer of a number of crack divisions from France and Italy. Panzer Grenadier

Division "Leibstandarte Adolf Hitler" ("LAH") was one of the elite formations which was ordered to move with best possible speed to join Army
Group Don and, specifically, the SS Panzer Corps. Upon its arrival
"LAH" was ordered to take position to the south-east of Kharkov and to
form a defensive front east of the River Donets, between Smiyev and
Kotomlya. The military situation at that time was assessed by SS Corps as
follows: "The 69th Red Army and 3rd Tank Army have gained the line of
the Upper Oskol and Valuiki and are pressing forward in conjunction with
6th Red Army, towards Kupyansk...while Popov's Army is closing in on
Slaviansk. The German 320th Division is fighting a fierce defensive battle
at Ssvativo. The intention of OKH to use the SS Panzer Corps in a concentrated counter attack has been thwarted by the speed of the Soviet
advance..." Three facts in the above appreciation are of importance to the
narrative which is described below. First, the intention to use the SS
Panzer Corps in a massive counter-attack. That fact locates the area in
which the corps was operating. Second, the speed with which the Red
Army was driving westwards for that has a bearing on the third fact, that
the hard fighting 320th Division was cut off from the main body of the
army group. It is the rescue of that division, by a battle group from the
Panzer Grenadier Division "LAH", with which the following description
deals.

The Division which KG Peiper, the reinforced 3rd (Armoured Personnel Carrier) Battalion of the Leibstandarte's 2nd Panzer Grenadier
Regiment, was to rescue had been on the right flank of the SS Panzer
Corps but during the first days of February 1943, it had been cut off and
stranded behind the advancing Red Army. Regrouped by its commander,
General Postel, as a wandering pocket the 320th, the Berlin Green Heart
Division, so named from its divisional sign, reached the area of Ssavinzy
on 7 February. Two days later Postel demanded immediate help for his
formation but was told that corps could not undertake such a relief operation until 12 February, at the earliest. The Army sitrep of 11 February
stated that, "The enemy, a force of four armies, has crossed the Donets
and is heading in a south-westerly direction [to the south of Kharkov].
Another enemy group is thrusting to the north of Kharkov." Paragraph 5
of that sitrep announced that the "...320th Division has been ordered to
advance to Smiyev via Liman, where it will be picked up by the SS
Panzer Corps". During the afternoon of that day the 320th reached Grig-
orievka and was directed to reach the railway line to Sidki where KG
Peiper would escort it back into the German lines.

Two hours before it was due to gain touch with the 320th, Peiper's
battle group left the Kolkhoz at Podolkov where it had been billeted. The
entry in the regimental war diary confirms that the Kampfgruppe vehicles

moved out at 04.30hrs and 45mins later crossed the River Udy and entered enemy held territory. The task which faced Peiper was no easy one. The 320th was behind the enemy front and could move only slowly, burdened as it was with a great number of wounded men, many of them seriously, which Peiper, in his post-battle report estimated to number over 1,500. As can be readily appreciated that burden of wounded so slowed the daily march rate vis-a-vis the faster pace of the Red Army units, that with every passing day the 320th was deeper and deeper behind the Soviet lines, thus making the rescue operation a longer and more dangerous operation. It was known that most of the wounded of the 320th were being carried in panje carts — in fact the greatest number of vehicles in service with the Green Heart Division were such waggons, the ubiquitous one- or two-horse carts whose beasts seemed to be tireless, impervious to cold and unaffected by shortages of food. In order to bring the wounded quickly into German lines, where they could undergo surgery, Peiper's KG had with it every available medical team, ambulance and a great number of empty trucks to carry the exhausted infantrymen.

The front line in the sector held by 1st Battalion of 2nd Panzer Regiment, ran along the River Udy which was spanned by a long wooden bridge. The village of Krasnaya Polyana which lay on the river's eastern bank was held by the Russians. The most recent intelligence reports which Peiper received showed that the 3rd Red Army with 6th Cavalry Corps on its left flank had crossed the River Donets and its spearhead detachments were 40km deep inside German-held territory. The whole area below Krasnaya Polyana had to be considered as enemy held, except for the small enclave to the north of Liman where the 320th was positioned. Peiper's Kampfgruppe had, therefore, to cross the Udy and then strike southwards through Russian-held areas and across the thrust line of 3rd Red Army until it reached Smiyev on the west bank of the Donets. East of that river was Postel's division which had a distance of some 15km to cover before it would be able to gain contact with the battle group.

Before the start of the operation, Peiper concealed his APCs in the houses around the wooden bridge across the Udy and at H-Hour led the advance across that bridge and into the village of Krasnaya Polyana. The half-track vehicles raced across the flimsy structure and with all weapons firing charged through the village. Opposition was light and soon the armoured column, together with most of the ambulances and lorries, was heading towards Smiyev. Some of the tail end of the lorry column, which had arrived late for the start of the operation, came under fire from Soviet troops in Krasnaya Polyana who had recovered quickly from the surprise of the battle group's attack and had gone back into action again. Six German lorries were destroyed by the Soviet fire but their drivers were picked up and carried into safety by those men whom Peiper left behind to form a small garrison in the village. The Kampfgruppe then thrust through to the southern area below Krasnaya Polyana and, although it was cutting across the Red Army's lines of advance, there were very few clashes with the enemy and those Soviet groups that were met were quickly attacked and just as swiftly overrun, dispersed or destroyed. At 06.00hrs, only 85mins after crossing its start line, KG Peiper had reached Smiyev where it learned from "LAH" divisional HQ that the 320th had not advanced past the Liman area. At 08.00hrs Peiper's orders were changed. He was no longer to halt on the western bank of the River Donets but was to advance to Liman and there make contact with Postel's formation. That was an order that Peiper was unable to execute. In the middle weeks of February the ice sheet across the river was thinning and was no longer able to bear the weight of the heavy APCs. Neither was there a bridge across the Donets, nor had his battle group any pioneer detachment that could construct one. He would have to remain on the western bank.

From that bank Peiper could only wait for the 320th to reach him. The first group to arrive was, in Peiper's words, Postel and a great number of officers who demanded to know why the battle group had not crossed the river as ordered. The young commander's reply that the ice was too thin was brushed aside as a nonsense until an SP of the 320th, having successfully negotiated the steep eastern bank, reached the ice and immediately broke through it. Then the main body of the 320th came into full view of the watchers on the eastern bank. It was no longer a fighting formation although some of its units still presented a martial appearance. But it was plain to see that even those units were at the end of their tether. Behind the unwounded formations came a stream of lightly wounded followed by the severe cases. These had been piled into panje carts or onto sledges and, where there was no room for them to be carried, they had been tied with ropes to be dragged behind the carts, often face downwards, through the snow. The doctors with the battle group worked all night treating those who needed the most urgent attention and amputating, in primitive surgical conditions, the limbs of those whose wounds had turned gangrenous. The remainder of KG Peiper took up defensive positions around the survivors of the 320th. All waited anxiously for dawn when the drive back to the German line could begin. One thought dominated them all. The battle group and the 320th had reached the Donets having encountered only light opposition from the Russians. Would they be equally as fortunate on the run home?

The lorried column bearing the wounded and the infantry of the 320th set off. Ahead of it and on either side the battle group's AFVs secured the flanks. At Krasnaya Polyana, the bridge across which Peiper's men had driven to begin the operation had been set alight by the Russians and was burned out, leaving only wooden stumps smouldering in the cold morning air. The village itself was now in the hands of a Red Army ski battalion which had recaptured it from the garrison which Peiper had dropped off. The APC battalion opened an attack and recaptured the village after desperate house to house battles. Then the pioneers from the "LAH" Division came into the area and quickly erected a temporary bridge — not a strong one but one capable of bearing the weight of a lorry filled with wounded. The infantry of the 320th crossed the ice-bound River Udy on foot and into the perimeter of the "LAH". By 16.00hrs on 13th the ambulances and lorries filled with wounded soldiers were back in the German lines. At 08.25hrs on 14 February, Postel sent off the signal that his rearguard battalion had crossed the river and that the 320th would be ready once again for active service. Peiper's battle group had completed its given task but he still had to bring his men and machines back into the divisional perimeter. He was still on the enemy side of the Udy at Krasnaya Polyana and could not use the flimsy bridge, nor cross the thinning ice sheet. The option left to him, other than abandoning the heavy machines, was to drive back into Red-held territory and to drive westwards to Mirgorod, where there was a German-held bridge which his vehicles could cross to gain their own lines. Kampfgruppe Peiper reached the divisional perimeter soon after midnight on the 14th and at 07.00 hrs on the 15th was back in action again fighting on another sector of the "Leibstandarte" battle line. The anabasis of KG Peiper was over and the 320th had been rescued, but Postel was grudging with his thanks and in his report claimed his men had fought their way back without help from anyone. It is a bitter postscript to a slick and skilfully executed operation.

At a time when the crumbling Eastern Front was being pulled together again it is clear that KG Peiper was not the only battle group to have been created in the "LAH" Division. Among the catalogue of battle group names which mark the progress of the division's battle for Kharkov are those of Dietrich, Dahl and Schuldt. The exploits of these and indeed of all the others, deserve to be recorded. In the case of Dietrich he and his battle group were eating a meal inside a house when a T34 smashed into the building. Before the Soviet driver could manoeuvre his vehicle free, Dietrich leapt onto the tank's foredeck and killed the crew with machine pistol fire aimed through the tank's vision slits and turret. KG Dietrich later expanded to become a battalion and Schuldt's battle group became a brigade. Throughout the whole divisional area and across the entire time period a mass of battle groups was created, most of them short-lived — often of a few hour's duration.

Battle Group Fullriede
in the Tunisian Mountains,
spring 1943

The war in Africa which had, from 1940, been confined to the deserts of Libya and Egypt, expanded in November 1942 out of those sandy wildernesses and into the mountains of Algeria and Tunisia. Those two countries, both French colonial territories, had been neutral since the Franco-German armistice of June 1940, and the Axis Powers had respected that neutrality. Allied planners realised however, that if they could land an army at Rommel's back his forces could be crushed between British 8th Army in the desert and an Anglo-American host operating in French North Africa. It was obvious that the Vichy French government would never give authority for landings and military operations in its territory so, without asking for that permission, the Allies decided to breach Algerian and Tunisian neutrality. Early in November their forces began to disembark in ports along the whole North African coastline.

Hitler's immediate reaction was to order a blocking force to be sent without delay and the speed with which this directive was carried out surprised the Allied leaders. Within a day German paratroop contingents had been flown in to secure airfields, ports and the principal cities of Tunisia. A constant trickle of men and material came in to hold the bridgehead perimeter and to ensure that Rommel's Italo-German army, withdrawing out of Libya, could reach the bridgehead and reinforce the troops in Tunisia. Germany's speedy reaction to the Allied invasion — and which had countered the Anglo-American strategy — was based on the simple and obvious premise that for as long as Axis forces held the capital city and Bizerta, the country's major port, the Allies could not use Tunisia as a springboard for military operations in the western and central Mediterranean. To maintain that spoiling victory which would thwart the Allied plans, required men and supplies. Hitler supplied both.

General von Arnim, the German commander in Tunisia, had to hold back the Anglo-American forces driving into Tunisia from the West while at the same time co-ordinating operations with Field Marshal Rommel, whose Panzer Army in the south of Tunisia was being driven back by British 8th Army. Von Arnim's most urgent military problem was to prevent the Anglo-American forces from seizing the mountain passes through which they would gain access to central Tunisia and, thereby, split Rommel's army from that of von Arnim. The defence of those passes fell chiefly upon army divisions, but many others were the responsibility of battle groups. One of the most successful Kampfgruppen was led by Lieutenant-Colonel Fritz Fullriede. During February 1943, the colonel was flown to Africa and briefed by von Arnim on the task which his new command was to carry out. This was to defend the Fondouk passes, part of the battle group's 65km-length of front. Battle group Fullriede was, to begin with, low in number and poorly equipped. It was made up of three companies of Italian infantry, nine German companies, 14 Italian field guns and three German infantry guns. A well-armed nucleus around which the Kampfgruppe had been built was Captain Duevers' 334th Armoured Car Battalion which also included some engineers, a pair of 88mm guns and a few light anti-aircraft weapons.

Fullriede saw as his first task the need to make himself known to the men he would be leading in battle, as well as gaining a clear picture of their fitness for combat. For the first few days after taking up position in his allotted sector he visited each of his units. Fullriede was fortunate in that he had arrived in Tunisia during a period of comparative inactivity. Both sides were exhausted from the strain of the winter battles and in that brief lull he was able to impress upon the soldiers of his Kampfgruppe the force of his personality. Between November and January the Allies had sought to crush the German bridgehead and the German-Italian forces had fought to hold the perimeter which had been created in the earliest days of the campaign. Fighting in the Tunisian mountains had been bitter, hard and wasteful but had been brought almost to a standstill by the mud produced by the heavy rains of January and February. The energetic Fullriede was determined to give the American units on his sector no rest at all. He sent out battle patrols to dominate No Mans Land and often accompanied these, learning at first hand the advantages and disadvantages of the local area. On those sectors where aggressive American commanders mounted their own small-unit operations, Fullriede soon reached the spot to inspire his men to master the situation.

Slowly the strength of Kampfgruppe Fullriede grew. On 4 March an Arab battalion, "Tunisia", came under command. The officers and NCOs of that unit were Germans who had served with the French Foreign Legion and had left it to serve with Panzer Army Afrika. The rank and file were native Tunisians.

The peace which had endured along Fullriede's sector was broken on 5 March by a heavy artillery barrage which fell onto an isolated forward position in front of the small native town of Pichon. First reports from the men in the front line indicated that the artillery fire was the opening of a major new American offensive. There had been a change of command in US II Corps and the new corps commander was the aggressive George

Patton. Fullriede drove into the forward positions to judge the situation on the spot. There he saw that American tanks had outflanked the German advanced strongpoint and had almost surrounded it. There was no time to lose if the men in that outpost were not to be cut off and destroyed. The commander ordered his reluctant soldiers to pull back to the main defensive positions in the village of El Ala and under heavy tank and machine gun fire the defenders withdrew. But before El Ala could be prepared for defence, US tank forces had swept down upon them and in a swift assault had captured the village.

Fullriede's worries were a little alleviated when a group of reinforcements came up — a platoon of commandos from the Brandenburg regiment. It was exactly the type of support that Fullriede would have wished for himself, combat veterans of proven ability. Fullriede knew that the Americans had not yet had time to consolidate their positions in El Ala and that until they had done this their hold on the village was tenuous. The German Army's standard response to the loss of ground was to counter-attack immediately — and here the battle group commander had the men available to retake the lost village. There was no time to organise even a mortar barrage and to issue artillery fire orders would have taken too much time. The need to counter-attack was an immediate one and the Brandenburg commandos claimed they needed no artillery support. They fought best in close-quarter battles.

The commandos melted away into the growing darkness leaving Fullriede's men to wait for a given signal — a Very light. Minutes passed and then there was a series of explosions from inside the village where two companies of American tanks had laagered for the night. Those explosions were followed by fires as the vehicles blew up, one after the other. The commando platoon was in action. The dark of the night was pierced at intervals by sudden brief flashes as hand grenades exploded or machine pistols fired bursts of bullets at the surprised Americans. Impatiently, Fullriede and his soldiers waited upon the signal and then, finally, it came: a green flare rising fast into the night sky. The battle group commander ordered his men to follow him and led them at the charge to where the Brandenburg platoon was driving the last American troops out of the houses which they had sought in vain to convert into strongpoints. The light of burning tanks showed a pair of American light howitzers with their crews lying dead around them. Immediately Fullriede called to a group of commandos asking whether they could operate the enemy guns. They could. Detachments of the battle group swung the weapons round, the commandos took post on the guns and within a few minutes they were in action firing at a pair of Grants which, attracted by the sound and sights of battle, had driven into El Ala. Three shots from the howitzers and both vehicles lay immobile and out of action. The remaining Americans realising the hopelessness of their position either surrendered or fled into the night.

The passes at Fondouk had been a sensitive sector since the earliest weeks of the campaign. Now, in March, their importance had increased with the build-up of Allied — chiefly American — forces facing them. The Axis High Command in Africa, aware of Allied preparations for a major offensive, reinforced Fullriede's battle group once again, and this time with Captain Kahle's 190th Reconnaissance Battalion.

We have seen in earlier pages that it was a favourite tactic of Field Marshal Rommel to launch pre-emptive strikes to upset his opponent's military preparations. He determined to launch such an attack against the US troops holding the El Zhagales Pass. That pass lay in the sector of front held by Fullriede's battle group and it says a lot for the confidence which the commander had in his men that for this spoiling attack he proposed to use just three platoons of infantry and three armoured reconnaissance vehicles. The task of that small fighting group was to advance across the 10km-wide No Mans Land, reach the mouth of the pass and then to fight a way through it.

The elan of Fullriede's soldiers proved irresistible and after a short but intense fire-fight the US defenders, who greatly outnumbered the German attackers, were forced back. One small American group took up positions on a ridge of high ground behind the pass. Tactically, this was an unsound move and was one which Fullriede quickly exploited. Combining some armoured cars, a detachment of motor cyclists and a couple of SPs mounting 7.5cm guns, his units encircled the American group on the ridge. The only immediately available artillery to support the infantry attack was a single mortar, the crew of which fired a short barrage. Under that flimsy fire cover Fullriede led his men in a charge. Five American officers and 65 other ranks were taken prisoner, but more welcome booty was the lorry park with a number of serviceable vehicles.

Rommel's pre-emptive attack had two consequences. The first of these was that the Americans had been forced out of the El Zeghales Pass. The second was that it woke the front on that sector and throughout the succeeding fews days US troops made a series of attacks against the Kampfgruppe and the units on either flank. Slowly, that burst of American activity died away to leave reconnaissance and battle patrols as the principal activity. It was, however, a false lull. On 20 March, a US armoured thrust broke through at Maknassy and at first Fullriede was ordered to clean up the situation, but those orders were revoked two days later. Then, instead of undertaking a new attack his battle group received further reinforcements, a small battle group whose principal formation was the 961st Penal Regiment.

Fighting flickered fitfully along Fullriede's front with US thrusts succeeded by battle group counter-thrusts. One particularly serious breach was made by the Americans on 28 March, on a neighbouring sector. That attack was the opening move of a general offensive to capture the passes. The first penetrations made by the US troops into the German positions were extended to become wide breaches. A break-through was imminent and it seemed that nothing could halt the American onrush.

Fullriede decided to swing across onto the neighbouring sector and open a counter-attack. Shortly before last light on 29 March, he explained his battle plan to the men of the two infantry companies and the 334th Battalion whom he intended to lead in person in the forthcoming battle. The mission was, he told them, to recapture a dominant hill, Jebel Gridyina, which had been lost the previous day. He led the column of infantry to the foot of the Jebel and then ordered his men to take up attack formation. He himself took post in the centre of the short line and led the companies into the attack. Swiftly and efficiently the battle group infantry swept up the hill, recaptured it and took as prisoners most of the US defenders. The remainder managed to escape into the night. Determined to recover all the ground which had been lost in the opening moves of the American offensive, Fullriede struck at the US forces holding another mountain top, Point 603, and used for this mission a battalion of the penal regiment and No 2 Company of the 334th Battalion. The attack opened at first light on 30 March and its speed and weight flung the US defenders off the peak and recaptured it.

There was a regrouping of forces on the Allied side and US II Corps was pulled out of the line at Fondouk and sent to the northern sector of the Tunisian battle front. That corps was replaced by British 6th Armoured Division and detachments from a French colonial division. Fullriede decided to launch a spoiling attack to roll up the Allied line, but his best unit, the 334th, was taken from him and posted to another sector. Now lacking the strength to undertake large scale missions, he and his battle group had to be content with local operations. Reinforcements were promised but few arrived. One which did was an Italian machine gun battalion.

The first major assault by 6th Armoured Division came in on 7 April and broke into the German main defensive line, but only at its second attempt; the first, an infantry attack, was beaten back. The second was a tank attack and succeeded. During the fighting one battalion of the Penal Regiment was almost totally destroyed. Only 150 men escaped from the battlefield. Immediately, Fullriede ordered a counter-attack using his SPs whose 7.5cm guns outranged the British tank guns. Five British machines were soon wrecked or burning and the advance by 6th Armoured was brought to a temporary halt.

By this time Rommel's Panzer Army had been driven out of the positions it had held at Mareth in southern Tunisia and was moving into the central part of that country. In order that the desert veterans could reach and take up fresh sectors in the battle line, it was even more essential that the western passes be held. The most important of those passes was Fondouk and the little town of Pichon, through an accident of war, had now become a place of strategic importance. A town so vital to the battle plans of the Axis High Command as Pichon had now become, needed to be defended by a strong formation and the withdrawal of the 334th had left Fullriede's battle group dangerously weak. Aware of that fact, High Command returned the 334th which took up position ready to meet the Allied offensive which would soon come in, now that 8th Army had linked up with the Allied forces in Tunisia.

It was stressed upon Fullriede that his Kampfgruppe had to hold Pichon and the Fondouk Pass until Rommel's Army had passed through Kairouan and into the security of the central area of the bridgehead. Only then could his unit leave its positions and pull back northwards. The scale of fighting on Kampfgruppe's front diminished for a day and then grew again. The opening moves of 6th Armoured Division's offensive were air and ground bombardments followed by infantry probes testing for weak points in the battle group's front. The weight of those British attacks and the fury of the artillery barrages and air- raids were too much for some of the battle group's soldiers. The native battalions — "Tunisia" and "Algeria", together with the Italian machine gun battalion — were the first to break and either abandon their positions or else surrender en masse to the British troops. Only the Foreign Legion NCOs and officers of the native battalions stayed to fight.

Pressure grew on the battle group's remaining units and under that pressure Fondouk was eventually taken, but 6th Armoured's attempts to bring their advance forward were stopped by Fullriede's last SPs and those companies which had been with the KG since it was created. There was a brief lull as both sides regrouped after the recent bitter fighting. Then came the news that the last elements of Afrika Korps had passed through Kairouan. Kampfgruppe Fullriede could now leave the battlefield and during the evening of 9 April, the commander issued orders to the groups which had served under him, that they were to detach themselves from the enemy and were to pass through Kairouan to take up fresh positions around Enfidaville, where a fresh defensive line had been set up. Not all the groups were able to detach themselves cleanly and were overrun by Allied armour.

Although Kampfgruppe Fullriede was later employed on other sectors, chiefly in the Pont du Fahs area, it is at this point that we leave it. The end of the war in Africa was now only a matter of weeks away and with that defeat ahead lay years of captivity as prisoners of war for the veterans of the African campaign.

Battle Groups of 315th Grenadier Regiment (167th Infantry Division) on the Eastern Front, October 1943

On 24 October 1943, 167th Infantry Division was moved to the Sybkoe area of the Eastern Front. This was a move dictated by the fact that, to the south-east of Kremechug, the Red Army had established a bridgehead on the west bank of the Dniepr out of which it intended to strike towards Kirovgrad. German 40th Corps was ordered to prevent that south-westwards thrust by destroying the Red bridgehead, but to conduct that operation it needed elite units. One of the formations which 40th Corps demanded was SS "Totenkopf" Division, and for the SS formation to be free to move to its new operational area, it had first to be relieved from the line at Sybkoe. The 167th Division was ordered to take over "Totenkopf's" positions and it is the action of 167th's 315th Grenadier Regiment in the fighting around Sybkoe which is described here.

As was the norm in the German Army by that stage of the war, a petrol shortage meant that infantry units had to foot march to new operational areas. No fuel could be spared to transport infantrymen who could walk. But by scrimping and saving and using methods that would not bear too close investigation, the divisional quartermaster's department had collected sufficient petrol to "lift" the Grenadier regiments to the Sybkoe sector and the first convoy set out loaded with troops. The truck drivers were instructed to return post-haste to carry the other regiment but the convoy did not return. A staff officer, seeing the exhausted state of the drivers and the lorries badly in need of servicing, ordered the columns off the road. The 315th Grenadier Regiment had, therefore, to reach its new sector on foot. To add to the Grenadiers' burden, the Red Air Force had superiority in the air and there was a great deal of partisan activity. German columns on the march, therefore, had to carry enough weapons and equipment to fight off those types of attacks. In addition, tent halves, blankets and all the standard requirements of winter campaigning had to be portered on the backs of the Grenadiers. Unit transport carried only food and ammunition.

The urgent need to relieve "Totenkopf" Division became an acute one when intelligence reports showed that the Russians intended to pre-empt 40 Corps' offensive. The 167th Division conducted final reliefs during the early hours of 26 October, and became responsible for a long perimeter running between the villages of Alexandriva and Popelnastoye. At Sybkoe, on the sector held by 315th Regiment, in the southern part of the perimeter, regimental patrols found evidence of a massive Russian build-up, presaging a major offensive. Soviet infantry probes grew in weight and from 18 November were made by both infantry and tanks. Division, realising the threat which faced it, asked for Stukas to attack the Soviet positions but were told by the Luftwaffe liaison officer that aircraft could not fly in such poor weather conditions. The division's rank and file noted bitterly that the weather conditions in no way affected Red Air Force operations.

During 19 November, the signs grew clearer that an attack against 315th Regiment was imminent. Reconnaissance patrols reported that the Russian trenches opposite were crammed with drunken, noisy soldiers and division asked for reinforcements which produced from corps three SPs, but no Grenadiers. During that day there were reports from regiment's forward positions of engine noises coming from "Kasten" wood. That night the Grenadier sentries peered anxiously into the darkness but heard no sound until, at 04.00hrs on 20 November, a heavy barrage fell on the regimental sector and grew within an hour to a hurricane of fire concentrated upon the area between Point 182 and Sybkoe-South, indicating the precise area where the main Soviet assault would be made.

While the shells still crashed down, out of "Kasten" wood a line of T34s emerged moving off in the direction of Losavatsky. There it was joined by a second line of tanks supported by infantry. That combined force shook out into battle formation and as it advanced another Soviet artillery barrage blanketed the "break-through" area. Then, out of the dense curtain of dust and smoke, a third group of tanks rolled forward. In the divisional area there were now only two SPs to oppose that Russian armoured concentration. The third SP had fallen out with transmission problems.

Red Army infantry undertook their first heavy attack at 06.15hrs, advancing towards two companies holding the ground around Point 192. The Grenadiers stood to arms and smashed that initial assault with rifle and machine gun fire. The Soviet commander switched the point of his attack to another piece of high ground, but before that new assault could unfold the divisional artillery had laid a "curtain" barrage which destroyed the Red infantry. At 07.00hrs, under cover of a fresh enemy bombardment, 30 T34s which had been concealed in dead ground, raced to gain the area between Point 184 and Sybkoe-South. The first of three waves of tanks rolled towards 2nd Battalion's slit trenches and when the vehicles reached them, Red Army infantry riding on their outsides leaped down. There then began a bitter hand to hand struggle between the infantry of both sides and it seemed, at first, as if the Grenadiers were gaining the upper hand. Then the second wave of tanks and infantry rolled forward and swept across the German trenches. According to the regimental war diary the Russian infantrymen were drunk, for they did not take cover when they came under fire. They were shot down in batches but the survivors continued to advance behind the T34s, instinctively closing the gaps which German fire tore in their ranks. A third Red Army wave followed the first two and 2nd Battalion's resistance died under that smothering blanket of enemy forces. Across the battlefield on which the battalion had perished there remained only individual and isolated German soldiers battling their way through the masses of Red Army infantry surrounding them.

Near Point 192, in 1st Battalion's area, 16 Red tanks raced downhill towards Devitche Pole aiming for the regiment's main artillery positions. The gunners loaded, aimed and fired like automata at the oncoming Reds but, within minutes, two of the battalion's batteries had been overrun and under the weight of the Russian attack, the rest of the artillery battalion went under, firing to the last. Resistance by the Grenadiers holding Devitche Pole, now lacking the support of the guns, could not long endure. It had been an unequal match. Under the assault of three waves of infantry and armour, the 315th Regiment shattered, with its survivors forming small islands of men, sub-battle groups, determined to resist the enemy who swarmed through the broken German front. The regimental commander, Major Pilgrim, ordered his HQ group to make for the gun pits, now well behind the Russian spearheads, and from those positions to continue their resistance. Theirs was a gallant but short-lived effort.

The tempo of the Soviet thrust slowed when it changed direction to advance towards Solotaryevka and the nearby Point 184. To support the Grenadiers holding positions there the two SP guns, which corps had allotted, opened a rapid and well aimed fire which stopped the enemy advance. In the fury of that fire-fight those Grenadiers of 315th Regiment, who had filtered through the Russian masses, joined with other survivors to take up the fight again.

The Red Army's plan to destroy the 167th Division had succeeded in smashing the front of 315th Regiment and at this time of desperate crisis the corps commander ordered divisional HQ to furnish a detailed, written explanation of the regiment's failure. The explanation was clear. Three Russian Guards infantry regiments, together with a tank regiment and supported by units of the 6th and 9th Guards Airborne Divisions had attacked the 315th. That great weight of enemy forces had been flung against a single German regiment whose strength numbered only 927 men, holding a 10km-long battle front. Under that pressure the line had ruptured. Appeals to corps for reinforcements were turned down and the regimental commander put into battle his B Echelon units formed into a Kampfgruppe. This took up a blocking position on either side of Solotaryevka. A second battle group formed from No 1 Company of the pioneer battalion was ordered to counter-attack in a north-westerly direction towards Devitche

Pole, while a battle group from No 2 Company was to strike in a south-westerly direction. The hope of smashing the Russian penetration was a forlorn one as the average strength of the pioneer companies had shrunk to only 35 men. At 08.15hrs corps promised a reinforcement of six SPs, but that was subsequently reduced to four with the caveat that those machines would not be able to reach the threatened area until 11.10hrs at the earliest. Patrols reported to the commander of 315th Regiment that the right wing was holding firm, that the centre was a wide gap filled with enemy forces and that the situation on the left wing was unclear.

The mental confusion at corps spread to division which ordered the shattered 315th Regiment to recapture Devitche Pole. This was an impossible mission. Regiment had difficulty enough in finding men to hold the blocking position at Solotaryevka, and the forces there which Pilgrim had hoped to hold the Red assault were very weak. They consisted of a number of small battle groups, the two largest of which were Kampf, located 6km behind Voroshilovka and a mixed group of artillerymen and the survivors of 1st Battalion, positioned north-west of Solotaryevka.

At 08.50hrs the Russian infantry and armoured forces resumed their advance towards that village, covered by an artillery barrage. They quickly entered the place but were then held by Kampfgruppe Ferstl, a mixed KG, which prevented the Soviets from exploiting the 1km-wide gap which they had created between Karbaumer's Grenadier Kampf-gruppe, defending the northern side of the village and KG Kampf to the south. Those two weak Kampfgruppen stood in danger of being isolated and regiment had no reserve to send up in support. Shortly before 09.30hrs the Soviets broke through south of Sybkoe and their advance, spreading out fan-like across the countryside, gained ground rapidly against diminishing German resistance. Soon the Reds had cut off the blocking force. To restore the situation and to close the gap in the line, both KGs then launched counter-attacks at 10.15hrs which drove the enemy out of Solotaryevka but which were too weak to carry the advance any farther.

There was a sudden lessening of pressure when the Soviets regrouped for a new attack while, on the German side, the battle groups of the blocking force received a few reinforcements. Then, between 10.00hrs and 11.00hrs, masses of Russian troops — infantry, artillery and horse-drawn carts — could be seen moving northwards through the breached line and creating a critical situation on Division's left flank, north of Solotaryevka. Within 45mins the Soviets had taken Chervona because the German sub-battle groups, now concentrated to form KG Pilgrim, lacked the strength to strike effectively into the flank of the enemy advance. It was a confused battle. While German units sought to attack on one sector the Russians were making their own assaults on another. Once again regiment received bizarre orders from Corps. The 315th was directed to halt the enemy's westwards advance but both KG Pilgrim and KG Kampf were fighting for their very existence. Although the four SPs eventually reached Pilgrim's battle group they had no accompanying infantry and had, therefore, only limited value. Corps next proposed an attack to cut off the enemy armour, using 106th Infantry Division to strike south-westwards from Ivanovka while the remnants of 167th Division, together with Pilgrim and Kampf battle groups attacked the left flank of the Soviet penetration. In view of the unclear situation, the onset of darkness and the exhausted state of his men, the Corps Commander postponed his attack until 21 November. One of the factors which influenced that decision was that the artillery battalions, intended to support the 315th's attacks, had not reached their allotted area.

During the late afternoon of the 20th, a strong Russian assault struck KG Pilgrim, and by 21.00hrs the barrage falling on the battle group's left flank reached a high pitch of intensity and was followed by a massive tank and infantry assault which was beaten off only with the greatest difficulty. An unusual feature of the attack was that the enemy lorried columns were each led by a truck carrying a huge searchlight. In view of the fact that the Soviet attack had pre-empted Corps plan and, because the enemy had numerical superiority, Corps cancelled the attack ordered for the 21st but demanded that the present line be held at all costs. During the night a few reinforcements came in and were formed into battle groups, or even sub-battle groups. Among the new Kampfgruppen formed at this time were Nikoleit: No 13 Company of the regiment's 2nd Battalion and parts of the anti-tank battalion, with a total strength of 120 men. The arrival of a reinforcement detachment, Kampfgruppe Knobelsberger, enabled KG Kampf to move to new positions around Point 177. The forces then deployed on regiment's left flank were the divisional Fusilier battalion, a total of 220 men; No 3 Company of the Pioneer Battalion, some 50 men; a miscellaneous group of 1st Grenadier Battalion and a few gunners, numbering 100 men, together with alarm detachments and signals detachments with a strength of only 80 men. Finally, there was an 80-man strong group of a replacement battalion formed into KG Zutt and the divisional reserve of 100 men.

The gap in the divisional line was temporarily closed by fighting patrols and during the night of the 21st-22nd, reinforcements arrived together with food and ammunition. The situation had been restored in the 715th's sector and it only remained for regiment to recapture the ground which it had lost. The attacks, when they were launched, were carried out not by battle groups but by formal units. It is, therefore, at this point that the account of the Grenadiers of 315th Regiment comes to an end.

Battle Group Krause of the Hitler Youth Division in the fighting at the approaches to Falaise, Normandy, during the late summer of 1944

One of the German divisions which fought in Normandy when the armies of the Western Allies invaded in June 1944, was 12th SS Panzer Division "Hitler Youth", ("Hitler Jugend" or "HJ"). By any standards this was an unusual formation. Not just because the rank and file were all very young. Nor in the fact that they were all volunteers, but because the training they received was designed exclusively to fit them for bloody battle. All field exercises were carried out using live ammunition and in the first few mock battles there were many casualties. But soon the recruits had learned the truth of the old soldiers' tales that a properly dug slit trench will protect against anything but a direct hit and that sweat saves blood. Once those lessons had been learned and absorbed, losses on training exercises sank to below 2 per cent, many of which were caused by road accidents. Being thus trained for battle and dedicated to combat, the "Hitler Youth" Division did not learn parade ground drills or the rituals of military minutiae. The rank and file had served, as the unit name proclaims, in the Hitler Youth organisation and most had been junior commanders. They had all been very young children when the Nazi Party came to power and their formative years had been influenced by that party's attitudes and education. In the Hitler Youth they had learned the basics of military discipline, had received weapons instruction and had had their bodies toughened with physical exercise and route marches. In 1934, Hitler had demanded that the youth of Germany be as hard as Krupp steel. Ten years later on the battlefields of Normandy, those who served in the 12th SS Division were certainly that, and in fanatical fighting on both the Western and later on the Eastern fronts, demonstrated their willingness to battle to the death for the man whose name they bore.

The officers and many of the NCOs for the division were seconded from other SS units, chiefly the "Leibstandarte SS Adolf Hitler" (1st SS Panzer Division), and were highly decorated veterans of the fighting on the Eastern Front. By conventional military standards these commanders were also young, but their combat experience gave them authority beyond their years. They had learned that to fight aggressively brought victory on the battlefield and the grafting of their experience onto the enthusiasm of the rank and file produced a body of men who were dedicated to the concept of victory in battle. Colin Gunner in his excellent book "Front of the

Line" described one of the SS units which he met in southern Austria at the end of the Second World War. Those men were, he wrote, "...the most formidable unit I saw at any time I wore the King's coat. They had passed from being soldiers into fighting machines..." It is interesting to reflect what his opinion would have been had he met the young lads of the "HJ" Division in the first battles of Normandy. And they were young: lads whose average age was 17 years. Indeed they were so young that they did not qualify for a cigarette issue nor were they eligible to receive the coveted ticket which gave them entry into military brothels.

During April 1944, "HJ" Division moved into Normandy and while the rank and file settled in, their commanders carried out an inspection of the ground between the mouth of the Seine and Bayeux, the sector held by General Marcks' 84th Corps. Brigadefuehrer Witt, commanding the "HJ" Division, concluded at the end of his inspection of the ground that neither division in the coastal sectors would be strong enough to withstand the forces that would be put in against them on D-Day. In his opinion the Allies would launch a sea and air assault with the aim of capturing Caen, its network of roads, and the nearby Carpiquet airfield. The terrain to the north and to the north-west of Caen had the best "going" for armour in the whole area. Therefore, it was in Witt's opinion the logical place for the Allies to land.

At 15mins past midnight on 6 June 1944, the first air landings were made in the invasion area and these were followed several hours later by assault landings from an armada of naval vessels. The 12th SS Division was ordered to move into the area held by 711th Division and hold itself ready to participate in the counter-attack which OKW had planned, but en route received a new order, deflecting it into 716th Division's area. The 7th Army war diary directed: "The 12th SS Panzer Division will take up a line running from Alencon to Crelouges-Flers... and will come under command of 84th Corps. Its task is to gain touch in the west with 21st Panzer Division and to throw back into the sea the enemy who has landed west of the Orne river..."

The commanders of the 12th had only a very general and, in places, totally inaccurate picture of the situation along the coast. All that was known was that Allied airborne units had been dropped east of the Orne and that to the west of that river an Allied beachhead had been set up. The "HJ" moved forward into the unknown but even before it entered the combat zone suffered its first casualties. The war diary of 1st/ 25th Regiment reported that its columns were attacked by low-flying aircraft firing machine guns and rockets. On that first day of the "HJ" Division's war service it lost 22 men killed in action, 40 wounded and one missing, and had engaged no enemy except the Allied aeroplanes.

Delays brought about by air-raids, diversions and traffic jams brought the division late and fragmented into its concentration area south-west of Caen. The 7th Army's intention was to launch a counter-attack on 7 June. Employing the three nearest available Panzer divisions — 12th SS, Lehr and 21st — they were to advance from the Caen sector towards the sea at Lion-sur-Mer. The plan was unrealisable. A joint attack by the three divisions during 7 June was out of the question. The 21st Panzer was already involved in the fighting east of the Orne, Panzer Lehr was 70km from the assault area and of the "HJ" Division only 25th Panzergrenadier Regiment and 2nd Panzer Battalion had reached the divisional concentration area. A major offensive involving three Panzer divisions was thus dramatically reduced to an attack carried out by the 25th Panzergrenadier Regiment and a single Panzer battalion. From the first week of June "HJ" played its part in holding the perimeter around Caen until the time that the Allies broke out of that confinement in August. This narrative dealing with the "HJ" Division in Normandy, does not open on 7 June, when its men were still green and unblooded. Rather it is the fighting which took place in August when, by now veteran soldiers, the remnant of 26th Panzergrenadier Regiment, forming Kampfgruppe Krause, was given the task of holding Falaise — 200 men against an entire Canadian infantry brigade backed by two squadrons of Sherman tanks.

Montgomery's Operation "Totalize", the combined Canadian, British and Polish offensive which opened on 8 August, failed to achieve the capture of the important road and rail communications centre of Falaise, a town of considerable strategic importance. In the first weeks following the invasion, for the Germans it had been the pipeline through which their forces were fed into the beachhead perimeter. By August, when the Allied armies broke out of their beachheads, the town had ceased to be a source to nourish the German divisions surrounding the Allies but had become, instead, an escape route out of a pocket in which they were all but completely enclosed. Falaise, with its network of first class roads, was a place through which most German units had to pass to escape towards the Seine. Inside the town there were roads of special importance, as for example the north-south highway from Caen to Argentan, permitting lateral movement across the width of the pocket and also the east-west road which ran along its length to the open neck of the pocket, around Trun and Chambois. A town of such importance as Falaise inevitably becomes a victim of war and, in addition to the Allied air bombardments which it had suffered before "Totalize", during the operation the town came within range of the guns of the Canadian artillery and had suffered badly.

"Panzer" Meyer commanding 12th SS Division, delegated the defence of Falaise to Kampfgruppe Krause, a formation numbering less than 200 men, made up, principally, of the remnant of 1st Battalion 26th Panzergrenadier Regiment, the divisional escort/battle patrol company and a couple of Panzer VI (Tigers) seconded from the 102nd Panzer Battalion. Krause group's anti-tank defences rested upon just two 7.5cm Paks for long-range fire, and for close-combat defence upon the bravery of its Grenadiers armed with anti-tank rockets. The task given to the battle group was to hold Falaise — to deny the town to the Allied forces for as long as possible.

Krause positioned his infantry along the town wall on a line running north-west to north-east with the Grenadiers of 1st Battalion on the left sector and the divisional HQ group on the right sector. One of the two anti-tank guns under his command was positioned on the right side of the Autes road to cover the river bridge, while the second was placed near Port Mariscot guarding the south-eastern road. Aware that the defence of the town wall could only be short-lived, Krause had the men of his group convert houses along the town's principal streets into strongpoints. Inside, each of these small groups would hold out. Krause realised that he would have to depend absolutely upon the resolution of his young Grenadiers who would be fighting without prospect of relief or reinforcement and under constant attack from superior forces. From his experience of the Russian Front, Krause knew that small groups of determined defenders had a value out of all proportion to their numbers when it came to fighting down an enemy's attacks. He knew his Grenadiers and was confident that they would fight to the last. It is the story of Kampfgruppe Krause which is narrated here.

As a justification for the length of time which it took the Canadians to capture Falaise, various sources have mentioned that 6th Brigade was not at full strength, that the casualties it had suffered during "Totalize" had not been made good, and that its men were tired from the strain of battle. This is, of course, true but the Grenadiers of the "HJ" Division had been fighting for a much longer period without reinforcement, without rest and without the assured supply of rations and ammunition upon which the Canadians could depend. Both groups of men were volunteers. Both were of high morale and of proven fighting quality. Yet the SS were able to blunt the Canadian assault. Other things being equal it can only have been the Grenadiers' intensive training during which they had experienced the sights, the sounds and the horror of battlefield conditions that gave them the edge. It was a charge frequently levelled against the German soldier that he could not think for himself or act upon his own initiative. The staunch defence of Falaise by groups of Grenadiers, or even by individual men, demonstrated how false was that accusation.

The 2nd Canadian Division's 6th Infantry Brigade, backed by two squadrons of armour and supported by both anti-tank and field artillery, was given the task of capturing the town. The brigade plan was for a swift thrust by two infantry battalions each supported by a squadron of Shermans. Divisional HQ set D-Day for the operation as 16 August and H-Hour at 13.00hrs, but such an early time was unrealistic given the road conditions and traffic jams through which the marching troops had to pass. Made aware of the difficulties, division put back H-Hour until 15.00hrs.

The advance to battle by the companies of the Canadian South Saskatchewan Regiment down the road towards Falaise, was contested by the pair of Tigers who were supporting Krause group as well as by a number of Grenadiers given the task of protecting the AFVs. Under the German fire the Saskatchewans went to ground and did not resume their advance until their own tank squadron had come forward to deal with the enemy armour. In the brief fire-fight which followed two Shermans were knocked out, but more importantly the Tigers and the Grenadiers were forced back closer to Falaise and no longer dominated the main road. The Canadian infantry companies were waved forward again and the interrupted advance resumed only to be halted for a second time as the files of men, now approaching the outer suburbs of the town, came under fire from an anti-tank gun detachment and its Grenadier defence group. The 7.5cm Pak took aim as one Sherman rounded the bend in the road and rumbled towards the river bridge. The gunners of the "HJ" held their fire until the tank was so close they could not miss. Their first shot scored a direct hit making this the first of the day's victims. During the course of less than an hour the crew of that gun knocked out two more armoured vehicles. The squadron which had begun the day's battle with 10 machines was now down to only five "runners". But Canadian pressure was telling upon 1st Battalion's Grenadiers who were holding the battle group's left sector. Under that pressure they abandoned their positions along the town wall and moved into the first of the strong-point houses.

On the Kampfgruppe's right flank, too, the escort company men had come under such furious armoured and infantry attack that they had been forced back from the wall. A runner reported to Sturmbannfuehrer Krause that the enemy had broken through and was working down towards the centre of the town. The commander's response was instinctive and immediate. He took the men of KG HQ, some 20 in all, and led them into a counter-attack, picking up small numbers of Grenadiers as the storming charge drew closer to the Canadian companies. Flinging hand grenades and firing machine pistols Krause's counter-attack group, with him at its head, rushed the Canadians. Then it was a matter of hand to hand fighting, of entrenching tool blades versus rifles and bayonets. It was a short but bloody fight but at its end the Canadians had been driven out of Falaise and the Grenadiers had, once again, taken up their former positions along the town wall. It was only a temporary respite.

On their respective sectors both Canadian battalions spent the remainder of the morning regrouping their companies. Late in the after-noon the leading company of the Saskatchewans reopened the attack, crossed the Aute and gained the eastern bank, but as its leading files climbed over it and prepared to advance towards the centre of the town, they came under the fire of a single machine gun sited inside a strong-point house and were pinned down. A troop of Shermans was ordered for-ward and shells from their tank guns set the house alight. The Grenadier defenders held out until the heat became unbearable and then moved their machine gun to a new position. Out in the streets handfuls of young men from the "Hitler Youth" fought their lonely battles. Their instructors had taught them well on the Beverloo training fields and those lessons had been reinforced with experiences gained over the past two months of unceasing combat. One basic lesson learned was that if infantry can be separated from their accompanying armour, then both can be destroyed in detail because neither can support the other. That tactic was employed by little groups of young SS men who, sheltering in the ruins of houses or hiding behind broken walls, waited until the Shermans had rumbled past them and then stood up to fire at pointblank range upon the Canadian infantry moving up the street and some distance behind the tanks.

It took a very long time for the Canadians to clear the north-eastern area of Falaise. Hour after hour was spent moving slowly and carefully through the streets of the old town, losing men killed and wounded as the rifle companies fought their way forward. Shortly after midnight, brigade ordered the Saskatchewans to clear the eastern suburbs and then to move down the railway line to take up defensive positions facing east. The advance, already slow, was continually affected by sniper and machine gun fire as the Canadians moved through the parkland of the Chateau de la Fresnay. The artillery FOO who was up with the Saskatchewan leading company, directed fire on the troublesome groups of Grenadiers stub-bornly contesting the advance and under those smothering barrages the SS were driven back. Slowly retreating but seizing every opportunity of strik-ing back at the Canadians, the men of KG Krause reached Falaise railway station in whose shattered buildings they had intended to make a stand. That intention was thwarted by the Saksatchewan advance which forced the "HJ" back into the town's public park. There one Grenadier sniper climbed a tree and opened fire on men in the open Bren carriers. It took some time for the Canadians to establish the location of that single sniper and then more time to kill him. Not until he was dead could the advance resume but it made little ground. A pair of machine guns firing from positions on the south side of the rue Clemenceau halted it again. More time was needed before that opposition could be beaten down and then the companies' advance resumed.

Delayed and obstructed by small numbers of determined SS men and very often by just individual Grenadiers, it was not until 03.00hrs on the morning of 17 August, that the Saskatchewans reached the railway and it took them another hour to gain the Trun road crossing. It was a relief to the exhausted Canadian infantrymen that resistance began to lessen after midnight and then grew even weaker. That resistance was diminishing because Krause considered that he had fulfilled his battle orders and that he could do no more. He had, thereupon, ordered his Panzers and Grenadiers to pull out of Falaise and to regroup at Resne la Mise. His order was not received by every one of his sub-units and this led to tragic consequences for his men.

In the western part of Falaise the Cameron advance was obstructed by the "HJ" 1st Battalion group and made only slow progress. Although the Saskatchewans had succeeding in crossing the Aute in their sector, the Camerons had been halted by a barricade across the roadway of the river bridge. Efforts to tear down that obstruction were met with bursts of fire from MG42s and from snipers in houses dominating the bridge. There could be no advance on the Cameron sector until the Shermans had come forward and either pushed the obstacle aside or, better still, concentrated their fire upon the machine gun nests and the snipers in the houses opposite. A squadron of tanks was ordered forward but the bombing raids of the previous days had created huge craters into which every one of the tank squadron's 10 Shermans "bellied". The infantry was unsupported and the Cameron colonel would not risk the lives of his men in so suicidal an enterprise as advancing along bullet-swept streets. He halted the attack until the tanks reached the river bridge. The day wore on. Night fell. During the hours of darkness the infantry, no longer willing to wait for the armour to arrive, moved forward and dismantled the barricade. The road forward was now clear and the Cameron attack to move into the centre of the town was set for 02.00hrs on 17 August.

The battalion moved off but within minutes was hit by such determined resistance that its assault faltered and died. The Camerons had struck a very determined group of Grenadiers whose resistance they could not overcome. Acting on the principle that one does not attack the enemy at his strongest point but that one bypasses it, the battalion's main effort tried to swing around the pocket of Hitler Youth defenders. On the German side that small Grenadier detachment had attracted to itself other small groups and a makeshift defence line was set up. Canadian probes undertaken to find a way round the original group then came up against the new defenders. Division, aware of how bitter was the fighting for the town, ordered another infantry brigade, the 4th, to "immediate alert" status ready to support the 6th Brigade in Falaise should this become necessary. Within the town the battalion of Fusiliers Mont Royale were brought out of 6th Brigade reserve and put into action to beef-up the assaults of other two battalions. The Camerons were given a new objective. The area of St Clair.

That fresh attack moved over its start line at 11.45hrs headed by armoured cars and armour. The assault had scarcely begun to roll when a single Grenadier rose up out of the rubble of a house. In his right hand he was carrying a Panzerfaust. With a single shot he destroyed an armoured car and before the astonished Canadians could react he had ducked back into the rubble only to re-emerge carrying a second projector. With his second shot he knocked out a Sherman. It was an inauspicious start to the Cameron attack but it was pressed home despite machine gun fire, attacks by anti-tank rocket teams and individual snipers. Shortly after midday the Camerons had reached St Clair, their given objective and moved on into Couvrigny. They consolidated in the large park of that suburb and began to dig in. A deep, heavy silence hung over the area; the fighting seemed to have died away and the exhausted soldiers had begun to relax when a shot rang out. There was a sniper in the area and his first shot had claimed a victim. To be under short-range sniper fire is particularly unnerving. At long range he may be inaccurate — but at close-range, every shot hits its target and there were a great many targets in the town park. Not until the sniper has fired a couple of shots can it be established from where he is firing and counter-action taken, but when a sniper opens up infantrymen usually go to ground and search for the source of the fire.

In this instance the SS Grenadier was using a trick which his instructors had seen applied by Red Army soldiers on the Eastern Front. The sniper had strapped himself halfway up a tree trunk and was firing from that position. His victims were chiefly those whom he could identify as officers. After a couple of shots the Camerons had narrowed their search to a particular section of the park and brought forward Shermans which lined up and swept the trees with machine gun fire. The tank gunners were ordered to cease fire. The sniper let off another round, probably an act of defiance to show that he was still active and, as he moved in the tree, a Bren gun carrier driver saw the movement. A long burst from a Bren gun, then another and then a third. This time there was no answering shot and a couple of officers deliberately walked about in the open. There was no response and a quickly formed patrol swept the suspect area. Below one tree they found fresh blood stains and looking up saw drooped in its upper branches the body of the Grenadier sniper. At that point the Cameron attack was halted to let the Fusiliers Mont Royale pass through to take up the running and to clear the southern part of the town.

The Fusilier advance was moving well when there was a sudden and unpleasant surprise. The Mont Royales had expected that the fighting for Falaise was almost at an end but they struck fanatical opposition. The group of SS Grenadiers confronting them were from 1st Battalion who had not received Krause's orders to pull back to Resne le Mise and who were defending a couple of houses and the area around them. The Fusiliers were up against men who must have known that they had no chance of living through this day, but who were determined to fight to the last. Individual SS men stood up and fired Panzerfaust and Panzerschreck rockets at the Shermans while others attacked the Canadian armour with explosive charges. Little groups of machine gunners swept the Fusilier positions with bursts of machine gun fire and a few Grenadiers closed with the Canadians firing machine pistols and then battling hand to hand. As the resistance by this group of SS men was beaten down, fire was opened upon the Fusiliers from another block of houses which dominated two main roads. It was essential that those two houses be taken without delay. Until they were the whole brigade advance on that sector was halted. Companies of Fusiliers were put in and were driven back. Tanks advanced and were destroyed. But, slowly, almost inevitably one feels, the Canadian effort began to succeed and men of one Fusilier company saw groups of the "HJ" running from the houses, both of which were now in flames, and into a girl's school, part of the Abbey of St Jean Baptiste.

The Fusiliers reported that the groups had numbered no more than 50 men, but whether these were a reinforcement to a garrison already in position or the surviving remnant of the defenders of the burning houses moving to new positions, they did not know. What was certain was that machine gun and sniper fire was now coming from the school building. Tanks came forward and standing off from the school opened up using armour-piercing shells to bring down the building upon the heads of its defenders. A battle patrol of 10 Fusiliers stormed into the school yard but were forced back under concentrated machine gun fire. With the main German resistance in Falaise now reduced to the school house, 6th Brigade could mount a well-planned attack. H-Hour was set for 02.00hrs. Inside the school the senior Grenadier NCO commanding the group held a ballot to decide which two men would be sent out to find Krause and to report what was happening in the town. A ballot was necessary, because not one of the "HJ" Grenadiers wanted to leave his comrades in this last fight.

The tank gun barrage destroyed the fabric of the school building and casualties among the SS defenders mounted. Those who were only lightly wounded were bandaged and insisted upon going back to man the guns or to fill ammunition belts. The unequal fight between the survivors of Kampfgruppe Krause and the Canadian Brigade continued but it could have only one outcome. Incendiary shells set the school ablaze and in time resistance faltered and then died altogether. The war diary of 6th Canadian Infantry Brigade reported "...only four defenders escaped on the South Saskatchewan sector. No prisoners were taken. Only dead and burned bodies were found..."

Although the Kampfgruppe went on to fight further battles in Normandy, it is at this point that our story of its struggle in Falaise ends for the town itself fell very shortly after. Krause and his 200 men had held out for over two days and nights gaining time for German formations of 5th Panzer Army and of 7th Army to escape from the Falaise pocket.

That staunch defence delayed the collapse of the northern wall of the Falaise salient and, to quote the Canadian official history of the campaign: "...a German force far smaller than our own [was] able to slow our advance to a point where considerable German forces made their escape [out of the pocket]...".

The eventual capture of Falaise followed by a swift Allied advance to Trun, at the neck of the pocket, caused the situation for the trapped German units to become critical. By 18 August, with the escape route nearly closed, the orderliness which had been a feature of the pocket's early days disappeared and units jockeyed for position to pass through the gauntlet of Allied fire and to escape northwards. When the Falaise operation was finally completed it was estimated that 40,000 German soldiers had been taken prisoner and more than 10,000 had been killed in action, but that a greater number had escaped to fight another day. That mass of men was heading for the River Seine behind which they hoped to escape the pursuing Allied tank armadas. As had been the case in the pocket, the first units to reach that river had arrived and been sent onwards in good order, but when the disordered mass of 5th Panzer Army and 7th Army flooded up to the Seine there were too few bridges across the river and a crush of vehicles built up around the approaches to every crossing place. Rumours of approaching Allied spearheads produced mild panic in some units which abandoned their heavy weapons and AFVs on the south bank and marched northwards towards Belgium in small, ad-hoc groups whose men were armed only with personal weapons. From prisoner of war interrogations, wireless intercepts and "Ultra" reports it was clear to the Allied planners that there was no defence line prepared north of the Seine and that no cohesive German front faced the Allied armies.

Montgomery, confident that victory lay within his grasp, proposed to Eisenhower, the Allied Commander-in-Chief, that the 12th (American) and 21st (British/Canadian) Army Groups should drive northwards together as "...a solid mass of forty Divisions...cross Flanders and seize Antwerp...". Eisenhower, likewise convinced that German resistance was crumbling, responded positively, hinting at the employment of the entire Airborne force, "...to speed...the missions...in the north-west...". Confidence grew among the senior Allied commanders that the war might well be ended in a matter of weeks and, indeed, the situation facing OKW was as serious as the Allies believed it to be. The German forces were heading northwards into Belgium and eastward towards Germany and that vast movement began to take on the character of a rout. As the divergent retreats continued, command staffs observed with alarm a gap appearing in the battle line between the right flank of 1st Army, which was pulling back to the area between Luxemburg and Nancy, and the left flank of 15th Army, which had withdrawn from the Pas de Calais area into positions around Antwerp and the Scheldt.

The gap between the 15th in Antwerp and the 1st in Luxemburg should have been closed by elements of 5th and 7th Armies, but these had been so badly mauled in the fighting in Normandy that the entire 5th Panzer Army had been withdrawn from the line for refitting and the scattered infantry remnants of the 7th had little defensive capability. There was another German Army in France, the 19th, but this was far away in the south and has no relevance to this account of military developments in Flanders and the Low Countries.

By 31 August, British forces had captured Amiens and could claim among the prisoners of war, General Eberbach, commanding 7th Army. Of greater importance to the Anglo-Canadian Army Group was that with the seizure of Amiens the last German defence line between the Somme and the Marne had been breached and ahead of Montgomery's armies there remained only the smaller water barriers of the Albert Canal and the River Maas. Although it was known that both were strong defensive positions, the euphoria at Supreme HQ Allied Expeditionary Forces (SHAEF) led to the belief that the German military machine would be unable to find sufficient soldiers to hold those lines and thus capitalise upon their natural defensive capacity. In the first days of September the formations of 21st Army Group were closing up to the Albert Canal expecting to meet little opposition. In his book, " A Full Life" General Horrocks, 30th Corps Commander, wrote that on 4 September, "...the only troops available to bar our passage northwards consisted of one German Division, the 719th, composed mainly of elderly gentlemen who hitherto had been guarding the north coast of Holland and had never heard a shot fired in anger, plus

BATTLE GROUP KRAUSE, NORMANDY

one battalion of Dutch SS and a few Luftwaffe detachments. That meagre force was strung out on a 50-mile front along the Albert Canal..."

On 3 September, Montgomery ordered Horrock's corps to halt its advance for 72hrs. While Horrocks and his men waited to be released from their enforced inactivity, on the other side of the battle front Hitler had taken action to plug the gap between 1st and 15th Armies. A Fuehrer Order was issued to Field Marshal Model who was not only the General Commanding Army Group B, but also carried the burden of Supreme Commander West. Despite the lack of information coming through to Model from the formations of his two commands, enough of a picture had emerged to convince him that if the German Army in the West was to be saved it was imperative to give ground and withdraw to the Siegfried Line. Model demanded, in addition, a reinforcement of 25 fresh infantry divisions and six Panzer divisions if he was to carry out the Fuehrer Order and hold the Westwall.

Hitler was very aware of the strain under which Model was placed and in order to relieve him of the more onerous burden, recalled to duty as Supreme Commander West, Field Marshal von Rundstedt, the officer he had replaced only months earlier. If there was any officer able to restore the confidence of the forces in the West, Gerd von Rundstedt was that man. The Fuehrer was also aware that he had to hold both the Albert Canal-Maas line in order to protect the approaches to the Saar and the Ruhr. He also had to retain his hold on Antwerp and Holland in order to deny the port facilities to the Allies. The Fuehrer Order mentioned in the previous paragraph directed that the canal was to be held as far as Maastricht, where a regrouped 7th Army was moving into position, and that the troops to defend the open gap would be Student's 1st Fallschirm (Para) Army, which he had only recently created but which was not completely raised. Hitler's orders to the para army were that it was to contest every foot of the ground in a stubborn delaying action.

The title, 1st Para Army, was a grand name for a formation which controlled the 3rd, 5th, 6th and eventually 7th Para Divisions. These, too, were grand names but the divisional and the Army description were hollow titles. Each of the first three units had suffered badly in the fighting in Normandy and had, in fact, been taken out of the line for reinforcement. None had expected to return to active service until November. Instead, the first week of September saw those burnt-out formations back in action again. German official reports on the para divisions stated that the 3rd had almost insignificant numbers, that 6th had the strength of just two infantry battalions backed by a few heavy calibre artillery pieces, and that 5th was in little better shape. In addition Student could count on three regiments of recruits who were grouped together as 7th Para Division, as well as 6th and 18th Para Regiments, the 1st Battalion of 2nd Para Regiment, an anti-tank battalion and a number of replacements amounting to approximately three regiments. Around that nucleus of Fallschirmjaeger formations, General Student grouped the remnants of two divisions from 88th Corps: 719th — Horrocks's elderly gentlemen — and 347th. Those formations, like the Fallschirmjaeger, were little more than fragments. In addition to them there were also detachments from SS replacement depots and from the base depot of the "Hermann Goering" Division. In support of the infantry contingents were 30 heavy and 10 light anti-aircraft batteries.

By the time that Horrocks' 30th Corps resumed its advance, von Rundstedt had reached the Western Front and had begun to restore the situation. His command was made up of two Armies, B and G, which numbered between them 48 infantry and 15 Panzer divisions. But here there is a qualification: very few of the armoured divisions was at full combat strength and in some cases did not have more than 10 "runners". Rundstedt's experience, Student's drive and the German staff system accomplished a military miracle. The para General, acting on his own initiative had borrowed staffs, confiscated personnel and had taken arms from units retreating through his sector. In anticipation of von Rundstedt's order he flung the gallimaufrey of formations described as 1st Para Army, along the length of the Albert Canal in a mass of very small Kampfgruppen. In most cases these groups were no more than a handful of men holding a machine gun position backed by tank-busting teams armed with Panzer-faust and Panzerschreck rocket launchers. Outnumbered and outgunned though the Jaeger of 1st Para Army knew themselves to be, Student had so imbued them with the will to fight and win that the battle groups, isolated and out of touch with each other though they were, and desperately short of heavy weapons, fought with unexampled bravery.

Volume 2 of the British official history, "The Victory Campaign", recorded that "...the retreat of the German armies had been a remarkable achievement...". Although their fighting strength had been reduced and the replacements they received lacked adequate training, they were able to seriously delay the Allied advance. Soon the gaps in the battle line had been closed, by 10 September, Army Groups B and G had gained touch and there was, once again, a continuous line running from the North Sea to Switzerland. By 11 September, German units which had been retreating were active again, ready to undertake offensive operations.

Battle Group of the 2nd Fallschirmjaeger Regiment in north-west Europe during the autumn-winter of 1944

A personal account of those days was given to me by my old friend, Adi Strauch. He had volunteered to return to front line service with his para unit, although the wounds he had received in Russia were still so raw that he could not operate any type of weapon. A new 2nd Fallschirmjaeger Regiment was being created and Strauch was posted to No 8 Company of its 2nd Battalion.

Because of his unhealed wounds he was posted to Company HQ where he was told that if the company commander was knocked out then he, Strauch, was to take over and lead the unit. The first inspection of No 8 Company was for him a depressing experience:

"There they were on parade. Standing alongside young volunteers were old NCOs, Luftwaffe men taken away from their company office desks and from headquarters duties. The nucleus of the company consisted of just eight trained paratroops. We were soon to go into action so there was little time; a few days at the most, in which to give them weapon training.

"On 5th September, we moved out: two heavy machine gun platoons, a mortar platoon, a half-platoon of infantry guns and two Panzerschreck [rocket launcher] sections and company headquarters. The battalion moved up on the following day to the Maaseik area, where it was to prepare for an attack on the village of Helchteren, near the Albert Canal. Our battalion reached the form-up area during the morning of the 7th and was soon involved in fighting against a British armoured division."

It was not long after that first clash that the swampy nature of the terrain and the intensity of the fighting broke up the battalion's formal hierarchy into battle groups, although Strauch continued to use the formal terms of "company" and "battalion". I shall do the same, but complement these by using the expression "battle group" when relating the actions which Strauch describes.

The military situation on the Western Front during that first week of September 1944 was that the Albert Canal, which 1st Para Army had been ordered to hold, had been crossed by British armour before the German units which were to defend it had reached the waterway and taken up position. To wipe out the British bridgehead, Student had ordered into action the only units immediately available, von der Heydte's 6th Para Regiment and Finzel's battalion of 2nd Para Regiment, the unit with which Strauch was serving. Student then ordered the other formations of the newly created 7th Para Division to march to the combat zone at best possible speed and enter the battle. To carry out the General's order, the young recruits completed a forced march and went straight into the attack against 11th British Armoured Division. The para formation recaptured the villages of Hechtel, Helchteren and Zonhoven but could not destroy the bridgehead. Student, accepting that the British were now across the canal in force, between Herentals and Haselt, ordered 1st Para Army to pull back behind the Maas-Schelde Canal so that by the middle weeks of September the army's front ran from Antwerp to Herentals and along the northern bank of the Maas-Schelde Canal to Maastricht on the Albert Canal. Those first operations are described by Strauch in his opening account:

"Our No 8 Company battle group suffered no losses in that first engagement and took up position in front of Helchteren...On 8 September and for the next few days the British attacked again and again but each assault was beaten back, although there were now heavy losses to both sides. An 88 which had been in action in front of the company headquarters house, was withdrawn without warning, leaving us with no support except for mortars and an infantry gun group which was under the command of an NCO from the Flak. The enemy attack on 11 September, was supported by flame-throwing as well as bulldozer tanks. That attack was able to gain ground because all our Panzerfausts, Panzerschreck missiles and the shells from the infantry guns had been fired off. The company commander had been wounded and evacuated so, according to orders, I took over and led the company battle group. The battalion's Jaeger Company had been almost wiped out and was no longer able to hold its positions. My old comrade, who had led No 1 Platoon, was fatally wounded at this time and enemy tanks began to work round our left flank. Over the field telephone which was still working I was ordered to pull back. British tanks were only a few metres away as I, together with five others, worked our way back to battalion headquarters which enemy tanks were now nearing. Our close-quarter tank-busting teams went into action and the enemy advance on that sector was quickly halted.

"We evacuated the wounded, putting them into very small, two-wheeled, horse-drawn carts. We did not so much load them as heap them into the available space. I was told to take some men and set up a trawl-line which would collect all those who had been separated from their units so that they could be reformed into new battle groups and put back into action. Armed with Panzerfausts, the battalion commander, accompanied by the CO of No 5 Company, then went out to attack the British tanks. Both officers fell in action. I led the remnant of the battalion battle group back across country and late in the night reached a bridge across the Maas-Schelde Canal. A General to whom I reported ordered me to take the men back to Kinrooi where he proposed to regroup our battalion's surviving members."

After action on the Albert Canal sector the battalion battle group was put in against US Airborne troops at Son and Veghel. Strauch records that the battle group was officered by men who had no Fallschirmjaeger experience but who had been seconded from the Flak arm of the Service. As a result of their lack of knowledge in siting defensive positions, the battle group lost men killed, wounded and captured. As Strauch remarked, in cases where officers from other arms of the Service were in command of paratroop units, their good intentions and personal bravery were no substitute for training and combat experience. Forced to retreat again the battalion battle group reached Deurne where the inexperience of the unit's officers once again resulted in unnecessary casualties. By the end of September the remnant of 2nd Battalion was in position in Helenhaven, which was reputed to be a quiet sector of the Front. It was not and fighting went on throughout October with a drain of losses that were never made good.

Strauch's battle group, the old No 8 Company, pulled back across the Maas and took up positions in the bend of the river between Herten and Linne. Not until December did the battalion battle group come, once again, under the command of an officer with front line experience, although even he was not a paratroop officer. Strauch then described a battle group operation which he led, a long-range patrol carried out during 5-6 January, on the far side of the Maas:

"On the enemy side of the river we worked towards Heel on compass bearing and several times brushed the enemy's positions but were not challenged and so were able to bypass them. On the Venlo-Maastricht highway we carried out road watch duties, counting the flow of Allied tanks and guns...[and] recrossed the river in the boat we had left in hiding. My report stressed that the Allies were building-up for a new offensive. At that time I was told that the recommendation for my promotion to Officer Cadet had been approved."

The history of 3rd Battalion South Wales Borderers which was holding positions opposite the German paras and describing the events of those days, included the following extract:

"...the enemy staged a most successful raid...A hail of mortar fire and shells fell on the three houses...each of which was occupied by a Section of men. These were driven to take cover by the ferocity of the enemy fire...a runner...returned with the news that one house was completely deserted; the Germans had cleverly spirited away a section of six men..."

The history then goes to state that the enemy: "...had shown a high degree of offensive spirit, which was proved by his patrolling activities on the battalion side of the river. Every credit must be given to him for carrying the battle into 'enemý' territory..."

The actions in which Strauch's unit had been engaged from the first week of September were, of course, very much those which had been fought by all the German battle group units which had been flung into the defence of the Albert Canal. By the end of that month Student was able to reintroduce a formal organisation so that most units could no longer be correctly described as Kampfgruppen. That hierarchical arrangement was a situation which did not last long and when Montgomery's Army Group thrust across the Maas and advanced towards the Rhine in the last two months of the war, the formal identity was lost again as most units fragmented into battle groups.

The February 1945 issue of the Para Army's news sheet "Fallschirmjaeger", described the fighting in which Strauch had been engaged, of which the following is but a brief extract: "It is a battle for villages...villages which have been turned into fortresses to block the advance of the enemy's tanks... Out of the ruins and from cellars the German defenders emerge and let their weapons speak. Hundreds of English tanks lie in this area — all knocked out. But no villages have been so bitterly fought for as Joost and Montfort, which act as breakwaters to the British flood. Those villages are defended by Z's para battalion... In the night 20 tanks accompanied by infantry moved forward and had soon gained a foothold in Joost..." The article concludes with an account of the heroism of the regimental commander and the quotation that "...the front is where the CO is".

By 1 February Fallschirm Army, now commanded by Schlemm who had replaced Student before Christmas 1944, held a sector from the Reichswald in the north to Roermond in the south. Most units were so weak that companies often numbered no more than 50 men. The 7th Para Division which had fought in the Hagener Forest, had suffered crippling losses but still retained its high morale. The number of "old sweats" — the men who had been trained in the first years of the war — were very few indeed, but an awareness of para traditions inspired the 18 to 20-year-olds of the Flak and Luftwaffe units who now formed the greater numbers in the regiments.

Other Fallschirmjaeger Divisions, notably 5th and 6th, had also needed to create battle groups until the divisions had reached full strength and could enter the war on the Western Front as homogeneous formations. The 1st Para Army then fell back under Allied pressure and fragments of units, formed into a great number of KGs, finished the war in north-western Germany.

Battle group Langkeit of "Grossdeutschland" Panzer Corps in the fighting east of the River Oder, January 1945

It was not on the Western Front alone that the armies of the Third Reich suffered military defeats in the autumn and winter of 1944. An Allied advance in Italy, slow but maintained, drove the German defenders from below Cassino, northwards and almost to the plain of Lombardy, while in Greece Loehr's Army Group began its long overdue withdrawal. Every theatre of operations had witnessed disasters but it was on the Eastern Front that Hitler's hosts suffered their severest defeats in that autumn of reverses.

By the end of 1944, the vast expanse of Soviet territory which the Wehrmacht had conquered during 1941 and 1942, had been retaken by the Red Army until only a thin buffer, the western half of Poland, separated the spearhead forces of the Red Army from Germany's eastern provinces. The Soviet summer offensive of 1944, Operation "Bagration", had smashed Army Group Centre (soon to be renamed Army Group "A") and had brought the Russian forces to the province of East Prussia which STAVKA was now preparing to take out in a major offensive. The once powerful Army Group North, by this time reduced to just a handful of divisions in Courland, had been forced back until it had the sea behind it and the Russians to its front and on both flanks.

Colonel-General Guderian, Chief of the General Staff at OKH, demanded that Hitler use the 30 experienced divisions in Courland to break through the Russian encirclement and to link up with other German formations in East Prussia where they, and the forces in East Prussia, would threaten the northern flank of any Soviet advance towards Berlin. Hitler rejected Guderian's demand with the result that by December 1944, the encircling Red Army was so strong that an attempt at a link-up between the German forces in Courland and those in East Prussia had absolutely no chance of success. Guderian then proposed that Army Group North be evacuated by sea from Courland and moved to bolster the last remaining German-held sectors of western Poland. That suggestion, too, was turned down by the Fuehrer.

General Gehlen, head of the General Staff Department (Foreign Armies East) and a recognised expert on the Soviet Union, produced figures which showed that the Red Army's Supreme STAVKA had planned for its nine military fronts to launch attacks between the Carpathian mountains and the Baltic Sea. The first blow would be undertaken by the 2nd

Above: A German soldier, dressed in a Russian sheepskin coat, crosses a battle site on the way to Moscow. The black stripe on his arm identifies him as German, despite the jacket.

Below: Men of a machine gun battalion bringing forward their machine guns on sledges during the advance upon Moscow, winter 1941.

Norddeutsche Ausgabe

Norddeutsche Ausgabe

Berlin, Freitag, 10. Oktober 1941

VÖLKISCHER BEOBACHTER

Kampfblatt der nationalsozialistischen Bewegung
Großdeutschlands

Die große Stunde hat geschlagen:

Der Feldzug im Osten entschieden!

Heeresgruppen Timoschenko und Woroschilow eingeschlossen — Heeresgruppe Budjenny in Auflösung

Neuer Kessel bei Brjansk
Die letzten voll kampfkräftigen Divisionen der Sowjets gesprengt

Das militärische Ende des Bolschewismus

Top left: The Nazi Party newspaper announces in the 10 October 1941 edition that the campaign in the East has been decided and the military end of the Bolshevist system.

Left: Soldiers in camouflage man a German 88mm gun in action during Operation "Typhoon", to the west of Moscow.

Above: Russian infantrymen, killed in action during the first winter of the war; victims of the Soviet military doctrine of shoulder to shoulder attacks.

Left: German infantry and armour moving forward during the first winter of the war in the East.

Below: The German Army's supply organisation broke down during the winter of 1941 and clothing supplies did not reach the forward troops. To keep the advance upon Moscow moving forward the most bizarre methods were used. This soldier, whose boots have long since fallen apart, has had to wrap his feet in rags to keep them warm.

Above: Werner Ostendorff, here seen in the rank of colonel, who commanded Kampfgruppe "Reich" during the winter battles to the west of Rhzev and in the bend of the Volga river in 1942.

Left: A dead German soldier who froze to death by the side of a field kitchen during the retreat from Moscow.

Right: Heinz Harmel, here seen in the rank of brigadier, who commanded Panzer Grenadier Regiment D of Kampfgruppe "Reich" during the winter battles of 1942-43.

Below: An SP gun protecting the thrust line to Losovaya in February 1943.

Below: Grenadiers of battle group "Reich" after they had captured Stytshevka, during the fighting to the west of Rzhev, 1942-43.

Left: "Jochen" Peiper, who led the mission to rescue the 320th Infantry Division cut off to the south-east of Kharkov in February 1943. Peiper is seen here with the rank of major and wears the Oak Leaves to the Iron Cross. The photograph thus dates sometime after January 1944.

Above: The officers of battle group Peiper at an "O" Group before an operation in November 1943. Peiper is the officer in the middle of the group wearing the Knight's Cross.

Below: A 7.5cm Pak being served by soldiers of the "Hitler Jugend" ("HJ") Division in Normandy in 1944.

Above: Fritz Witt, commander of the "HJ" Division in Normandy (right) with Axmann, the leader of the Hitler Youth organisation. Witt was killed by shellfire on 15-16 June and was succeeded by "Panzer" Meyer. Both men were amongst the youngest General officers of the German forces in the Second World War.

Above: "Panzer" Meyer (right), here seen with SS General "Sepp" Dietrich, served in the elite "Leibstandarte" before being posted to 12th SS Panzer Division. He took command of that formation after the death of Witt.

Right: "Panzer" Meyer in Normandy.

Right: General Heinrich Eberbach, who commanded Panzer Group West, a formation later renamed Panzer Group Eberbach, on 10 August 1944. Eberbach who then went on to command 7th Army, was captured during the British advance into Belgium and Holland at the end of August 1944.

Far right: Colonel Langkeit and officers of the "Grossdeutschland" Panzer Corps planning a new attack.

Right: Colonel Langkeit (2nd left) here seen with General von Manteuffel (to his left) during an operation on the Eastern Front.

Above: Colonel Willi Langkeit, commander of battle group Langkeit of the "Grossdeutschland" Panzer Corps, who led his battle group in the fighting at the approaches to Frankfurt-am-Oder, January 1945.

and 3rd Byelo-Russian Fronts against East Prussia. The second blow would be launched from a start line in the bend of the Vistula by Zhukov's 1st Byelo-Russian and Koniev's 1st Ukrainian Fronts. STAVKA's strategy on that sector, was to isolate and destroy Army Group A (formerly Army Group Centre) and to advance as far as the River Oder, a distance of some 300km. The STAVKA effort would employ 2.25 million soldiers on just Zhukov's and Koniev's Fronts. Between them they would control 163 infantry divisions, 32,143 guns and 6,500 AFVs. On the narrow but vital Baranov sector of the Vistula bend where the main attack was to be made, the Soviets enjoyed a superiority over the Germans of 9:1 in infantry, 6:1 in armour and 10:1 in guns. The Order of Battle of Army Group A was 9th and 17th Infantry Armies and 4th Panzer Army, controlling a force of 30 infantry, four Panzer and two motorised divisions. Strong though that Army Group seemed to be, most of its divisions were burned out and they were, in any case, too few in number for the battle which lay ahead.

In an effort to increase front-line strengths, Guderian ordered a thorough comb-out of rear echelon units and this, together with a regrouping and a thinning-out of formations produced 14 divisions. These he formed into a strategic reserve for he proposed, when the current Russian offensive eventually lost its momentum, as it must do after the mighty advances of the previous autumn, to launch a counter-offensive. That riposte would not be able to match the Red Army's effort in size and weight, but the Chief of Staff was confident that it would gain Germany a valuable breathing space. Guderian was not able to deploy and use that strategic reserve as he wished. Hitler who had planned the offensive on the Western Front, which has become known as the Battle of the Bulge, promptly ordered that Eastern reserve to be sent westwards, assuring his Chief of Staff that its divisions would be returned as soon as it was clear that the Battle of the Bulge was being won. Hitler also comandeered all the construction and road building battalions which Guderian had assembled, together with the heavy artillery he had brought together to support the sectors of the battle line which in his opinion were most under threat. With the removal of so many of the formations essential to its defences the Eastern Front, already understrength, was so dangerously weakened that it would be certain to shatter when the new, major, Russian assault was launched.

Gehlen then reported that the Soviets had concentrated in their 90km-wide bridgehead at Baranov, in Poland, five infantry armies and six armoured corps as well as a number of independent infantry and armoured formations. The imbalance of forces had now risen in favour of the Red Army to 11:1 in infantry, 7:1 in AFVs and 20:1 in artillery. The Russian superiority in artillery was so high that the local commanders could mass

250 guns on each kilometre of front. Back in the Ardennes it had become clear by the end of December that Hitler's gamble had failed and that the German forces, which had advanced in the first days of the Battle of the Bulge, were now withdrawing in disorder. Guderian demanded the return of his Panzer divisions to enable Army Group A to meet the imminent Russian offensive. Hitler refused and instead reduced Guderian's forces still further by despatching Panzer Corps Gille, Guderian's sole reserve in the bend of the River Vistula, southwards into Hungary where he planned to open a new offensive.

The Chief of Staff sent Hitler a final piece of intelligence: "The new Russian winter offensive will open on 12 January". Still the Supreme Commander refused to reinforce the Eastern Front. Then in the early hours of that day a barrage opened on the Baranov sector which lasted from 01.30 to 06.00hrs. When it ceased a deep silence endured for 30mins after which the bombardment began again. Behind the barrage as it marched across the cratered landscape, special Red Army detachments, punishment units put in as a human sacrifice, advanced to kill those German soldiers who had survived the shellfire. Behind the so-called "Strafbats", an armada of tanks rolled forward followed by divisions of conventional Red Army infantry. That huge assault broke through the front of 4th Panzer Army and crushed all but the most minimal resistance in the front line sectors. Here and there a German machine gun went into action against the flood of Soviet soldiers marching across the open plains. But it was only machine guns which retaliated. Not one piece of German artillery had survived to fire back at the oncoming Russians. However, the rear units of 4th Panzer Army were not affected by the Russian attack and were able to retreat westwards.

Realising, at long last, the need to take action on the Vistula sector Hitler ordered the elite "Grossdeutschland" Panzer Corps, together with a few divisions from Hungary and the Western Front, to restore the situation in 4th Panzer Army's area. It was a movement undertaken by too few forces and too late in time. Zhukov's armies were advancing along a thrust line which aimed directly at Frankfurt-am-Oder and were moving with such speed that the probability existed they would reach the east bank of the river before the slower-moving German units and would destroy them before those units could cross to the safety of the west bank. Supreme STAVKA had planned the battle of Berlin as the final operation of the war in Europe and, to prepare the ground for that advance, Zhukov ordered his armies to race for the Oder and to establish bridgheads on the river's western bank — springboards out of which the Red Army would make the advance to the Reich's capital.

The race to the Oder can be said to have begun when, in the second week of January 1945, Zhukov's armies stormed across the Vistula. Within a matter of days there was no longer a solid German battle line in that area. On 20 January, Colonel-General Schoerner, the new commander of Army Group A, committed 11th and 24th Panzer Corps to a counterattack to knit up the ruptured front of 4th Panzer Army. It was an effort too weak to achieve any sort of success. The Red Army counter-attacked 24th Corps and cut it off. It then became a "wandering pocket" trying to fight its way back to the German lines. "Grossdeutschland" was ordered to rescue 24th Corps and its assault made such good ground that by 22 January the advance guards from both formations had gained touch.

The Eastern Front was collapsing and, faced with that catastrophe, the only solution which suggested itself to the Reich's leadership was that the creation of a few large and flexible battle groups would have greater offensive/defensive potential than several smaller battle groups. The latter had always lacked heavy weapons and had also experienced difficulties in the matter of supplies and replacements. In accord with that solution High Command directed "Grossdeutschland", resting after its rescue mission, to create a strong all-arms battle group. Kampfgruppe Langkeit was created on 26 January 1945 and its chief infantry constituent, Corps Panzer Grenadier Replacement Brigade, was a unit unusual for that time since it was at almost full establishment. The other component of Langkeit's KG was Major Petereit's Alarm Group Schmeltzer, which also had sufficient soldiers to flesh-out the new, elite and very specialist battle group.

To counter the Russian race to the Oder, the German military commanders, lacking sufficient men or weapons, had only the advantages of familiarity with the terrain and an awareness that their officers and men were determined to defend their native soil. It was believed that a system of field fortifications had been set up to the east of the Oder, resting upon a chain of lakes, the so-called Tirschtiegel positions. A water barrier, such as a lake system, has the advantage that it compels an attacker to advance across areas of ground — land bridges — which the defenders can hold in strength. In the case of the Tirschtiegel positions this was not the case. There had been almost no work undertaken and responsibility for constructing the trench lines had been left to Nazi Party political officers who had deserted their posts and fled as the Reds approached. Such positions as had been constructed were rudimentary — a few trench lines, dug-outs and in some places an anti-tank ditch. All showed evidence of hasty and unplanned work. A second line of trenches and dug-outs was in a worse state than the first line, with only the most basic work begun but not completed. The military commanders withdrawing into the Tirschtiegel positions were thus faced with the dual problems that they must not only somehow find sufficient labour to complete the trench systems, but must also man those positions before the Soviet offensive reached them. The only military units immediately available were local militia and Volkssturm detachments, made up of poorly armed men who would be no match for Zhukov's veterans. In an effort to fill the defence lines with troops the High Command raised units out of any available bodies of men. In some cases officers were appointed to take up Staff positions in formations which had been given grandiose titles but which had no troops. To begin with it was a nightmare scenario but slowly the efficiency and pragmatism of the German military system manifested itself and order was produced out of chaos.

The newly-created Kampfgruppe Langkeit was one of the formations which should have manned the Tirschtiegel positions. Its infantry component was renamed Kluever's Panzer Grenadier Regiment, with Schmeltzer's Alarm detachment, three Grenadier companies and a machine gun company forming its 1st Battalion. The men, although chiefly young recruits, had veteran instructors, officers and NCOs. Schoettler's 2nd Battalion had three Grenadier companies, a machine gun and a mortar company. Few of that battalion's rank and file were "Grossdeutschland" soldiers. No 7 Company, for example, was made up of men from other units who had been taken off trains passing through Cottbus, and taken onto the strength of the "Grossdeutschland" unit. The battle group's artillery component had been, to begin with, just two heavy field howitzers. Then a battery of light field howitzers was formed and, finally, a light Flak battery with four 2cm guns, four twin-2cm guns and four 3.7cm motorised anti-aircraft pieces, came onto strength. A small SP gun detachment was also created. To obtain AFVs, Langkeit was not so much pragmatic as piratical. He comandeered machines from the factories in which they had been made and requisitioned other vehicles from the "Grossdeutschland" training depots. Many of these latter were powered by charcoal gas engines, others had no turrets and some had no guns — in short, the only factor which made them AFVs was the plating they carried. Nevertheless, Hudel, commanding the Panzer detachment, had soon created an HQ squadron, a Panzer company, a recce platoon, two tank destruction troops each armed with Panzerschreck rocket launchers, and two more troops armed with Panzerfausts. There was also an anti-tank company and a motor cycle company.

During the night of 26-27 January the Kampfgruppe, in no way completely raised or forming a homogeneous group, began to move towards the front. The divisional history records that despite the obvious shortcomings and deficiencies in equipment, the morale of the men marching out to give unequal battle was first-class. They were determined to win, even though they knew the enemy was vastly superior to them in number and equipment. Langkeit was ordered to concentrate his Kampfgruppe around Reppen and then to strike north-eastwards into the flank of the Red Army forces advancing upon Stettin. Following on from that operation the KG was next to take up its allotted positions in the Tierschtiegel defences. A few days later the entire battle group set out for Reppen, to undertake its first mission, to attack the flank of the Red Army advancing towards Stettin.

On its approach march it was surprised and attacked by strong Russian forces. The principal reason for the surprise encounter was that Langkeit had been given no information on the location of the Soviet forces. His battle group fought back and restored the situation and was then advised that Bittrich's SS Corps was encircled somewhere near Sternberg. On 30 January, Langkeit sent a battle group, the 2nd Battalion of his Panzer Grenadier regiment, to break through the Soviet encirclement and to bring out Bittrich's trapped formations. The battalion reached Pinnow and formed two small motorised battle groups to carry out the rescue operation. The Grenadiers were heartened as they carried out their attack to hear the sounds of small arms and artillery fire, believing these to be made by the SS. About midday the true explanation of those battle noises came when Soviet tanks appeared from the north-east and began firing into Pinnow. Patrols then reported to Langkeit that Russian armour and infantry, outflanking the Kampfgruppe to the north, were making for Reppen. Langkeit decided that his priority was to bring out the SS Corps and ordered 2nd Battalion to continue with its attack. By last light on 30 January, the Panzergrenadiers had smashed the Red ring and gained touch with the SS. Not long after that an independent tank-destroyer company of armoured vehicles also broke the encirclement, was immediately taken onto the strength of Bittrich's group and went into action.

Covered by a rearguard formed by 2nd Battalion, the remnant of SS Corps, escorted by the tank-destroyer company, then pulled back towards Frankfurt. Langkeit's 2nd Battalion then prepared to defend Reppen. Meanwhile, the situation in which the main body of the Kampfgruppe was placed had deteriorated with the report that Russian forces had now outflanked it both to the north and the south. There could now be no question of an advance to Sternberg and 1st Panzergrenadier Battalion, backed by 88mm guns and other artillery weapons, moved towards Reppen to reinforce the 2nd Battalion.

It had a nightmare journey. The Reppen road was blocked by columns of slow moving refugees who panicked when JS tanks appeared on the crest of the ridge north of the road and opened fire upon them.

North of the road where there was good going, the Red Army commander concentrated the mass of his tanks. To the south of the road where thick woodland made the terrain unsuitable for armoured operations, he put in his infantry. At a point well behind Langkeit's Kampfgruppe, Russian tank columns cut the road so that the battle group which had been put into action to smash one encirclement was now itself in danger of being surrounded and cut off. It was also dangerously split up. The 2nd Panzergrenadier Battalion was in Reppen, 1st Battalion was on the road to that place and the heavy vehicles and tanks of the main body were isolated from both those battalions.

Langkeit formed that main body into two columns and intended to lead them in a mass charge to break the Soviet ring. Such an attack did not and, indeed, could not, succeed because the columns could not deploy off the road and into open country. Trapped fast among the civilian carts they were the principal targets of Soviet infantry and tank gun-fire from north and south of the road — fire that smashed down into the press of carts and people and created enormous casualties. Here and there a few Panzers forced their way out of the press of civilian carts and charged the enemy road blocks but died in the concentrated fire of the Soviet tank guns. Back in Reppen the Panzergrenadiers of 2nd Battalion, squatting in their slit trenches, patiently endured strafing from the air and barrages from mortars and from tank guns. The houses in the town were soon in ruins. The Red commander, thinking that the German troops were now either dead or demoralised, ordered tanks and infantry to mop up the remnants. His decision gave the Panzergrenadiers the chance at last to exact revenge for the punishment they had suffered. A wave of 10 T34s was shot to pieces by the 88s and a Red Army infantry battalion which came in against No 6 Company was wiped out almost to a man. But it was clear the battalion's ability to resist was nearly at an end and Langkeit ordered it to destroy its vehicles and fight a way through to the main body. During the night of 31 January, covered by a barrage, the heavy weapons were destroyed and the Grenadiers and artillerymen marched to join the main body.

The situation in which the KG was placed was desperate and Langkeit decided to make a break-out attempt through the woods south of the road. Once his units had grouped in the forest they would be faced with a difficult, tiring march but the Russian infantry in the woods were less strongly armed than the tank units on the main road. It should, therefore, be easier for the Kampfgruppe to fight its way through and escape. The battle group's last surviving eight-wheeled armoured car went into the forest to reconnoitre the route and, although the first reports were encouraging, the situation deteriorated again during 1 February. The units filtering along forest rides and secondary roads, once again became closely entangled with civilian columns and came under fire from Soviet infantry forces which had now entered the woods in strength. Langkeit's light Flak groups, heavy machine guns and Pak poured fire along the edge of the forest to beat back the Red Army units and to aid the slow-paced withdrawal. Stuka aircraft of Colonel Rudel's tank-busting squadron were brought in to aid the escape but their efforts had little success.

Langkeit's "O" Group during the night of 2 February, heard a bleak report. The guns were down to two rounds each and the break-out through the woods had not succeeded. He proposed that the Kampfgruppe make a swift, direct thrust along the road. This might succeed so long as it was covered by a strong rearguard. Spearheaded by a Panzer detachment, the first attack was made in the early hours of the morning of 3 February, but failed to smash through. Meanwhile, on the northern side of the road, 1st Grenadier battalion attacked and destroyed the Russian forces opposing them in hand to hand combat and drew the attention of the Red commanders to that sensitive area. That gave the chance for the "Hetzers" of the tank destroyer unit and the last of Hudel's Panzers to carry out a second, and this time successful, thrust up the road. By 14.00hrs the Soviet ring had been ruptured and the westward withdrawal began. It was a short-lived move. At Kunersdorf more Soviet tanks had cut the road but, once again, the Panzer/SP group struck and destroyed them. During that battle Sergeant Riedmuller won the Knights Cross for destroying four T34s with successive shots and when the lie of the land prevented him from destroying the fifth, climbed out of his Panzer and "killed" it with a Panzerfaust.

A stream of military and civilian vehicles was now pouring through the broken ring and 2nd Battalion gave flank protection to the main body of the battle group as it pulled back towards Frankfurt. The artillery units, positioned in the streets of Damm, a suburb of that city, fired barrages to cover the retreating formations. Some detachments of KG Langkeit were first held in Damm but were then ordered to cross to the Oder's western bank and take up defensive positions there. The remainder of the battle group continued to hold the bridgehead.

That eastern group fought bitterly to prevent the capture of Kunersdorf airfield which the Soviets needed as a forward base for the next stage of their offensive. In that fighting the bridgehead group suffered severe losses and even their most determined defence and skillfully mounted attacks could not prevent the Red Army from eventually crushing the Damm perimeter. On 3 February, an order was issued upgrading Kampfgruppe Langkeit to "Kurmark" Panzergrenadier Division. It is at this place, therefore, that we leave the battle group and consider another one which fought in the east when the Third Reich was in its death throes.

Battle Group Porsch, a bicycle-mounted, tank-busting detachment in the fighting in the eastern provinces of Germany, April 1945

The approaching end of the Second World War in Europe saw the distintegration of whole German armies, the destruction of entire corps and the annihilation of divisions. Those units were wiped so completely from the situation maps at Army Group HQ and in the Fuehrer bunker that it was as if they had never been. The Germans do not use, as we do, the expression, "To put the troops through a mincing machine". Their expression is a single and terrifying word — incinerated.

As the Eastern Front fell apart under the hammer blows of the Red Army, formation after formation was "incinerated" and their ashes blew away into nothingness. On the High Command maps other names appeared: those of Kampfgruppen. As Joachim Schulz-Naumann wrote in his work, "Die letzten dreizig Tage", the War Diary of OKW from April to May 1945, "to delay the enemy advance he had to be attacked by individual battle groups...". Most of those newly created and individual battle groups fought the last battles with bitter intensity. Some were detachments of Skorzeny's Jagdverbaende which had long since ceased to operate partisan-type missions behind the Russian front lines. Now they were fighting as infantry, yet still employing all the special skills they had learned and used to good effect on those guerilla-type operations. Among the battle group names on the High Command maps were many which were composed of SS men: KG Solar, Jagdverband Mitte and KG Schwendt, a unit skilled in counter-attacks and storming assaults. Then there was KG Wesler, a company of snipers whose specialist activities and high "kill" rate had so dominated one Russian bridgehead on the River Oder that enemy activity on that sector was held in check. The exotically named KG "Thousand and one Nights", was a mixed battalion formed round the 560th Jagdpanzer Battalion. Then there was, in approximately brigade strength, Kampfgruppe Lebedur. At this time, too, KG Speer made its appearance. This was the escort unit of the Reichs Armaments Minister and just one of the formations which were handed over by the Nazi leaders for employment on active service.

In the previous chapter which dealt with battle group Langkeit it was mentioned that the Reich's leadership considered a single strong Kampfgruppe to be more effective than a number of smaller ones. That had still been a true assessment in January 1945, when there remained an effective front in the East, but it no longer obtained in the final weeks of the war. In those last critical weeks any battle group which could be scraped together was put into action and some battle groups were smaller in size than a battalion. One such Kampfgruppe is the subject of this account — a company of 500/600th Punishment Battalion, whose soldiers became tank destruction specialists under the leadership of Untersturmfuehrer Porsch.

In April 1945, the Red Army broke out of the confines of its bridgeheads on the Oder and soon two vast Soviet Fronts were overrunning the eastern provinces of Germany and thrusting towards the Reich's capital, Berlin. The destructive power of that giant Soviet offensive caused the Eastern Front to unravel and as Schulz-Naumann has described, battle groups was just one method which command staffs at all levels employed to knit the ruptured front together. These KGs were inserted into the battle line. Small groups of highly trained and absolutely determined soldiers who would stiffen the combat efficiency of neighbouring and perhaps less resolute units. It was with such "corset" units as the 500/600th Bewaehrungs — or Punishment — Battalion of Skorzeny's organisation that the Front was held together, and it is with Porsch's company of that battalion that this account deals.

In the British Army during the Second World War, men who were criminals in the military sense were confined in detention barracks, far removed from the dangers of the front line and were fed and well housed. This was not the case in continental armies where those types of men were grouped into special units and sent out on such dangerous missions as clearing minefields, leading death or glory charges or in other perilous ways, seeking to redeem their lost military honour. The 500/600th had carried out a number of spectacular operations and as a result of these successes its original role as a punishment detail was overlaid and hidden, the fighting skills of its soldiers becoming more prominent. In the last weeks of April, Russian pressure separated the company whose exploits we are to follow, from its parent battalion, part of Sturmbannfuehrer Milius's Kampfgruppe Solar, and that company became an independent command, a specialist, mobile, anti-tank detachment. In the great and heady days of Germany's military might mobile anti-tank units had been Panzer and heavy Panzer SP formations whose awesome, high-powered guns had "killed" enemy armour up to 1km distant. By April 1945, the picture had changed and now this mobile, anti-tank company, known either as DORA II or as Kampfgruppe Porsch, was mounted on bicycles and armed with either short-range, rocket launchers or else with explosive charges. Once there had been centimetres of armour plate to protect the SP gunners. Now, the bicycle-mounted battle group went unarmoured into the fight, either firing its rocket weapons at ranges below 70m, or clambering onto the outside of moving tanks to affix a charge on the vehicle's outside, or to throw a grenade into its open turret.

Porsch, the young commander of the KG, had risen from recruit in 1941 to become, by 1945, a company commander decorated with the 2nd and 1st Classes of the Iron Cross, the German Cross in Gold, the golden close-combat badge, a mention in the German Army's Book of Honour and four badges on his arms signifying the single-handed destruction of that number of enemy tanks. He had led his company with flair and courage in past battles. In those of the last weeks of the war which he was to fight as a battle group leader, Porsch was to carry out spectacular acts of bravery which went unreported in the chaos which attended Germany's collapse.

During the last weeks of April 1945, the German hold upon the heights of Seelow, west of the River Oder, was broken and when that strong defensive line was swept away it released Russian formations which stormed across Brandenburg heading west towards Berlin. Those advancing spearheads, over-runing and dispersing what little opposition they met, had soon encircled in a number of pockets the German units which had had little chance to escape from the Seelow area. One of those pockets held DORA II. The local Red Army commander, believing that the German troops opposing him were broken and ready for the "kill", sent in a regiment of armoured vehicles to destroy any last vestiges of resistance. The first wave of that Russian advance was made up of heavy JS tanks with the lighter T34s forming the second wave. At high speed the armoured phalanx thundered towards the encircled Germans, intending to overawe the defenders and to force their quick surrender. To influence that decision, the tanks halted some distance from the German trench line and opened fire with their main armament and with on-board machine guns. Although the men of KG Porsch were well-dug in, the barrage inflicted casualties which had to be borne. The Grenadiers knew that they had to be patient; soon the enemy would close in and then their time would come. Within minutes the great steel machines had reached to within a few hundred metres of DORA II slit trenches. Above the battlefield noises Porsch shouted orders to his men, identifying for them the vehicles they were each to destroy. Then the first wave tanks were within killing range of the Panzerfaust and Panzerschreck launchers. Responding to the blast of the young commander's whistle, the soldiers of KG Porsch stood up, aimed their weapons and fired. Streaks of flame erupted from the tubes. The projectiles struck the Russian machines and other flames were born as the heavy tanks caught fire. One, two, three — single "kills" were burning, but then as the melee between the German Grenadiers and the Russian tanks became general, a small group of machines which had penetrated as far as Porsch's company HQ was hit and set alight by satchel charges stuck to their exteriors.

Surprised by the fury of the battle group's opposition, the Soviet commander pulled back his tank regiment, changed its thrust line and sought to take DORA II from the right flank. That change of direction brought the Russian machines across a sector held by another of Skorzeny's units, other men who were specialists in close-quarter tank destruction techniques. Once again the Soviet armour recoiled. The defeat of his tanks decided the Red Army general. He would take out those troublesome Germans with artillery and infantry.

Although the Red Army commanders were well aware that the rate of fire of German machine guns was now as high as 2,000 rounds per minute, they still sent in their infantry in dense waves, shoulder to shoulder using the tactics employed in battles fought a century or more earlier. The long lines of Red infantrymen marched stolidly forward towards Porsch's battle group. Ahead of the first line of Russian soldiers the shells of their Army's violent creeping barrage crashed down, a barrage aimed at destroying the German defenders. Between that slowly advancing line of explosions and DORA II's slit trenches, fell a rain of rockets as batteries of Katyusha projectors saturated the area. The explosions of the creeping barrage and the thunder of the Katyusha rocket projectiles had soon coalesced into a single blanket of noise, but at last the creeping barrage passed over the trench line. The Grenadiers knew that the time had come. The Red infantry formations were closing in. There was neither time nor need to set up the machine guns on tripods. The German machine gunners, resting their bipoded weapons on the crumbling earth parapets of the slit trenches, opened fire while others of the battle group projected grenades from rifle cup dischargers or flung hand grenades into the oncoming masses of men now only a few metres distant. The hysterical chattering of the MG 42s — their rate of fire so high and the sound they made so distinctive that Red Army soldiers called the weapon "Hitler's Saw" — traversed the Russian infantry line. The enemy fell in groups, bodies piling upon each other as the follow-up lines seeking to bring the advance forward were cut down in their turn. Under that murderous fire the Soviet infantry halted and began a slow retreat.

Gallant though the defence by KG Porsch had been, such isolated examples of selflessness and devotion to duty could not alter the fact that they could not hold out indefinitely and that a westward retreat had become inevitable. The battle group pulled back and was placed in reserve, a period of rest which was soon ended. A crisis at Lebus, where Russian tank masses were concentrating to attack the town, needed the immediate employment of Porsch and his men. The battle group set out but the press of refugee carts on the road forward delayed it for so long that the town had fallen before the KG reached it. Another retreat westward had to be made, all the time harried by Soviet armoured advance guards and fighter-bomber assaults from the air. The exhausted bicycle-riders reached the German main battle line, passed through this and billeted for the night in a farm building only 300m behind the front line. During the night the detachments holding the line were either pulled back by order or were driven back by enemy assault. Porsch was awakened with the alarming news that the farmyard was filled with Russian soldiers. His men were quietly wakened, given their orders and put into battle. A few minutes of fast firing action was all the time it took to kill the enemy soldiers in the area and then, undertaking a cautious reconnaissance, the KG discovered that a neighbouring village was held by some combat engineers, the first of two groups of reinforcements to be taken on strength that day. The second was a group of Grenadiers belonging to the Dutch SS Division "Nederland". Made confident by this increase in the strength of his tiny command, Porsch decided to attack the surrounding Russian enemy and in a short, sharp action forced him back to Neu Zittau. During the fighting which marked the course of those early spring days was the celebration of the battle group's 125th "kill" and Porsch's 17th victory. On 26 April he learned he had been awarded the Knights Cross. One victory which his KG then gained, as if to celebrate their commander's honour, was a swift thrust through a Russian battalion position, an assault which captured the HQ staff of that enemy unit. Another successful operation, made together with some survivors of the "Frundsberg" Division, destroyed the men of a battery of Russian mortars and captured eight of the projectors.

From the sounds of battle heard on every side and especially from behind the Kampfgruppe's front, as well as from the weight of Russian artillery fire which now poured out upon it, it was clear that the group was projecting as a salient into the Russian line. It was time that a fresh attempt westwards was made to gain the German lines but they were never reached. Groups of civilians poured into the small salient held by KG Porsch, a German-held area in a country swarming with Red Army soldiers. The civilians were hoping to find in that small enclave some respite from the rapes and murders that were endemic in Red-held territory. Porsch could not abandon the defenceless civilians to the barbarities that would await them and delayed his withdrawal. Soon it was too late. A swift, precise Russian tank thrust cut the neck of the salient turning it into a pocket within which was trapped DORA II, the civilians and fragments of other German military units which had elected to join Porsch and fight

Collecting his small group into a compact whole, Porsch led it in a march westward hoping to gain touch with the German battle front. In this attempt the KG men fought and defeated one Soviet unit after another as these tried to bar the slow-paced retreat. Attacked from the air, subjected to artillery barrages, tank assault, cavalry charges and infantry attack, the pocket wandered across the heathland of Brandenburg seeking — not always successfully — to gain the protection of its few forested areas. It was at this point that the civilians left KG Porsch and without that burden the military units made better progress.

Although the Soviet main effort was concentrated upon Berlin and on destroying the last formal resistance in and around that city, there were a great many Russian units employed on "tidying-up" operations to take out the remaining pockets of German resistance now cut off and isolated far behind the Soviet front line. One such pocket of resistance was battle group Porsch and the strength of the original group had been reduced by the fury and constancy of the Red Army's assaults until it was made up of just 48 men.

The last act in the life of KG Porsch was played out between Markisch-Buchholz and Toepchin. A Russian infantry battalion surrounded the area and the officers of the German units trapped with the battle group accepted the Soviet ultimatum to surrender or be destroyed. Porsch gathered his few men and told them that there was the choice of surrender and captivity or certain death if they remained with him. All chose to stay with the young commander.

On the bitter field of Toepchin the Red Army battalion moved forward to attack the remnant of DORA II, now just a handful of men. The first in a series of Russian infantry attacks brought the KG losses. Seven men fell in that first assault and 18 were killed in the second. Attack after attack was made by the Red unit, but all failed without achieving the victory for which the Russian colonel was determined to achieve. At dawn on 28 April, the Soviets began a new series of attacks. The first of these was opened by a furious mortar barrage behind which Soviet infantry advanced to wipe out the defiant survivors of DORA II. The first attack was flung back but the end of the battle group's military life was fast approaching. Fully aware of the situation and also of what would face them as prisoners of war in the Soviet Union, those men who were badly wounded killed themselves with hand grenades or by pistol shot. When the Red battalion came in for a new assault the battle group had only one round of ammunition left and that its owner used to shoot himself.

Now there was nothing left but the hand to hand struggle, man against man and Porsch, raising the staff he had carved in the 1941 battles around Volkhov, led the last 11 of his men into their final attack. Furious though that charge was, it could have only one end. The battle group commander and a few of his men still alive when the scrimmage ended, obtained permission from the Russian colonel to bury their dead comrades. Kampfgruppe Porsch died on the battlefield of Toepchin, only a couple of days before Berlin fell, bringing with it the end of the war in Europe. Porsch endured more than a decade of solitary confinement in prison and returned to Germany, one of the very last to be repatriated.

EPILOGUE

Battle groups were in action until the last day of the war. Then hostilities ceased and the need for them was gone. The last entries in the text of this book are taken from two histories of the Second World War. One extract was written by an Englishman and the other by a Frenchman.

The Englishman, writing in Volume 3 of the official history of the war in the Mediterranean and the Middle East, although not mentioning battle groups specifically, used words which describe their actions very accurately: "... It would be unfair and ungenerous not to recognise the considerable achievements of the German troops [in Africa]... Small groups and sub-units were constantly being flung together for some desperate enterprise — usually to plug some gap — and it is astonishing how often they brought it off. The German soldier always seemed capable of making one more supreme effort..."

The French author of *Histoire de Falaise*, after commending the courage of the Canadians who fought for that town in August 1944, then wrote of the men of Kampfgruppe Krause: "... Ought we not [at the same time] wonder at those 18 year-old Germans who held out in their positions until the Canadian infantry and tanks reached them, often with a thirty to one superiority. They waited for the moment to fire when it would have most effect although knowing full well that such delay diminished their own chances of survival but who accepted death to defend their Fatherland..."

BIBLIOGRAPHY

PUBLISHED WORKS

Bielefeld & Essame, *The Battle for Normandy*, Batsford

Blumenson, *Break Out and Pursuit*, US Army, 1961

Buschleb, H. *Feldherren und Panzer im Wuestenkrieg*. Vowinckel, 1966

Ellis, *Victory in the West*, HMSO, 1968

Esebeck, H. von, *Helden der Wueste*, Heimbuecherei, Berlin, 1942

— *Sand, Sonne, Sieg*, Heimbuecherei, Berlin, 194

Guderian, H. *Errinerungen eines Soldaten*, Vowinckel, Heidelberg, 1951

— *Die Panzertruppen und ihr Zusammenwirken mit den andreren Waffen*, Mittler, Berlin, 1940

Gunner, C., *Front of the Line*, Greystone, 1992

Harrison, G. A., *Cross Channel Attack*, US Army, 1951

Hillgruber, *KTB der OKW*, Bernard & Graefe

Lehmann, R. *Die Leibstandarte*, Munin, various dates

Mellenthin, F. W., *Panzer battles*, Vowinckel, 1953

Meyer, H. *Kriegsgeschichte der 12ten SS Panzer Div. "Hitler Jugend"*, Munin, 1982

Meyer, "Panzer", *Grenadiere*, Munich, 1965

Middelldorf, E., *Taktik im Russischen Feldzug*, E. S . Mittler, 1956

Munzel, O., *Panzertaktik*, Vowinckel, 1959

Nehring, W. K., *Die Geschichte der deutsch Panzerwaffe, 1916-1945*, Motorbuch Verlag, 1974

Playfair, I. and Molony, C., *The Mediterranean and the Middle East*, Vols 1–4, HMSO, 1956–66

Randel, A., *A Short History of 30 Corps*, Buende

HQ 2nd Army, *A History of Operations*, Bielefeld

Stacey, C. P., *The Victory Campaign: The Canadian Army in World War Two*, HMSO, Ottowa, 1966

Selbstverlag, *Geschichte des Panzer Korps "Grossdeutschland"*, Berlin, 1958

Tessin, G., *Verbaende und Truppen der deutsch. Wehrmacht und Waffen SS, 1939–1945*, Biblio Verlag

Traditionsverband der Division, *Geschichte der 3ten Panzer Division*, Richter, Berlin, 1967

Tschimpke, A., *Die Gespenster Division*, Zentralverlag der NSDAP, 1941

Yerger, M., *"Das Reich"*, Volume 1

Unpublished Sources

Afrika Korps, *KTB. Afrika Korps & Panzer Armee Afrika*
Army Group "B", *KTB*, 1944
BAOR, *Intelligence Reviews.* Various dates.
7th Army, *KTB*, 1944
Simon, *Experiences Gained in Combat against Russian Infantry — Soviet Infantry and Armoured Forces*

US Army, *Effects of Climate on Combat Conditions in European Russia*
War Diary, *The Nova Scotia Highlanders*
War Diary, *27th (Canadian) Armoured Regiment*

As well as interviews and correspondence with former German soldiers and officers.

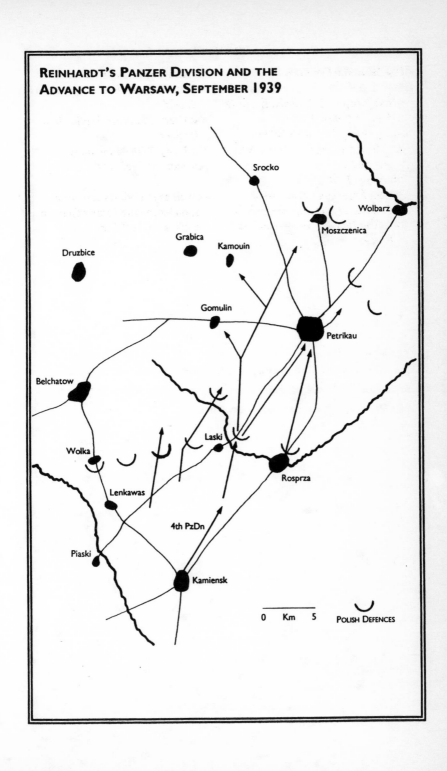

REINHARDT'S PANZER DIVISION AND THE
ADVANCE TO WARSAW, SEPTEMBER 1939

Srocko

Wolbarz

Moszczenica

Grabica

Kamouin

Druzbice

Gomulin

Petrikau

Belchatow

Wolka

Laski

Rosprza

Lenkawas

4th PzDn

Piaski

Kamiensk

0   Km   5   POLISH DEFENCES

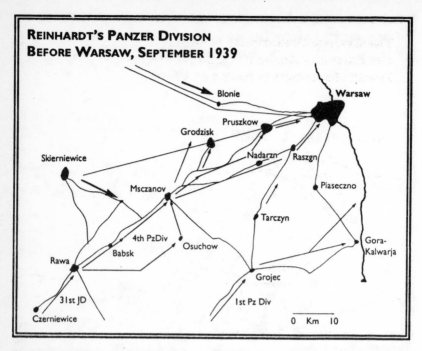

REINHARDT'S PANZER DIVISION BEFORE WARSAW, SEPTEMBER 1939

Blonie

Warsaw

Pruszkow

Grodzisk

Skierniewice

Nadarzn

Raszgn

Msczanov

Piaseczno

Tarczyn

4th PzDiv

Osuchow

Babsk

Rawa

Gora-Kalwarja

Grojec

31st JD

Czerniewice

1st Pz Div

0   Km   10

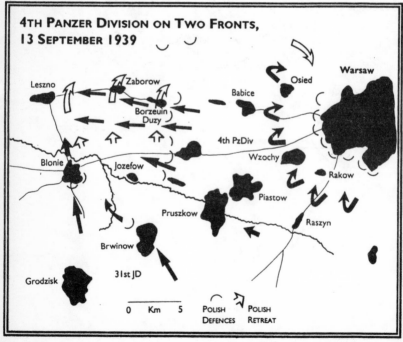

4TH PANZER DIVISION ON TWO FRONTS, 13 SEPTEMBER 1939

Leszno

Zaborow

Osied

Warsaw

Babice

Borzeuin Duzy

4th PzDiv

Blonie

Wzochy

Jozefow

Rakow

Piastow

Pruszkow

Raszyn

Brwinow

31st JD

Grodzisk

0   Km   5

POLISH DEFENCES

POLISH RETREAT

THE GERMAN OPERATIONAL PLAN FOR THE CAMPAIGN AGAINST POLAND, SHOWING PINCER MOVEMENTS IN EAST AND WEST

BALTIC SEA

LITHUANIA

Danzig

• Königsberg

• Vilnyus

EAST PRUSSIA

• Minsk

RUSSIA

Bygerszcz • • Torum

• Bialystok

Kutno • • Warsaw

• Brest-Litovsk

Lodz •

Gora Kalwarja

Radom

Lublin

• Luck

GERMANY

Sandomierz

Zhitomir •

Krakow

Przemsyl

Lvov

GERMAN ATTACKS

RUMANIA

0   Km   200

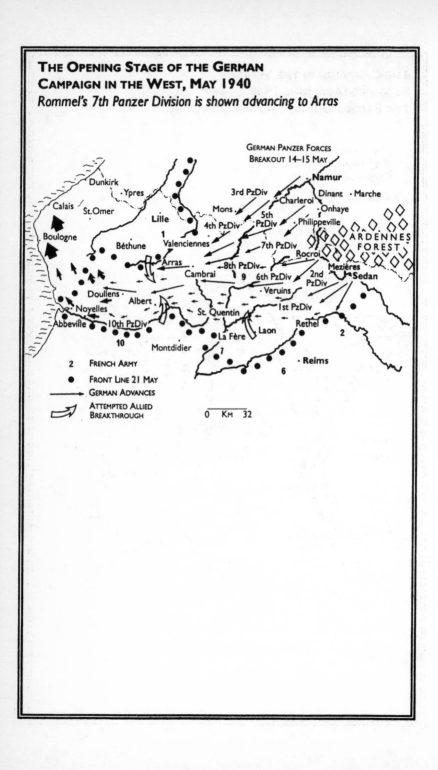

THE OPENING STAGE OF THE GERMAN CAMPAIGN IN THE WEST, MAY 1940

Rommel's 7th Panzer Division is shown advancing to Arras

GERMAN PANZER FORCES
BREAKOUT 14–15 MAY

Dunkirk
· Ypres
Calais
St.Omer
Boulogne
Béthune
Lille
Valenciennes
1
Arras ·
Cambrai
9
Doullens ·
Albert
Noyelles
Abbeville
10th PzDiv
10
Montdidier
St. Quentin
La Fère
Laon
Veruins
6th PzDiv
2nd PzDiv
Mézières
Sedan
1st PzDiv
Rethel
2
7
Reims
6

Namur
Dinant · Marche
Charleroi
Onhaye
Mons ·
Philippeville
3rd PzDiv
4th PzDiv
5th PzDiv
7th PzDiv
Rocroi
8th PzDiv

ARDENNES FOREST

2	FRENCH ARMY
●	FRONT LINE 21 MAY
→	GERMAN ADVANCES
	ATTEMPTED ALLIED BREAKTHROUGH

0   KM   32

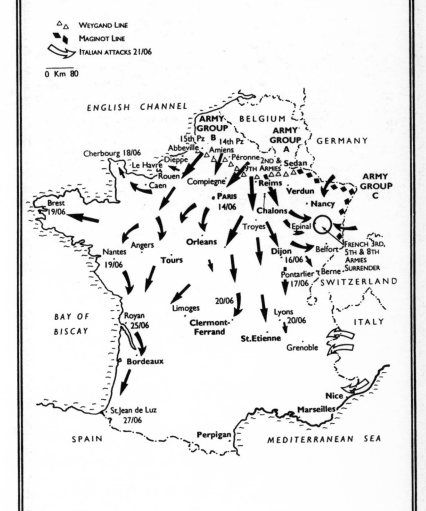

THE CAMPAIGN IN THE WEST:
SECOND STAGE, JUNE 1940.
7TH PANZER DIVISION ADVANCES TO CHERBOURG

△△ Weygand Line

◆◆ Maginot Line

⇨ Italian attacks 21/06

0 Km 80

ENGLISH CHANNEL

BELGIUM

ARMY GROUP B

ARMY GROUP A

GERMANY

ARMY GROUP C

15th Pz   14th Pz

Abbeville   Amiens   Péronne   2ND & 9TH ARMIES   Sedan

Cherbourg 18/06

Dieppe

Le Havre

Rouen

Caen

Compiegne   Reims   Verdun   Nancy

Brest 19/06

PARIS 14/06

Chalons

Troyes   Epinal

FRENCH 3RD, 5TH & 8TH ARMIES SURRENDER

Angers   **Orleans**

Nantes 19/06

Tours

Dijon 16/06   Belfort

Berne

Pontarlier 17/06

SWITZERLAND

BAY OF BISCAY

Royan 25/06

Limoges   20/06

Lyons 20/06

ITALY

Clermont-Ferrand

St.Etienne

Grenoble

Bordeaux

St.Jean de Luz 27/06

SPAIN

Perpigan

Nice

Marseilles

MEDITERRANEAN SEA

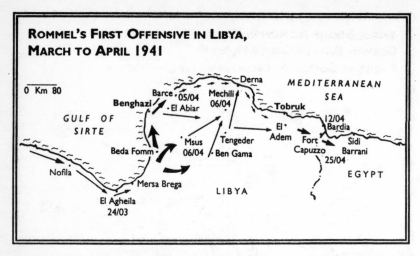

ROMMEL'S FIRST OFFENSIVE IN LIBYA, MARCH TO APRIL 1941

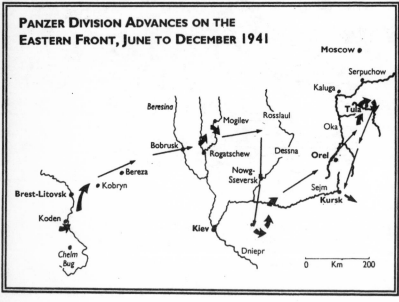

PANZER DIVISION ADVANCES ON THE EASTERN FRONT, JUNE TO DECEMBER 1941

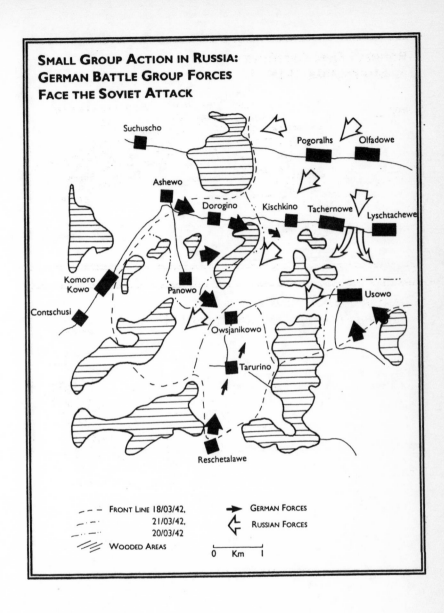

SMALL GROUP ACTION IN RUSSIA:
GERMAN BATTLE GROUP FORCES
FACE THE SOVIET ATTACK

Suchuscho

Pogoralhs   Olfadowe

Ashewo

Dorogino   Kischkino   Tachernowe
Lyschtachewe

Komoro
Kowo

Panowo   Usowo

Contschusi

Owsjanikowo

Tarurino

Reschetalawe

FRONT LINE 18/03/42,   GERMAN FORCES
          21/03/42,   RUSSIAN FORCES
          20/03/42,
WOODED AREAS

0   Km   1

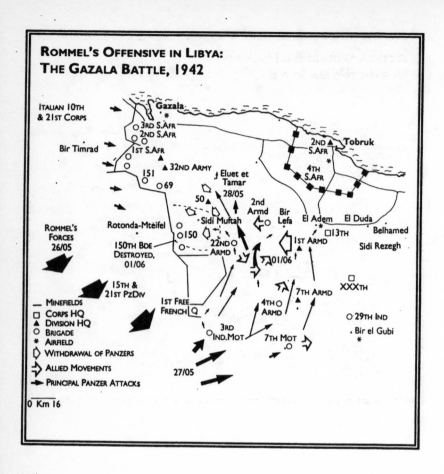

ROMMEL'S OFFENSIVE IN LIBYA:
THE GAZALA BATTLE, 1942

ITALIAN 10TH
& 21ST CORPS

Gazala

3RD S.AFR
2ND S.AFR

Bir Timrad

1ST S.AFR

32ND ARMY

2ND S.AFR

Tobruk

4TH S.AFR

151

69

Eluet et Tamar
28/05

50

2nd Armd

Bir Lefa

El Adem

El Duda

13TH

Belhamed

ROMMEL'S FORCES
26/05

Rotonda-Mteifel

Sidi Muftah

1ST ARMD

Sidi Rezegh

150

150TH BDE DESTROYED,
01/06

22ND ARMD

01/06

15TH & 21ST PzDIV

7TH ARMD

XXXTH

MINEFIELDS
CORPS HQ
DIVISION HQ
BRIGADE
AIRFIELD
WITHDRAWAL OF PANZERS
ALLIED MOVEMENTS
PRINCIPAL PANZER ATTACKS

1ST FREE FRENCH

4TH ARMD

29TH IND

3RD IND.MOT

7TH MOT

Bir el Gubi

27/05

0 Km 16

ACTION AROUND BIR HACHEIM
DURING THE GAZALA BATTLE, 5-11 JUNE 1942

SOLARO ESCARPMENT

6TH S.AFR

Tobruk

2ND S.AFR

2ND S.AFR

16TH AFR

1ST S.AFR

Acroma

4TH S.AFR

Alem Hamza

32ND ARMY TANK

11TH INDIAN

151

50

TOBRUK PERIMETER

69

• Eluet et Tamar

RIGEL RIDGE

1ST ARMOURED

ITALIAN 10TH CORPS

21ST PzDIV

SIORA RIDGE

22ND ARMOURED

BATRUNA RIDGE

2ND ARMOURED

EL ADEM

"ARIETA" DIV

201ST GUARDS

7TH ARMOURED

• SIDI MUFTAH

Rotonda • Mteifel

15TH PzDIV

4TH ARMOURED

29TH INDIAN

BIR EL HARMAT

0   Km   16

7TH MOT BDE

○ ALLIED BRIGADE

▲ ALLIED DIVISION

— MINEFIELDS

➤ PANZER BREAKOUT

⇨ ALLIED REDEPLOYMENT

⇦ ALLIED ATTACK

1ST FREE FRENCH

Bir Hacheim

Bir Bevid

4TH S.AFR ARMD. CAR REGT

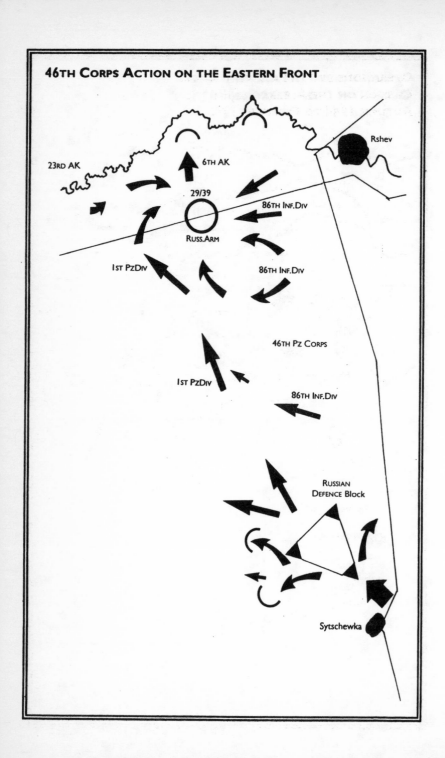

46th Corps Action on the Eastern Front

Rshev

23rd AK

6th AK

29/39
Russ.Arm

86th Inf.Div

1st PzDiv

86th Inf.Div

46th Pz Corps

1st PzDiv

86th Inf.Div

Russian Defence Block

Sytschewka

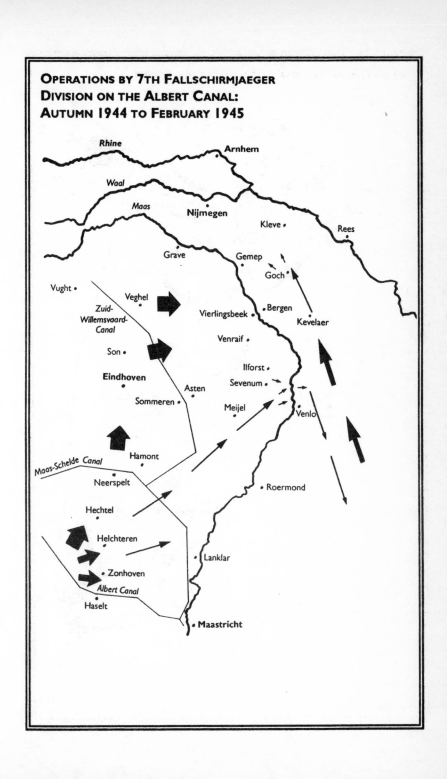

OPERATIONS BY 7TH FALLSCHIRMJAEGER
DIVISION ON THE ALBERT CANAL:
AUTUMN 1944 TO FEBRUARY 1945

Rhine   **Arnhem**

Waal

Maas   **Nijmegen**

Kleve •

Rees

Grave •   Gemep •

Goch •

Vught •

Veghel •

Zuid-
Willemsvaard-
Canal

Vierlingsbeek •   Bergen •

Kevelaer

Venraif •

Son •

Ilforst •

Eindhoven •

Asten •

Sevenum •

Sommeren •

Meijel •

Venlo •

Hamont •

Maas-Schelde *Canal*

Neerspelt •

Roermond •

Hechtel •

Helchteren •

Lanklar •

• Zonhoven

Albert Canal

Haselt •

• **Maastricht**

INDEX